Rural Credit in Western India
1875-1930

WESTERN INDIA

Rural Credit
in
Western India
1875-1930

Rural Credit and the
Co-operative Movement
in the Bombay Presidency

I. J. CATANACH

UNIVERSITY OF CALIFORNIA PRESS

Berkeley   Los Angeles   London
1970

University of California Press
Berkeley and Los Angeles, California
University of California Press, Ltd.
London, England
Copyright © 1970, by
The Regents of the University of California
Library of Congress Catalog Card Number: 72–94986
International Standard Book Number: 0–520–01595–9
Printed in the United States of America

Acknowledgments

This book has been long in the making; it would be impossible to list all those, in India and elsewhere, to whom I owe a debt of gratitude. I must thank here, first of all, Professor Kenneth Ballhatchet of the School of Oriental and African Studies, University of London, under whose guidance a first version of part of the book took shape as a doctoral thesis. Reconsideration of the argument, and much additional research, has been financed by the University of Canterbury, the Research Committee of the New Zealand University Grants Committee, and the Australian National University. For permission to consult unpublished records I have to thank especially the Government of undivided Bombay, the Director of the National Archives of India, and the Librarian and Keeper of the India Office Library and Records, London. For much good advice I am grateful to Professor Mahadeo L. Apte, Dr. R.G. Kakade, Professor D.A. Low, Dr. S.R. Mehrotra, Professor Morris David Morris, Shri M.V. Sovani, and Professor Daniel Thorner. I should like to record, too, my indebtedness to three persons who figure prominently in this book: the late Harold H. Mann, the late Vaikunth L. Mehta, and Sir Robert Ewbank. It has been a privilege to know such men. The University of California Press have been the most patient of publishers, and my wife and family have cheerfully tolerated for almost a decade the absences and absent-mindedness of one who has tried to combine the responsibilities of author, university teacher, husband, and father.

I.J.C.

Christchurch
December 1969

[v]

Contents

Abbreviations

The following abbreviations have been used in the footnotes: those in the first list are the same on the whole as those used in Bombay Government correspondence; those in the second list refer to bibliographical sources such as files, and to record offices.

Admin.	Administration
Ag.	Acting
Agric.	Agriculture
Asst.	Assistant
Bom.	Bombay
C.D.	Central Division
Ch. Sec.	Chief Secretary
Collr.	Collector
Confl.	Confidential
Co-op.	Co-operative
Cttee.	Committee
D.A.	Director of Agriculture
Dep.	Deputy
Dept.	Department
D/O	Demi-official
encl.	enclosed
G. of B.	Government of Bombay
G. of I.	Government of India
Govr.	Governor
Govt.	Government
G.R.	Government Resolution
Jt.	Joint
L. Rev.	Land Revenue
N.D.	Northern Division
Offg.	Officiating

R. & A. Dept.	Revenue and Agriculture Department (Government of India)
R.D.	Revenue Department
Regr.	Registrar
Rept.	Report
Rev.	Revenue
S.D.	Southern Division
Sec.	Secretary
U. Sec.	Under Secretary
B.C.Q.	*Bombay Co-operative Quarterly*
B.M.	British Museum
Bom. L. Rev. Admin. Repts.	*Government of Bombay Land Revenue Administration Reports*
Bom. Prov. Banking Enquiry Cttee. Rept.	*Report of the Bombay Provincial Banking Enquiry Committee, 1929–30.* Vol. I
B.P.C.B.	"Bombay Provincial Co-operative Bank"
B.P.C.I., III	"Bombay Provincial Co-operative Institute, III"
B.R.O.	Maharashtra State Record Office, Bombay
B.S.C.B.	Maharashtra State Co-operative Bank, Bombay
Caird Papers	Indian papers of James Caird
Deccan Riots Rept.	*Report of the Committee on the Riots in Poona and Ahmednagar, 1875*
G.D. Vols.	General Department Volumes
I.O.L.	India Office Library
I.O.R.	India Office Records
J.D. Vols.	Judicial Department Volumes
L. Rev. Procs.	India (Government of India) Land Revenue Proceedings
Maclagan Cttee. Rept.	*Report of the Committee on Co-operation in India.* 1915
N.A.I.	National Archives of India, New Delhi
N.C. & C.B.	"Nira Canal and Central Bank"
Patiala	From the Punjab Record Office, Patiala
Poona	Office of the Registrar of Co-operative Societies, Maharashtra State, Poona. Record Room

Poona C.C.B.-A.	"Poona Central Co-operative Bank—A."
Poona, Registrar's Library	Office of the Registrar of Co-operative Societies, Maharashtra State, Poona. Registrar's Library
P.P.	*Parliamentary Papers*
Prov. Co-op. Conf. Procs., 19—.	*Proceedings of the Co-operative Conference held in Bombay, December 15–18, 1908,* and semi-annually under varying titles, to 1929
R.D. Vols.	Revenue Department Volumes
Regr.	"Registrar" 1920–30. Correspondence
Regrs.' Conf. Procs., 19—.	*Proceedings of the Conference of Registrars of Co-operative Societies,* 1906 and semi-annually to 1928
Rept., 19—.	*Annual Report relating to the Establishment of Co-operative Credit Societies in the Bombay Presidency during the year ending 31st March 1905,* and the following years, under varying titles, to 1937
Rev. Despatches to India	Revenue Despatches from the Secretary of State for India to the Governor-General of India
Rev. Letters from India	Revenue Letters from the Governor-General of India to the Secretary of State for India
S.P.G.	Archives of the Society for the Propagation of the Gospel in Foreign Parts, London
S.R. G. of B., N.S.	*Selections from the Records of the Bombay Government, New Series*
S.R. G. of I.	*Selections from the Records of the Government of India*
Temple Papers	Private papers of Sir Richard Temple

Introduction

Much of the real stuff of Indian history is peasant history; for centuries most Indians have lived in the rural areas. That being so—the British were inclined to argue, even in the later days of the raj—most Indians were primarily concerned with the business of winning a living from the soil; they were not interested in politics. A British-dominated government, many Englishmen thought, could concern itself with the welfare of the Indian peasantry—the majority—in a way that a government dominated by Indian "urban politicians" would not. "I do not think that the salvation of India is to be sought in the field of politics at her present stage of development," proclaimed Lord Curzon in 1904.[1] His viceroyalty at one and the same time sums up much of the imperialist tradition of the previous century and looks forward to the economic concerns of Indian governments in the post-Independence years. It was during Curzon's viceroyalty—in 1904, in fact—that the first Indian Co-operative Societies Act became law.

Yet that Act did not spring unassisted from the mind of a mere temporary visitor to India, fertile though Lord Curzon's mind was. To a very considerable extent the Act was the result of deliberations amongst permanent officials extending over a number of years, at least as far back as the so-called Deccan Riots of 1875. These disturbances were generally assumed to be a protest against a supposed tendency for land held by peasant cultivators to pass into the hands of money-lenders-cum-traders; the Co-operative Societies Act of 1904 is one of a series of measures which, while by no means intended to extinguish the money-lender, did aim to put some fairly definite limits on his activities. This study examines— in a spirit of sympathy as well as, at times, of scepticism—first, the

[1] Budget Debate speech, 30 March 1904, quoted Edna R. Bonner, "The Economic Policy of the Government of India, 1898–1905" (M.A. thesis, University of London, 1955), p. 227.

diagnosis of the rural credit situation in the Bombay Deccan which
was offered in the years after 1875, and, then, the working in
Gujarat and the Bombay Karnatak, as well as in the Deccan, of the
co-operative societies which were intended to provide a remedy
for the supposed problem of agricultural indebtedness.

The history of rural co-operatives in the Bombay Presidency is,
at least to some extent, part of peasant history. But peasants—
especially, perhaps, Indian peasants—have not normally been particularly literate. Inevitably, most of the material available for a
study such as this will not be the work of peasants. Government
records, both published and unpublished, must provide the basis
for many of our conclusions, although for so recent a period as ours
non-official material, such as bank records and newspapers, has
managed to survive the vagaries of climate and managerial calls
for space with encouraging frequency. Just occasionally it is possible to piece together from these sources the stories of individual
co-operative societies. At such times the historian may feel that he
has really begun to come to grips with peasant history. But in India
peasant history is not made only on the plots of the single extended
family, or at the level of the individual co-operative society or the
individual village. Peasants are members of castes, and the caste
may be a more important unit of social organization in India than
the single village.[2] The increasing politicization of caste in our
period, in part through the growth of caste associations covering
large stretches of territory, had an important bearing on the success or failure of co-operatives. Even nationalism—whatever contemporary British officials might have claimed—became of interest
to some peasants, especially in Gujarat; co-operative societies were
sometimes affected as a result. Above all, when we consider peasant
history as a whole in western India in the fifty or sixty years prior
to the great depression of the thirties, it appears to be concerned
with a considerable amount of economic change. This was a period
when, for example, "trade by rail and wire" (as a contemporary
account aptly put it)[3] was being rapidly extended; by no means was
every peasant a "subsistence" farmer. Rural credit and the co-
operative movement have to be studied in this broad context of
economic change.

2 See Louis Dumont and D. F. Pocock, Editorial in *Contributions to Indian Sociology*, No. 1, April 1957.
3 *Gazetteer of the Bombay Presidency*, Vol. XII, *Khandesh* (1880), p. 194.

The co-operative movement in India was, to begin with, the creation of the state. This fact alone makes it inevitable that government officials, as well as peasants, will figure largely in this study. There is little doubt that the development of co-operative societies was at first foisted upon a somewhat unwilling Government of Bombay by the Government of India. (The two southern Presidencies of Bombay and Madras had in any case traditionally assumed a certain amount of independence from the Government of India.)[4] We must therefore concern ourselves, at least to some extent, with Government of India—Government of Bombay relations. We must even consider, at times, relations between the Government of India and the India Office in England. But we must concern ourselves, too, with relations within the Bombay administration, relations between the so-called Secretariat in the city of Bombay and the men, based on the Deccan city of Poona, who acted as Registrars of Co-operative Societies in the first thirty or so years of this century. The Registrars were always drawn from the élite administrative service, the Indian Civil Service, that supposedly omnicompetent body of men working within the characteristically British "literary generalist" tradition.[5] Two of the first four Europeans to hold the position of Registrar were rather notable eccentrics: the Registrar's office sometimes provided a place for the official who was both brilliant and enthusiastic but at the same time something of an odd man out. Sheer economic and administrative necessity, as well as, perhaps, "Indianization" of the I.C.S. in the 1920s, eventually brought a slightly more staid, if equally clever, brand of administrator to the fore as Registrar. The Registrars, of course, in the almost inevitable Indian bureaucratic way, soon gathered a "department" about them: the Co-operative Department formed a fairly typical sample of a vital "hinge group," the army of minor Indian officials who made it possible for a few thousand Europeans to administer a sub-continent. Yet, for all these tendencies towards bureaucratization, many senior officials connected with the co-operative movement in Bombay genuinely

---

[4] See Curzon's complaint about this state of affairs in his letter to Lord George Hamilton, 7 June 1899, reproduced in *The Evolution of India and Pakistan, 1858 to 1947: Select Documents*, ed. C. H. Philips, pp. 70–71.

[5] The phrase is used by Ralph Braibanti in "Reflections on Bureaucratic Reform in India" in *Administration and Economic Development in India*, ed. Ralph Braibanti and Joseph J. Spengler, p. 10. Braibanti contrasts this tradition with "the more technical empirical disposition of American public administration."

believed in the need to promote non-official leadership of the movement; indeed they asserted (after the initial hesitancy) that the
co-operative movement could be used to promote the virtues of
"democratization," a democratization which might well be a pre-
requisite of self-government for the country. Especially in the days
before the Government of India Act of 1919, relations between
"state" and "co-operative movement" in Bombay meant the inter-
action of British and Indian officials, and Indian and occasionally
British non-officials, on a level of intimacy rarely reached in other
fields, even in the field of so-called local self-government.[6]

What we are examining, of course, is an attempt to put a "development" programme into effect long before "development"
became fashionable. India was the first non-Western country to
experiment with rural co-operatives; many of the approaches to
co-operation now taken for granted were painfully worked out in
India. We are studying the effect of an "innovation" introduced
from the West—this one happened to come from the Rhineland
area of Germany—on an essentially "traditional" society.[7] One of
the main questions we must ask ourselves is this: Was the modesty
of the success of co-operative societies in the Bombay Presidency
primarily the result of inertia within Indian society, or was it the
result of the essential unsuitability of the innovation offered? The
question has a familiar enough ring about it in these development-
conscious days; perhaps in this case the cool analysis of the historian can contribute something, if only indirectly, to the solution of
the problems of the present.

A word is necessary about the coverage of this study, both in
time and in space.

The year 1930 was chosen as a terminal point mainly for reasons
of the availability of documents from government sources. But
1930 also represents, approximately, the onset of the full force of
the economic depression, and in some respects the end of an era
in Indian economic history. The introduction of a measure of
economic protectionism in India during the depression—in the
sugar industry in 1931, for example—helped to give the years that

6 The term came into use during Lord Ripon's viceroyalty, 1880–84. See Hugh
Tinker, *The Foundations of Local Self-Government in India, Pakistan, and Burma.*
7 For some wise cautionary words on the use of such terms as "tradition" and "modernity" see the introduction to Lloyd I. Rudolph and Susanne Hoeber Rudolph,
The Modernity of Tradition: Political Development in India.

followed a rather different character from the period before 1930, even if many changes did not become fully apparent until the war years.

This volume is concerned with Gujarat, western Maharashtra (the Konkan and the Bombay Deccan), and the Bombay Karnatak: three constituent regions of what was officially known as the Bombay Presidency. Administratively speaking, these areas corresponded approximately with the so-called Northern, Central, and Southern Divisions of the Presidency. Although, formally speaking, Sind was part of the Bombay Presidency until 1936, it is not discussed here. Conditions in that arid though increasingly irrigated land were much closer to those of the Punjab than to those of what was often called the Presidency proper.

Most of the Presidency proper had come under British rule at about the same time, in the early years of the nineteenth century. In most parts of the Presidency proper the dominant form of land tenure was rayatwari: the peasant paid revenue direct to the government without the intervention of intermediaries. In each of the administrative districts of the Presidency a Collector was in charge of both revenue matters and law and order. All three main areas of the Presidency proper were united to some extent, too, in looking towards the growing commercial and industrial city of Bombay. Bombay was their administrative capital and their main port; their roads and their railways eventually made for Bombay, and many a countryman found temporary or permanent employment there; much of the business of the regions centred on the city. But the regions, especially Maharashtra, looked somewhat uneasily at the growth of the metropolis. For one thing, much of the real commercial power in Bombay was in the hands of Gujaratis, and those Gujaratis tended to have their links with fellow Gujarati traders and money-lenders in the non-Gujarati hinterland. The extent of anti-Gujarati feeling in Maharashtra in our period can be exaggerated. Nevertheless, such feeling was there. There were, in fact, three major languages in the Presidency—Gujarati, Marathi, and Kanarese—three different though sometimes related histories, three different and potentially conflicting cultures.

Gujarat and the Gujaratis owed their commercial position in the Bombay Presidency largely to their tradition of entrepreneurship in trade with west and southeast Asia and, indirectly, with Europe. This tradition dated back at least to Roman times. Probably not a great deal of the profit of trade was normally invested in the rural areas of Gujarat;[8] nevertheless, Mountstuart Elphinstone, at the time of the introduction of British rule, had marvelled at the "extraordinary prosperity" of the peasantry of Gujarat.[9] Gujarat had—and still has—its dark-skinned Kaliparaj eking out an existence on its poorer soils, and in the hilly parts of the Gujarat-Maharashtra borderland area of Khandesh there were many semi-aboriginal Bhils. But the Patidars of the fertile and reasonably well watered Charotar plain of Gujarat generally reaped good rewards from their skilled farming. The Patidars made up the "dominant castes" of the region;[10] Brahmans there were in Gujarat, but, partly because Anavla Brahmans were the most prominent group amongst the revenue farmers, who lost most of their power with the coming of the British, there was never, in modern times, a "Brahman problem" in Gujarat.

The situation in Maharashtra was very different. Apart from the Konkan—the narrow, isolated littoral on the western side of the Ghats, south of Bombay—and the Mawal area in the foothills on the other side of the range, most of Maharashtra, for most of the year, presented a picture of occasional lightly cultivated valley areas amidst an arid, sparsely covered, eroded series of "mesas and buttes, the tops remarkably accordant, often as if sliced off with a knife."[11] East of Poona, in fact, lay the great Deccan "famine belt," a region of limited and (perhaps more important) frequently ineffective rainfall: a region "highly prosperous in a good year but with very frequent years of failure or partial failure of crops."[12] There was much truth in the assertion in 1892 of an official report

8 At least not until the 1770s, according to recent research: see Ashin Das Gupta, "The Character of Traditional Trade" (Paper presented to the Conference on Modern South Asian Studies, Cambridge, July 1968), p. 5.

9 Minute by the Governor (Elphinstone), 6 April 1821, on Ahmadabad and Kaira districts, *Select Committee on the Affairs of the East India Company, Minutes of Evidence*, Vol. III, Appx., p. 641. *P.P.* 1831–32 (735–III) xi.

10 The term is derived from the work of Professor M. N. Srinivas. See his "The Dominant Caste in Rampura," *American Anthropologist*, Vol. LXI, No. 1 (February 1959).

11 O. H. K. Spate and A. T. A. Learmonth, *India and Pakistan: A General and Regional Geography*, 3d ed., p. 692.

12 Harold H. Mann, *Rainfall and Famine: A Study of Rainfall in the Bombay Deccan, 1865–1938*, p. 4. The words quoted are actually used about Ahmadnagar district but are equally applicable to Sholapur district and parts of Satara and Poona districts. See also Mann's evidence to the *Royal Commission on Agriculture*, 1928, Vol. II, pt. i, *Evidence taken in the Bombay Presidency*, p. 16 (iii–viii).

on the area that "the main cause of indebtedness would appear to be the capriciousness of the climate."[13] This unpromising territory had been the headquarters of the warrior-peasant power of the Marathas in the seventeenth and eighteenth centuries. Here, the influence which certain Brahman elements had obtained during the rule of the Peshwas in the eighteenth century had scarcely diminished under the British in the nineteenth.[14] For Brahman rights to education and administrative posts had been largely preserved in Maharashtra.

Some parts of the Bombay Karnatak, to the south of Maharashtra, had physical characteristics similar to those of the Bombay Deccan. But in the Dharwar and Belgaum districts this description by a Karnatak geographer was frequently appropriate: "Prosperous villages, high land values, frequency of litigation in civil courts, the number of times this region changed hands under the Peshwa rule . . . indicate the agricultural wealth of the region, past and present."[15] The reference to the Peshwa period reminds us that though the Karnatak had seen frequent intrusions from Maharashtra, the Marathi-speaking elements, Brahmans and Marathas, remained very definitely a minority amidst Kanarese-speaking peasant groups. The most notable of these groups was that of the so-called Lingayats, followers of the reformist Vira-Saiva sect, founded in the twelfth century.

It was amidst these very diverse regions, then, that the Registrar of Co-operative Societies was expected to work. He had generally had previous experience of only one or at the most two regions, and he often knew only one regional language; now the whole Presidency was his "touring" area. Whatever else may be said about the work of the Registrars, especially the early Registrars, it must be admitted that the tasks they faced were very considerable.

The Indian co-operative experiment has certainly been written about before. The works of Hubert Calvert, C. F. Strickland, and

[13] *Report of the Commission appointed to Enquire into the Working of the Deccan Agriculturists' Relief Act, 1891–92,* pp. 30–31.

[14] The Peshwas were theoretically the chief ministers of the descendants of the great Maratha leader, Shivaji, but in fact the real rulers of the Poona-based state. The Peshwas were Chitpavan Brahman by caste.

[15] C. D. Deshpande, *Western India: A Regional Geography,* p. 105.

(especially) Sir Malcolm Darling became known to a wide circle
of readers in the twenties and thirties.[16] But these men were all,
at various times, Registrars in the Punjab, where co-operation appeared to have somewhat more success than it did in Bombay—
although sometimes, one suspects, appearance belied reality. Certainly in reality there was less emphasis in the Punjab on non-
official participation than there was in Bombay; the Punjab tradition of "paternalism" died hard. It is worthwhile examining
another, rather different tradition.

It cannot even be claimed that nothing has been written on co-
operation in Bombay. There is a useful government-sponsored
fiftieth-anniversary volume,[17] which concentrates, however, on the
period after the depression of the thirties. Another carefully com-
piled fiftieth-anniversary volume was published by the Bombay
State Co-operative Union.[18] The authors of these books do not appear to have made much use of unpublished or manuscript material, however. Probably they did not feel the need to explain the
social and economic background of the co-operative movement,
since it was perhaps already to some extent known to their readers
simply because they were Indian. Yet another brief study of the
history of the co-operative movement in the Bombay area was
made by Dr. K. N. Naik in his volume entitled *The Co-operative
Movement in the Bombay State*. This work was published in 1953;
its historical sections were criticized by the late V. S. Bhide, an
Indian who was Registrar at the end of the twenties, as being "over-
charged with emotion" in their "patriotic eagerness to castigate
a foreign regime."[19] It ought to be possible now, over twenty years
after Independence, to take a balanced view of an era that has
gone. "The events covered in this book," writes Dr. Gopal in the
Preface to his study of Lord Irwin's viceroyalty, "are now as much
a part of history as, say, the Norman Conquest. Contemporaneity is
a matter of mood as well as of time."[20]

16 Hubert Calvert, *The Wealth and Welfare of the Punjab* (1922); C. F. Strickland,
An Introduction to Co-operation in India (1922); Malcolm Lyall Darling, *The Punjab
Peasant in Prosperity and Debt* (1925), *Rusticus Loquitor, or The Old Light and the
New in the Punjab Village* (1930), *Wisdom and Waste in the Punjab Village* (1934).
See also, for another well-known Punjab "development" project, F. L. Brayne, *Socrates
in an Indian Village* (1929).
17 [N. V. Nayak.] *Fifty Years of Co-operation in the Bombay State* (1957).
18 K. N. Naik, ed., *Fifty Years of Co-operation: Golden Jubilee Souvenir* (1954).
19 Review, *Bombay Co-operative Quarterly* [*B. C. Q.*], July 1953, pp. 33–38.
20 S. Gopal, *The Viceroyalty of Lord Irwin, 1926–1931* (1957).

Some men who figure in this study are still alive; some have only recently died. When an historian has met some of those, both British and Indian, whose decisions he may at times have to criticize, he perhaps approaches his task with a little more humility. In writing this book I have often been reminded of Professor Butterfield's complaint that he has known many students who could easily find fault with the diplomacy of Bismarck, but who themselves were quite incapable of wheedling sixpence out of a college porter.[21] I hope that I have not treated anyone completely unjustly.

[21] Herbert Butterfield, *History and Human Relations*, p. 169.

I

The Deccan Riots and Deccan Indebtedness, 1875-1904

The Disturbances of 1875

The first outbreak of rioting against money-lenders in the Deccan in May 1875 appears to have taken place in Supa, a village about forty miles from Poona. Twenty-fours later there was a disturbance in another village, fourteen miles away, and over the next fortnight at least thirty more villages (quite possibly twice as many) were similarly affected.[1] The wrath of the rioters was directed chiefly against the Marwari and Gujarati money-lenders; the Maharashtrian Brahman money-lenders, far fewer in numbers, were usually left alone. The riots did not spread with startling rapidity;[2] as a result, police and army units were sometimes forewarned and arrived in time to avert outbreaks in a number of villages.

The pattern followed in most of the riots was that men began congregating in the afternoon, sometimes within a village, often just outside it. When dark came, there was a noisy rush on the money-lenders' houses. Often a hundred or more men took part;

[1] According to the official *Report of the Committee on the Riots in Poona and Ahmednagar, 1875* [*Deccan Riots Rept.*], p. 4, disturbances "took place" in thirty-three villages in the two districts, and were "threatened" in thirty-one more villages in Poona district and in many other villages in Ahmadnagar district. Shivram Hari Sathe, Hon. Sec., Poona Sarvajanik Sabha, claimed that riots had actually taken place in a number of villages which are not mentioned in government reports: Sathe to Ch. Sec., Bom., 28 June 1875. (B.R.O., J.D. Vol. 82 of 1875.)

[2] They took a fortnight to spread over an area of only about forty miles from north to south and sixty miles from east to west. One of the biggest and quickest leaps taken by the riots seems to have been the first—fourteen miles in a day. Even the *Grand Peur* of the early days of the French Revolution does not seem to have moved at more than walking pace: Georges Lefebvre, *La Grande Peur de 1789*, p. 182.

the money-lenders of Supa—which was really more of a market-town than a village—claimed in a petition, probably with the hyperbole not unusual in such documents, that eight hundred had participated in the disturbance there.[3] The money-lenders were generally warned of what was to come; many of them seem to have complied with the rioters' demands, which were normally limited to the surrender by the money-lenders of their "bonds" and other documents—the written evidence of indebtedness—and the destruction of those documents. Little violence followed. One group of villagers was even reported to have paid the railway fare of their money-lender to a safe haven.[4] There was, in fact, evidence of the "discriminating purposefulness" which has been noticed as a mark of somewhat similar disturbances in Europe.[5] If the money-lenders did not comply with the rioters' demands, or had left the village earlier, the rioters would use their lighted torches to set fire to the money-lenders' haystacks (here again there are European parallels), ladders would be brought so that the rioters could enter the money-lenders' comparatively opulent two-storied houses, doors and shutters would be prised open with iron bars, and then the money-lenders' houses would be set on fire. Even in these cases, however, there was little real violence: according to government records, only one money-lender was seriously injured.

Peasants and Money-lenders

Although the Government of India may have feared a "general Maratha uprising,"[6] the Government of Bombay do not appear to have taken quite such an alarmist view of the situation.[7] For one thing, apart from an isolated and possibly hardly related riot in Satara district in October 1875, the disturbances appear to have

---

[3] Petition of the Supa Sowkars to Govr., Bom., 23 September 1875. (B.R.O., Vol. cited.)

[4] S. H. Sathe to G. of B., letter cited.

[5] George Rudé, *The Crowd in History*, p. 253. For a more extended attempt to compare the Deccan Riots with other agrarian disturbances in India and Europe, see I. J. Catanach, "Agrarian Disturbances in Nineteenth Century India," *Indian Economic and Social History Review*, Vol. III, No. 1 (March 1966).

[6] The words used by Thomas R. Metcalf in his useful but somewhat brief article, "The British and the Moneylender in Nineteenth-century India," *Journal of Modern History*, Vol. XXXIV, No. 4 (December 1962), p. 395.

[7] See notes of W. Lee-Warner, Ag. U. Sec., Bom. R.D., 13 and 14 June 1875, and A.R[ogers]., Member of Council, G. of B., 13 June 1875; there is no sign of panic. See also the careful drafting by J. Gibbs, Member of Council, and E. W. Ravenscroft, Ch. Sec., of Bom. R.D. letter to G. of I., R. & A. Dept., No. 4072 of 16 July 1875. (B.R.O., Vol. cited.)

been virtually confined to certain talukas of only two districts,
Poona and Ahmadnagar. It was thus only as a result of some prod-
ding from Simla that the Government of Bombay appointed a
four-man commission, with some of its membership drawn from
outside the Bombay Presidency, to enquire into the riots.[8] The
Deccan Riots Commission duly reported, and some time after-
wards their report was made public. It was obvious, the Commission thought, that the riots were in some way connected with agricultural indebtedness. Agricultural indebtedness seemed to have
many causes, including the irregularity of the monsoon in the
Deccan and the consequent precarious nature of cultivation in the
area, and also the supposed "improvidence" and "extravagance"
of the rayat, especially at such times as weddings.[9] But the Commission devoted most of their attention to what they believed to
be a deterioration in the relations between peasants and money-
lenders, brought about largely as a result of the coming of British
notions about land and law. In particular, the Commission were
concerned about what they thought to be one of the most important signs of these deteriorating relations, an increase in the rate of
transfer of land from agriculturists to non-agriculturists.

Until recently most students of Indian history would have been
inclined to accept the Commission's analysis without much hesitation. After all, it was money-lenders' houses that were burnt to
the ground in 1875. But in the past few years there have been some
hints of the necessity for revising our concepts about agricultural
indebtedness in nineteenth century India, and, in particular, our
concepts about the transfer of land from agriculturists to non-
agriculturists. Dr. Dharma Kumar, for example, claimed, in a book
published in 1965, that in the Madras Presidency, in the last two
decades of the nineteenth century, "there seems to have been no
large-scale dispossession of the peasantry by money-lenders and

8 Telegrams, Viceroy to Govr., Bom., 2 and 6 August 1875; Notes of Rogers, 4 August, and Gibbs, 7 August 1875. (B.R.O., Vol. cited.)
9 *Deccan Riots Rept.*, p. 49. It is extremely difficult to find reliable data on the
proportion of rural indebtedness which resulted from expenditure on marriages and
other ceremonial and social occasions. In 1929–30 estimates for two villages in
Gujarat and three villages in the Karnatak varied from 14.1 per cent to 45.8 per cent.
See *Report of the Bombay Provincial Banking Enquiry Committee, 1929–30*, Vol. I
[*Bom. Prov. Banking Enquiry Cttee. Rept.*], p. 49. See also the Committee's cautionary
words about the reliability of these estimates, ibid., p. 50.

traders."[10] This assertion prompted Professor Morris David Morris to assert that "most of the evidence that is cited about land transfers comes from periods of famine and may therefore not be representative."[11]

Recently we have had some indications that Professor Morris's queries may be justified. Dr. Eric Stokes has begun to show us that in the North-western Provinces, at least in the first half of the century, many of the land transfers took place within the so-called landholding castes rather than between agriculturist and non-agriculturist groups.[12] And in some painstaking work on the Punjab—the seat of many of the fears about land transfer in the nineteenth century—Dr. P. H. M. van den Dungen has demonstrated that the traditional picture of indebtedness in that part of India is in need of modification. In the Punjab, too, it seems, land was often transferred within the cultivating "tribes," rather than to Hindu trading castes. When land did pass to Hindus in the Punjab, its new owners sometimes showed themselves, by the end of the century, to be "improving" landlords.[13] Professor Bernard Cohn has now taken the argument a step further. He claims that, at least so far as "political" power in the villages was concerned, it was frequently of no great consequence who, legally speaking, owned the land in nineteenth century India. The new owners often merely had "some rights over land and its product." The old landed castes remained in real control in the villages.[14]

What, then, have we to say about the Deccan? It is clear that long before the British assumption of power the peasants were heavily indebted to Gujarati and, to some extent, to Marwari money-lenders. The Gujaratis had come first, mainly in the seven-

[10] Dharma Kumar, *Land and Caste in South India: Agricultural Labour in the Madras Presidency in the Nineteenth Century*, p. 179.

[11] Morris David Morris, "Economic Change and Agriculture in Nineteenth Century India" (a review article on Kumar, *Land and Caste*), *Indian Economic and Social History Review*, Vol. III, No. 2 (June 1966).

[12] Eric Stokes, "Traditional Elites in the Great Rebellion of 1857: Some Aspects of Rural Revolt in the Upper and Central Doab" (Paper presented to Conference on South Asian Elites, Cambridge, April 1968), and "Agrarian Indebtedness and the Great Rebellion of 1857 in India: A Study of the Saharanpur District" (forthcoming).

[13] P. H. M. van den Dungen, "Changes in Status and Occupation in Nineteenth Century Panjab," in *Soundings in Modern South Asian History*, ed. D. A. Low, pp. 76, 81.

[14] Bernard S. Cohn, "Recruitment of Elites in India under British Rule" (Paper presented to the Conference on Modern South Asian Studies, Cambridge, July 1968).

teenth and eighteenth centuries. The Marwaris had come later,
but still, it would appear, to some extent in pre-British times.[15]
The Marwari and Gujarati money-lenders had come because
Maharashtra to a large extent lacked *bania* (money-lending) castes.
The Poona Peshwas, it was true, borrowed from local Brahmans,
and doubtless some Deshasth Brahman *kulkarnis* (village accountants) lent money in the eighteenth century, as they did under
the British.[16] But, generally speaking, money-lending was in the
hands of non-Maharashtrians, even before the British assumption
of power. Peasant debts were of two kinds, individual debts and
village debts. In the days of the Peshwas the village "money-
lender" did not in fact deal in money to any great extent. He supplied the cultivator with seed, and supplied him with food grains
while his crop matured, in return for a portion—sometimes a
considerable portion—of the harvest. He was thus primarily a
small-scale trader, a source of loans in kind and a disposal agent
for the peasant's "surplus." Only occasionally did he give cash
loans—when, for example, a peasant had to provide a dowry for his
daughter. Other, larger money-lenders, often urban "bankers,"
lent to whole villages, through the village headmen, at those times
of the year at which revenue payments were due from the villages.[17]
Rates of interest were high; a British official, William Chaplin,
Commissioner in the Deccan, had commented on the fact as early
as 1822.[18] As the Deccan Riots Commission realized, high interest

15 *Gazetteer of the Bombay Presidency,* Vol. XVII, *Ahmednagar,* pp. 76–79; 294–95.
16 A distinction must be made between Chitpavan Brahmans and Deshasth
Brahmans. The Chitpavan Brahmans appear to have come originally from the
Konkan; they had been placed in positions of considerable responsibility in Maharashtra by the Peshwas. The Deshasth Brahmans belong to the *Desh,* that is the
Deccan plateau. One group of Deshasth Brahmans, the Madhyandin Brahmans (who
may originally have come from central India) were particularly notable for trading
and money-lending activities in pre-British times, and formed the main body of
those Brahmans who lent money to the Peshwas. See I. Karve, *Maharashtra—Land and
its People,* pp. 18–19, 81. Yet another Maharashtrian Brahman community which
deserves notice at this point is that of the Sarasvat Brahmans. They come now from
the Konkan, but they possibly originated in Bengal and, even before that, in the
region of the south Punjab through which the now non-existent river Sarasvati used
to flow. They form a vigorous trading and intellectual community in modern Bombay. See Karve, *Maharashtra,* p. 18, and also Selig S. Harrison, *India: The Most
Dangerous Decades,* p. 105.
17 *Ahmednagar Gazetteer,* pp. 305–6; Ravinder Kumar, "The Deccan Riots of
1875," *Journal of Asian Studies,* Vol. XXIV, No. 4 (August 1965).
18 William Chaplin, *A Report exhibiting a view of the Fiscal and Judicial System
of Administration introduced into the Conquered Territory above the Ghauts under
the Authority of the Commissioner in the Dekhan* (1824), pp. 174–75.

rates had always been to a considerable extent the result of irregular rainfall: the money-lender could never be sure of repayment.
But indebtedness had to be combined with—indeed, to some extent it had to be the result of—a system of free sale and mortgage
for large-scale transfer of land from one set of persons to another
to be possible.

It cannot be said that the British were altogether responsible
for introducing such a system to the Deccan. Under the Marathas
the so-called *mirasdars*—probably a majority of the cultivators in
Ahmadnagar and Poona districts[19]—had certain rights of "sale"
and "mortgage," although the rights of individual *mirasdars* or
mirasdar families are supposed to have been heavily circumscribed
by their fellow *mirasdars* and by the government. We must beware,
however, of giving too much credence to the idealized versions of
the situation in the Deccan presented to some of the early British
administrators by their Brahman advisers (just as we must beware
of some of the early reports prepared by Indians for the British
conquerors of Bengal.) A recent study by a Japanese scholar shows
quite clearly that the rights of alienation of *mirasdars* in the Deccan, especially of those who did not hold official positions in the
village, were not *in practice* so greatly circumscribed by the end of
the Maratha period.[20] This state of affairs may well have been an
indication of a trend towards independent proprietary right—a
trend emphasized in the disturbed conditions of the later eighteenth century. Certainly such a tendency is observable in later
seventeenth century and eighteenth century North India.[21]

19 Mountstuart Elphinstone, "The State of the Conquered Territories" (1823), para.
420. *Select Cttee. on the Affairs of the East India Company, Minutes of Evidence,*
Vol. III, Appx., p. 653. *P.P.* 1831–32 (735–III) xi.

20 Hiroshi Fukazawa, "Lands and Peasants in the Eighteenth Century Maratha
Kingdom," *Hitotsubashi Journal of Economics,* Vol. VI, No. 1 (June 1965), especially
p. 40. Probably the most reliable of the accounts presented by the earliest British
administrators were those by Lt. Col. W. H. Sykes, "Statistical Reporter" to the
Government of Bombay, 1824–31. In *Land Tenures of the Dekkan* (1835), pp. 11–12,
he makes the distinction between *mirasdar* and *watandar*. A *mirasdar* was simply an
hereditary landholder. A *watandar* held hereditary office in the village. As a representative of government he was given a *watan,* that is, land upon which revenue did
not have to be paid but which in theory—because office went with it—could not be
alienated without the permission of the village leaders and of the government.
Popular usage tended to confuse *mirasdar* and *watandar,* but, as Sykes put it: "The
Watandar was always a Mirasdar; but the Mirasdar, simply as such, was not
necessarily a Watandar."

21 See S. Nurul Hasan, "The Position of the Zamindars in the Mughal Empire,"
Indian Economic and Social History Review, Vol. I, No. 4 (April–June 1964); Irfan
Habib, *The Agrarian System of Mughal India,* p. 162; B. R. Grover, "Nature of Land-

Of course, when scholars, after a great deal more enquiry, have satisfied themselves about rural conditions in the last years of the Peshwas, they will doubtless still have to admit that British policy, and especially the "Survey Settlement" of 1836 and the following years (which conferred unrestricted rights of transfer on all who paid land revenue), upset to some extent the traditional pattern of lending in the Deccan. Furthermore—and probably more importantly—the British brought with them their civil courts; mortgage bonds could now be enforced through foreclosure or the threat of foreclosure. The custom of sitting *dharna* at a debtor's door in order to recover a loan soon largely disappeared;[22] so, too, did the principle of *dam dapat*—the belief that the total interest should not exceed the sum originally lent. The introduction of a strict rayatwari revenue system, under which individuals rather than villages were liable for the payment of land revenue, put an end to the activities of those bankers who lent to whole villages. The local money-lender-cum-trader now added to his activities. He now often became an unofficial tax-gatherer, making payments of land revenue on his individual clients' behalf. Local money-lenders became more numerous and possibly more unscrupulous. Yet such a situation was not altogether detrimental to the peasant's welfare. His credit had been enlarged because of the increased mortgage value of his land, and this, together with the increase in trade caused by the construction of better roads and of railways, brought about the great extension of cultivation which took place in the Deccan in the forty or so years preceding the riots of 1875. For example, in Petha Supa—the area where the riots first broke out in 1875—the cultivated area increased from 114,000 acres at the time of the first survey settlement to at least 142,000 acres in 1873. In the same period, it was calculated, population increased by 43 per cent, working bullocks by 10 per cent, carts by 220 per cent, ploughs by 31 per cent, and wells in use by 71 per cent.[23] Since

Rights in Mughal India," *Indian Economic and Social History Review*, Vol. I, No. 1 (July–September 1963), p. 15; Tapan Raychaudhuri, "The Agrarian System of Mughal India," *Enquiry*, New Series, Vol. II, No. 1 (Old Series No. 10) (Spring 1965), pp. 96–97.

[22] A creditor, or, more often, his servant, would sit at a debtor's door telling passers-by the reason for his sitting there. Sometimes less peaceful methods were used by the servants of money-lenders.

[23] W. G. Pedder, "Leading Points Regarding Revision Settlements," and Bom. G.R.R.D. No. 5739 of 29 October 1874. (N.A.I., Revenue, Agriculture and Commerce [L. Rev.] A Procs., March 1875, No. 18.) For the extension of cultivation in other Deccan areas in the early nineteenth century, see N. V. Sovani, "British Impact on

the numbers of bullocks and ploughs—vital to the peasant's prosperity—had not kept pace with the increase in population, it can hardly be claimed that this part of the Deccan had undergone all-round economic growth. Nevertheless, in some respects there had obviously not been stagnation.[24]

The Deccan Riots Commission did not give a great deal of attention to such wider changes. They concentrated instead on their main theme of agricultural indebtedness. They noted, for example, the considerable increase in the numbers of mortgage and sale deeds registered between 1869–70 and 1873–74 in two of the affected talukas. They found evidence, too, of a considerable increase in Poona and Ahmadnagar districts of the number of suits for debt. More specifically, they noticed a distinct rise in the number of suits for mortgaged land. At Talegaon, in Poona district, for instance, there were six such suits in 1854. In 1872 there were 192; of these, 143 were suits against cultivators. And in the twelve villages in the Ahmadnagar district which the Commission specially investigated, it was found that, according to Revenue Department records, about an eighth of the so-called occupancies were held by money-lenders, and that the money-lenders had acquired these occupancies within the past twenty years, and for the most part within the last ten years.[25]

At first sight such a case for the growth of agricultural indebtedness is convincing enough; it certainly has to be said that in its statistical detail the report was a model for its time. It is worthwhile noting, however, that the Poona Sarvajanik Sabha (one of the earliest of the Deccan's "proto-nationalist" political organizations) had claimed in 1873 that "three quarters of the suits for small debts in all the Civil Courts of the country are instituted not

---

India before 1850–57," *Cahiers d'histoire mondiale,* Vol. I, No. 4 (April 1954), p. 868. We must be somewhat wary of statistics for "cultivated area," since in Bombay these represented area on which land revenue was paid rather than the area actually farmed. But the intention of "cultivation" was presumably there, otherwise the land would have been surrendered.

24 Morris, "Economic Change," p. 205, speaks of "the clearing of forests, the elimination of the waste, the suppression of the fallow, not to mention the growing regional specialization and the shift of output from lower to higher value crops which seem to have marked the 19th century." He could also have mentioned the growth of double-cropping: in the ten years prior to 1891–92 double-cropping in the Bombay Presidency rose by 28 per cent. *Statement Exhibiting the Moral and Material Progress and Condition of India during the decennial period from 1882–83 to 1891–92,* p. 423. *P.P.* 1894 (43) lix.

25 *Deccan Riots Rept.,* pp. 55–59.

with a view to secure their payment, but to obtain a renewal of
the bonds that would otherwise be time-barred."[26] There may
have been a certain amount of exaggeration here, but the charge
was still significant. It would seem, too, that not all "sales" registered in the years before 1875 were genuine; some were probably
no more than very secure mortgages.[27] The Deccan Riots Commission appear to have been at least to some extent aware that in the
Deccan the registration of a "sale" deed did not necessarily lead
to a change of "occupant" (*khatedar*); that is, it did not necessarily
lead to a change in the person from whom, according to revenue
records, land revenue was due. As the Commission put it, the
money-lender was reluctant to assume the "responsibilities of recorded proprietorship."[28] A man whose status, though he still
worked the land that had been his, was now in fact that of a tenant-
at-will of a money-lender, might still be theoretically liable for the
payment of land revenue. This situation suited the money-lender;
and it suited the former owner to think that, since he was still the
"occupant" so far as the Revenue Department was concerned, he
had not completely lost his connection with his ancestral lands. It
is possible, then, that in the twelve Ahmadnagar villages investigated by the Deccan Riots Commission the number of holdings in
effect transferred to money-lenders over the twenty years before
1875 was even higher than the figure of one-eighth of the total
quoted in the Deccan Riots Report. For the Commission's calculations were based on the number of recorded transfers of "occupancies." But there was, of course, no guarantee that a money-
lender, having gained an "occupancy" right, was going to keep it;
he might well keep it only until he could find a buyer—perhaps, in
fact, the former owner. Furthermore, the Commission admitted
that most of the transfers in its twelve sample villages had taken
place in the ten years or so before the riots. It could well be argued
(bearing in mind Professor Morris's strictures) that these transfers

26 *Report from the Sub-Committee of the Poona Sarvajanik Sabha appointed to
collect Information to be laid before the East India Finance Committee on matters
relating to India*, p. 64. (I.O.L., Temple Papers, MSS. Eur. F.86/214: "Native Opinion
in India." I owe the reference to this rare pamphlet to Dr. S. R. Mehrotra.) Bonds
became "time-barred"—unenforceable at law—after six years, or after three years if
they were unregistered, under the Limitation Act of 1859.
27 H. B. Boswell, Collector of Ahmadnagar in 1875, thought that "not 30 per cent"
of the sales recorded in the registration records were bona fide. See his Administration
Report, 1874–75, quoted *Deccan Riots Rept.*, Appx. A, p. 224.
28 *Deccan Riots Rept.*, p. 83.

were the result of the contraction of trade after the bonanza conditions of the American Civil War period,[29] a contraction which
coincided with conditions of scarcity, if not of famine, in 1870–71
and 1871–72; these conditions, therefore, did not necessarily represent a long-term trend. It is difficult, however, to dismiss completely the rather harrowing reports by various officials which
were quoted by the Commission, some of them coming from years
well before the Civil War. Many of these reports asserted that dispossession was taking place or that the threat of it was ever present.[30] Furthermore, the fact that many peasants, though legally
dispossessed, still tried to retain in the revenue records at least
some of the prerogatives of ownership indicates that, whatever may
have been the case in the rest of India, in the Deccan the possession
of land mattered a great deal in terms of individual peasant psy-
chology. A twentieth century Director of Agriculture in Bombay
summed matters up when he said that a man would "really rather
get Rs.10 a month by cultivating his own lot, than get Rs.15 a
month and work for somebody else."[31]

So far as the Deccan as a whole is concerned, then, it seems that
we must accept, on the combined evidence of the statistics and the

[29] Professor Morris, in his major work, *The Emergence of an Industrial Labor
Force in India: A Study of the Bombay Cotton Mills, 1854–1947*, p. 18, n. 40, claims
that at the time of the war "rising prices of cotton apparently affected only those
districts of India where cotton was grown." This may have been so, strictly speaking,
but in Deccan districts where comparatively little cotton was grown, such as Poona
and Sholapur, there does seem to have been a considerable rise in the prices of
basic millets, in sympathy with cotton prices. See graph showing fluctuations in
prices of *bajri* and *jowari* at Sholapur, 1821–75, in R. D. Choksey, *Economic Life in
the Bombay Deccan (1818–1939)*, p. 30.

[30] *Deccan Riots Rept.*, Appx. A., pp. 84–98, are of special significance: George
Wingate to Registrar of Court of Sadar Dewanee Adalat, No. 319, of 24 September
1852. Wingate was one of the architects of the Survey Settlement and has been
called "one of J. S. Mill's most unquestioning disciples" (Eric Stokes, *The English
Utilitarians and India*, p. 127). But already by 1852 he was alarmed by a situation
in which lands held by "uneconomic cultivators," which it had been hoped would
fall into the hands of "traders, pensioners and other parties having capital" under
the new arrangements, appeared in fact to be passing into the hands of money-
lenders.

[31] Harold Mann, 1927: *Royal Commission on Agriculture in India*, Vol. II., pt. i,
Evidence taken in the Bombay Presidency, p. 32. Mann also claimed (p. 77) that he
had had cultivators coming to him saying "This land does not belong to us, and
we are not going to bother to do more than get our one crop from it." A modern
survey carried out in western India comes to the conclusion that "even if we combine
the expenditures incurred by the landlords and the tenants, the per acre expenditure on improvement of the tenant cultivated lands would be only about one third
of that incurred on the owner cultivated lands." V. M. Dandekar and G. J. Khudanpur, *Working of the Bombay Tenancy Act, 1948: Report of Investigation* (1957),
pp. 143–45.

official reports, the notion that land transfer from agriculturist to
non-agriculturist classes was occurring, and probably occurring
increasingly, in the twenty or thirty years preceding the Deccan
Riots. We must accept the notion, too, that this situation was regarded seriously by the Deccan peasantry. But this is not to say
that the Deccan Riots were necessarily a result mainly of increasing land transfer. For when one actually comes to examine why
riots ocurred in, say, one village in a specific area but not in another, one finds that one has to take into account such factors as
the presence or absence of suitable leadership, the timing of
weekly markets, and the power of rumour. Fears seem to have been
produced by an epidemic of cholera. Fears and expectations seem
to have arisen also from the conduct of enquiries by government
officials, in connection with the compilation of the District Gazetteers, into the activities of money-lending groups. Here, perhaps, is
one reason for the existence, at the time of the riots, of the belief
that the government in some way supported the rioters. According
to one Indian newspaper, the story circulated that "a Marwadi
creditor bought an attachment on the gown of a European lady.
The gentleman was greatly enraged at the insolent proceeding of
the Marwadi, and reported the same to Government, which has
issued a circular order to plunder Marwadis wherever they may be
found." Some villagers were reported to have restrained themselves temporarily from riot while they waited for the mythical
government order to be received.[32]

When all is said, of course, it still has to be admitted that the
Deccan Riots were related, to a considerable extent, to grievances
against money-lending groups. These were not necessarily long-
term grievances, however. One very important factor in triggering
off the riots had been in existence only since February 1875. At
this time, as a concession to a certain amount of vaguely Poona-
inspired agitation against revised revenue settlements, the Government of Bombay announced that, in future cases of non-
payment of land revenue, peasants' "moveable" property—their
cattle and implements—rather than their land, would be confis-
cated first. But the money-lenders, pressing hard for recovery of

---

[32] For elaboration of this paragraph see Catanach, "Agrarian Disturbances," pp.
70–75. For the story of the Marwari and the European woman, see *Dnyanodaya*, 10
June 1875, quoted "Report on the Native Papers of the Bombay Presidency," week
ending 19 June 1875.

loans given in the near-famine years of the early seventies, and themselves often being pressed by larger urban money-lenders-cum-bankers, found a way to take advantage of this concession. Those money-lenders who paid the land revenue on the peasants' behalf had generally done so by instalments. But now, because the money-lenders no longer considered the peasants' land, the money-lenders' chief security, to be in immediate danger of government attachment, some of them refused to pay the second instalment of the land revenue demand, even though the peasants' surplus had already been delivered to them in the belief that this instalment would be paid. The money-lenders, since they often already had all the peasants' "surplus," and sometimes more,[33] presumably felt that only they could benefit from any eventual remission of revenue payments; some peasants, however, were apparently not prepared to let them play this game. But even this explanation of the riots cannot be taken too far, since the Government order of February 1875 applied to areas in which riots did not occur, as well as to areas that were riot-stricken in May and June.[34] Again, then, we are forced to return to some extent to what might be described as psychological reasons for the riots.

When one looks carefully at the sort of people who took part in the riots, one finds again that the simple "economic" explanation of "poverty" and "indebtedness" is insufficient. The isolated riot in the Satara district in October 1875, long after the main series of riots, does seem to have been, at the outset, the work of comparatively poor people—not, however, of cultivators by caste but of Mangs, ropemakers, men, incidentally, with a reputation for rebelliousness.[35] But the leadership of the riots of May and June was generally, it would appear, in the hands of men from old *mirasdar* groups. These men were not necessarily the wealthiest in the vil-

---

[33] The notions of "surplus" and of "subsistence" are extraordinarily difficult to define. In India today the very small peasant, thoroughly indebted to his money-lender-cum-trader, is often compelled to make "distress sales"; it can be argued, therefore, that he sells more than his "surplus." See Dharm Narain, *Distribution of Marketed Surplus of Agricultural Produce by Size-level of Holding in India, 1950–51,* pp. 34–37. See also Harry W. Pearson, "The Economy Has No Surplus: Critique of A Theory of Development," in *Trade and Market in the Early Empires,* ed. Karl Polanyi, Conrad M. Arensberg, and Harry W. Pearson.

[34] Catanach, "Agrarian Disturbances," pp. 68–69.

[35] Thomas Coats, "Account of the Present State of the Township of Lony . . ." (Paper read 29 February 1820), *Transactions of the Literary Society of Bombay,* Vol. III, 1823, p. 189; also Henry Orenstein, *Gaon: Conflict and Cohesion in an Indian Village,* p. 119.

lage, but they were certainly not normally amongst the poor. *Patils*, village headmen, were the most common leaders. The position of the headman in the Deccan system of administration was a difficult one: he was both village leader and the servant of government. The Deccan Riots showed that at a time of conflict the headman was liable to assume his traditional leadership role in the village, or at least to forget his duties as policeman and informant. And yet, as the Deccan Riots Report itself pointed out, very acutely, "an assembly of villagers acting with their natural leaders for a definite object, was a less dangerous body than a mob of rioters with no responsible head would have been."[36] When the riots were not in the hands of *patils* they were occasionally led by relics of the pre-British order. On one occasion a man who probably traced his ancestry to a Maratha *subhedar* family appears to have taken a good deal of the initiative.[37]

It is more difficult to generalize about those who followed these leaders. But perhaps some indication may be obtained from the depositions of seventy-four rioters, which were published in an appendix to the Deccan Riots Commission's Report.[38] These must be used cautiously, as almost all who made statements took the opportunity to protest that they had absolutely nothing to do with the riots; certainly they may not form a cross-section of the rioters. But they make up virtually the only sample we have—most unfortunately, records of cases such as these, which were dealt with summarily, do not seem to have survived in Bombay or in the Collectors' offices. Of the seventy-four convicted rioters about whom we know something we can roughly distinguish the economic and social position of fifty-six. Thirteen were village servants, *balutedars*, or village artisans, many—but probably not all— in fairly poor circumstances. They may have been amongst the "bad characters" who appear with monotonous regularity as a vague category in reports of the Deccan Riots, as they do in reports of many other Indian disturbances—but there is no real reason to

[36] *Deccan Riots Rept.*, p. 6. See also Catanach, "Agrarian Disturbances," p. 74.

[37] The most important leader at Supa appears to have been one "Rungrow Narayen Soobhedar" (Rangrao Narayan Subhedar): Petition of the Supa Sowkars, 23 September 1875. (B.R.O., J.D. Vol. 82 of 1875.) For the role of the *subhedar* in the Maratha system, see Surendranath Sen, *Administrative System of the Marathas*, 2d ed., p. 94. The *subhedar* was perhaps the nearest Maratha equivalent of the modern Collector.

[38] Appx. B.

think that *balutedars* were especially lawless. Several of the convicted *balutedars* claimed, probably truthfully, that they had simply picked up odd pieces of property in the confusion after the riots and were arrested when it was found in their possession. Eight more of the fifty-six whom we can place appear to have been landless (one or two of these had recently become landless). Ten had an assessment of under twenty rupees. But twenty-eight of the fifty-six, and probably another nine, paid twenty rupees or more in land revenue every year. Amongst these were several who had no mortgage debt whatsoever. An assessment of twenty rupees would mean almost certainly a holding of at least twenty acres, and probably more. In 1875–76 the average assessment per "occupied" acre in Poona district was 8 annas 3 pice.[39] But the Deccan Riots Commission claimed, with some evidence to back them up, that "of the occupants in embarrassed circumstances about two thirds hold land of less than twenty rupees assessment."[40] If the depositions of the convicted rioters provide any indication at all, the sort of people who took part in the Deccan Riots may well have been mainly from the solid middle group of the peasantry, with holdings of, say, twenty to fifty acres. Such men were, by the standards of the Deccan of the time, neither very wealthy nor very poor.[41] Some of them may, in fact, have had few connections with money-lenders; after

---

[39] *Jamabandi* [Land Revenue] *Rept., S.D., Bombay Presidency, 1875–76*, p. 31.

[40] *Deccan Riots Rept.*, p. 59.

[41] Rural Maharashtra in the nineteenth century could perhaps become almost as controversial as Tawney's and Trevor-Roper's sixteenth and seventeenth century England; there is a similar paucity of reliable information. But Dr. Ravinder Kumar seems to go a little too far when, in "The Rise of the Rich Peasants in Western India," in *Soundings in Modern South Asian History*, ed. D. A. Low, p. 55, he contrasts the wealth of a small group with "the poverty of the overwhelming mass of the cultivators, who bore a crippling burden of debt, whose position became increasingly desperate with the passage of time and who rose against their oppressors in 1875." Part of Dr. Kumar's argument appears to be that when in the late 1860s Colonel Francis spoke of the increased prosperity of the rayats he was in fact judging on the basis of what he saw of the standard of life of a small minority, the "rich peasants." The official statistics, for what they are worth, of number and extent of holdings (including *inam* land) in government villages in Poona and Ahmadnagar districts in 1875–76 are given in Table 1, p. 237. It must be emphasized that these statistics and other similar series over the years tell us virtually nothing about the size of the actual cultivated units. See below, pp. 187–88, and *Royal Commission on Agriculture*, Vol. II, pt. i, *Evidence taken in Bombay*, pp. 76–78: evidence of Dr. Harold Mann. It is worthwhile noting also that in 1921 twenty acres of (largely dry-crop) land in the Deccan were considered, by the same authority, to be the minimum necessary to support an average family without recourse to subsidiary occupations: Harold Mann and N. V. Kanitkar, *Land and Labour in a Deccan Village*, Study No. II, p. 43.

all, the Deccan Riots Commission thought that only one-third of all the occupants were, as they put it, "embarrassed by debt."[42]

The Deccan Agriculturists' Relief Act

The Deccan Riots Commission felt that there were two possible ways of dealing with the problem of agricultural indebtedness. One was to put checks on the activities of the money-lender; the other was to compete with him in the provision of credit.

The Commission found themselves to be in favour of some legal restraint on the activities of the money-lender. As a result, the Government of India brought into being the Deccan Agriculturists' Relief Act of 1879. Significantly enough, in view of past and future attitudes of the Government of Bombay, the Government of India seems to have acted in this instance only after a certain amount of pressure had been brought to bear on it, from Bombay, by Sir Richard Temple's government.[43] Temple had served his apprenticeship in the Punjab, where official attitudes to agricultural indebtedness tended to be more clear-cut than they were in Bombay. The Deccan Agriculturists' Relief Act was one of the first of many pieces of legislation in various parts of India which attempted to halt transfer of land (real, or occasionally, perhaps, supposed) from the "agriculturist" to the "non-agriculturist" classes. Under the Act, in indebtedness cases in which agriculturists were involved, the Civil Courts were to investigate the whole history of the transactions; they could reduce interest rates if they saw fit, and order the repayment of debts by instalments. Only in the direst of circumstances were the courts to permit the sale of a debtor's land, and then only if the land had been pledged as a security. But it was hoped that many cases would not reach the courts; provision was made for specially appointed local conciliators and village *munsifs* (low-ranking Indian judges) to settle cases wherever possible. In the four districts to which the Act originally applied—Poona, Ahmadnagar, Sholapur, and Satara— the documents respecting all loans, leases, mortgages, and sales in which agriculturists were concerned, no matter how small the sum involved, now had to be registered if they were to be recognized by the courts. Provisions was made for the registration of small trans-

---

[42] *Deccan Riots Rept.*, p. 55.
[43] Minute by Temple, 30 August 1878, quoted *Agricultural Indebtedness in India and its Remedies, being Selections from Official Documents*, ed. S. C. Ray, Appx. I.

actions by "village registrars." At first these were the *kulkarnis*, that is, the village accountants.[44] These, however, were soon thought to be inefficient. Registration by village *kulkarnis* did not last beyond 1882; the "circle registrars" who took their places were probably—at first, at any rate—little more efficient.[45]

There is some evidence of a shortage of agricultural credit in the Deccan in the years immediately following the introduction of the Deccan Agriculturists' Relief Act.[46] The explanation of this phenomenon offered at the time was that the money-lender felt that his ultimate security, the peasant's land, was no longer sure and therefore, on occasion, he would not lend. No one at this time seems to have considered the possibility that the new investment opportunities which were gradually opening up in the industrializing city of Bombay, after the booms and crashes of the sixties, might have been attracting capital, especially Gujarati capital, which before the late seventies and the eighties would have been invested in the rural sphere.[47] Opinions differed as to the degree to which the Deccan peasant was deprived of the capital which had normally been at his disposal. Mahadev Govind Ranade, notable as a political figure and also as one of the judges specially appointed to supervise the working of the Act, insisted that the shortage was a legacy of the 1876–77 famine and that in any case all who were really credit-worthy could obtain their requirements.[48] One suspects, however, that Ranade's definition of "credit-worthy" was one which excluded a majority of the Deccan peasants; Ranade does not appear to have had a great deal of sympathy for the per-

[44] For outlines of the Deccan Agriculturists' Relief Act and its amendments, see K. G. Sivaswamy, *Legislative Protection and the Relief of Agriculturist Debtors in India*, chapter II; for a legal approach, see K. S. Gupte, *The Dekkhan Agriculturists' Relief Act. . . . As modified up to the 31st March 1928.*

[45] A. D. Pollen, "Report on the Operation of the Deccan Agriculturists' Relief Act during the year 1882." (I.O.R., Lee-Warner Political and Miscellaneous Private Papers, "Deccan Ryot, Series II," f. 221. I owe the reference to these papers to Dr. Richard Tucker.)

[46] Pollen, f. 226; also M. G. Ranade, quoted by Pollen, f. 223; H. Woodward, on Special Duty, to Ch. Sec., No. 30 of 25 June 1883, *Papers relating to the Deccan Agriculturists' Relief Act during the years 1875–94*, S.R. G. of I., Home Dept., No. cccxlii, Vol. I, p. 337.

[47] A very likely explanation, which does not appear to have been suggested until 1912: "Report of the Deccan Agriculturists' Relief Act Commission 1912," p. 7. (I.O.R., Bom. Legal Dept. Notification No. 1019 of 20 August 1914, Bom. Legal Procs., Vol. 9608.)

[48] Ranade, quoted Pollen, "Report on the . . . Relief Act . . . 1882," pp. 223–24. Cf. "Observations" by Raymond West, 27 July 1883, *Papers relating to the . . . Relief Act*, I, 387–96.

petually struggling small man.[49] It would seem that the eventual effect of the Relief Act was to increase considerably the number of ostensible "sales."[50] A sale of this variety meant that the Act was circumvented. It also meant, however, that the money-lender had what he regarded as reasonable security, and the peasant could have his loan. The Act does not appear to have led to any permanent impairment of the credit machinery of the Deccan. Some of those professional money-lenders whose business depended mainly on borrowed capital may have withdrawn.[51] More loans may have been given "on account," without any security, except, possibly, a promise on the part of the debtor to deliver produce to the creditor. But, if contemporary reports are to be believed, in the years after the passing of the Relief Act, there was a notable increase in the importance of "agriculturist money-lenders," men who belonged to the "agriculturist" classes and who were therefore not subject to the rigours of the Act. Such men (mainly Maratha by caste and many of them genuine cultivators as well as lenders of money) probably largely redressed any imbalance which the Act at first created.[52]

Agricultural Banks

As far as actual competition with the money-lender was concerned, the Deccan Riots Commission were somewhat shy of going

---

[49] Ranade, Note, 2 August 1883, on West's "Observations": "Much has been made of the statement contained in Mr. Woodward's report that the better classes of agriculturists have benefited more from the protection afforded to them than the less self-dependent classes. This result is in strict accordance with all reasonable human expectations. If it had been otherwise, there might have been grave cause for anxiety." *Papers relating to the . . . Relief Act,* I, 398. See also Richard P. Tucker, "M. G. Ranade and the Moderate Tradition in India (Ph.D. diss., Harvard University, 1966), pp. 205–34.

[50] *Report of the Commission appointed to Enquire into the Deccan Agriculturists' Relief Act, 1891–92,* p. 12.

[51] A. F. Woodburn, "Report on the . . . Relief Act" (1889), *Papers relating to the . . . Relief Act,* II, 37; "Report of the . . . Relief Act Commission, 1912," p. 8.

[52] Woodburn, p. 40; *Report of the Commission appointed to Enquire into the . . . Relief Act, 1891–92,* p. 6; "Report of the . . . Relief Act Commission, 1912," p. 8. See also West's prophetic "Observations," 27 July 1883, *Papers relating to the . . . Relief Act,* I, 389. There is unfortunately no detailed statistical basis to contemporary assertions; each report, one feels, tends to follow the previous one. Woodburn was rightly sceptical of the notion that increases or decreases in the number of occupancies of various sizes could be ascribed mainly to the working of the Relief Act (p. 61). A comparison of the statistics for the number of holdings in the 25–100 acres range in 1884–85 and 1895–96 (the most widely spaced years after the Act and before the famines for which there are directly comparable figures) shows that there was

beyond the age-old provision of government financial assistance
to the rayats—*takkavi*—in times of need. It is significant, however,
that they gave some attention to another possible method of competing with the money-lender: "agricultural banks." Schemes for
state-sponsored or state-encouraged banks in the rural areas had
been under intermittent discussion for a good many years in the
North-western Provinces.[53] The Deccan Riots Commission came
to the conclusion, however, that banks in the rural areas which
they were investigating could be of little use to the peasant, since,
the Commission claimed, probably correctly, most of his transactions were still in kind rather than in cash.[54] The Commission
assumed that "agricultural banks" could not deal in kind. In an
appendix they gave an indication of what was almost certainly
another reason for the rejection of the proposal. They quoted without comment the correspondence which had ensued when, in 1858,
a suggestion that the government itself should set up banks in the
rural areas had first been put forward in the Deccan. H. E. Jacomb,
then an Assistant Collector in the Ahmadnagar district, had proposed, as an experiment, the setting up in one or two districts of
loan banks in conjunction with rural savings banks; there was to
be a "committee" and a Manager in the district town, and "cor-
responding agencies" in the smaller centres. At the basic level the
village officers would act as agents. Loans were to be recovered in
the same way that revenue demands were collected.[55] The Bombay
Government of the time had agreed that such banks ought to be
encouraged, but they had added that it was "not likely that the
Home Government would countenance any scheme which, although deserving encouragement on its merits, ought, according

---

a sizeable increase in Ahmadnagar district but a slight decrease in Poona district.
(*Jamabandi Reports, S.D., 1884–85*, p. 41, and *1895–96*, p. 44.) In Poona district, at
any rate, there may well not have been in this period any considerable "aggregation"
on the part of "agriculturist money-lenders."

53 J. Strachey, Offg. Collr., Moradabad, Minute of 19 May 1859. (I.O.R., India
Judicial Procs., Range 206, Vol. 66: 16 September 1862, No. 55.) I owe this reference
to the article by Thomas R. Metcalf, cited n. 6 above, pp. 396–97. Strachey continued
to interest himself in agricultural banks when he was Lieutenant-Governor of the
North-western Provinces: see Sayyid Ahmad Khan, "On the Improvement of the Land
. . . and on the Establishment of Agricultural Banks," *Indian Famine Commission
Report*, Appx. I, p. 195. *P.P.* 1881 (C.3086–I) lxxi, pt. i.

54 *Deccan Riots Rept.*, p. 71.

55 H. E. Jacomb, Asst. Collr., Ahmadnagar, to Collr., Ahmadnagar, No. 13 of 6
December 1858 and No. 2 of 29 January 1859, quoted *Deccan Riots Rept.*, Appx. A.,
pp. 112–28.

to acknowledged principles, to be left entirely to private enterprise."[56]

Yet the notion of "agricultural banks" of some variety was to
have a long life ahead of it. One who became interested in the
matter in the early eighties was Evelyn Baring, the Finance Member of Ripon's Government of India. Baring came from a notable
merchant banking family and he had already had some experience
of the supply of credit to Eastern peasants during his time as Commissioner of the Public Debt in Egypt.[57] His interest in the matter
in India may at first have been independent, but it was certainly
heightened by news of a scheme put forward by William Wedderburn, later to become an enthusiastic supporter of the Indian National Congress, but then a somewhat unconventional District
Judge at Ahmadnagar.[58] Wedderburn's interest, in turn, was forti-
fied by the encouragement offered by a number of Indian—largely
Poona Brahman—"promoters."[59] (Indeed, one may perhaps see
this group's support of Wedderburn's scheme as evidence of a
desire on the part of the displaced traditional "banking" elements
in Poona, and of those who had adapted themselves so that their
wealth was increasing through the practice of law, to strengthen
their position vis-à-vis that of the immigrant money-lending groups
out in the villages.)[60] With the coming into force of the Deccan

[56] Ag. Sec., Bom. R.D., to Commr., S.D., No. 932 of 8 March 1860, ibid., pp. 108–09.

[57] Evelyn Baring, Lord Cromer: Service in Royal Artillery from 1856; Private
Secretary to Lord Northbrook, Viceroy of India, 1872–76; Commissioner, Egyptian
Public Debt, 1877–79; Finance Member, India, 1880–83; Agent and Consul-General,
Egypt, 1883–1907. Baring was not a member of the family merchant banking firm
(Robert L. Tignor, *Modernization and British Colonial Rule in Egypt, 1882–1914*,
p. 57), but he undoubtedly had influential "contacts" in the financial world.

[58] Baring had previously had a good deal to do with the founding of the Crédit
Foncier in Egypt. A letter from Baring to Ripon, 6 September 1881 (B.M. Add.
MSS. 43596, ff. 169–72), suggests that this fact, the enquiries of the 1880 Famine Commission, and the writings of Wedderburn all combined to bring about Government
of India interest in the possibilities of agricultural banks. For Wedderburn's early
activities in the matter see "Your Peripatetic" in "Current Philosophy" column,
Bombay Gazette, 21 February 1881; Wedderburn, letter to Editor, *Bombay Gazette*,
2 March 1881; Note by James Caird, 28 April 1881, on Wedderburn's activities while
on leave in England (I.O.L., Caird Papers); and Wedderburn, "Agricultural Banks
for India," *Bombay Gazette*, 22, 26, 29 August, 2 September, 1881 (later published
in pamphlet form).

[59] See report of meeting at residence of Chintamanrao Visvanath Natu, 20 November 1882, *Copy of Correspondence respecting Agricultural Banks in India*, p. 5.
P.P. 1887 (340) lxii. Wedderburn had recently moved to Poona as District Judge; he
and J. G. Moore, Collector of Poona, attended the meeting.

[60] Chintamanrao Visvanath Natu was described as a "savkar" by C. Gonne, Ch. Sec.,
G. of B., Note, August 1883, *Papers relating to . . . the Relief Act*, I, 405. So too was
another "promoter," Govind Mahadev Gadhre. In 1880–81 Natu was Treasurer of the

Agriculturists' Relief Act, Wedderburn claimed, the professional money-lender was finding it increasingly difficult to bring successful suits against agriculturist debtors for the possession of land taken in mortgage. In these circumstances the money-lender, according to Wedderburn, would in many cases "gladly" sell his claim to an agricultural bank. The amount owing would be recovered by instalments which would be so small, Wedderburn announced somewhat airily, as to make the rayat "at once solvent," but which would be a profitable proposition for the heavily capitalized bank.[61]

The Poona promoters claimed that the money-lenders in Purandhar taluka, in Poona district, had agreed to their scheme.[62] It was one for complete "debt redemption." Wedderburn's aim was not simply to supply the peasants with the short-term credit needed for meeting the seasonal costs of cultivation; he also hoped to provide for land improvement and the repayment of long-standing—sometimes ancestral—debts. The bank was to be not only the work of "Poona capitalists." Wedderburn had notions of introducing Bombay and British capital, as well. During a period of leave in England Wedderburn crusaded for his scheme; John Bright, the old radical warrior, even chaired a meeting on the subject at Exeter Hall.[63]

Baring and Ripon gave Wedderburn's scheme their cautious endorsement. Indeed, Baring went so far as to propose grafting a scheme for agricultural banks on to legislation, then being drafted, which was to make the granting of *takkavi* loans somewhat more elastic.[64] But at the same time Baring was not enthusiastic about the role which Wedderburn had marked out for the state in his much publicized scheme.[65] The government was to guarantee the capital of the bank and was to be the debt-collecting agency; as in

---

Poona Sarvajanik Sabha, and Gadhre was Auditor; Shivaram Hari Sathe and S. H. Chiplonkar, two other "promoters" of the bank, were Secretary and an Hon. Secretary, respectively, of the Sabha. See list of office-bearers in front of *Quarterly Journal of the Poona Sarvajanik Sabha*, Vol. III, No. 1 (July 1880).

[61] Wedderburn, *Agricultural Banks for India* (Pamphlet), p. 1.

[62] Chairman, Poona Committee for the Establishment of Agricultural Banks, to Wedderburn, 9 January 1883: *Copy of Correspondence*, p. 33.

[63] *The Times*, 5 July 1883, quoted *Copy of Correspondence*, pp. 12–13.

[64] See speech of Sir Steuart Bayley, Imperial Legislative Council, 26 October 1882, quoted *Agricultural Indebtedness,* ed. S. C. Ray, pp. 57–58.

[65] Baring to Ripon, letter cited; also S. Gopal, *The Viceroyalty of Lord Ripon, 1880–1884,* p. 188, n. 4.

Jacomb's earlier scheme, the bank's dues were to be collected at the same time that the land revenue was collected. This aspect of the scheme met with complete condemnation from some. William Lee-Warner, then a young Assistant Collector,[66] but due to rise to considerable heights in his official career, was scathing about the proposal for government provision of "cork jackets" for the bank's share-holders: "The inevitable crash will come," he said. "Can anyone pretend that agricultural banks would succeed in a famine-stricken tract where scarcity recurs once in every 11 years and severe famine appears once in every 50 years?" He was very suspicious of the part the Poona promoters—many of them associated with the Poona Sarvajanik Sabha—would play. "The Poona capitalists would get a whole village into debt, foreclose mortgages, and zamindars would take the place of the peasant proprietory."[67] Others doubtless had their suspicions of Wedderburn's co-sponsors,[68] but basically it was the role which Wedderburn proposed for government which caused the scheme's rejection by the India Office.[69] The radical interest in England kept up their pressure, eventually succeeding, in 1887, in having the papers relating to the scheme "laid upon the table" of the House of Commons. But it was stated quite firmly that no further action was to be taken in the matter.[70]

There is little justification for claims that Wedderburn's scheme was for banks "on the co-operative principle."[71] In the scheme submitted to the Government of Bombay and the Government of India, there was no suggestion of putting the bank or banks under

[66] William Lee-Warner: Asst. Collr., Private Sec. to Govr., Ag. U. Sec., 1869–76; Asst. Commr., Sind 1876–78; Member Education Commission, Calcutta, 1882; Ag. Junior U. Sec., G. of I., Foreign Dept., 1884; Ag. Political Agent, Kolhapur, 1886; Sec., G. of B., Political Dept., 1887; Member, Governor-General's Council, 1893–94, 1895; Resident, Mysore and Chief Commr., Coorg, 1895; Sec., Political and Secret Dept., India Office, 1895; Member, Council of India, 1902; K.C.S.I., 1898; G.C.S.I., 1911.

[67] Lee-Warner, Asst. Collr., Satara, to Ch. Sec., 4 October 1883, *Papers relating to the . . . Relief Act*, I, 457.

[68] For the official suspicion of the Poona Sarvajanik Sabha and its members at this time see James C. Masselos, Synopsis of Bombay University Ph.D. thesis, "Liberal Consciousness, Leadership and Political Organization in Bombay and Poona, 1867–1895," *Indica*, Vol. II, No. 2 (September 1965), p. 163.

[69] Sec. of State to Viceroy No. 8 (Legislative) of 15 February 1883 and No. 95 (Rev.) of 23 October 1884: *Copy of Correspondence*, pp. 3 and 55.

[70] *Hansard's Parliamentary Debates*, Third Series, Vol. 319, p. 922 (18 August 1877).

[71] S. K. Ratcliffe, *Sir William Wedderburn and the Indian Reform Movement*, p. 37. The claim is repeated by Gopal, *Lord Ripon*, p. 188, and by Philip Woodruff [Mason], *The Men Who Ruled India*, Vol. II, *The Guardians*, p. 162.

the local control of the peasants themselves, or of raising at least some of the capital from the peasants. Such organizations could not, therefore, be called "co-operative." The distinction between "agricultural banks" and "co-operative societies" is a vital one, although it was not always seen by many who came after Wedderburn. Wedderburn was not unaware of the existence of the Raiffeisen co-operative societies in Germany,[72] but he did not publicly advocate their introduction into India. While his scheme was under discussion, however, an editorial appeared in a newspaper, the *Bombay Gazette*, which specifically suggested the development of Raiffeisen societies in India, although only as supplementary to the work of "agricultural banks." Part of the editorial introduced a notion that was to recur many times in future years.

The idea of joint responsibility of the village community still occurs, and although there may be no village communes in the Deccan, there is still a feeling of joint responsibility in village debts; and in the early days of British rule instances of Soukars producing bonds binding upon the village for advances made to it were not uncommon. Might not this feeling be revived in some measure? Might there not be a *panch* of village elders who could pledge the credit of the whole village as an association to repay a loan made by one of its members? Village life is so open and public.[73]

These words may well have been, at least to some extent, the inspiration of a proposal put forward by Charles Gonne, Chief Secretary to the Government of Bombay, in 1883. This proposal resembles the *Bombay Gazette* scheme of 1881 in most of its essentials, except that it was not put forward simply as supplemen-

[72] Wedderburn, *Agricultural Banks for India*, p. 13.

[73] *Bombay Gazette*, 1 September 1881. It is just possible that Wedderburn himself wrote this editorial for the newspaper. It included these Wedderburn-like words: "We cannot expect much from Members of Council and Revenue Commissioners; their intelligence is fossilised, and prevents them from understanding and assimilating new ideas, and their position makes them hostile to nobler manners and better laws." If Wedderburn was responsible for this editorial, it would be untrue to say that he never advocated the introduction of co-operative societies in India. The writer of the editorial professed to expect more from "Governors," "accustomed to the free inquiry and restless curiosity of the House of Commons." The Governor of Bombay of the time, Sir James Fergusson, did indeed support the Wedderburn scheme; he appears to have had the somewhat extraordinary belief that it was basically similar to schemes for "land companies" in New Zealand which he had been helping to promote before he left England. (Fergusson had been Governor of New Zealand, 1873–74). These companies were in extreme financial difficulties by the 1890s. Had Wedderburn's scheme been permitted, there would have been undoubtedly a number of gullible Englishmen who would have invested in it some of Britain's "surplus" capital.

tary to a plan for agricultural banks.[74] But Gonne's scheme—
whether or not it was his own—was not greeted with enthusiasm by
the Government of India; indeed, T. C. Hope, the Bombay representative on the Imperial Legislative Council, thought it to be
"totally unworkable, in a rayatvari country at any rate." There was,
he believed, "no common bond of interest" amongst the Deccan
villagers.[75] The battle over the real nature of the "Indian village"
—or at least the western Indian village—was being fought yet again.

"Statistics, Averages, and Ratios"

As a result of discouragement from the India Office, and of some
lack of enthusiasm even at Simla, the Government of India did
not, in the eighties, pursue the subject of agricultural banks. In
the field of provision of credit they contented themselves with
passing two acts which made the procedure for granting *takkavi*
slightly more elastic: the Land Improvements Loans Act of 1883
and the Agriculturists' Loans Act of 1884.

But the Government of India remained concerned about agricultural indebtedness, and especially about land transfer. There
was, for example, one question that was always being asked by the
Government of India about the Deccan Agriculturists' Relief Act:
Was the Act in fact reducing the amount of land transfer between
agriculturist and non-agriculturist? The working of the Act was
investigated briefly on behalf of the Government of Bombay by a
Civilian, Hillersden Woodward, in 1883,[76] and in a good deal
more detail by another Bombay Civilian, A. F. Woodburn, in
1889.[77] The Government of India were dissatisfied both with the
1889 Report and with the Government of Bombay's reaction to it.
C. J. Lyall complained that the members of the Bombay Government were "hopelessly at variance over the effects of the Act";
Woodburn's report appeared to him "to rely too exclusively on
statistics, averages, and ratios." Woodburn was a revenue officer; a
man from the judicial "side," Lyall claimed, would have come up

---

74 Gonne, "Note on the Working of the . . . Relief Act," *Papers relating to the . . .
Relief Act,* I, 416–17.

75 Hope to Gonne, 6 September 1883, ibid., Vol. I, p. 439.

76 H. Woodward, on Special Duty, to Ch. Sec., No. 30 of 25 June 1883, ibid., Vol. I,
pp. 335–60.

77 "Report by A. F. Woodburn, on Special Duty, to Consider the Deccan Agriculturists' Relief Act, 1889," ibid., II, 12–130.

with a simpler and rather different story.[78] So the Government of India proceeded in 1891 to appoint their own Commission to investigate the Act, made up mainly of men from the judicial "side," and drawn largely from provinces other than Bombay.[79]

But even this Commission could do little more than demonstrate with considerable clarity that, in the absence of what were known as a Record of Rights and a Mutation Register in the Bombay Presidency, there were no sets of reliable figures to which one could turn if one wished to discuss land transfer. This was still the case even in the four Relief Act districts where there was now virtually compulsory registration of all deeds. Registration records referred to contracts between people and were indexed under the names of individuals. Revenue records referred basically to pieces of land. The two types of records could not be used together without great difficulty.[80] Registration figures for mortgages and sales of land, it is true, though they continued to rise somewhat fitfully in the four Relief Act districts, rose more rapidly in the Deccan districts not covered by the Act.[81] Many at the Government of India level thought that, whatever one's doubts about the accuracy of specific figures, here was an argument for the extension of the Act to all districts.[82] But the reports of the Bombay Registration Department from the late seventies show that there were many reasons for rises and falls in registrations; registration could rise because of prosperity, because men had money they wished to invest, as well as a result of scarcity.[83] The Government of India failed to consider whether lands in those Deccan districts which were not covered by the Act, being on the whole less prone to famine than those that were covered by the Act, were quite simply more saleable than those of the famine belt. The operation of mar-

[78] C. J. Lyall, Note, 29 November 1890. (I.O.R., Lee-Warner Political and Miscellaneous Private Papers, "Series V," f. 441.)

[79] India G.R. Home (Judicial) Dept. No.17–1497–1502 of 20 November 1891, *Papers relating to the . . . Relief Act*, II, 256–87.

[80] *Report of the Commission appointed to Enquire into the Deccan Agriculturists' Relief Act, 1891–92*, especially pp. 6, 71. See also G. of I., *Note on Land Transfer and Agricultural Indebtedness in India*, 1895, pp. 25–26, 36, 61.

[81] Woodburn Report, 1889, *Papers relating to the . . . Relief Act*, II, 34.

[82] *Note on Land Transfer*, 1895, pp. 61–62. See also Minute by Sir Charles Crosthwaite, 28 November 1892, G. of I., *Selection from Papers on Indebtedness and Land Transfer*, 1895, p. 123.

[83] *Reports on the Administration of the Registration Department in the Bombay Presidency 1877–78*, p. 9; *1878–79*, pp. 2, 3; *1880–81*, p. 5.

ket forces in the field of genuine sales tended to be forgotten. The
men at the Government of India level were prepared, however, to
take up the challenge offered by those who pointed out that many
sales were not genuine. They felt that an indication of the real
position could be obtained from a perusal of the statistics in the
settlement reports of various dates regarding the amount of land
which was, as they put it, sub-let.[84] (By "sub-letting" they appear
to have meant what would be called letting in the West; the officials
were working on the theory that the state was the ultimate landlord
in India.) Where statistics for sub-letting showed a rise, they implied, money-lenders were increasingly obtaining the land and
letting it, often to its original proprietors. Unfortunately, however, such statistics could not be trusted either. For, as the years
went on, it became increasingly clear that quite considerable
amounts of land were being let by "agriculturists" to "agriculturists."[85] Sometimes, no doubt, those who let land were of the "agriculturist money-lender" variety. But from about 1877 it gradually
dawned on Bombay officials that a man classified as an "occupant"
might in fact have let part or all of his land and be working
temporarily or permanently as a labourer in prosperous Khandesh,
that great frontier area of the Bombay Presidency for much of the
nineteenth century.[86] Or, increasingly, he might be working in
Bombay. "Even in 1881," it was claimed, "when there was no railway nearer than about 60 or 70 miles, the Satara labourer mi-
grated in large numbers to Bombay. In 1881 the Deccan districts
together furnished one half again as many inhabitants of Bombay
as they did in 1872, and very nearly as large a proportion as the
Konkan."[87] Tales—probably slightly exaggerated—began to drift

---

84 *Note on Land Transfer*, 1895, p. 63.

85 "The peasant proprietors now sublet about one-fourth of their lands": Sir
Richard Temple, Govr., Bom., Confl. Minute of 29 October 1878 on "Condition of
the Peasantry in the Central Deccan (Districts of Poona, Ahmednagar, Sholapur and
Satara)." (I.O.R., Lee-Warner Political and Miscellaneous Papers, "Deccan Ryot,
Series II," f. 121.) Temple says that his assertion has been "verified by the Settlement Commissioner," but no further details are given. See also *Revision Settlement
of 126 Villages in the Old Bagalkot Taluka of Bijapur District, S.R. G. of B., N.S.*,
No. clxxvi, p. 6: "The period for which land is mortgaged or sublet, together with
other minor conditions are, of course, factors of great importance in determining the
significance of the transaction."

86 Temple, Minute cited, and enclosed letter from J. G. Moore, Collr., Satara,
D/O to Private Sec. to Govr., 30 October 1878; C. H. Jopp, Ag. Asst. Collr., Ahmadnagar, D/O (to C. Gonne?) 26 August 1883, *Papers relating to the . . . Relief Act*, I,
458–59; *Ahmednagar Gazetteer*, p. 240; *Khandesh Gazetteer*, p. 134.

87 "Report on the Economic Condition of the Masses of the Bombay Presidency

in of whole villages virtually abandoned at the time of famine only to be reoccupied when better times dawned.[88] And even if the Deccan peasant stayed at home in his village for the whole year, he might still be engaged at certain times in so-called subsidiary occupations: labouring for another landholder or carting. In the long run, it is worth noting, the coming of the railway probably did not make a great deal of difference to the amount of carting in some areas: even in the 1920s it was still reputed to be more profitable to cart produce forty or fifty miles to a large market town than to cart it five miles to a railway station where the price offered by an agent with a quasi-monopoly over produce brought to that station would generally have to be accepted.[89]

Few attempts were made to quantify these economic trends in the later nineteenth century. The question of the amount of income which the ordinary Deccan peasant obtained from subsidiary occupations, both rural and urban, was dealt with especially superficially;[90] the existence of such vague sources of income in addition to cultivation provided, of course, suitable ammunition for use against those "agitators" who insisted increasingly that the ordinary Deccan peasant simply could not survive on his income from cultivation alone. But it is little wonder that the 1891–92 Commission on the working of the Relief Act, realizing the importance of at least some of the qualifications that had to be made when Deccan statistics were quoted, and not feeling bound to make a case against the complaints of nascent nationalism, at one stage threw up their hands and declared plainly that it was "impossible for Government to know what the land question really is."[91] All that they could recommend was a few minor amendments to the Relief Act.

---

by the Director, Land Records and Agriculture" (J. W. P. Muir-Mackenzie), p. 33, encl. Viceroy to Sec. of State No. 3 (Rev., Agriculture & Famine) of 30 October 1888. (I.O.R., Parliamentary Collection No. 221.)

[88] Jopp, letter cited; Woodburn, Report, 1889, *Papers relating to the Relief . . . Act*, II, 84.

[89] Collr., E. Khandesh, quoted *Bom. L. Rev. Admin. Rept.*, *1925–26*, p. 37. Cf., however, *Kalpataru* (Sholapur newspaper), 20 December 1875, quoted "Report on the Native Papers of the Bombay Presidency," week ending 1 January 1876.

[90] Nevertheless, Dr. Ravinder Kumar's assertion about the Deccan in 1875 is hardly accurate, even for that year: "Without an outlet to the urban world, the dispossessed peasant was forced to live as a landless laborer, often on those very fields which he had formerly cultivated as an independent proprietor." "The Deccan Riots of 1875," *Journal of Asian Studies*, Vol. XXIV, No. 4 (August 1965), p. 619.

[91] *Report of the Commission appointed to Enquire into the . . . Relief Act, 1891–92*, p. 71.

The modesty of these recommendations brought a notable declaration from Lord Lansdowne, the Viceroy. "I desire . . . to place on record my opinion that legislation of this kind will only touch the fringe of agricultural indebtedness. . . . It is to my mind impossible to read the mass of evidence which has come to us from Bombay, from the Central Provinces, from the Punjab and even from parts of Bengal, without coming to the conclusion that remedies of an entirely different kind are indispensable if the evil is to be held in check."[92] Lord Lansdowne, in other words, looking at India as a whole, believed that it was by no means impossible to know what the land question really was. In 1895 the Government of India informed the Secretary of State that the whole question of agricultural indebtedness, "than which none more difficult or more important has of late years arisen in connection with our internal administration," was receiving their serious attention. "Meanwhile," they added, "public opinion is ripening on the subject; the conviction that something more than mere palliative measures is required is no longer confined to officials, but is shared by some of the most advanced representatives of native opinion, and it is advisable that action should not be unnecessarily delayed."[93]

Pressure from the Punjab

Lord Lansdowne's concern was doubtless to some extent a reflection of his personal realization of the political dangers to which a land problem might give rise. After all, he was an Irish landlord. Lansdowne's concern was also, it would seem, to some extent a reflection of the concern of his own Revenue and Agriculture Department. The leading members of this department of the Government of India over a period of thirty years—men such as Edward Buck, Denzil Ibbetson, James Wilson, and Edward Maclagan—appear to have come from either the Punjab or, less frequently, the North-western Provinces.[94] In the Government of India, then,

---

[92] Lansdowne, Note on the Report of the Deccan Commission, 3 January 1894: G. of I., *Selection from Papers on Indebtedness and Land Transfer,* 1895, p. 131.

[93] Viceroy to Sec. of State, No. 20 (L. Rev.) of 27 March 1895. (I.O.R., Rev. Letters from India, 1895.)

[94] Edward Buck: Asst. Collr., Offg. Sec., Board of Rev., N.W.P., 1863–75; Sec. G. of I., R. & A. Dept., 1881; K.C.S.I., 1897. Lord Dufferin told Sir Walter Lawrence that he regarded Buck as "the great genius of his administration" (Lawrence, *The India We Served,* p. 51).

the views on agricultural indebtedness of men from North India increasingly dominated. Punjab official concern in the matter was probably more political than economic. Muslim peasants, it was felt by many officials, were being oppressed, and Muslims had their connections with the men of the Frontier, and beyond; furthermore, the Indian Army relied to a considerable extent on recruits from the Punjab peasantry.[95] Concern about land problems was also very much a part of the continuing Punjab tradition of "paternalism." S. S. Thorburn, for example, published in 1886 a book entitled *Musalmans and Money-lenders in the Punjab*. Thorburn appears almost to have called for a British-sponsored holy war on behalf of "monotheistic agriculturists" against the *banias*, "men of miserable physique and no manliness of character."[96] Yet the effect of such writing can be exaggerated. The intemperance of Thorburn's language apparently did not altogether assist his case (or his career).[97]

There were undoubtedly other factors involved in the formation of the Government of India's attitude on the agricultural indebtedness question. The ideas of T. H. Green, and of his disciple Arnold Toynbee, were beginning to have some influence.[98] Laissez-faire was no longer fashionable—and it is doubtful whether most officials in India had ever given their full allegiance to that philosophy.[99] One can overemphasize the importance of theory:

Denzil Ibbetson: Asst. Commr. and Settlement Officer, Punjab, 1870–81; Deputy Superintendent, Census, Punjab, 1881; Compiler, *Punjab Gazetteer*, 1883; Member, Deccan Agriculturists' Relief Act Commission, 1891–92; Offg. Sec., R. & A. Dept., G. of I., 1895; Sec., R. & A. Dept., 1896; Member, Governor General's Executive Council, 1899; Ag. Lt. Govr., Punjab, 1905; K.C.S.I., 1903. "The greatest of Indian Civilians of my day" (Lawrence, p. 34).

James Wilson: Asst. Commr., Punjab, 1875; Offg. Sec. to Financial Commr., 1885 and 1886; Offg. Sec., G. of I., R. & A. Dept., 1903; Sec., 1906; Financial Commr., Punjab, 1908; K.C.S.I., 1909.

Edward Maclagan: Asst. Commr., Punjab, 1886; Offg., U. Sec., G. of I., R. & A. Dept., 1890; Dep. Commr., Punjab 1896; Offg. Ch. Sec., Punjab, 1906; Sec., G. of I., R. & A. Dept., 1910; President, Cttee. on Co-operation, 1914–15; Govr., Punjab, 1919–24; K.C.S.I., 1921.

[95] See Norman G. Barrier, *The Punjab Alienation of Land Bill of 1900*, especially pp. 25, 34.

[96] S. S. Thorburn, *Musalmans and Money-lenders in the Punjab*, pp. 1, 37.

[97] Barrier, p. 20, n. 43.

[98] For Toynbee's influence on the Indian Civil Service entrants whom he tutored at Balliol—they included James Wilson—see Benjamin Jowett, Memoir of Toynbee, in Arnold Toynbee, *Lectures on the Industrial Revolution*, London, 1884.

[99] Professor Thomas R. Metcalf rightly observes that "in India, where the Government played such a dominant role in society, laissez faire was usually honored more in the breach than in the observance." *The Aftermath of Revolt: India, 1857–1870*,

there was an element of pragmatism in India's end-of-century "administrative revolution," a pragmatism not altogether different from that which appears to have characterized the "administrative revolution" which Britain underwent rather earlier in the century.[100] Nevertheless, the fact remains that in the last years of the century an increasingly vocal group in the Government of India were somewhat dogmatically convinced that agricultural indebtedness and especially land transfer were serious problems. One cannot avoid the impression that these officials were more and more determined to find an India-wide justification for their policies—whatever the southern presidencies might think. In October 1895 the Government of Bombay were requested to forward their "final views and definite proposals" for action in the direction of imposing restrictions on the transfer of land from agriculturists to other classes of the community.[101]

It was not until 1898 that the Government of Bombay came to reply to this rather stern letter. They were inclined to think that the "staying power" of the peasant, even in the Deccan, was much better than it had been: "any officer who was witness of the famine operations in 1876–77 and also those of 1896–97 can testify to this fact." But the famine of 1896–97, and the enquiry that followed, had created an atmosphere of shock in some Bombay Government circles. After all, even Gujarat was stricken with conditions of dire scarcity for the first time since the 1820s. As in the Punjab, the basis of the fears of officials in Bombay was to some extent political. According to the Government, Brahman "agitators" had tried to

---

p. 172. See also Sabyasachi Bhattacharya, "Laissez faire in India," *Indian Economic and Social History Review*, Vol. II, No. 1 (January 1965).

100 See Oliver MacDonagh, "The Nineteenth-century Revolution in Government: A Reappraisal," *Historical Journal*, Vol. I, No. 1 (1958); also MacDonagh, *A Pattern of Government Growth, 1800–1860: The Passenger Acts and their Enforcement*, and G. Kitson Clark, *The Making of Victorian England*, passim. Dr. Barrier's study of the background to the Punjab Land Alienation Act of 1900 shows very clearly that, at the Government of India level, government in late nineteenth century India was similar to government at the time of the mid-nineteenth century "administrative revolution" in Britain in another way: much of the initiative was taken not by the "politicians" at the top—not even by Curzon—but rather by civil servants, faced with the necessity of finding reasonably humane solutions to day-to-day problems. See Barrier, especially pp. 96–99.

101 D. Ibbetson, Offg. Sec., G. of I., R. & A. Dept., to all Local [Provincial] Govts., No. 24–75–1 (L. Rev.) Confl. of 26 October 1895. (I.O.R., India L. Rev. Procs., Vol. 4762.)

induce cultivators to withhold payment of their land revenue at the time of the famine. Such a situation, thought Lord Sandhurst,[102] the Governor of Bombay, was "fraught with alarm." Sandhurst did not gain the agreement of all the members of his Council to his advocacy of the grant of a type of "tenant-right," on the Irish model. (Sandhurst was a devoted Gladstonian Liberal.) Nor did the Civilians of his Council agree with his advocacy (again perhaps with Ireland in mind) of grants to assist the dispossessed in regaining possession of their ancestral lands. Nevertheless, in October 1899 the Government of Bombay were on paper prepared to follow Sandhurst in recommending legislation which would virtually prohibit all sales or other permanent alienations of land in the Presidency except to "agriculturists" or those with hereditary interests in the land in question.[103] Such a measure, of course, would have gone far beyond the provisions of the Deccan Agriculturists' Relief Act, which was concerned only with cases actually brought before the courts or local "conciliators."

Bombay Stubbornness

But the Government of Bombay's next move in the matter does not appear to have arisen directly from the 1899 proposals. Nor does it appear to have arisen from a close consideration of the Punjab Alienation of Land Act of October 1900. To a large extent, rather, it was the result of the Bombay Government's experience in dealing with another famine, that of 1899–1900, and especially of their difficulties in collecting arrears of land revenue in the season that followed. Very suddenly, in May 1901, the Government of Bombay brought forward a bill for amending the Presidency's Land Revenue Code. The bill would have allowed the government to revert to what was pre-British practice in some areas of Gujarat (and to what was still the practice in parts of the Konkan) and grant permission to occupy "waste" or hitherto unoccupied lands on a tenure that it would be necessary to renew annually. The holder of such land would have no permanency of tenure and thus could not mortgage his land. A proposal of this nature had

---

102 Lord Sandhurst: Son of William Mansfield, 1st Baron Sandhurst, soldier and Liberal politician; service in Coldstream Guards; Lord in Waiting, 1880–85; U. Sec. for War, 1886, 1892–94; Govr., Bom., 1895–99.

103 J. W. P. Muir-Mackenzie, Sec., Bom. R.D., to Sec., G. of I., R. & A. Dept., No. 7100/168 Confl. of 7 October 1899. (I.O.R., Bom. L. Rev. Procs. Vol. 5777.)

been under serious consideration since 1898.[104] But the 1901 bill would also have permitted the government to grant to the original occupants, on a restricted tenure, land which had become forfeit to the government because arrears of revenue had not been paid. It would not have been possible to alienate land granted under such circumstances without obtaining government permission. This latter proposal appears to have been very hastily thought out. The bill was introduced at a specially summoned meeting of the Legislative Council at the end of May 1901. Neither the Government of India, who had been informed of the bill only twelve days before, nor the India Office, were fully aware of what the bill involved. It was only after the bill had been introduced that the Government of India learnt, to their dismay, that the proposed measures could affect 50 per cent of the area of certain districts and 20 per cent of the entire area of the whole Presidency. Those who were in arrears in land revenue payments, they protested, ought at least to be given the opportunity to make up those arrears over a period of time. The Government of India were suspicious, furthermore, that the Government of Bombay, now no longer headed by Lord Sandhurst, intended their bill to take the place of legislation along the lines of the Punjab Alienation of Land Act.[105] The Government of Bombay replied confidentially that the bill was aimed in part at contumacious money-lenders,[106] who, presumably, were refusing to pay land revenue "on behalf of" rayats, in the hope of obtaining a remission. It is difficult to avoid the conclusion that to some extent it was for this very reason that a well-organized agitation against the bill sprang to life. Over five hundred vernacular petitions and numerous English petitions, from Gujarat as well as the Deccan and the Karnatak, reached the Bombay Government and the Viceroy.[107] A petition from Poona (as usual assumed by the authorities to be the centre of conspiracy) complained that

104 See F. S. P. Lely, Commr., N.D., to Ch. Sec., No. 1061/21 Confl. of 25 March 1898. (I.O.R., India Legislative Procs., Vol. 6172: August 1901, Nos. 4–23, Appx. H.) Lely was a controversial figure, who became Chief Commissioner of the Central Provinces, 1905, and a member of the Decentralisation Commission, 1907–08.

105 J. B. Fuller, Offg. Sec. G. of I., R. & A. Dept., to Ch. Sec., Bom., No. 1518 of 9 July 1901. (I.O.R., Vol. cited: August 1901, No. 16.)

106 Ch. Sec., Bom., to Sec., G. of I. Legislative Dept., Telegram No. 134 of 4 August 1901. (I.O.R., Vol. cited: August 1901, No. 21.)

107 Vernacular petitions are summarized, and many of the English petitions are given in full, in the Appendices to India Legislative Procs., October 1901, No. 24. (I.O.R., Vol. cited.)

"The principal feature of the Bill is to take advantage of the famine forfeitures of land and reduce the status of poor cultivators, who have been unable to pay the assessment during the last year owing to sheer inability, to that of daily labourers or tenants at will."[108] It was reported that some cultivators in Nasik district, who had hitherto had no encumbrances on their lands, were mortgaging land in order to pay their revenue arrears. The Collector of Sholapur believed that "misunderstanding" was "complete." It was "hopeless" to try to convince cultivators that in the normal course their lands would not be threatened.[109] And in the Legislative Council the opposition of Indian elected members, led by Pherozeshah Mehta, culminated in the first "walk-out" in the Council's history; even G. K. Gokhale, the so-called Moderate, rather apologetically left the Chamber.[110] The Government of India gave their consent to a somewhat modified piece of legislation with reluctance and only on condition that the provisions which related to forfeitures would be administered with "extreme care."[111] They followed this up with a letter insisting that in future the Government of India should be given ample time to consider provincial bills involving "matters of principle" before they were introduced into the provincial legislative councils.[112]

It is not surprising that the agitation against the 1901 legislation, and the Government of India's rebuke, should have brought many in the Government of Bombay to resolve that they would have nothing more to do with major legislation on agricultural indebtedness. Bombay officials commented caustically on the recommendation of the 1901 Famine Commission that legislation along the lines of the Punjab Alienation of Land Act should be brought down in Bombay.[113] They claimed, correctly, that the statistics

[108] "Petition of the inhabitants of Poona assembled in a public meeting held on 7 July 1901," to Govr., Bom. (I.O.R., Bom. Legislative Procs., Vol. 6237.)

[109] Collr. Nasik to Commr., C.D., No. 9996 of 3 August 1901; Commr., C.D., to U. Sec., R.D. Telegram No. 9996 of 3 August 1901. (I.O.R., Bom. L. Rev. Procs., Vol. 6239: September 1901, No. 269.)

[110] See his speech immediately before leaving the Chamber, 24 August 1901, quoted *Speeches and Writings of Gopal Krishna Gokhale*, ed. R. P. Patwardhan and D. V. Ambekar, Vol. I, *Economic*, p. 444.

[111] H. W. C. Carnduff, Offg. Sec., G. of I., R. & A. Dept., to Sec., Bom. Legislative Dept., No. 1514 of 27 September 1901. (I.O.R., Bom. L. Rev. Procs., Vol. 62–93: October 1901, No. 24.)

[112] Offg. Sec., G. of I., Legislative Dept., to Ch. Sec., Bom., No. 1692 of 22 October 1901. (I.O.R., Bom. Legislative Procs., Vol. 6237.)

[113] *Report of the Indian Famine Commission*, 1901, p. 111. *P.P.* 1902 (Cd. 876) lxx.

which had been set out in the Bombay Government's 1899 letter
on land transfer by no means supported the Commission's conten-
tion that a quarter of the agriculturists in the Presidency had lost
their land to the non-agriculturist classes. "It is not known," they
added, "on what basis is framed the estimate of the Famine Commission that less than a fifth are free from debt."[114] The Bombay
Government now adhered strongly to the argument put forward
by R. A. Lamb, Collector of Ahmadnagar, that it would be unwise
"under the very recent and strong impression of an exceptionally
bad series of years, to hurriedly adopt . . . measures which would
introduce into the revenue system changes of which no one can
forsee the ultimate results."[115] And, recalling the troubles of 1901,
the Government of Bombay asserted that "a more substantial
ground for dangerous agitation can scarcely be conceived than an
authentic intimation that cultivating occupants were to be deprived of a right which they and their ancestors have, whether to
their advantage or not, held and highly prized for centuries." In
any case, they continued, a measure such as the one proposed by
the Famine Commission would not deal with the "Agriculturist
land-grabber." But in 1903 they offered no plans for seriously
limiting the agriculturist money-lender's activities, or those of the
professional money-lender. All that they recommended was a continuation of "palliative" measures and, in particular, persistent
attempts at voluntary liquidation and composition of debt.[116]

It was in this sceptical and somewhat uncompromising mood
that the Government of Bombay, and many officials in the Bombay
districts, greeted further Government of India proposals, also
backed by the Famine Commission, for the establishment of co-
operative societies.

"Find Raiffeisen"

Frederick Nicholson, in 1890 Collector of Tinnevelly in the
Madras Presidency, was something of an enthusiast. In fact, long
after he had officially retired he was still in India, dabbling in

114 W. T. Morison, Ag. Sec., Bom. R.D., to Sec., G. of I., R. & A. Dept., No. 719
of 2 February 1903. (I.O.R., India L. Rev. Procs., Vol. 7068: October 1905, No. 37.)
115 R. A. Lamb, Collr., Ahmadnagar, to Commr., C.D., No. 1574–R of 29 April 1902,
encl. Morison to G. of I., letter cited.
116 Morison to G. of I., letter cited.

schemes for the economic betterment of the country.[117] At the end of 1890 and the beginning of 1891 Nicholson wrote a series of articles for the *Madras Mail* proposing the setting up of Raiffeisen-type co-operative societies in India.[118] It is difficult to say exactly where Nicholson obtained his information on developments in Germany;[119] certainly his *Madras Mail* articles show him to be by no means ill-informed on the subject. Nicholson knew about the rejection of the Wedderburn scheme in Bombay; he was aware of the differences between co-operative societies and Wedderburn's proposal for "agricultural banks." Like Gonne in Bombay, he felt that it was possible to build a credit structure on supposedly still existent traditions of "joint village action." Village headmen and the "chief residents" would be the officers of the associations which he proposed. "Village courts"—and by these he meant so-called panchayats—could, he believed, assist in the recovery of loans; there would be no need of Revenue Department assistance in the matter. Shortly after writing these articles Nicholson went to Europe on sick leave and gathered more information on the whole subject. On his return he was invited by the Madras Government to utilize his material in the writing of a report. The leading spirit in this invitation appears to have been Lord Wenlock, the Governor, a man who, though he hardly distinguished himself in that post, at least managed, as befitted a Yorkshire landlord, to interest himself in "agricultural matters."[120] Nicholson's report was pub-

---

[117] Frederick Nicholson: Asst. Collr. and Collr., Madras, 1869–97; Member, Imperial Legislative Council, 1897, 1900; Member, Madras Board of Revenue, 1899; Member, Famine Commission, 1901; K.C.I.E., 1903; retd., 1904; Hon. Director, Govt. Fisheries, Madras, 1906–20.

[118] "Popular Banks for India," *Madras Weekly Mail*, 25 December 1890, 1, 15, and 22 January 1891. Nicholson was acknowledged to be the author of these articles in an editorial in the *Madras Weekly Mail*, 9 September 1891. See also, ibid., 26 August, 2 September, 17 December 1891, 24 March 1892.

[119] He possibly obtained his first ideas on the subject by reading some articles in *Chambers's Journal*: "Popular Banking," 22 September 1883; "People's Banks," 24 November 1883; and "People's Banks," 6 October 1883. See P. N. Driver, "The Co-operative Developments in the Bombay Presidency with Special Reference to the Bombay Deccan," M.A. thesis, University of Bombay, 1932, p. 4.

[120] Lord Wenlock: Liberal Unionist Whip in House of Lords; Govr., Madras, 1891–96. *The Complete Peerage*, Vol. XII, pt. i. p. 487, quotes the *Times* obituary notice of 16 January 1912: "As he laid no claim to gifts of high statesmanship or intellectual power, his rule [in Madras] was not marked by brilliance or originality ... [but] he is remembered with affection by the depressed and backward classes of the Presidency." Wenlock had set up a co-operative society in his own village in Yorkshire before going out to India; on his return he formed an association for the

lished in 1895; its burden was, in Nicholson's own words, "Find Raiffeisen."[121]

Raiffeisen was the burgomaster of the village of Heddesdorf, near Neuweid, in Germany. He was not wealthy, but he was inspired by a spirit of Christian philanthropy. From the time of the 1848 famine he had experimented with various forms of co-operative association amongst the villagers, designed to eliminate the middleman and the money-lender, but it was not until 1864 that the loan society which became a model for many others was set up. From about 1879 Raiffeisen's co-operative ideas began to spread fairly rapidly in Germany, Italy, and the Austrian Empire.

The Raiffeisen societies were fundamentally self-governing associations of borrowers, who all, or practically all, subscribed a share of the capital of the society, and who made use of the further capital attracted to the society through the combined credit of the members. Their area of operation was limited as a rule to a single village; members, it was claimed, thus knew the faults and good points of every potential borrower; administration was gratuitous, by an elected committee, only the clerical work being paid for; the liability of members was unlimited; the amount of share capital an individual could hold was usually limited so as to avoid a "dividend-seeking" spirit, any profits over a certain sum being allocated to a reserve fund; loans had to be utilized for productive purposes. The aim of the societies, according to Nicholson, was to supply "confidence, courage, the spirit of thrift, of self-help," to a peasantry that was "enfeebled, suspicious and dispirited."[122] The societies, he claimed, provided "an education in many of the finer social and economic faculties";[123] they "not merely popularized but democratized credit."[124]

Such was the system which Nicholson proposed to transfer from the Rhineland villages to the Madras Presidency. He was emphatic that he did not want to establish state banks—"an unheard of ex-

---

organization of agricultural co-operatives in England, similar to Horace Plunkett's Irish Agricultural Organization Society. See H. W. Wolff, *Co-operation in India* (1919 ed.), p. 44, n.

[121] F. A. Nicholson, *Report Regarding the Possibility of Introducing Land and Agricultural Banks into the Madras Presidency.* Vol. I, 1895; Vol. II, 1897.

[122] Ibid., I, 163–64.

[123] Ibid., p. 151.

[124] Ibid., p. 150.

periment in State socialism." But the functions of the state would be considerable with regard to co-operative societies. It would "suggest and favour" their establishment, it would provide efficient supervision, and it might grant "some moderate loans either as working or as mere starting funds."[125]

Nicholson's report is written in an impressive though somewhat repetitive style. By the time it was presented Lord Wenlock had left Madras. The government of his successor opposed Nicholson's schemes with a vehemence that was at times almost abusive. Mr. Nicholson's "408 closely printed quarto pages," they said, showed an "absence of definiteness in conception. . . . The extremely undesirable conditions which are reported to prevail in Bombay and other provinces not so favoured, or" (the Madras Board of Revenue added patronizingly) "not so well administered as Madras," did not obtain in their territories. "There is far too much loose talk about the indebtedness of our ryots," they asserted, probably with some truth. The professional money-lender in the Madras Presidency was "not oppressive." "Happily," the Government of India were not likely to favour such a "race for ruin" as would be brought about by the establishment of co-operative societies.[126]

"Little Republics"

But the expostulations of the Madras Government apparently did not reach, or went unheeded by, certain officials in northern India. Copies of Nicholson's report began circulating in the Punjab and the North-western Provinces at the turn of the century. Edward Maclagan at Multan and T. J. Crosthwaite at Dera Ismail Khan in the Punjab made a few very tentative experiments in the organization of associations somewhat approximating those contemplated by Nicholson. Crosthwaite collected capital, in the first instance, in the form of grain.[127] Then, H. E. L. P. Dupernex, a Civilian in the North-western Provinces, became extremely enthusiastic about village banks, as he called them. After a rather brief look at Italian co-operative societies during a home leave, he produced a book on the whole subject of fostering co-operative

125 Ibid., pp. 23–24.
126 Madras Board of Revenue Resolution No. 412 of 4 November 1896, encl. Bom. G.R.R.D. No. 7407 of 26 November 1900. (Poona, ADM. S.O.7.)
127 *Indian Agriculturist*, 1 July 1901.

societies in India.[128] Its purpose was frankly propagandist. Dupernex's first premise was contained in the well-known passage from
the early British administrator, Charles Metcalfe, which he
quoted: "The Village Communities are little Republics, having
nearly everything they want within themselves, and almost independent of any foreign relations." The essential characteristics of
the village community, Dupernex claimed, were "brotherhood"
and "joint responsibility," its "democratic character," its system of
public accounts, its strict rules about the admission of strangers,
its opposition to the idea of individual profit, and the gratuitous
nature of the services rendered by the members of the community.[129] All these, Dupernex said, were also essential features of co-
operative societies. It was therefore possible to think of "grafting
on to" the village community "the new growth of co-operative
credit."[130] Here was the fullest statement of what had already become a recurrent theme. Yet in spite of this emphasis on the village,
Dupernex believed that the first move in the setting up of a successful co-operative movement would have to be made in the
district towns. There, "people's banks" should be set up which
would provide capital for the societies. "To occupy the vacant
ground immediately next that already taken up by the joint-stock
bank and from that point to work gradually downwards is the
system which, if slow in its progress, is the likeliest in the long run
to attain the desired end."[131]

It was natural that Ibbetson and his friends in the Government
of India should become interested in such schemes. They sent
Nicholson's report and Dupernex's book to the provincial governments for brief consideration in October 1900. The Government
of Bombay were not at all enthusiastic. They saw "little or no indication of such mutual trust among members of rural communities
in this Presidency as would make co-operative credit possible."[132]
In December, after an informal meeting of a committee in Calcutta—Nicholson and Dupernex were amongst those at this meeting—the appointment of a Select Committee to study the question

128 H. Dupernex, *People's Banks for Northern India: A Handbook to the Organization of Credit on a Co-operative Basis.* H. E. L. P. Dupernex: Asst. Collr., N.W.P.,
1889; Asst. Commr. and Jt. Magistrate, 1897; District Judge, 1901; retd., 1913.
129 Ibid., pp. 63–70.
130 Ibid., p. 78.
131 Ibid., p. 111.
132 Bom. G.R.R.D. No. 7407 of 26 November 1900. (Poona, file cited.)

fully was announced and further opinions were requested from provincial governments.[133] This time the Government of Bombay consulted the men out in the districts. The Collector of Ahmadnagar replied that he believed that conditions in the Deccan were vastly different from those in Dupernex's North-western Provinces. In the Deccan, he claimed, there was no class of large landholders who might take up positions of leadership in co-operative societies, gratuitous service was completely unknown in the villages, and joint responsibility beyond the limits of the family group was something that it would be difficult for the Maratha *kunbi* to understand.[134] On the other hand, the Collector of Surat, in Gujarat, claimed that in his district "combinations" to build such works of public utility as temples and bridges were frequently to be found in the villages. This might be interpreted as a hopeful sign for co-operative societies, but the Collector went on to claim that in fact there was "too great rather than too little confidence between man and man" in the villages.[135] The Survey Commissioner and Director of Land Records and Agriculture (some of whose many functions were soon to be distributed to other officials) felt that a few societies could no doubt be started amongst the Patidars of Gujarat, and in the Karnatak. But he considered that the people in these comparatively prosperous areas could well take care of themselves.[136] The Commissioner of the Southern Division wondered if co-operative societies could do much to help men already in debt. Such people, he feared, formed a large proportion of the population. He also noted that (unlike the Survey Commissioner) the Collector of Dharwar was not sanguine about the prospects of co-operative societies in the Karnatak. The Collector claimed that the majority of agriculturists in his district, who belonged to the Lingayat sect, quarrelled frequently amongst themselves and were unlikely to work with the Marathi-speaking Brahmans of the district.[137] The Collector of Nasik, writing in a genially cynical strain not uncommon at the time, thought that perpetual failure in the sphere of co-operative societies could be deduced

---

[133] G. of I., R. & A. Dept., to Local Govts. Nos. 258–262–326–12 of 30 January 1901. (Poona, file cited.)

[134] Collr., Ahmadnagar, to Commr., S.D., No. R 898 of 25 March 1901, encl. Bom. G.R.R.D. No. 4073 of 30 May 1904. (Poona, file cited.)

[135] Collr., Surat, to Commr., N.D., No. 517 of 6 February 1901, encl. Bom. G.R. cited.

[136] Survey Commr. to Ch. Sec. No. A.—1071 of 2 April 1901, encl. Bom. G.R. cited.

[137] Commr., S.D., to Ch. Sec. No. 1273 of 14 April 1901, encl. Bom. G.R. cited.

from what he saw as the complete failure of measures to promote "local self-government" in India.[138]

Only James McNeill, the Acting Collector of Poona, replied both somewhat optimistically and in detail about the prospects of co-operative societies. He thought that the wealthier irrigated areas of his district probably offered the best scope for the development of societies. The two main difficulties would be to secure a capable managing body and to enforce prompt repayment of loans. He did not think that it would be impossible to find philanthropically minded landowners, and lawyers in the district towns, who would help with leadership. To bring about prompt repayment it might be necessary to allow debts to societies to be recovered as arrears of land revenue. The objection of the "political inexpediency" of such a policy "would probably have less weight now than twenty years ago."[139]

The Co-operative Societies Act

Replies such as these, from district officers all over India, were considered by the Select Committee, which met in Simla in June and July 1901. This Committee drafted a bill "of a permissive character" which would do little more than provide a legal framework for a co-operative movement. But the bill was withdrawn from the Committee's report after that report had been printed,[140] and a second Select Committee set up. The Report of the Famine Commission of 1901 had appeared. Nicholson had been a member of this Commission; it was therefore not surprising that the Commission's Report had called for more positive government measures to encourage a co-operative movement.[141] And although the India Office's chief adviser in the matter, Henry Wolff, the President of the International Co-operative Alliance in London, was in general theoretically opposed to state subventions of any kind in the co-operative sphere, he had come to the conclusion that in India some initial advances from government funds might be in order.[142]

---

[138] Collr., Nasik, to Commr., C.D., No. 5213 of 26 April 1901, encl. Bom. G.R. cited.

[139] Collr., Poona, to Commr., C.D., No. 2877 of 28 March 1901, encl. Bom. G.R. cited.

[140] See end of *Report of the Select Committee on the Establishment of Co-operative Credit Societies in India,* 1901.

[141] *Report of the Indian Famine Commission, 1901,* pp. 98–99. *P.P.* 1902 (Cd. 876) lxx.

[142] Henry Wolff to Sec. of State, 26 June 1900, encl. Sec. of State to Viceroy No. 19 (Rev.) of 8 February 1901. (I.O.R., Rev. Despatches to India, 1901.) Wolff was pri-

Meanwhile, the Government of Bombay continued to make discouraging comments on the very notion of co-operative societies, and came to light with an alternative scheme for the supply of agricultural credit. Legislation should be undertaken, they thought, to extend the law relating to *takkavi* to loans made, under government supervision, by private persons or "associations for productive purposes."[143] The meaning of this hastily drawn up proposal is not altogether clear. But, whether by accident or by design, there are some notable resemblances to Wedderburn's scheme of the eighties.

That scheme had, in fact, been kept in public view in the nineties largely through the exertions of a number of Indian "nationalists," amongst whom Ranade, Pherozeshah Mehta, Dinshaw Wacha, and Gokhale—all from western India—appear to have been the most prominent.[144] To some extent these men took their cue from their mentor in the Congress, Wedderburn. Furthermore, insofar as "agricultural banks" became a "national" cry of the Congress, that cry provided a convenient counter to the criticism that the Congress did not concern itself with the affairs of the ordinary people of India. The President of the Indian National Congress in 1901, Dinshaw Wacha, was well aware that the Government of India were considering proposals for setting up co-operative societies. And he was well aware—in a way that perhaps, by that time, Wedderburn was not—that co-operative societies were not the agricultural banks for which the Congress had been calling for so many years. "The Sowcar, I mean the honest usurer, is not likely

marily a journalist and publicist rather than a practical co-operator; he was somewhat sententiously sure of himself and his theories. He never visited India, though in later years he was to produce a book about co-operation in that country. Wolff was to exercise an influence over the early development of co-operation in India which was possibly out of proportion to his real stature. Yet at the beginning, when officials were still floundering in their efforts to grasp the fundamentals of co-operation, his influence on the whole was helpful.

143 Bom. G.R.R.D. No. 5574 of 12 August 1902.

144 For a long list of calls for agricultural banks from Indian politicians and papers in the last years of the nineteenth century, see Bipan Chandra, *The Rise and Growth of Economic Nationalism in India: Economic Policies of Indian National Leadership, 1880–1905*, p. 485, n. 162. Dr. Bipan Chandra's conclusion that a great many differing economic interests were represented in the "Indian national leadership" at this time (p. 752) is amply borne out by his earlier statement that "the Indian national leaders generally adopted somewhat complex, many-sided, ambivalent, and sometimes divergent attitudes towards the problem of rural indebtedness" (p. 466). For a brief but very useful discussion of the subject, see John R. McLane, "Peasants, Money-lenders and Nationalists at the end of the 19th Century," *Indian Economic and Social History Review*, Vol. I, No. 1 (July–September 1963).

to view his rival with anything like friendliness or favour," he told the Congress. The money-lender was essential to the rural economy; after all, he added, with some truth, "without his aid it would become impossible that the crores of land revenue could be so punctually gathered from year to year." Wacha was inclined to favour a scheme such as that of the Egyptian Agricultural Bank.[145] He wrote privately to Baring, who now, as Lord Cromer, was the de facto ruler of Egypt and intent on putting into practice the ideas which the less free conditions of India had prevented him from experimenting with. Cromer replied that "Co-operative Credit Societies in the East are all nonsense. Anyone who knows the natives knows they will never co-operate."[146] In spite of Wacha's views, however, the Congress went on record at the end of 1903 with a resolution praising the Co-operative Credit Societies Bill, which was then before the Imperial Legislative Council.[147] It is possible that this apparent volte-face was the result of a certain decline in the power of Wacha's political chief, Pherozeshah Mehta, consequent to some extent on his replacement on the Imperial Legislative Council by Gopal Krishna Gokhale.[148] Certainly Gokhale, in his days in the Bombay Legislative Council, had taken a somewhat more independent line than had Mehta and Wacha over the 1901 amendment to the Land Revenue Code.[149]

The Co-operative Credit Societies Bill was finally passed on 25 March 1904. The creation of a framework for a co-operative movement had taken much time. But, as Denzil Ibbetson, the bill's

---

[145] *Report of the Seventeenth Indian National Congress held at Calcutta on the 26th 27th and 28th December 1901*, p. 47. For the Egyptian Bank see chap. 2.

[146] Quoted in "Agricultural Banks in India" (originally contributed as an article to the *Indian Journal of Economics*, January 1916), *Speeches and Writings of Sir Dinshaw Edulji Wacha*, p. 363.

[147] *Report of the Proceedings of the Nineteenth Indian National Congress held at Madras on the 28th 29th and 30th December 1903*, pp. 142–44. But one of the seconders of the motion, Charu Chunder Ghose, quite obviously did not see the difference between co-operative societies and the "agricultural banks" which Congress had previously proposed.

[148] In 1903 Gokhale was elected Joint Secretary of the Congress in addition to Wacha (who for some years had been the working member of a partnership with Wedderburn—now a figurehead). See ibid., p. 147. For Gokhale's replacement of Mehta, see Stanley A. Wolpert, *Tilak and Gokhale: Revolution and Reform in the Making of Modern India*, p. 141.

[149] In his speeches and writings on that bill he had skilfully insisted that he would support the bill if it would really help the rayat. He called for new, positive measures such as "the promotion of non-agricultural industries" and the foundation of "Agricultural Banks." See Patwardhan and Ambekar, eds., *Speeches and Writings of Gokhale*, pp. 425–44.

sponsoring Member, had to admit in the Imperial Legislative Council, there was "hardly a provision of any significance in the Bill which some of our advisers do not regard as of critical importance, and others condemn as a fatal defect."[150] In the West, co-operatives had grown up with a good deal of spontaneity, and normally without the help of the state. It was decided in India that, to begin with, anyway, co-operation would have to be actively fostered from above. In the Indian situation, it came to be believed, the only body suitable for this task was the state. That decision having been made, it was at first proposed simply to add to the duties of the District Collector: to appoint him "Registrar" of co-operative societies for his district.[151] Ideas changed by March 1904. The Resolution which was published at the same time as the Act[152] said that while the Collector and other Revenue officials could be of assistance in the organization of societies, the Government of India attached "much importance to the appointment of a special officer in each province to guide and control the movement, especially in the early days of the movement." Each provincial government should appoint a Registrar, "who should be selected for his special qualifications, and should, for the first few years at least, be constantly visiting societies and watching their progress. . . . Upon the selection of this officer the success of the experiment will very largely depend." The Government of India believed, however, that gradually "the fostering care of the Registrar" would be less required until his duties became "purely official." In deciding to ask the provincial governments to appoint a special officer for co-operative work, the Government of India made a choice which was to influence the whole development of co-operation in India and, in fact, in many other Asian and African countries which have since followed the Indian model. The official Registrar, working out overall policy and intervening frequently in co-operative affairs, was to be no mere temporary phenomenon. In Bombay each Registrar was to leave his own special imprint on the co-operative movement, so that to some extent, in the first

150 *Abstract of the Proceedings of the Council of the Governor-General of India assembled for the purpose of making Laws and Regulations, 1903–4,* p. 29 (4 March 1904).

151 *Select Cttee., 1901, Rept.,* p. 5.

152 India G.R., R. & A. Dept. (L. Rev.) No. 1—63-3 of 29 April 1904. The remainder of this paragraph and the next three paragraphs are based on this resolution; quotations are from it unless it is otherwise stated in the footnotes.

twenty years especially, the history of the co-operative movement became the history of the "reigns" of individual Registrars.

It was proposed in 1904 to concentrate on the encouragement of societies for the supply of agricultural credit. It had been originally intended to limit membership to men of small means; membership was now thrown open to all, though precautions ought to be taken, the Government of India believed, against the Act's provisions being made use of "by persons for whom they were not intended." There was to be no declaration of war on the money-lender. Indeed Ibbetson, the driving force behind the operation of the Act in its early years, diplomatically expressed the hope that "money-lenders would in the end help the movement. They have often been unjustly abused as a class."[153] Co-operative societies were intended to make small, short-term loans for "productive purposes." The implication was, of course, that the money-lender was to be left to handle long-term business and loans for the ever present and in some cases ever increasing expense of marriages and social life generally. Such an emphasis was to have important repercussions.

Unless a provincial government specially ruled otherwise, the liability of rural societies was to be unlimited; this, it was considered, would promote careful and watchful habits amongst the members of the village societies. Deposits from members and non-members were to be encouraged: there was a strong feeling amongst many (probably not completely unjustified)[154] that there was plenty of capital in the villages of India, which needed only to be prised out of its hiding-places. The object was to stimulate the Victorian virtues of "thrift and self-help." It was only when these virtues had been displayed, when in fact some deposits had been collected by a society, that the Government would consider making it a loan, on a rupee-to-rupee basis, to a maximum of Rs.2000. Such loans would not be granted automatically. They were to be given primarily as "an earnest of the reality of the interest taken by

---

153 *Proceedings of the Conference of Registrars of Co-operative Societies held on the 25 September 1906 and the following days*, p. 9. It is worthwhile noting that Ibbetson's hostility (unlike Thorburn's) was never directed towards the money-lender as such, but rather against the system which allowed him to flourish. See his classic settlement report, *Report on the Revision of Settlement of the Panipat Tahsil and Karnal Parganah of the Karnal District, 1872–1880*, pp. 110–111, and also his letter of 7 March 1889, quoted Barrier, *Punjab Alienation of Land Bill*, Appx. C.

154 See P. G. K. Panikar, "Rural Savings in India," *Economic Development and Cultural Change*, Vol. X, No. 1 (October 1961). Dr. Panikar includes under the heading "rural savings" the capital of all rural money-lending and trading groups.

Government in the movement"; it was not intended to grant loans to new societies indefinitely. It was hoped that urban societies, "lending with the approval of the Registrar to rural societies," would soon come into being.

Societies were not to be permitted to make advances against standing crops: "no form of security would be more unsuitable." Competition in this particular preserve of the money-lender was therefore not intended, either. Transactions could be conducted in grain, however, as in Crosthwaite's experimental societies. After a great deal of argument it had been decided that loans against the security of jewelry should be allowed only in very special circumstances. The question of mortgages on land was "even more difficult." On the one hand it was obviously desirable that a cultivator should be able to substitute a mortgage upon reasonable terms for one that was on exorbitant terms; on the other hand, "personal credit" was felt to be the basis of the short-term loan system which was contemplated. Mortgages in India often led to court cases: it was "above all things desirable" that societies should "keep out of the law courts." The final conclusion was that loans on mortgage should as a general rule be permitted, but that provincial governments should be given extensive powers to prohibit or restrict such loans. The Act was intended to be characterized by "simplicity and elasticity." Provincial governments and Registrars were given a wide range of discretionary powers. It was hoped that the co-operative movement would "neither suffer from the absence of that official guidance without which a successful start cannot be hoped for in this country, nor be prevented by too much supervision and too many restrictions from attaining its full development."

So ran the long and carefully worded Resolution which was sent to provincial governments and publicized widely throughout India. By no means had all the arguments about the need for a co-operative movement or the mode of its operation been settled. In the early days, in fact (the Royal Commission on Agriculture had to admit in 1928), "the leaders of the blind were themselves often amongst the afflicted."[155] There were many, especially in Bombay and Madras, who thought that the whole idea of co-operation in India was sheer folly: Dupernex himself told the International Co-

---

[155] *Royal Commission on Agriculture, Rept.,* p. 444.

operative Alliance meeting in Budapest in 1904 that the general opinion in India was that co-operation would never succeed there.[156] Some of the less sceptical perhaps misunderstood the nature of co-operation. As an early Bombay Registrar put it, "The truth is—we were talking of 'Agricultural Banks' and we have been landed with 'Co-operative Societies.' "[157] And yet it must be said that, so far as Bombay was concerned, in the generally hasty memoranda that government officials had produced on the subject in the years immediately preceding 1904, a number of the problems that were to face the co-operative movement in the future had, in fact, been identified in their essentials.

What was perhaps the most basic of questions about the co-operative movement had been posed: had the problems of agricultural indebtedness and land transfer been exaggerated, at least so far as Bombay was concerned? The Government of Bombay (when they had recovered their equilibrium after the famine) had rightly disputed some aspects of the Government of India analysis of this matter. But supposing co-operatives were to be introduced, in spite of the protestations of the Government of Bombay. Could they ever succeed in the Deccan "famine belt"? It was significant that James McNeill, Acting Collector of Poona in 1901, had singled out the irrigated tracts of his district—not very considerable in extent—as being the most suitable areas in which to promote co-operative societies. What were the chances of the success of co-operatives in other parts of the Presidency, such as Gujarat and the Karnatak? It had been asked whether the comparative wealth of at least some castes in those regions was such as to make it doubtful whether co-operatives could be of much use to them.

It had been asked, too, whether there was any real basis of indigenous "co-operation" in the villages of the western Presidency. If co-operation did not come naturally, if in reality the co-operative movement was something essentially new, then were the peasants capable of appreciating whatever virtues co-operative societies might possess? In 1893 the visiting agricultural expert J. A. Voelcker had asserted that "the Native, though he may be slow in taking up an improvement, will not hesitate to adopt it if he is convinced

---

[156] H. R. Crosthwaite, "Recollections and Reflections," *B.C.Q.*, June 1917, p. 16.
[157] C. S. Campbell to Govt. (through Director of Agriculture), No. 1464 of 17 October 1907. (Poona, Decentralisation.)

that it constitutes a better plan and one to his advantage."[158] But as one scans the correspondence which preceded the Co-operative Societies Act one comes to doubt whether the average district officer, at least in the Bombay Presidency at this time, had quite the same faith in the Indian peasant, though he might be genuinely interested in his welfare.

[158] J. A. Voelcker, *Report on the Improvement of Indian Agriculture*, p. 11.

II

Some False Starts, 1904-1911

An Irishman Frustrated

The Government of Bombay had no desire to make a full-scale quarrel with the Government of India over such a matter as the Co-operative Societies Act, which, after all, was a comparatively minor piece of the policies and politics of the time. The *Bombay Government Gazette* of 14 July 1904 therefore announced the appointment of "Mr. J. McNeill, I.C.S., to be Registrar of Co-operative Credit Societies, Bombay Presidency."[1]

McNeill, it will be remembered, had been the only Collector in 1901 to write both fully and favourably on the prospects of co-operative societies. Like a good many others in the Indian Civil Service, he was an Irishman. He was eventually, in fact, after retirement from the Service in 1915, to enter Irish politics; he became Irish High Commissioner in London and then Governor-General of the Irish Free State.[2] In 1904 all that was in the future. Yet it was his Irish connections which drew him into co-operative work at the beginning of the century. An annual report of the Irish Agricultural Organization Society, the organizing body for Irish co-operatives, had been amongst papers circulated to Collec-

---

[1] Bom. G.R.R.D. No. 5269 of 11 July 1904, *Bombay Government Gazette*, pt. i, 14 July 1904, p. 962.

[2] James McNeill: Asst. Collr., Bom., 1890; Regr. Co-op. Socs., 1904; Collr., 1906; Settlement Commr., 1911; conducted enquiry into situation of Indians overseas, 1913–14; Offg. Commr., C.D., retd., 1915. "An able Indian Civil Servant" (Lord Hardinge, *My Indian Years, 1910–1916*, p. 73). McNeill's brother, Eoin, was a Sinn Feiner and was jailed by the British; this led James McNeill into Irish politics. (See his letter to Sir Horace Plunkett, 7 June 1917, Plunkett Papers, Horace Plunkett Foundation, London.) His subsequent career was as follows: Chairman, Dublin County Council, 1922; High Commissioner for the Irish Free State in London, 1923–28; Governor-General, 1928–32. A number of letters in the Plunkett Papers provide an interesting commentary on this part of McNeill's life.

tors in Bombay in 1901.[3] McNeill must have noticed this. Realizing that co-operative societies were coming in India whether the Bombay Government liked it or not, he utilized part of his leave in 1901–2 to learn something of the societies which had been set up in his homeland. He visited Horace Plunkett, the apostle of Irish agricultural co-operation and, becoming caught up in the prevailing enthusiasm, helped in the work of the I.A.O.S.[4] On his return to Bombay he was the obvious man to appoint as Registrar. He was an avowed optimist about the chances of success of co-operative societies in Bombay; he could be allowed to chance his hand.

At first it seemed as though the official scepticism was going to be justified; McNeill failed to start any societies at all during his first "season." Admittedly, he had to spend much of his time at the beginning in gathering a staff around him, in obtaining office accommodation in Poona, and in drafting leaflets and having them translated. Admittedly, too, it was a bad season, and McNeill had taken up his position when the season had already begun and basic loans had been obtained from the money-lenders. But McNeill seems to have realized fairly soon that the task before him was rather more difficult than he had thought in 1901. According to the grandson of an early co-operator, McNeill, "having lost all hopes of organizing any society,"[5] went down to Betigeri-Gadag, in Dharwar district in the Karnatak. There he met Canon C. S. Rivington, an Anglican missionary, who seems to have instilled some new hope in him. Eventually Rivington, together with an Indian friend, Shivaji Ramchandra Kulkarni, organized the first co-operative society in the Bombay Presidency, the Kanaginhal Agricultural Co-operative Credit Society, Unltd., in Gadag taluka. Kulkarni appears to have been a Maharashtrian Brahman; his successful intervention at this point perhaps illustrates the fact that anti-Brahman feeling, which was to be strong in the Karnatak within fifteen years, was as yet not at all prominent in that area.

[3] Encl. Bom. G.R.R.D. No. 2110 of 29 March 1901. (Poona, ADM. S.O.7.)

[4] McNeill to Plunkett, 24 November 1931, 8 January 1932. (Plunkett Papers.) See also G. K. Gokhale to McNeill, 24 October 1901, for an oblique reference to these activities. (N.A.I., Gokhale Papers. I am grateful to Shri Satyapal, of the National Archives, for drawing my attention to this letter, which incidentally shows the breadth of Gokhale's interests and the range of McNeill's acquaintances.)

[5] H. M. Kulkarni, "A Peep into Pioneering Days—Shri Shivaji Ramchandra Kulkarni and Shri M.S. Kulkarni," *B.C.Q.*, July 1954, p. 74.

Certainly his main contact in the village of Kanaginhal was one
Shiddangavda, the headman, obviously a Kanarese-speaking man.
Shiddangavda later helped in the organization of several other
societies in the surrounding area.[6] Rivington was a devoted and
humble man, who came from the family which had been publishers to the Tractarians.[7] There were not many conversions in the
Karnatak in his time; he felt, however, that his work for co-
operative societies and in the municipality was justified as a method of "showing our interest in our neighbours."[8] McNeill himself
was posted on "special duty" as Acting Collector of Dharwar between the months of May and August 1905. (Early Registrars were
likely to be regarded as reserve strength whose services could occasionally be called upon for other work.) When at last he found
time to write his report for the year ending 31 March 1905 he
could say that eight societies had been registered in Dharwar district since the close of the official year; in five of these "the work
was being carried out excellently."[9] At the end of March 1906
there were thirty-one societies registered in the Presidency; of
these, ten were working satisfactorily.[10] But the Punjab Registrar
had in the same year toured one district and had registered sixty-
five societies there alone.[11] In some ways, he thought, "encouraging thrift among the Punjabi peasants might be likened to bringing coals to Newcastle."[12]

It was clear that some fundamental thinking had to be done over
the question of co-operative societies in Bombay. McNeill fairly
soon came to the conclusion that the Government of India's idea
that societies should not be hampered at the beginning by too
many rules was a false one so far as the Bombay Presidency was
concerned. "Village communities, so far from resenting restrictive
rules, are timid about undertaking responsibility without directions as to its exercise."[13] There should be no ambiguity about

[6] *Annual Report on the Working of Co-operative Credit Societies in the Bombay
Presidency, 1905–6*, p. 4. Hereafter the titles of such reports are abbreviated in footnotes as *Rept.*
[7] Information from the Ven. S. A. Mara.
[8] Rivington, "Report for the year ending 31 October 1909" (S.P.G., Missionary
Reports Received, 1909, Reference 31.)
[9] *Rept., 1904–5*, p. 5.
[10] *Rept., 1905–6*, p. 2.
[11] *Annual Report on the Working of Co-operative Credit Societies in the Punjab
for the year ending 31 March 1906*, p. 2.
[12] *Punjab Report, 1906–7*, p. 3.
[13] *Rept., 1904–5*, p. 2.

rights and duties, otherwise few would join the societies. And so detailed model rules for societies were drafted, on the lines of those McNeill had known in the Irish Agricultural Organization Society.[14] The Government of Bombay were somewhat doubtful as to the necessity for such rules;[15] nevertheless, McNeill's rules served as a basis for some years. McNeill also decided that it was of little use relying on the Collector and his revenue officials in each district to organize viable societies. He felt from his own experience that a Collector generally had quite enough to do in getting through his work in the law and order realm. But at the same time it was clear that the Registrar himself could not personally foster each society. "Even when the people [of a village] are anxious to have a society and are willing to subscribe capital they expect to be gently pushed through every step and to be given a little breathing time between successive steps."[16] It was for this reason that McNeill evolved a system of "honorary organizers" of co-operative societies.

Ideally, honorary organizers were to be "non-officials" who lived in the rural areas, men with some education and leisure and of some standing in their comunities, who would volunteer, as a social service, not only to organize societies but also to keep a friendly eye on them once they had been started. They were to receive no pay, but were to be given a travelling allowance on a reasonably generous basis. In the village, McNeill claimed, advice from honorary organizers came "not as an official proposal but as a friendly suggestion to listeners usually prepossessed in favour of the adviser."[17] The use of Indian honorary organizers in the co-operative movement made Bombay in this respect practically unique amongst Indian provinces for some years. Wilberforce, the Punjab Registrar, saw little need for them.[18] This was perhaps not only for the reason that he was quite successful without them; there is evidence that the Punjab Government feared that once they released their paternalistic grip on co-operative societies—which, of

---

[14] Ibid.

[15] Bom. G.R.R.D. No. 351 of 13 January 1906, on *Rept., 1904–5*.

[16] *Rept., 1904–5*, p. 4.

[17] *Rept., 1905–6*, p. 7.

[18] *Proceedings of the Conference of Registrars of Co-operative Credit Societies held at Simla on the 25th September 1906 and the following days*, p. 10. The proceedings of Conferences of Registrars are hereafter cited in the footnotes as *Regrs.' Conf. Procs., 19–*.

course, were in competition with Hindu money-lenders—they could well become Muslim anti-Hindu organizations.[19] In Bengal the honorary organizers were frequently Europeans;[20] there may have been semi-political fears behind this state of affairs, too. Even in Bombay there was probably some significance in the fact that the first "non-official" honorary organizers were in fact all retired officials of the "rank" of Deputy Collector; official caution perhaps increased when it was reported in 1908 that members of the Poona Sarvajanik Sabha were renewing "agitation" in the countryside under the guise of promoting "agricultural improvement."[21] The changing position of honorary organizers in the movement in Bombay, and the changes in the sorts of people who were asked to become organizers, together make up one of the most important themes of the next twenty-five years.

McNeill also set the tone for much of the controversy of the following years in his unambiguous expression of his views on the questions of the supply of funds to co-operative societies and the recovery of loans from recalcitrant debtors. The 1904 Government of India Resolution on co-operative societies had promised an initial loan to deserving societies, on a rupee-to-rupee basis, up to a maximum of Rs.2000. McNeill believed that this sum was insufficient; the amount which villagers could subscribe to qualify for this grant was, he claimed, "only a fraction" of the amount required to finance the year's agricultural operations. "I think that if less importance be attached to stimulating thrift and effort and more to testing the capacity of village communities to manage funds raised on their joint credit the results of the first few years' working may be much more valuable."[22] Here, in fact, was a direct challenge to the public philosophy of the Co-operative Societies Act. The question of summary recovery came up at the Registrars' Conference at the end of September 1906. In the face of opposition from a number of other provincial Registrars, McNeill insisted that societies should not have to go through the long processes of

19 See note of P. J. Fagan, Offg. Financial Commr., Punjab, 21 October 1913, attached to *Punjab Report, 1912–13*. See also Michael O'Dwyer, *India As I Knew It, 1885–1925*, pp. 255–56.

20 *Report on the Working of Co-operative Credit Societies in Bengal for the year 1906–1907*, p. 26.

21 *Bom. L. Rev. Admin. Rept., 1907–8*, pt. ii, p. 27.

22 McNeill to Govt., No. 996 of 13 September 1906, encl. Bom. G.R.R.D. No. 11378 of 1 December 1906. (Poona, Spare Copies.)

the Civil Courts in order to recover loans from wayward members.[23] He was not to have his way in his time as Registrar.

Charlie Campbell

C. S. Campbell took over the position of Registrar in October 1906. He was a younger man than McNeill; since his arrival in India in 1899 he had been Assistant Collector and Special Famine Officer in Satara, working in the thick of village life, and Assistant Collector and Personal Assistant to the Collector of the then still undivided district of Khandesh. He had not been out of India since he had arrived, having spent four months' privilege leave in Satara, possibly undertaking voluntary work of some variety.[24] He once wrote that he had twice been asked whether he would like the position of Registrar, and on both occasions he had declined it. "I was informed, however, later, that I was to study under and take over from Mr. McNeill."[25] This was not, it might seem, a particularly promising beginning. But Campbell's attitude in this matter was not one of sullen compliance. "I entered a free billet; and began to identify myself with it."[26]

Charlie Campbell was an essentially Victorian figure: a "muscular Christian" who reminds one very much of Tom Hughes of *Tom Brown's Schooldays* fame. A strong, utterly fearless man, he had a warm, susceptible heart and was immensely moved by poverty and misery. He gave away a considerable portion of his salary as private benefactions; he was frequently to be seen followed by a troop of small Indian boys, orphans, whom he was "educating."[27] He brought to bear on the co-operative movement what can only be described as a missionary spirit; indeed, it is not surprising to find that he, like McNeill, retired early from the Indian Civil Service—he to become a Christian missionary. Campbell was a superb linguist. To quote the words of his successor as Registrar, R. B. Ewbank: "He could even speak [Marathi] with the inflec-

23 *Regrs.' Conf. Procs., 1906*, p. 16.
24 Campbell's draft "Statement of Career" for the Royal Commission on Decentralisation in India, 1907. (Poona, Decentralisation.)
25 Campbell's draft "Memo on the position of the Registrar of Co-operative Societies." (Poona, Decentralisation.)
26 Ibid.
27 Information from C. S. Campbell's nephew, Brigadier Lorne Campbell, V.C., Sir Robert Ewbank, Sir Stanley Reed, and the late Dr. Harold Mann. Charles Campbell: Asst. Collr., Bom., 1899; Regr. 1906–11; Collr., 1916; Recruiting Officer, 1916–18; C.B.E., 1919; retd., 1925.

tions of (say) Satara, Nasik or the Desh, and was familiar with the shades of dialect of unlettered rustics."[28] On the face of it, then, Campbell was an ideal Registrar. But was he? In Campbell, one fears, pity was combined with a certain amount of gullibility. His undoubted brilliance was of the erratic variety. Single phrases or sentences from his writing read better than the strangely punctuated whole. His tremendous energy was combined with a large measure of personal sensitivity. He simply did not fit in with many of the more hard-headed of his fellow Civilians. Still, the energy of the man, coupled with his occasional prickliness, have left us with a mass of reports, memoranda, and long plaintive letters which, put together, give us an extraordinarily valuable picture of the co-operative movement in its early days in Bombay.

At least two hundred days of Campbell's year were spent in travelling. This was not the normal sort of "touring" in which the District Officer indulged; the whole Presidency was the Registrar's territory. "The pace one has to go," commented Campbell, "is certainly telling, if not killing."[29] Such travel involved "stays where expedient and possible; in village or city (or Railway Station!)."[30] Yet not all Campbell's touring difficulties need to have been faced. The fact was that virtually nothing was planned in advance. "The 3 months during which I travelled round with him learning the job," Sir Robert Ewbank has written, "were the most uncomfortable of my life. . . . We used to arrive at some wayside station, waste an hour in getting transport for our very meagre kit, find the dak bungalow occupied, go and sleep in a bug infested chora (chavdi), make our supper on some baked beans out of a tin and so on. There was no necessity at all for all this—very bad for health and temper. But he just smiled and neither complained nor tried to plan things properly."[31]

Campbell always combined his visit to a village co-operative society with a visit to the local school: "Unfortunately school education and methods of teaching have often little in common with co-operative ideas," but still, education, he believed, was a necessi-

28 Letter to the author from Sir Robert Ewbank.
29 *Rept., 1906–7*, p. 1.
30 Campbell, Memo. A, Draft Evidence for Decentralisation Commission. (Poona, Decentralisation.)
31 Letter to the author from Sir Robert Ewbank. A *chora,* or *chavdi,* is a building to accommodate travellers.

ty if co-operation was to succeed on a wide scale.[32] He preferred, in fact, to sum up his work "in the general language of education; rather than in statistics and in figures of 'finance.' "[33] And, indeed, one has to search quite extensively in his reports before one finds that there were about three hundred societies at the end of his period as Registrar, in 1911,[34] as compared with thirty-one when he took up the position. Many of the three hundred societies that he left behind him were not very sound. There were the Satara societies, for example. In 1907–8 there was plague in that district, and Campbell was sent down on special duty in order to help in administering inoculations. His sympathetic personality soon made itself felt amidst "the inevitable hustling and heckling" of the Deccan villages. Everywhere he went, he claimed, he was asked for help, for "a society." He decided on a new policy. Almost overnight the total number of societies "registered" in the Presidency nearly doubled.[35] Campbell seems to have believed that by registering these famine-belt societies and thus confronting the Government of Bombay with a *fait accompli* he could force that government to grant large loans to the societies.[36] But government loans on the scale Campbell had hoped for were not forthcoming. The Government of Bombay were able to obtain from the Government of India a slight relaxation of the equal-deposits rule in certain special cases, but in practice most of the Satara societies failed to obtain loans. Much of the rest of Campbell's career as Registrar is the rather sorry story of his efforts to make these societies work without any money. Then there were the societies for the Kaliparaj tribal people of Mandvi taluka of Surat district. These societies had money to begin with. But the money came from the members' old money-lenders.[37] This was in accordance with the Government of India's official pronouncements, but in reality, "after organizing village societies, the money-lenders man-

[32] *Rept., 1906–7*, p. 11.

[33] *Rept., 1909–10*, p. 2; cf. *Rept., 1906–7*, p. 1.

[34] Campbell gave up the position at the end of November 1911. The figure for March 1911 was 252 (*Rept., 1910–11*, p. 3), and for March 1912, 368 (*Rept., 1911–12*, p. 20).

[35] *Rept., 1907*, p. 2.

[36] *Rept., 1907–8*, p. 8.

[37] Khandubhai Desai, Evidence, Committee on Co-operation in India, 1914–15. (Punjab Record Office, Patiala.) Hereafter this Committee will be cited as Maclagan Cttee.

aged to get the loans advanced to the members in satisfaction of their swollen claims. The result was that the loans were not used for productive purposes and they could not be repaid."[38]

The Karnatak

It was, in fact, only in the Karnatak, and especially in Dharwar district, that a viable co-operative movement began to come into being in the Bombay Presidency before 1911. In Canon Rivington, Campbell doubtless found something of a kindred spirit. But it is impossible to explain the fortunes of the co-operative movement in Dharwar, even in these early years, simply in personal terms. It is tempting, indeed, to opt for another explanation: to ascribe the success of the co-operative movement in the Karnatak, and especially in Dharwar, solely to the peculiar ethos of the dominant cultivating group, the Lingayats. From the beginning of the century, if not before, they had been joining together for the provision of western type education for their young men,[39] though education in English was not yet a marked characteristic of the Lingayats. In 1915 the Collector of Dharwar wrote:

The district is still mainly one of small holders—a sort of peasant state —and these small holders are maintained in contentment largely by the absence of any sharp cleavage, as in other districts, between the agricultural and commercial classes. The prevailing caste, the Lingayats, are generally cultivators and traders and the small holder readily passes into the rank of the well-to-do and the well known. This condition makes against social bitterness and for general confidence and solidarity, which perhaps accounts for the remarkable progress of the district in co-operation, sanitation, improved agriculture, and other advanced movements.[40]

But this picture was not altogether adequate. The Lingayats, in spite of their virtual rejection of the caste system,[41] were, as the

[38] C. M. Gandhi, "Glimpses of the Co-operative Movement," *B.C.Q.*, April 1954, p. 14.

[39] William McCormack, "The Forms of Communication in Virasaiva Religion," in *Traditional India: Structure and Change*, ed. Milton Singer, pp. 126–27. In 1915 J. N. Farquhar, in *Modern Religious Movements in India*, p. 302, claimed that the "Lingayat Education Association" had been in existence for some thirty years. On the Lingayats, see also N. C. Sargant, *The Vira-Saiva Religion*.

[40] A. E. L. Emmanuel, Collr., Dharwar, quoted *Bom. L. Rev. Admin. Rept., 1914–15*, pt. ii, p. 33.

[41] See William McCormack, "Lingayats as a Sect," *Journal of the Royal Anthropological Institute of Great Britain and Ireland*, Vol. XCIII, pt. i (January–June 1963),

Collector of Dharwar in 1901 had noted, a somewhat quarrelsome group—as puritans in religious matters are perhaps inclined to be. Above all, the ascription of such success as the co-operative movement had in Dharwar solely to the "solidarity" supposedly inculcated by Vira-Saivism ignores the fact that in Dharwar a more reliable rainfall than that of the Deccan provided the basis of a reasonable prosperity which was so often lacking amongst the peasantry to the north and east. The Lingayats were the dominant social group in the district of Bijapur. But in the first thirty years of its operation the co-operative movement was never very strong in this district. The explanation must surely lie largely in the fact that Bijapur, like so much of the Deccan, suffers from a highly irregular rainfall. This simple matter of rainfall cannot be forgotten in any discussion of western India.[42]

The Village Society

The committee of a society, Campbell once wrote, was "generally composed of men who (so it would seem from a distance) have naturally fallen into their places. . . . Committees or Panches (for such they may often literally be) exist *ipso facto* in the body of villagers assembled." To the villager "the process of popular election is hardly comprehensible in theory, and superfluous in practice. As long, then, as we get honesty we need not press for technicalities and strict compliance with Western formulas."[43] At least in his early days as Registrar, Campbell normally worked with the leading men of the village, considered in terms of caste, wealth, and prestige. But what might be called the "hinge group" between the government and the people in the organization of co-operative societies was not always the same as that between the government and the village in the normal course of administration. "The old Maratha proverb classes the Kulkarni [village accountant] with the Sonar [goldsmith] and the Shimpi [tailor] as one of those who take their perquisites on the way. . . . The better village officers, of course, are ready enough to help; but we must reckon with all sorts of hosts: and in a village the Patil and Kulkarni assuredly are

---

pp. 59–71. But there remains a distinction—which the British perhaps tended to emphasize—between the Jangams or "priests" of the Vira-Saiva religion and the "laity": *Gazetteer of the Bombay Presidency*, Vol. XXII, *Dharwar*, pp. 102–15.

[42] On the subject of rainfall in Bijapur district see Harold H. Mann, *Rainfall and Famine*, passim.

[43] *Rept., 1906–7*, p. 10.

such. We are practically reintroducing the 'Panch' system and courting, in part, opposition from the Patil."[44] This is not to say that the *kulkarni* in the Deccan, and the *talati* in Gujarat (a personage who was often accountant for several villages), were not extensively used as "secretaries" for the societies. But sometimes the committee of a society were persuaded to appoint the local schoolmaster as secretary. As children from all the factions in a village usually went to the school, it was in the schoolmaster's interest not to become connected with any of these factions. On the whole, Campbell thought, the schoolmaster was more trusted by the villagers than the *kulkarni*. After all, the *kulkarni* was sometimes a petty money-lender himself. The secretary was usually paid. Sometimes, as in Satara district, the only way of raising enough money to employ a literate secretary was to give such a person the oversight of several societies.[45] As for the ordinary members of the society, "The General Body meets sometimes; but it is seldom met."[46] They were, of course, usually out in the fields at the time of day the official chose to make his visit. Only by staying overnight in the village could the visiting government officer hope to make much contact with the members of a society. "The Secretary and Chairman may suffice for ordinary questions," wrote Campbell, "and the books may reflect the Societies [sic] work and use."[47]

Campbell drew a distinction, in the later years of his career as Registrar, between societies that he termed "aristocratic" and those that he termed "democratic." In "aristocratic" societies there were, generally, "one or two big men of the village" who to a very large extent controlled the society. They supplied the capital; the more they supplied the more the society obtained from the Government under Campbell's system of almost automatic subsidies on a rupee-to-rupee basis up to the maximum of Rs.2000. The leaders themselves were usually non-borrowers; "all the lower villainage [sic] . . . being more or less of a dead level in their sight" naturally joined as soon as patronage was extended. The patrons became the leading committee members. Their policy was never questioned;

---

44 *Regrs.' Conf. Procs., 1907*, pp. 30–31; cf. *Rept., 1906–7*, p. 8.

45 *Rept., 1909–10*, p. 4.

46 Campbell, "Note on how far officials should take any part in organisation or supervision," composed for Agriculture Department subordinates. (Poona, Subordination of Regr. to D.A.)

47 Ibid.

they were re-elected from year to year. In these societies a secretary
was easily found; the accounts were well kept, at least formally.
But "democratic" societies, Campbell wrote,

begin sometimes very near or actually on the lowest round—minimum
of members (ten), all borrowers (though solvent), no deposits, dependent on a outsider for writing accounts, entrance-fee absent (by preference), redemption of usurious old debts a first claim on the Society.
Such little groups of little people, which come clamouring for recognition, are by no means confined in each case to a single caste: but the
members forming each are closely knit together. . . . Honesty and
honour seem natural to many of them, but their equality of status and
finance makes exercise of authority and discipline (by the "Panch")
more difficult: and it requires a strong "Secretary" from without to
keep them business-like.[48]

There were, of course, various intermediate stages between
these two types. One or two cases had occurred, Campbell reported in 1910, where societies had partly changed their character.
The original depositors had been required to guarantee, before
the government subsidy was given, that they would leave their
money invested in the society for five years. But "big" men soon
found that unlimited liability was often not an attractive proposition. Now that the first five years were up, they had sometimes
"withdrawn their deposits in a body."[49] This diminution of enthusiasm amongst the wealthier peasantry was to be significant for
the future.

A single man could be responsible for fostering dissension. He
could be a headman, or a village accountant, or a professional
money-lender. Or he could be an "agriculturist money-lender."
A man who had money to deposit in a society *ipso facto* presumably had money to lend.[50] Campbell's opinion of the agriculturist
money-lender was not high. He did not feel that the terms offered
by such a man were better than those offered by the person who
took no part in cultivation; rather, he thought, the reverse was
the case. "I think the proverbial Bania might be preferred to the
moneyed agriculturist."[51] Frequently, of course, dissension in co-
operative societies was the result of the working of "factions."

48 *Rept., 1909–10*, p. 9.
49 Ibid., p. 10.
50 *Rept., 1906–7*, p. 6.
51 *Rept., 1907–8*, p. 5.

Not every "group" in a western Indian village was necessarily a quarrelsome "faction." Nor were factions necessarily based upon a single caste.[52] But in co-operative societies, in the early years in Bombay, at any rate, factions tended to have a caste basis, which in turn represented to some extent economic cleavage within the societies. In the villages, Campbell wrote, it was "rather a matter of distinction to have a few low caste men on show with their receipt books, to show the amount of loan they have received."[53] But the "aristocratic" societies usually resented the presence of more than a few low caste men. And one society in Surat district insisted, not completely unjustly, on higher interest rates for low castes if they were admitted.[54] At times, Campbell thought, it might be necessary to have two co-operative societies in a village so that competing factions could be catered for.[55]

Such problems might eventually bring about the failure of a society. But the end of a society, Campbell recognized, might eventually come from "mere inertia or ergo-phobia; death by dying as it might be called. In such cases it is probably best to remove the corpse by 'cancellation,' to prevent neighbours being put off by the putrefaction."[56]

The Heart of the Matter

Campbell came to what was in some ways the heart of the problem of credit co-operatives in his Reports for 1908 and 1909. It was simply that the rayat was extremely reluctant to repay his loans from the society. To a large extent this was not because of any essential dishonesty. It was mainly because he persisted in regarding the co-operative society simply as another money-lender. The idea of repayment of principal as well as of interest was foreign to the rayat. According to Campbell, the "agreement" between debtor and creditor, which Westerners tended to interpret literally because it was in writing, was really "that the debtor will

52 Although cf. Oscar Lewis, *Village Life in Northern India. Studies in a Delhi Village.* He says that factions "follow caste lines" (p. 114) and claims that they "contribute to the compartmentalized and segmented nature of village social organization." Others would not emphasize so much the divisiveness of such groups, and would recognize the importance of what Lewis calls "alliances or blocs" of factions.

53 *Rept., 1906–7,* p. 5.

54 *Rept., 1908–9,* p. 12.

55 Campbell's Evidence, *Royal Commission on Decentralisation in India, Minutes of Evidence, Bombay,* p. 91. *P.P.* 1908 (Cd. 4367) xlvi.

56 *Rept., 1906–7,* p. 5.

get as much and repay as little as possible. The settlement is a working out of this agreement."[57] This view was carried over into the co-operative field. A good many peasants preferred the perpetual tussle with the money-lender to the cut-and-dried methods of the co-operative society. And furthermore, the co-operative society, as a business organization, with very real responsibilities to its members, could not possibly give the easy accommodation to the villager in the matter of loans that the individual money-lender could give. It might grant a lump sum at sowing time, to be paid back as a lump sum at harvest time. But in the meantime a child might be born, there might be a wedding, a bullock might die, the crop itself might fail. The money-lender could grant a new loan and an extension of time while perhaps raising his interest rates;[58] the society could not possibly do this while keeping its rates at a modest (for India) 9 per cent.

Could the co-operative society hope to beat the money-lender at his own game? Campbell believed that it could—given adequate government assistance. Essentially, he made many of the points that McNeill had made, but he made them more pungently, one might almost say irreverently. He believed that the precondition for a government loan—that there should be some deposits from members—was wrong. It was not easy, he wrote, to understand "how a man who is already in debt, has current calls on his cash (e.g. at assessment time), and wants further loans, can deposit any money whatever with profit or propriety." Even if a man by chance had a little money hidden away, he was not always ready to "give himself away to his Saukar," or to weaken his case for suspensions or remissions of land revenue payments, by displaying his wealth in the form of deposits in a co-operative society.[59]

What Campbell had in mind, in fact, was "the total transference of tagai [*takkavi*] to the 'Co-operative' Department."[60] In other words, the money that was at present lent by the revenue authorities under the Agriculturists' Loans Act and the Land Improvements Loans Act, should be lent to and through his own new little organizations. Campbell appears to have believed that the system of "joint-*takkavi*," under which money was sometimes lent to a vil-

[57] *Rept., 1907–8*, p. 5.
[58] *Rept., 1908–9*, p. 9.
[59] *Rept., 1906–7*, p. 6.
[60] Campbell to Govt., No. 494 of 28 February 1908. (Poona, Decentralisation.)

lage or a group within a village, could be applied to co-operative societies. He compared societies with the organizations of "local self-government" in India. The Indian governments were not supposed to wait until local boards had become more "polished" before trusting them with money. With supervision, Campbell thought, these organizations managed to "get on, more or less." Similarly, co-operative societies, given supervision as well as money, would "get on." It was quite obvious that what the people needed was money. The Government had the money. It was as simple as that. "We shall do more good perhaps in the East if we take people as they stand and help them where they are."[61] But the Government of Bombay were not going to make the radical alterations in their financial and administrative structure which Campbell suggested—certainly not while the Government of India continued to proclaim publicly that state financial aid to co-operative societies could be little more than a necessary evil, and a temporary one at that. In 1910, therefore, Campbell was still complaining, with some truth, that the conditions attached to loans from Government tended to encourage the formation of societies of the "aristocratic" kind, but that they "directly opposed the initial progress of democratic societies."[62]

There seems to be little doubt that the co-operative societies were placed at some disadvantage when it came to recovering unpaid debts. Under the Co-operative Societies Act, a society, in the event of a debtor's refusal to pay a debt, had no final resort except the Civil Court. The burden and cost of suing in a Civil Court and of having the Court's decrees executed were, Campbell thought, enough to break a society. Yet it was argued by some that it would not be right to give co-operative societies privileges which others did not have. That would savour of "favouritism." "I cannot help thinking that a point of view starting on these lines will end finally by logical procedure in negation of government altogether," replied Campbell. "Surely it is one of the highest privileges of Government to favour the good and disfavour the evil." It was also said that societies should not be "pampered." "But children and plants die without care," wrote Campbell, "and grown-ups too for

61 Ibid.
62 *Rept., 1909–10*, p. 10.

that matter."[63] It was foolish to say that societies should rely only on "moral pressure" to recover their debts. "It is almost as though one argued (after reading some treatise on the 'family' . . . or the like) that as the family should obviously be based on piety . . . no provision against impiety was required."[64] Summary procedure was the only answer to the societies' problems in this matter, Campbell believed. Summary procedure, he claimed, pervaded the administration of India.[65] And by "summary" Campbell meant anything "on the spot" as opposed to "an extraneous something that takes a long time in coming." It could be decision and execution by a Revenue authority; it could mean decision and execution by the society itself—by "Panch," as Campbell persisted in terming it.[66]

Decentralisation and Departure

Campbell's complaints about the Government of Bombay's attitude on these matters—and his complaints on several other more personal questions—came to a head with the enquiry promoted in 1907 by the Royal Commission on Decentralisation in India.

On the first government notification of the appointment of the Commission Campbell had written, "I suppose this hardly affects us at all."[67] A later Bombay Government circular invited officers to submit "lists of all cases in which they have to refer to this Government, or through them to the Government of India, for orders which they could, in their opinion, more suitably give themselves without submission to higher authority." "Have we anything whatsoever?" Campbell asked his Head Clerk.[68] Later, however, Campbell had fresh thoughts, prompted by a sense of grievance. Was there not very close at hand a situation where decentralisation was necessary? Was it not intolerable that his own reports and letters to Government should have to "pass wholesale through, or filter through, the Director of Agriculture" and be subjected to "jour-

[63] Campbell, "On the Question of summary-procedure for the recovery of co-operative societies' dues," *Regrs.' Conf. Procs., 1907*, p. 28.

[64] *Regrs.' Conf. Procs., 1908*, p. 29.

[65] Ibid., p. 28.

[66] Ibid., p. 27.

[67] Campbell, Note, undated, written on his copy of Bom. G.R. General Dept. No. 5307 of 28 August 1907. (Poona, Decentralisation.)

[68] G. of B., General Dept., Circular No. 5731 of 20 September 1907, and Campbell's note, undated, written on it. (Poona, file cited.)

nalistic criticism" on the way?[69] McNeill, a more senior man than Campbell, had had direct access to Government; it was perhaps an indication that the Government of Bombay at this stage attached no great importance to the post of Registrar that the second official to hold that post was not a man of full Collector's status. Nevertheless, the Government of India and the India Office had agreed to the change, and Campbell had been fitted into an appropriately subordinate place in the hierarchy in Bombay.[70] Campbell felt that principles were involved. "Minimize the man on the spot," he wrote, "and co-operation may run to theory and die. . . . When I desire to *encourage* I want (because the people need)—expedition, replies in no uncertain voice, and definite promises—from myself. Even if such are not required for general administration, yet assuredly are they when it is a matter of getting the down-trodden to trust, the suspicious to work, and the poor to stake their all in a strange device of government."[71]

This protest had no effect. So Campbell produced—with profuse "humble" apologies for its length—a collection of "notes" and "memoranda" for the Decentralisation Commission. His memorandum "On the position of the Registrar of Co-operative Societies, Bombay" figured prominently, of course. Practically the whole of the administrative system of the time came under discussion.

---

[69] Campbell to Govt. (through D.A.), No. 1464 of 17 October 1907. (Poona, Decentralisation.)

[70] See Viceroy to Sec. of State No. 11 (L. Rev.) of 16 April 1908, and enclosures. (I.O.R., Rev. Letters from India, 1908.) There is little point in delving deeply here into an issue which appears to have become, at least so far as Campbell was concerned, a matter of personalities. The whole sorry story is in the Poona file "Subordination of Regr. to D.A." Campbell claimed that he had no intimation of the subordination of the Registrar to the Director of Agriculture when he had first been appointed in an "acting" capacity. At the time the Director of Agriculture was P. J. Mead, I.C.S., but he was replaced late in 1907 by another Civilian, G. F. Keatinge, who held the position until his retirement in 1921. Keatinge probably summed up his relationship with Campbell fairly accurately in a note of December 1909: "It would cause endless friction and waste of time if I were to attempt to take any part in the control or supervision of the work in connection with Co-operative Credit Societies. . . . I seldom see Mr. Campbell, have practically no correspondence with him, and know nothing about his work, policy or movements except such information as I glean from his annual report. . . . So far as my control is concerned Mr. Campbell has the substance of what he wants without the name. I have the name without the substance. I had imagined this would satisfy him; but evidently it does not." (Keatinge's forwarding remarks—No. 8444 of 11 December 1909—on Campbell to Govt. (through D.A.) No. 2698 of 3 December 1909 encl. Bom. G.R.R.D. No. 936–28 Confl. of 28 February 1910.)

[71] Campbell, Draft Memo. for Decentralisation Commission, "On the position of the Registrar of Co-operative Societies, Bombay." (Poona, Decentralisation.)

Campbell wrote much on what he believed to be the uselessness of the office of Divisional Commissioner, on the necessity of keeping a Civilian in one language area (as Registrar, he had to cover three language areas), on the necessity of giving each Collector a Personal Assistant, on the folly of the prevailing governmental hankering after the numerical in reports. But when he came to develop his ideas about co-operatives he appeared to go beyond even his proposal that societies should be given charge of all *takkavi* operations. "I think in time the function of Co-operative Credit Societies, if they do their work well, may be extended with advantage. *For instance*—school board, agricultural schemes, management of water courses and even collections of assessments or arrears are all things that might come (in whole or in part) within their purview at some future date."[72]

When the Commission came to examine Campbell, however, they had very little to guide them as to the tendencies of his thought. For, much to its author's discomfiture, "Mr. Campbell's omnibus report"[73] had been returned to him *in toto* by the Bombay Government as "not likely to be of the kind wanted by the Commission." Instead, he had been asked to submit mere headings of his seven main points.[74] It was his heading "Reintroduction of the 'Panch' system through the medium of Co-operative Credit Societies" which most interested the Decentralisation Commission, although Campbell was not asked to explain it at great length.[75] It was probably not primarily as the result of Campbell's advocacy that the Decentralisation Commission came to the conclusion that formal village panchayats could be given rather more administrative powers than they had possessed previously[76]—a conclusion which, with its associated presuppositions about the pre-British past, appears to have provoked a good deal of disagreement amongst some Bombay officials.[77] In its final Report the Commis-

---

[72] Campbell, Draft "Note B" for Decentralisation Commission. (Poona, Decentralisation.)

[73] An Under-Secretary's note, 3 April 1908. (B.R.O., R.D. Vol. 80 of 1908.)

[74] Campbell to Govt. (through D.A.), No. 646 of 15 March 1908. (Poona, Decentralisation.)

[75] *Decentralisation Commission, Minutes of Evidence, Bombay,* pp. 95–96.

[76] See Hugh Tinker, *The Foundations of Local Self-Government in India, Pakistan, and Burma,* p. 85.

[77] This was the reason for the pronouncements of P. J. Mead and G. Laird MacGregor in *Census of India, 1911,* Vol. VII, *Bombay,* pt. i, p. 200, on the "village panchayat fallacy." See Tinker, p. 94.

sion rejected the suggestion that "panchayats should come under the Registrar of Co-operative Societies."[78] In the meantime, however, Campbell found himself "accused," so he wrote, of having started such a heterodox idea. This provided an occasion for him to re-submit to the Bombay Government his whole collection of memoranda on decentralisation. He claimed he had not said that panchayats should be bound up with a Registrar of Co-operative Societies as a person—"a policy which looks to me on the face of it more or less disastrous." He had merely pointed out the connection which he thought ought to exist between panchayats and the co-operative movement as such.[79]

Campbell's treatment was actually not quite as severe as he imagined; R. A. Lamb, now the Bombay Revenue Member,[80] was not content with his Under-Secretary's disparaging unwillingness to bother him with Campbell's report, and he specifically asked for it to be sent to him.[81] Obviously, what the Bombay Government disliked most was Campbell's attempt to make his personal feelings known by means of a submission to a Royal Commission. There was, however, a good deal of truth in Lamb's comment on Campbell's work: "Mr. Campbell is now our expert on co-operative credit; and like other experts he is a little apt, apparently, to think that—as to his subject at least—in him alone there is wisdom, and that anyone else's opinion is mere obstacle and hindrance."[82]

The first serious sign that Campbell's policy was not in accord with Government of India ideas came at a Conference of provincial Registrars held in January 1911. Edward Maclagan, from the Punjab, the new Secretary to the Government of India in the Revenue and Agriculture Department, believed that a spirit of competition between the Registrars was "not unhealthy." He noted, rather unfavourably, the small number of rural societies in Bombay as compared with the numbers of rural societies in other provinces.[83]

78 *Decentralisation Commission Report*, p. 240.
79 Campbell to Govt. (through D.A.), No. 646 of 15 March 1908. (Poona, file cited.)
80 Richard Lamb: Asst. Collr. Bom., 1879; Collr., 1892; Sec., Bom. R.D., 1904; Ch. Sec., Bom. 1907; Member of Council, Bom., 1908; Member, Governor-General's Executive Council, 1910; K.C.S.I., 1911; retd., 1915.
81 Lamb's remarks on Under-Secretary's note cited above, n. 73.
82 Lamb, Ch. Sec., Note, 22 December 1907. (B.R.O., R.D. Vol. 80 of 1908.)
83 *Regrs.' Conf. Procs., 1911*, pp. 4–5.

When it came to a discussion of government loans to co-operative societies the Registrars of Bengal and Madras said that, in compliance with the original Government of India precepts, now that the movement had taken root they were giving government loans very sparingly. Campbell, on the other hand, had to admit that he "appeared to have used more from this source of supply than other provinces." At present there was a sum of Rs.1,60,000 of government loans outstanding as compared with about Rs.41,000 in Bengal and Rs.45,000 in Madras. He considered that he was "morally bound to give the equivalent deposit, if the members deposited money with the society." Maclagan replied that Campbell was under an "entire misapprehension as to any moral obligation" to give equivalent government loans in such cases. Such a moral obligation would arise only "if the Registrar induced the members to deposit money by a promise of such assistance."[84] But this was, in fact, what Campbell had been doing.

When Campbell came to write his annual report in August it was fairly obvious that he was going. The report is a summing up, in a style rather more sober than Campbell's usual one, of his work as Registrar. He still maintained that this work should be seen in terms of "educational progress. . . . And I feel that we ourselves are included in the educational progress; and are perhaps the most important part thereof!" But he was now ready to say with the orthodox that "our best policy will be, probably, to concentrate on good centres and urge to perfection societies already good, rather than spend more money on doubtful returns. . . . We can afford to lop fairly heavily now." There is no doubt that he had in mind his societies for the poor of Satara district.[85]

A confidential Government Resolution, despatched on 18 December but dated 1 December, the date of R. B. Ewbank's appointment to the position of Registrar, made clear one of the reasons for the change. "No progress" had been made in "effectively associating" the work of the Registrar of Co-operative Societies with that of the Director of Agriculture. "It is not possible for Government to permit the indefinite continuance of arrangements in which

84 Ibid., pp. 29–30.
85 *Rept., 1910–11*, pp. 1–2, 4.

the work of the Registrar remains aloof and separate from the work of the Agriculture Department."[86]

Agricultural Banks Again: The Egyptian Model

Though co-operation's advent in India had been heralded with a good deal of publicity, other schemes for the alleviation of agricultural indebtedness were not completely forgotten. No sooner, in fact, had the Co-operative Societies Act been passed than there was a revival of interest in agricultural banks.

The main reason for this revival of interest was the apparent success of Cromer's Agricultural Bank of Egypt. This privately owned bank was founded in 1902, after several years of experiment by the National Bank of Egypt.[87] The Bank received some financial assistance from the Egyptian Government; it was supposed to distribute loans to the peasantry through its own officers, but the government tax gatherers collected the Bank's dues. Cromer had carefully considered the "political objection" to connecting the state in this way with the collection of debts,[88] as he had done in India when Wedderburn's scheme had been under discussion. But apparently he did not now believe this to be an overriding objection. In its time, the Egyptian Agricultural Bank was considered to be a noteworthy experiment; the authorities in Egypt had to deal with a large number of enquiries on the subject.[89]

The rule of Cromer in Egypt has been seen as part of the "Indianization" of Egypt: he himself had considerable Indian experience, and he brought to Egypt a number of key civil servants from India.[90] It might be said, however, that in the first decade of the twentieth century a process which showed signs of occurring in one sphere, at least, was the "Egyptianization" of India. The most important convert in India to the idea of agricultural banks was Frederick Nicholson, the same Nicholson whose report had lain be-

---

[86] Bom. G.R.R.D. No. 11391–257 Confl. of 1 December 1911. (Poona, Subordination of Regr. to D.A.)

[87] For the Egyptian Agricultural Bank's antecedents, see Gabriel Baer, *A History of Landownership in Modern Egypt, 1800–1950*, pp. 69, 87.

[88] *Report on the Finances, Administration and Condition of Egypt and the Progress of Reforms, 1895*, p. 8. *P.P.* 1896 (C. 7978) xcvii.

[89] *Report on . . . Egypt and the Soudan in 1903*, p. 13. *P.P.* 1904 (Cd. 1951) cxi.

[90] Robert L. Tignor, "The 'Indianization' of the Egyptian Administration under British Rule," *American Historical Review*, Vol. LXVIII, No. 3 (April 1963). See also Tignor, *Modernization and British Colonial Rule in Egypt 1882–1914*, and Roger Owen, "The Influence of Lord Cromer's Indian Experience on British Policy in Egypt 1883–1907," *St Antony's Papers*, XVII (Middle Eastern Affairs No. 4), 1965.

hind the Co-operative Societies Act. He visited Egypt to see for himself the working of the Agricultural Bank and returned enthusiastic about the possibilities of setting up similar institutions in India. He was, in fact, a man of enthusiasms, some of them possibly somewhat short-lived. He now wrote that "co-operative credit societies are only one form of credit system. . . . It has never been contended that they are or should be a sole system." He now asserted that "nothing but very slow progress" in the formation of co-operative societies in India could be predicted. Agricultural banks, he thought, could supply co-operatives with the capital they needed. But it is clear from Nicholson's report that he intended that the proposed agricultural banks' main source of business should be, as in Egypt, loans made direct to the cultivator, rather than loans to co-operative societies.[91] The Madras Government, of which Nicholson was now a member, were quick to agree to his scheme for promoting an agricultural bank in that province.[92] A change in administrative opinion—probably in part a result of a change of governors—had occurred in Madras in the few years since the fierce denunciation of Nicholson's report on co-operative societies. The Government of India also agreed to Nicholson's scheme, making very few provisos—Curzon had given up the viceroyalty, but Ibbetson, the energetic Punjabi, was still a member of the inner circle at Simla. They believed that the scheme merited a liberal measure of assistance, even acceptance of "a substantial degree of risk."[93]

The major portion of the capital of the Egyptian Agricultural Bank was provided by the British-backed National Bank of Egypt, an institution which was, as the Madras Government put it, "financially and politically strong."[94] The Government of India believed that the Madras venture should also be floated on the London market, the shareholders being guaranteed a minimum dividend of 3 per cent per annum for fifteen years. "Should the bank be started and prove a failure," the Government of India informed the Secretary of State somewhat airily, "then at the most Government will have lost on the guarantee a sum which cannot

[91] Nicholson to Govt. of Madras, 5 February 1904, encl. Viceroy to Sec. of State, No. 37 (L. Rev.) of 7 December 1905. (I.O.R., Rev. Letters from India, 1905.)
[92] Sec., Govt. of Madras R.D., to G. of I., R. & A. Dept., No. 1333 (Confl. No. 170) Rev. of 3 December 1904, encl. G. of I. Rev. Letter cited.
[93] G. of I. Rev. Letter cited.
[94] Govt. of Madras to G. of I., letter cited.

exceed 22½ lakhs of rupees spread over fifteen years." The Government of India was even prepared to agree to the bank's paying Revenue Department officials to collect its debts at the same time as the assessment, as in Egypt.[95] Possibly to the surprise of those in India, the India Office decided that the experiment was worth trying, and wrote that they were prepared to place the scheme "informally before financial houses of standing in London."[96] It was not long before the Secretary of State was approached by a syndicate of British financiers and businessmen with interests in India, led by Sir Ernest Cable of Bird and Company, the Calcutta jute exporters.[97] Their plan, which included provision for the guarantee of a 4 per cent interest rate, was accepted in principle by the Government of India while it was still being considered by the India Office.[98] It was the news that such an agricultural bank might soon be formed that prompted in two Gujarati businessmen from Bombay, Vithaldas Thackersey and Lalubhai Samaldas, the response which eventually led to the formation of the Bombay Central Co-operative Bank.

The Bombay Response

From the beginning the prime emphasis in the co-operative movement in Bombay had been, as the Government of India had hoped, on rural societies. But it had not been forgotten that Dupernex, and also the Government of India in 1904, had expected that eventually urban "co-operative banks" would be able to raise sufficient capital to meet both their own needs and the requirements of rural societies. As it happened, urban co-operation at first grew fairly rapidly in Bombay, without a great deal of official prompting. Indeed, at one stage, in 1910, there was more capital invested in the 50 "urban" societies than there was in the 122 "rural" societies; the position was reversed by 1911, however.[99] One caste group, the Sarasvat Brahmans of Bombay city, who were rising to a modest prosperity, soon found that co-operation pro-

95 G. of I. Rev. Letter cited.

96 Sec. of State to Viceroy, No. 82 (Rev.) of 27 April 1906. (I.O.R., Rev. Despatches to India, 1906.)

97 Cable had been a member of the Imperial Legislative Council from 1901 to 1903, representing the Bengal Chamber of Commerce.

98 Viceroy to Sec. of State, No. 17 (L. Rev.) of 9 May 1907. (I.O.R., Rev. Letters from India, 1907.)

99 *Regrs.' Conf. Procs., 1911*, pp. 4–5, 40–41, 50.

vided an outlet for their strongly corporate endeavours. But, apart
from a few government-sponsored societies for weavers, most of
the "urban" societies in the Bombay Presidency did not have a
caste basis. Investors in urban co-operative banks came on the
whole from "the intermediate classes between those who deal in
Government paper and smaller people who prefer to deposit in
the savings banks."[100] "Up country pleaders and depositors of that
class," it was asserted in 1914, were "nervous" about their investments; they preferred to have them invested locally, and co-
operative banks provided an outlet for them.[101] But the funds of
the urban societies were by no means always available to the rural
societies. We may perhaps surmise that some of the rather timid
petty capitalists who made up the membership of so many of the
urban societies would previously have invested directly or indirectly in agriculture; it is possible, then, that the new co-operative
banks had actually siphoned off capital from the rural areas. Certainly it was urgently necessary in some way to channel urban
capital, through the co-operative movement, into the countryside.

McNeill reported at the end of his first year that the establishment in Bombay of an urban co-operative which would attempt to
provide for the rural societies' needs had been suggested to "a few
native gentlemen" at the Oriental Club.[102] As a result, it would
appear, Vithaldas Thackersey organized the Bombay Urban Co-
operative Society. He was a Bhatia, the son of one of the first big
mill owners in Bombay; although he was still young he was already
a member of the Municipal Corporation and of the Legislative
Council, and, as an energetic and confident—perhaps over-confident
—financier, wielded great influence in those days of rapid commercial development.[103] McNeill and Campbell were also able to obtain some loans for various societies from individual businessmen
in Bombay. Most of these loans were of a modest variety. But one
of those who assisted, Lalubhai Samaldas, lent his money "at almost too kindly a rate to begin with," even Campbell was forced
to say. Yet Lalubhai was no mere soft-hearted philanthropist. His
background was different from that of Vithaldas. He came from a
family of Nagar Brahmans which had supplied Dewans to Bhav-

[100] Khandubhai Desai, Evidence, Maclagan Cttee.
[101] Vithaldas Thackersey, Evidence, Maclagan Cttee.
[102] *Rept., 1904–5,* pp. 1, 5.
[103] See H. L. Kaji, *Life and Speeches of Sir Vithaldas Thackersey,* passim.

nagar, a not unimportant Indian State in Saurashtra, since 1828. Lalubhai had risen to be Chief Revenue Officer of the State before his family had suddenly and somewhat inexplicably fallen from grace in the Maharajah's eyes.[104] The existence of his family estates meant that Lalubhai had no financial troubles. He could have retired to a life of leisure in Ahmadabad. But there he had felt restricted; rather than dwell "in the midst of middle-class lawyers and retired officials who were living lives on incomes a sixth of what he could expect,"[105] he had gone to Bombay and entered the business world. He was evidently a striking figure, with his turban and his broad, silk-bordered dhoti.[106] He brought a certain gentility to the commercial life of Bombay, too: "He said that even though he was in business he could look upon it as a Brahmin and not as a Vaisya."[107] In the Indian context this is perhaps the most significant comment which he could have made on his own life. In politics he had annoyed the man he had chosen to follow, Pherozeshah Mehta, by supporting some aspects of the Land Revenue Code Amendment Bill of 1901; his experience of revenue administration in Bhavnagar, where all land was held on an annual tenure, led him to believe that the bill had some virtues.[108]

It was probably his public refusal to support the politicians of the Legislative Council in their onslaught on the bill that had led to his being invited by the Bombay Government authorities to comment on the proposals of the 1901 Government of India committee on co-operation. He had felt that in setting up a co-operative movement it would be difficult to obtain capital from the rayats themselves, and that private capital would therefore be necessary. Furthermore, he had thought that it would be unwise to leave the running of co-operative societies in the hands of the villagers. "In the ryotwari tract," he commented, "the village panch does not

---

104 S. Natarajan, *Lalubhai Samaldas,* p. 19.

105 Ibid., p. 24.

106 D. A. Shah, "Let us remember our own pioneers in time," *B.C.Q.,* March 1946, p. 163.

107 Natarajan, *Lalubhai Samaldas,* p. 44. For some interesting observations on the role of the Nagar Brahmans in Bombay commercial life, and other relevant matters, see Mrs. D. P. Pandit, "Creative Response in Indian Economy: A Regional Analysis," *Economic Weekly,* 23 February and 2 March 1957, and Mrs. Hemlata Acharya, "Creative Response in Indian Economy: A Comment," ibid., 27 April 1957.

108 Natarajan, p. 27. (Lalubhai's "Notes on the Bombay Land Revenue Amendment Bill" are to be found in I.O.R., India Legislative Procs., Vol. 6172: October 1901, No. 24, Appx. E.18.)

exist, and for some years at least it will not come into existence."
Lalubhai had brought forward his own proposals for establishing
an "agricultural bank" in one of the talukas of Gujarat.[109] When
the Co-operative Societies Bill was passed, however, he was quite
eager to help in the government experiment, in spite of the rejection of his own scheme. He paid particular attention to the societies in Ahmadabad and Kaira districts and soon joined in the
work of Vithaldas Thackersey's Bombay Urban Society.

But it was not only their interest in co-operative societies which
led Vithaldas and Lalubhai to make their first joint proposal for
the financing of Indian agriculture. It was also the feeling that
British interests should not be allowed any further entry into that
most basic of India's industries, agriculture—the feeling, to quote
Vithaldas's biographer, that "foreign capital should not be allowed
to exploit the agriculturists of India."[110] The foundation of their
bank must be seen, in fact, as part of that great burst of swadeshi
commercial activity which India experienced from about the year
1906. In Bombay, it is true, most Indian commercial men looked
somewhat askance at the lengths to which the Bengal swadeshi
movement was being taken at the time. Nevertheless, it could be
argued, they had the experience and the capital to make the
swadeshi movement into something a little more lasting than the
rhetoric and flamboyant defiance of certain sections of the Bengal
bhadralok. In Bombay, these were the years especially of the
swadeshi banks. The directors of the Bank of Baroda, for instance,
founded in 1908, included many of those who later joined the directorate of the Bombay Central Co-operative Bank.[111]

Lalubhai and Vithaldas first learnt of Cable's scheme for an
"agricultural bank" during their visit to Calcutta in 1906 for the

109 Lalubhai Samaldas to Commr., N.D., 1 August 1902. (Poona, ADM. S.O.7.)

110 Kaji, *Thackersey*, p. 158.

111 The information about early Bank of Baroda directors has been gleaned from
advertisements issued by that bank at the time of its Jubilee in 1958. For the circle
about Lalubhai Samaldas and Vithaldas Thackersey, and their attitude to the Bengal
swadeshi movement, see A. P. Kannangara "Indian Millowners and Indian Nationalism before 1914," *Past and Present*, No. 40 (July 1968). It could perhaps be added
here that some of the swadeshi banks crashed in 1913—but Britain had her South
Sea Bubble at a somewhat similar stage of development. The men who launched the
first Indian shipping enterprise, Scindia, in the words of the biographer of Lalubhai
Samaldas, "knew only half of what they were doing and were completely ignorant
of ships and shipping" (Natarajan, p. 41). Sir Shapurji Broacha advised Lalubhai
against buying what became the company's first ship: he had had the misfortune to
travel on her to America thirty years before! (Ibid., p. 40.) Yet, with a certain amount
of state support, Scindia has succeeded.

second All-India Industrial Conference, itself to a large extent a swadeshi gathering, since it was held at the same time and place as the meeting of the Indian National Congress for the year. Lalubhai interviewed the Private Secretary to the Viceroy; Bombay businessmen, he said, could do what Cable's British syndicate proposed. When Lalubhai and Vithaldas arrived back in Bombay, Vithaldas set about publicizing an ambitious scheme for an Indian-financed agricultural bank. An article in the *Times of India Illustrated Weekly* outlined the plans of the two men. Share capital of twenty-five lakhs would be raised on the market in the usual way, and a government guarantee of 4 per cent interest on one hundred lakhs of debentures was requested. The bank would be registered under the Co-operative Societies Act. It would have an All-India field of operations, which, Vithaldas asserted, would "make for economy of management and security." Its work would not be confined to agriculture. "Every one of the Central Banks hitherto formed under such conditions," Vithaldas claimed, had "found it distinctly necessary to do other business to keep the 'pot boiling.' Co-operative societies' business is a capital addition where there is other business. However, the very undertaking given to do it at minimum rates makes it desirable, if not indispensable, that there should be a good flow of other business to earn a dividend and keep the Bank in strength." "A portion" of its capital was to be earmarked for agricultural purposes—apparently for loans to individuals as well as to co-operative societies. Vithaldas laid emphasis, as other proponents of "agricultural banks" had done before him, on long-term loans for "debt redemption."[112]

Not surprisingly, a great many objections were raised to this scheme. It seemed to some to be an attempt to obtain the privileges of a government guarantee, and registration under the Co-operative Societies Act, for what appeared to be in most respects an ordinary joint-stock concern.[113] In these circumstances it was something of an achievement for Lalubhai, who was invited by the Government of Bombay to attend the Conference of Registrars of Co-operative Societies held at Simla in 1908, to persuade the Registrars to agree to a resolution stating that if an agricultural bank were set up, all the capital should be issued in India in rupees. On the

[112] Thackersey, "Agricultural Indebtedness and How to Relieve It," *Times of India Illustrated Weekly*, 7 August 1907, p. 8.
[113] See *Prov. Co-op. Conf. Procs., 1908*, pp. 10, 26.

other hand, the majority of the Registrars believed that no government guarantees were necessary in order to set up such a bank.[114] Lalubhai and Vithaldas saw that their original scheme had little prospect of success. They decided to confine their attention in the meantime to co-operative societies in the Bombay Presidency. In a modified scheme for a bank they omitted the proposals for doing business with individuals and put the figures for share and debenture capital at one-fifth of the original estimates.

This scheme was first put forward at the Provincial Co-operative Conference in December 1908.[115] At this same Conference, however, McNeill, who was now Collector of Ahmadnagar but who had kept up his interest in problems of agricultural indebtedness, brought forward another scheme, a scheme which was thoroughly in the Wedderburn tradition. Significantly, McNeill appears to have lost much of his faith in the sort of co-operative societies which he had set out to found: "Under existing conditions it is very unlikely that co-operation will proceed beyond friendly discussions in which the official exponent will not add to his reputation for practical common sense," he had written in his annual administration report for 1907-8.[116] McNeill now called for the establishment of "Taluka Co-operative Credit Societies," financed partly from government sources and partly by money-lenders. Holdings and indebtedness would be checked and the recognized nominal indebtedness would be reduced by at least 25 per cent. (McNeill now recognized that such a reduction would be necessary in any scheme for the redemption of long-term debts.) The land would then be mortgaged to the government. Debt redemption should be undertaken only in cases where the operation could be completed within twenty-five years. Village societies would continue to exist, but they would operate only as the agents of the taluka societies. McNeill believed that experiments should be undertaken first in three or four villages, but he was thinking of a much wider field of operations as an ultimate goal.[117] His scheme met with a moderately warm reception, both from George Sydenham Clarke, the new Governor of Bombay, and from Muir-Mackenzie, the Revenue

---

114 *Regrs.' Conf. Procs., 1908*, pp. 14-15.
115 Lalubhai Samaldas, "A Scheme of a Central Financing Society," *Prov. Co-op. Conf. Procs., 1908*, pp. 25-27.
116 McNeill, quoted in *Bom. L. Rev. Admin. Rept., 1907-8*, pt. ii, p. 51.
117 McNeill, "Debt Liquidation," *Prov. Co-op. Conf. Procs., 1908*, pp. 22-25.

Member of the Governor's Council.[118] Muir-Mackenzie, who had at one stage been Director of Agriculture in Bombay and was generally sympathetic to the rayat's problems, put the total rural indebtedness of the Presidency at twenty-eight crores, or eighteen and a half million pounds sterling. This sum in itself, he wrote, was "not so very large." But then, rapidly withdrawing from such an adventurous position, he added that it could be taken that the money could not be found for McNeill's scheme. In the circumstances, he felt the scheme propounded by Vithaldas Thackersey and Lalubhai Samaldas was the better one.[119] Clarke agreed, and the Government of India was informed of Bombay's intentions.

The Government of India's reply was outwardly not very encouraging. A scheme for an agricultural bank on the Egyptian model was still being considered, they said; in the meantime, consideration of further schemes would have to be postponed. R. W. Carlyle, the Secretary of the Revenue and Agriculture Department, made the preliminary comment, however, that the proposal of Vithaldas and Lalubhai that the Registrar should sanction all loans to societies before they were made would mean the maintenance of a permanent "Co-operative Department," and such an eventuality, he claimed, the Government of India wished to avoid.[120] Nevertheless, in the consultations at Simla, Carlyle made it clear that he believed that there were strong "political" objections to Cable's scheme: "There is a very large number of educated Indians who would honestly believe that an attempt was being

---

118 G. S. C[larke]., Note, 30 December 1908. (B.R.O., R.D. Compilation No. 303, Vol. 60 of 1911.)

George Sydenham Clarke: Service with Royal Engineers, 1868–1904, including a period in Egypt; Sec. Cttee. on Imperial Defence, 1904–7; Govr., Bom., 1907–13; Baron 1911.

119 M-Mack[enzie]., Minute of 3 March 1909. (B.R.O., Compilation cited.) John W. P. Muir-Mackenzie: Asst. Collr., 1876; Ag. Director of Land Records and Agriculture, 1888; U. Sec., G. of I., R. & A. Dept., 1889–93; Offg. Sec. Bom. R.D., 1896 and 1898; Survey Commr. and Director of Land Records and Agriculture, 1897; Ch. Sec., 1900; Member Irrigation Commission, 1901; Rev. Member, Bom., 1905; K.C.S.I., 1909; retd., 1910. Muir-Mackenzie to some extent represented a "Simla" attitude to agricultural matters in the Government of Bombay. Measures against land transfer were never condemned while he was present in Bombay. *The Indian Social Reformer* said that he was responsible for "many measures of practical philanthropy" (10 January 1909).

120 Carlyle to G. of B. No. 971–110–5 of 20 September 1909. (B.R.O., Compilation cited.) Carlyle's experience was virtually limited to Bengal. "Secretariat work was never completely congenial to him" (*Dictionary of National Biography, 1931–40*); after he retired he wrote, with his brother, the well-known *History of Medieval Political Theory in the West*.

made to exploit Indian agriculture just as they would hold we have exploited Indian trade."[121] Bombay's case was assisted when Vithaldas Thackersey was elected a member of the Imperial Legislative Council; he had some fruitful meetings with Meston, the Finance Member of the Viceroy's Executive Council.[122] But the main reason for the increased interest in the Bombay scheme was the news that all was not well with the much vaunted Agricultural Bank of Egypt. Confidential and guarded comments from the Egyptian authorities reached the Government of India in the early months of 1909. Cromer had now left Egypt; his departure had roughly coincided with the end of a somewhat artificial period of prosperity in that part of the world. The Egyptian Bank had been put to the test for the first time. It now became apparent that a large proportion of the money borrowed from the Bank at cheap rates had been devoted to purchases of land rather than to increased production. Increasingly, the Bank was neglecting short-term small-loan business. Furthermore, arrears had begun to rise steeply, even though the Bank's dues were treated as the first charge on the combined instalments of land revenue and Bank debts collected by the government tax collectors.[123] By 1910, Sir Eldon Gorst, Cromer's successor in Egypt, was openly advocating the establishment of co-operative societies in that country.[124]

The Government of India were certainly not going to embark on Cable's scheme for an agricultural bank with such a warning before them. They now gave their support to the Bombay scheme. But the India Office, confronted with the Egyptian example, had become frightened of any scheme for a guaranteed bank, and in-

[121] Carlyle, Note, June 1909. (N.A.I., R. & A. (Agriculture) "A" Procs., July 1909, No. 53.)

[122] Meston to Lamb, D/O of 8 February 1910. (B.R.O., Compilation cited.)

[123] H. P. Harvey, Financial Adviser, Egyptian Government, Memo. of 15 March 1909, and comments thereon of C. A. Innes, U. Sec., G. of I., R. & A. Dept., 1 June 1909. (N.A.I., Proc. cited.)

[124] *Reports by His Majesty's Agent and Consul-General on Finances, Administration and Conditions of Egypt and the Soudan*, pp. 12–13. *P.P.* 1910 (Cd. 5121) cxii. I am grateful to Dr. Colin Eldridge for sending me the text of two relevant letters from Gorst to Cromer: 31 December 1909 and 22 January 1910. (Public Record Office, Cromer Papers, F.O. 633, Vol. XIV, p. 63.) It is evident that Gorst had to be discreet when writing to his predecessor on the subject of the Bank. But one passage in the letter of 22 January 1910 is revealing: "The main error in the past has been, to my mind, that the local agents of the Bank were given a percentage on all the loans they put out and thus got into the habit of encouraging the fellaheen to take as much money as possible. It was this, and not the Government guarantee of three per cent, which caused a certain amount of recklessness in the way loans were put out."

stinctively, perhaps, they were more wary of Indian schemes as such than they were of British schemes. The arguments between Whitehall and Simla were protracted; much time was spent on the theme of the proportion of debenture capital to share capital.[125]

Finally, the India Office agreed to what was virtually the 1908 proposal of Lalubhai and Vithaldas: the bank was to confine its lending activities solely to co-operative societies, share capital was to total seven lakhs, and authorized debenture capital (the interest of which was guaranteed) was to total twenty lakhs.[126] But the Secretary of State added certain qualifications. His agreement to the scheme, he said, was not to be construed as in any sense an abandonment of the co-operative principle, and should not stand in the way of the future organization of co-operative "unions," for the supply and joint guarantee of capital, by the societies themselves. His sanction was intended to lead to a demonstration of the profitable use to which loanable capital might be put in a dry area, which would encourage the formation of similar institutions in other parts of India without government assistance.[127] We seem to have evidence here of the personal attitude towards state intervention in economic matters of Morley himself, an attitude which the Indian Industrial Commission of 1916–18 found to be "deadening."[128] Nevertheless, for some years, it was possible to maintain that the guarantee of interest on the Bombay Central Co-operative Bank's debentures was "the most interesting departure from the general policy of government on the co-operative movement."[129]

The Nira Canal Scheme

Although negotiations for the formation of the Bombay Central Co-operative Bank were protracted, no great amount of thought was given, either by the Government or the promoters of the Bank, to the problem of the types of societies which the Bank would

---

125 Sec. of State to Viceroy No. 85 (Rev.) of 30 September 1910; V. Thackersey and L. Samaldas to U. Sec., G. of B., R.D., 17 November 1910. (B.R.O., Compilation cited.)

126 Telegram, Sec. of State to Viceroy, 21 March 1911. (B.R.O., Compilation cited.)

127 Sec. of State to Viceroy No. 85 (Rev.) of 30 September 1910. (B.R.O., Compilation cited.)

128 *Indian Industrial Commission Rept.* (1918), Vol. I, p. 4.

129 V. Venkatasubbaiya and Vaikunth L. Mehta, *The Co-operative Movement* (Servants of India Society Political Pamphlets, 1918), p. 164. Cf. Mehta's much later enunciation of the same notion in "Co-operation in Relation to Government," in *Changing India: Essays in Honour of Professor D. R. Gadgil,* ed. N. V. Sovani and V. M. Dandekar (1961), p. 182.

finance. The Nira Canal irrigated area of the Poona district had been in the minds of both parties from the beginning as one possible scene of operations.[130] But concentration of the Bank's resources in that area does not seem to have been envisaged until towards the end of 1910, when the possibility arose of a serious limitation of long-term debenture capital, through the unwillingness of the India Office to guarantee the interest on the required amount.[131] Thereafter, in spite of the Secretary of State's final agreement to the amount of debenture capital which had been proposed in 1908, the promoters appear to have been determined to press for rapid developments in the Nira Canal area. Sir Vithaldas was "in a great hurry," commented one of the Bombay Government's Under-Secretaries.[132]

There is evidence to suggest, however, that by this time elements in the Bombay Government were also in a great hurry—to get rid of their own somewhat unprofitable Canal finance scheme.

The Nira Canal had been opened in 1884. It had been intended primarily to provide relief in times of scarcity for those already inhabiting the surrounding area. The character of that area soon changed, however; it became one of Bombay's minor equivalents of the Punjab's "canal colonies," and the emphasis switched to cash crops. At first the most notable increase in production was in garden crops for the Poona market. But by the beginning of the twentieth century an incoming group, Malis, mainly from the Sasvad area of Poona district, were renting increasingly large areas for the production of sugar cane and generally making handsome profits.[133] The Malis were gardeners by caste, of about the same status as the Marathas. They had a reputation as a "progressive" caste, apparently taking easily both to education and to new agricultural pursuits.[134] In truth, their chief advantage in the Nira Canal area seems to have been their previous experience with irrigated crops; the original inhabitants of the area, mainly Marathas

---

[130] See P. J. Mead, Ag. D.A., to Ch. Sec., No. A/5356 Confl. of 2 October 1907 (Poona, D.A. 24); also Clarke, Note, 30 December 1908. (B.R.O., Compilation cited.)

[131] See R. A. L[amb]., Note, 28 November 1910. (B.R.O., Compilation cited.)

[132] R. D. Bell, Note, 4 October 1911. (B.R.O., Compilation cited.)

[133] Later in the century it was reported that the Sasvad *malis* "tend to rent out not parts of but the entire holdings of the old landholders." D. R. Gadgil, *Economic Effects of Irrigation: Report of a Survey of the Direct and Indirect Benefits of the Godavari and Pravara Canals,* p. 115.

[134] *Ahmednagar Gazetteer,* pp. 89–91, 241.

by caste,[135] frequently made exceedingly poor attempts at imitating the Malis' methods. They also did not have the Malis' capital resources. An annual capital outlay of Rs.500 per acre was often necessary for a good crop of sugar cane. Money-lenders could supply this capital, of course, on condition that they were given marketing rights over the crop. It was not altogether surprising that the inexperienced Maratha peasant often had to pay over 20 per cent for his capital.[136] In an attempt to ease the credit problem of the Maratha agriculturist in the Nira Canal area, J. P. Brander, the Assistant Collector in charge of that part of Poona district in 1907–8, strongly advocated the establishment in the area of a state-aided joint-stock bank, on the model of the Egyptian Agricultural Bank. Muir-Mackenzie interested himself in the scheme. But before making a decision on the scheme for a bank, the Government of Bombay sanctioned an experimental scheme for advancing *takkavi* loans to approved sugar-cane growers, interest being charged at a rate of 9 per cent. The scheme was intended to demonstrate the possibilities of success of an agricultural bank "in the hopes that some banking agency may be induced to step in and compete with the sowkars."[137] An Indian "Special Officer," with a small staff, was appointed to carry out the scheme. On the whole, B. B. Sahasrabudhe, the man appointed, performed his task well. The procedure for the grant of loans was worked out: enquiry into the borrower's security, inspection of his crops during the growing period, application of pressure on him to bring his produce to the Government depot for sale so that loans could be recovered. From the beginning,

---

135 *Maratha* is used here to cover both the original Maratha peasant-soldier group and the Kunbi group of generally poorer peasants. The social distinction between the two groups appears to have all but died out in the course of the first half of the twentieth century. (See Irawati Karve, *Hindu Society—An Interpretation*, pp. 19–21.) The *Ahmednagar Gazetteer* (1884) claimed that the Malis were once Marathas "who took to gardening and by degrees formed a separate community" (p. 89). But in the strict sense they are certainly a separate caste today; indeed there are signs of Maratha-Mali animosity, largely as a result of the Malis' success as agriculturists and their widespread purchases of land. (Karve, *Hindu Society*, pp. 153, 155.)

136 For the early years of the operation of the Nira Canal, see Harold H. Mann, "Economic Conditions in Some Deccan Canal Areas," *B.C.Q.*, December 1918, pp. 121–26. For a later assessment by Mann—in which the Malis are termed "invaders"— see Mann, "The Economic Results and Possibilities of Irrigation," in Mann (ed. Daniel Thorner), *The Social Framework of Agriculture: India, Middle East, England,* p. 329. (Reprinted from *Indian Journal of Agricultural Economics*, Vol. XIII, No. 2. 1958.)

137 Muir-Mackenzie, quoted B. B. Sahasrabudhe, "Interim Report for the First Crop Year 1908–1909 of the Nira Canal Tagai Loans Scheme, Poona District," p. 19. (Poona, Registrar's Library.)

however, arrears began to appear. Indeed, their appearance could hardly have been avoided: so as not to arouse opposition from the money-lenders, government clients were apparently not selected from amongst the money-lenders' clients.[138] In other words, the government gave every appearance of having elected to assist those who, from the start, were generally less credit-worthy. By 1911 there were three lakhs of outstanding debts,[139] and it seems to have been assumed that the *takkavi* scheme was radically faulty, to be consigned to oblivion, together with all schemes for agricultural banks. George Curtis, the new Commissioner for the Central Division, was only too eager to accept the suggestion of the promoters of the new Central Co-operative Bank that the Nira Canal area should be an important area of the Bank's operations.[140] So the Registrar was not altogether incorrect in claiming in 1912 that co-operative societies were formed on the Canal "at the desire of government."[141] Even in 1920 it was possible for a Registrar to maintain that the Bombay Government had special duties in connection with the Nira Canal societies because those societies had been "started by the Bank taking over the tagai liabilities of government at their request."[142]

Unwarranted Optimism

This willingness to hand over the Nira Canal *takkavi* scheme to the co-operative organization, youthful and not altogether satisfactory as that organization was, may at first sight seem somewhat paradoxical. Yet in reality the move was symptomatic of a deeper tendency in Bombay administrative circles. Certainly rather more was expected of the co-operative movement now that the Central Bank in Bombay had been launched and the impetuous Campbell had been replaced, and in this respect the Bombay Government

---

138 J. P. Brander, Asst. Collr., Poona, quoted *Bom. L. Rev. Admin. Rept., 1907–8,* pt. ii, p. 10.

139 R. B. Badve, "Report on the Working of the Nira Canal Societies up to the close of the co-operative year 1913–14," p. 2. (Poona, Registrar's Library.)

140 Personal communication from Sir Robert Ewbank. George Curtis: Asst. Collr., Bom., 1888; U. Sec., R.D., 1894; Postmaster General, 1896; Postmaster General, Madras, 1897–1901; Director of Land Records, Bom., 1906; Settlement Commr., 1907; Commr., C.D., 1911; Ag.Ch. Sec., 1914; Ch. Sec., 1915; Member, Governor's Executive Council, 1916–21; K.C.S.I., 1921.

141 Ewbank to D.A. No. 486 of 10 February 1912, encl. Bom. G.R.R.D. No. 7651 of 12 August 1912.

142 Otto Rothfeld, Regr., to Govt., No. E.S.T.–124 of 26 July 1920, encl. Bom. R.D. Order No. 2452 of 18 August 1920.

were not to be completely disappointed. But that Government, which in the earlier nineties had been, not unfairly, rather sceptical of the Government of India's assessment of the situation in the rural areas of the Presidency, appears twenty years later to have been to some extent a victim of false self-satisfaction. It is almost as though the Government of Bombay now felt that rural problems were so rapidly diminishing in number and intensity that the co-operative movement could be relied upon to take care of a good many of those that remained. "Co-operative Societies and Agricultural Associations are spreading in all directions," proclaimed a government resolution, concocted for public consumption, in August 1912[143]—this at a time when the movement in Bombay was in fact lagging seriously behind that in a number of other provinces. In private, Lamb, who had succeeded Muir-Mackenzie as Revenue Member, expressed the belief that "as the [co-operative] movement continues to spread and as the Act is amended to meet the altering conditions, Co-operative Credit Societies may be reasonably expected to reach a position in which they will be able not only to make advances to their members for financing their agriculture, but also to take over their existing debts and gradually liquidate them." Lamb did add, however, that he thought that the process would take "many years to reach its full development"; meanwhile, certain other measures to assist the "embarrassed cultivator" might be desirable.[144]

Others in the Bombay administration were not so cautious. Indeed, in the half dozen or so years before about 1912 there were some who concluded that the famine years had actually assisted in the development of those favourable tendencies which had been apparent in the earlier nineties. The reduction of population caused by plague and famine had brought about a shortage of labour; this at a time when the area of cultivation was still being extended, especially in Khandesh.[145] In this situation, it was claimed, agricultural labourers and even tenants, to some extent, could begin to dictate their own terms. (The vital fact that cattle in the Presi-

143 Bom. G.R.R.D. No. 7760 of 19 August 1912, attached to *Bom. L. Rev. Admin. Rept., 1910–11*, pt. ii.
144 R. A. Lamb, Minute, 8 November 1910, encl. Bom. G.R.R.D. No. 735 of 23 January 1914.
145 G. S. Curtis, Collr., Khandesh, quoted *Bom. L. Rev. Admin. Rept., 1903–4*, pt. ii, p. 8. See also W. T. Morison, Collr., Surat, ibid., p. 3.

dency took a decade to reach their pre-famine numbers[146] tended to be forgotten.) From Broach district it was reported that tenants were transforming themselves into peasant proprietors.[147] Prosperity came from emigration abroad, too. From Surat district, especially, there was frequent mention of large sums of money flowing back to the relatives of those who had emigrated to South and East Africa at the time of the famine.[148] And Curtis, the Commissioner of the Central Division, declared in 1912, in his exaggerated, rather flamboyant way, that in some of the Deccan talukas, agriculture had become merely the *"parergon,"* the pastime, of the "bulk of the population"; "their real means of livelihood is derived from labour in mills, docks and railway works in Bombay, Karachi and elsewhere."[149] Curtis, before he became the Commissioner of the Central Division, had been Settlement Commissioner and Director of Land Records, and it was he who had been largely responsible for initiating Bombay officials at all levels in the intricacies of the Record of Rights and Mutation Register. (The introduction of these long-called-for registers had begun in Bombay in 1903;[150] the Famine Commission Report of 1901 had provided the final stimulus.) Curtis, especially as Commissioner of the Central Division, used the information which the Record of Rights and the Mutation Register were at last beginning to provide in a vigorous campaign against further "shocks to title" in the form of additional restrictions on land alienation. "I need not dilate on the enormous importance of accurate statistics," he wrote in 1913. He continued, with obvious relish:

For want of them authorities like the late Mr. Justice Ranade who have written at length on the subject have been driven back on the registration records which record movements in one direction only and which take cognizance of sales and mortgages and none at all of redemption and reconveyances. . . . Is the land really moving from agri-

---

146 G. F. Keatinge, *Note on Cattle in the Bombay Presidency,* pp. 4–5.

147 R. P. Barrow, Commr., N.D., *Bom. L. Rev. Admin. Rept., 1907–8,* pt. ii, p. 60.

148 A. S. A. Westropp, Collr., Surat, *Bom. L. Rev. Admin. Rept., 1904–5,* pt. ii, p. 6; H. L. Painter, Collr., Surat, *Bom. L. Rev. Admin. Rept., 1906–7,* pt. ii, p. 10; F. G. H. Anderson, Collr., Surat, *Bom. L. Rev. Admin. Rept., 1909–10,* pt. ii, pp. 9, 19.

149 *Bom. L. Rev. Admin. Rept., 1911–12,* pt. ii, p. 28. Needless to say, Curtis did not quote Census data in support of his conclusion. For two very optimistic general surveys of rural economic conditions, see Bom. G.R.R.D. No. 8451 of 21 September 1910, on *Bom. L. Rev. Admin. Rept., 1908–9,* pt. ii, and Bom. G.R.R.D. No. 8695 of 15 September 1911, on *Bom. L. Rev. Admin. Rept., 1909–10,* pt. ii.

150 Under the Bombay Land Record of Rights Act of that year; this legislation was later incorporated in the amended Land Revenue Code of 1913.

culturists to non-agriculturists? Do the transactions recorded in the
registration offices represent permanent transfers: a lasting loss to the
agriculturists? Or do they merely represent temporary hypothecations
necessary to supply the former with capital which are incidental to
every system of agriculture in every country of the world? Was the impression conveyed by the registration figures in the period 1878–1903
wholly wrong? Is the Deccan Agriculturists' Relief Act a piece of panic
legislation which in existing conditions can be safely dispensed with?[151]

Curtis was by no means alone in his scepticism about the need
for further agrarian legislation, or, indeed, about the need for
the continuance of some of the agrarian legislation then in force.
In January 1911 the Government of Bombay replied, very be-
latedly, to the last Government of India request, made in 1905, for
a reconsideration of the Bombay decision not to proceed with legislation on the lines of the Punjab Land Alienation Act.[152] The
Government of Bombay now claimed that it appeared "from an examination of the index to the Record of Rights" that only about
one-sixth of the occupied land area in the Presidency—and one-fifth
in terms of land revenue assessment—was held by "non-agriculturists." They also claimed that, in reality, over the whole Presidency "the land held by non-agriculturists is not increasing but
is decreasing."[153] No actual statistics to back up these assertions
were quoted in the Bombay letter, although the results of certain
local investigations could perhaps have been given.[154] But generalizations on a Presidency-wide basis were hardly warranted at this
stage: it had taken some years to introduce the Record of Rights
into all districts, and the final format of the registers had been
settled only recently.[155] Generalizations about the whole Presidency, therefore, could be made on the basis of statistics for two

---

[151] *Bom. L. Rev. Admin. Rept., 1912–13,* pt. ii, p. 29. See also Curtis's statistics of
transfer (only for the years 1911–12 and 1912–13) appended to Bom. G.R. No. 4553 of
14 May 1914, on *Bom. L. Rev. Admin. Rept., 1912–13,* pt. ii.

[152] J. Wilson, Sec. G. of I., R. & A. Dept., to G. of B., No. 1548–76–2 of 10 October
1905. (I.O.R., India L. Rev. Procs., Vol. 7068.)

[153] G. Carmichael, Ch. Sec., G. of B., to Sec., G. of I., R. & A. Dept., No. 831 of
28 January 1911. (I.O.R., India L. Rev. Procs., Vol. 9219: April 1913, No. 1.)

[154] E.g. W. T. Morison, Commr., C.D., quoting S. R. Arthur, Collr., Satara, on land
transfer in his district, and G. Carmichael, Collr., Poona: *Bom. L. Rev. Admin. Rept.,
1907–8,* pt. ii, pp. 28–9, 61. Carmichael was probably thinking of his Poona experience
when, three years later, as Chief Secretary, he wrote to the Government of India on
the subject of land transfer in the Presidency as a whole.

[155] Bom. G.R.R.D. No. 9980 of 3 November 1910, and enclosures. (I.O.R., Bom. L.
Rev. Procs., Vol. 8592.)

years at most. Furthermore, the extraordinarily difficult question of defining "agriculturist" and "non-agriculturist" remained.[156] At Simla, Sir Edward Maclagan, Secretary of the Revenue and Agriculture Department after the "Bengal" interlude provided by R. W. Carlyle, was making a last stand for the old "Punjab" view on land alienation. He rightly queried the basis of the Bombay assertions. But in 1913 even Maclagan resigned himself to letting the Government of Bombay go its own way: the Government of India, he wrote, were "not prepared to press" for the introduction of legislation aiming at further restrictions on land alienation.[157]

The Government of Bombay had claimed, it was true, that the Deccan Agriculturists' Relief Act was now effecting "in large part the object of an Alienation of Land Act, *viz.*, the restriction of credit to the necessary financing of agriculture."[158] In 1903 certain key sections of the Act had been extended to all districts of the Bombay Presidency. Furthermore, in 1907 the Act had been amended so that verbal as well as written agreements could be taken into account by the courts, especially when they were dealing with "sales" that were really mortgages. But by 1912 a number of influential Bombay officials, following the example of Curtis, felt that the Act had little value and was a needless relic of the nineteenth century. Its working was therefore investigated yet again, this time by S. R. Arthur, a Civilian, and V. M. Bodas, a retired Subordinate Judge.[159] The "Arthur Commission" claimed that the introduction of the Relief Act in a district at first improved the position of the agriculturist.[160] But the system of conciliation and reduction of debts eventually led to "increasing demoralisation." Both creditor and debtor knew that a court or a "conciliator" would generally scale down a debt; the creditor therefore claimed that the amount owing was higher than it actually was, while the debtor claimed that it was lower. It did not pay to be honest in such circumstances.[161] The immediate result of

---

156 As C. W. M. Hudson, Commr., N.D., pointed out in *Bom. L. Rev. Admin. Rept., 1913–14,* pt. ii, p. 33.

157 Maclagan, Sec., G. of I., R. & A. Dept., to G. of B. No. 500–142–2 of 4 April 1913, encl. Bom. G.R.R.D. No. 735 of 23 January 1914.

158 Carmichael to G. of I., letter cited.

159 Their terms of reference are given in Bom. G.R. J.D. No. 979 of 2 February 1912. (I.O.R., Bom. Judicial Procs., Vol. 9078.)

160 "Report of the Deccan Agriculturists' Relief Act Commission, 1912," p. 3: Bom. Legal Dept. Notification No. 1019 of 20 August 1914. (I.O.R., Bom. Legal Procs., Vol. 9608.)

161 Ibid., p. 4.

the Arthur Commission's recommendations was the abolition of the system of "conciliation" by amateurs and the withdrawal of the privilege of remission of court fees in suits to which an agriculturist was a party.[162] Otherwise, however, the Deccan Agriculturists' Relief Act, in this attenuated form, was left to die a slow death.[163]

The Arthur Commission re-emphasized what they believed to be the increasing importance of the agriculturist money-lender. Such a person, Arthur and Bodas felt, could be as "grasping" and as dishonest as the professional money-lender. But, they continued,

he is subject to a powerful check in the public opinion of the village community of which he is a member, he springs from a class of whose difficulties and troubles he has intimate knowledge, he is more on a level with the debtor as regards intelligence, and, in the last resort, if the small holder's land does pass to him, the transfer is of no political moment, the cultivation is likely to be more expert and the debtor is relieved sometimes from a hopeless position and set free to earn his living otherwise.[164]

The transfer of land to the agriculturist money-lender was "of no political moment": this notion was to be prominent in the Government of Bombay's thinking on agrarian matters almost until the coming of provincial autonomy in 1937.

[162] Bom. J.D. Notification No. 3545 of 14 May 1913. (I.O.R., Bom. Judicial Procs., Vol. 9338.)
[163] See *Bom. Prov. Banking Enquiry Cttee. Rept.*, pp. 179–81.
[164] "Report of the Deccan Agriculturists' Relief Act Commission, 1912," p. 8.

III

The Registrar and the Societies, 1911–1919

Ewbank and the New Policy

R. B. Ewbank was a young man, and had served only four years before being appointed Registrar of Co-operative Societies in Bombay in 1911. In his previous service in Gujarat he had tried, as any ambitious young Civilian tried, to make a reputation for himself in a particular field. The field that he had chosen was agriculture, and he had to his credit participation in the organization of "agricultural associations" and co-operative societies in Surat district and the Panch Mahals in Gujarat.[1]

He had not been Registrar for very long before it became apparent that he was attempting to conduct the administration of the co-operative movement along lines that were different from those of Campbell. "In previous years," Ewbank wrote in his first administration report, "this Department claimed to be judged by an educational criterion rather than by statistical returns. Eight years have elapsed since the movement was first initiated and I think that the time has now come when this rather incommensurable standard should be abandoned and emphasis laid upon results."[2]

[1] Robert Benson Ewbank: Asst. Collr., Bom., 1907; Regr. Co-op. Socs., 1911–19; Sec., Cttee. on Co-operation in India, 1914; Dep. Sec., G. of I., 1920–24; Ag. Private Sec. to Viceroy, 1925; Sec., Bom. Back Bay Enquiry Cttee., 1926; Ag. Sec., G. of I., 1926–27; Representative of G. of I. in E. Africa, 1927–28; Sec., Bom. General Dept., 1929–34; retd. I.C.S., 1936; Member, Commission of Government, Newfoundland, 1936–39; at Dominions Office, 1939–41; Director, Brewers' Society, 1942–47. C.S.I., 1934; Kt. 1941.

[2] *Rept., 1911–12,* p. 2.

And indeed there were results—of the kind understood by the Secretariat—in the first years of Ewbank's regime. In 1912 Ewbank had to record that Bombay was now behind all the major provinces of India in the number of its societies.[3] But the number of co-operative societies in the Presidency had risen from 251 to 368 during 1911–12;[4] by 1913 there were 515 societies,[5] and by 1914 the total was 698.[6] Indeed, in 1914 the Government of Bombay began to fear that the movement might overreach itself, and it laid down the policy that no official pressure should be used to accelerate the formation of credit societies.[7]

This rise in the number of societies was partly the result of the opening of the Central Bank in Bombay. It was, too, partly the result of an increase of public confidence in the co-operative movement—an increase which appears to have come about quite suddenly, after seven or eight years during which the attitude of the public at large was best described as "one of some suspense."[8] Ewbank took up his position at an auspicious moment. But the rise in the number of societies was also the result of increased efficiency under the new Registrar. Procedure in the Registrar's office and in the districts became more standardized;[9] new model rules were promulgated, especially by means of a 200-page *Manual* in English,[10] which Ewbank laboriously prepared.

Ewbank's advent meant an end to the encouragement of societies for such people as sweepers and poor Satara agriculturists. On the Satara societies of the famine zone, Ewbank commented in his first report, with a certain amount of irony: "Mr. Campbell stated last year that the position was not without hope but required delicate handling, and this is undoubtedly the truth."[11] By 1914 Satara was, in Ewbank's opinion, "the plague spot of the Presidency." One hundred and thirteen societies had, at one time or another, been registered in the district. Already forty-six had had to be liqui-

---

[3] Ewbank to D.A. No. 2090 of 8 May 1912, encl. Bom. G.R. Finance Dept. No. 2931 of 6 September 1912.

[4] *Rept., 1911–12*, p. 20.

[5] *Rept., 1912–13*, p. 23.

[6] *Rept., 1913–14*, p. 29.

[7] Ibid., p. 2.

[8] *Rept., 1906–7*, p. 11.

[9] See Ewbank, Note, 19 January 1912, at side of Draft Circular to Auditors and Special Mamlatdars. (Poona, Miscellaneous XVIII, Orders on Audit and Inspection.)

[10] *A Manual for Co-operative Societies in the Bombay Presidency* (1914).

[11] *Rept., 1911–12*, p. 9.

dated, and there were still some fifteen "thoroughly bad" societies which would have to be wound up.[12] "For the submerged debtor, the loafer, or the hopelessly illiterate," Ewbank pronounced, "no system can create wealth or independence."[13] In this way were defined the lowest income limits to which in future the co-operative movement would reach. Ewbank did not define the upper limits, but it would probably be fair to say that if his best societies were not purely "democratic," in Campbell's sense of the word, neither were they "aristocratic." Doubtless Ewbank would have agreed with P. B. Haigh, who acted as Registrar in 1914, that "the man with 'the economic holding' who can do a little more than make ends meet is our most promising recruit."[14] The man with a very large holding, the man who often did no field work himself, was not to have an important place, on the whole, in the co-operative movement in Bombay in our period. Such a man, besides being afraid of unlimited liability, often did not need to borrow money at the rates at which co-operatives could offer it.

Ewbank was the first Registrar who was able to give respectability to the notion that a minor bureaucracy, of a reasonably permanent nature, was necessary to assist in the guidance and extension of the co-operative movement. Campbell had been able to obtain funds to employ two men to act as "auditors" of co-operative societies. They had the status of *mamlatdars*; they were, then, reasonably senior members of the Indian official hierarchy.[15] Campbell had also added to his establishment a couple of men of lower status to assist with the general oversight of the Gujarat Kaliparaj societies[16] and the Karnatak societies. But this was not before he had resorted for a time to the expedient, typical of Campbell, of paying for an extra assistant for the Karnatak himself.[17] The Government of Bombay had made appointments as auditors only because other provinces had such officials, and even at the beginning of 1912 the Government of India deprecated "the creation of anything resembling a regular service of subordinate officials

12 *Rept., 1913–14*, p. 3.
13 *Rept., 1912–13*, p. 4.
14 *Rept., 1914–15*, p. 9.
15 Bom. G.R. Finance Dept. No. 1990 of 23 April 1908 and enclosures. (Poona, Permanent EST.)
16 Campbell to D. A. No. 2502 of 6 November 1909, encl. Bom. G.R.R.D. No. 12356 of 22 December 1909.
17 *Rept., 1910-11*, p. 1; *Rept., 1911-12*, p. 9.

for the control of the co-operative movement."[18] However, in an India in which the notion of government as *Ma-Bap* (mother-father) was prominent, and in an India where the co-operative movement had come into being solely as the result of government initiative, a permanent "Co-operative Department" in each province was probably, in the end, virtually inevitable. In Bombay, Ewbank certainly hastened the process. His case for extra staff was always meticulously made, so that even in war-time he never seemed to be pitching his demands too high. He obtained the services, for example, of K. B. Bhadrapur, at first as an Auditor,[19] and then as an Assistant Registrar.[20] Bhadrapur was a member of the small Karnatak agriculturist community of the Raddis. He was "one of the rising hopes of his caste,"[21] being "the first Raddi M.A."[22] His position with the Raddis and the Lingayats was one of great influence;[23] indeed Ewbank, looking back in later life, went so far as to aver that it was he who "set the Movement really going in the Southern Division."[24] Then there was V. H. Gonehalli, who first worked with Ewbank in the capacity of an Extra Deputy Director of Agriculture, and later as an Assistant Registrar.[25] He was the son of a poor cultivator of the Kanara district; he himself had worked in the fields until he was fifteen. By dint of "remarkable powers of perseverance and self help" he had won his way by scholarships to a school teaching position, to Bombay University, and finally to Cambridge.[26] He died, at a comparatively early age, as

18 G. of I. R. & A. Dept. (L. Rev.) Circular Letter No. 1–402–3 of 2 January 1912, encl. Bom. G.R.R.D. No. 825 of 25 January 1912.

19 Bom. G.R. Finance Dept. No. 4038 of 7 November 1913.

20 Bom. R.D. Order No. 11855 of 1 December 1916.

21 Ewbank to D.A. No. 1182 of 3 February 1917, encl. Bom. R.D. Order No. 5434 of 1 May 1917.

22 Ewbank to D.A. No. 10941 of 1 November 1916, encl. Bom. R.D. Order No. 11855 of 1 December 1916.

23 Over half the Raddis were Lingayat by religion. See R. E. Enthoven, *The Tribes and Castes of Bombay*, III, 258. An 1884 Gazetteer says that though they are classed by the Brahmans as Sudras (of the lowest *varna,* or group of castes), they "rank with Lingayats, hold a high position, and will not eat from the hands of Brahmans." It adds that Raddis "seldom send their boys to school and take to no new pursuits. They are an intelligent well-to-do class with fair prospects." *Bijapur Gazetteer*, pp. 149, 155.

24 Ewbank, "Memories of the Early Days," *B.C.Q.*, April 1954, p. 5.

25 Bom. R.D. Order No. 11855 of 1 December 1916.

26 R. P. Barrow, Sec., Bom. R.D., to G. of I., R. & A. Dept. (Agric.) No.261–P of 13 July 1906, encl. Viceroy to Sec. of State No. 21 (Agric.) of 2 August 1906. (I.O.R., Rev. Letters from India, 1906.) See also *B.C.Q.*, December 1929, p. 183. The author has heard Gonehalli held up as an exemplar even today by an ambitious but not particularly high ranking government official.

a Collector of a district. Gonehalli's rise, which perhaps seems a little freakish, was probably to some extent due—in an increasingly caste-conscious era—to the very fact of his lowly origin. Nevertheless, he undoubtedly had considerable ability and tremendous enthusiasm. D. A. Shah, a Gujarati, who was appointed as an Auditor under Ewbank in 1918 and who soon became an Assistant Registrar, had a less unusual background, but he, too, was a man of great ability. He was a Bombay University Prizeman who, but for his health, probably could have been a member of the Indian Civil Service. In the uneasy 1940s he was to act as Registrar and as a Collector.[27]

Honorary Organizers

Although Ewbank was largely responsible for pruning the co-operative movement of many of its economically unviable branches, and for creating a "department," it would be a mistake to see his work only in terms of the operation of an efficient bureaucratic machine. For Ewbank, it is true, co-operation was not a mission in life in the sense that it had been for Campbell; it was primarily a government policy—to be vigorously put into action simply because it was government policy. But there was a streak of idealism in Ewbank, too, and he devoted much attention to cultivating the interest and enthusiasm of "non-officials."

Campbell's rather unbusinesslike methods had repelled some Indians, although the quality of his personality had attracted others. He had gone outside the ranks of retired officials for honorary organizers. Thus, G. K. Chitale, an Ahmadnagar Brahman "pleader" (lawyer), who was setting out on a career in local and Presidency politics, had been drawn into the co-operative movement. But on the whole it was not until Ewbank's advent that Indians who were also "politicians" were added to the list of honorary organizers.[28] The two greatest prizes were Gopal Krishna Devadhar and R. M. Sane. Devadhar was a foundation member of Gokhale's Servants of India Society, who—probably because of his

---

[27] Ewbank considered himself very fortunate to have obtained his services. See Bom. R.D. Order No. 10364 of 21 October 1918.

[28] As Sir Robert Ewbank himself has freely acknowledged, in conversation with the author, this policy was to some extent a reflection of the generally more relaxed political atmosphere that prevailed in Bombay between 1913 and 1918, during the governorship of Lord Willingdon. Cf. Gandhi, *The Story of my Experiments with Truth*, pp. 276, 279.

close contact with Christian missionaries in his youth—had been
largely responsible for having the constitution of the Society
which Gokhale set up changed so that it would be not only a political organization but also a group of "national missionaries."[29]
Hadapsar society, which Devadhar organized very near Poona,
became a model; for years to come, any visiting dignitary could not
leave Poona without a visit to Hadapsar. Its success—or, rather, its
seeming success, for its collapse in the late twenties was to be disastrous—was mainly the result of Devadhar's ability to wheedle
deposits from his Poona friends. Sane, another Chitpavan Brahman, had rather different political and social leanings from Devadhar; he was friendly with the militant Tilak as well as with the
"moderate" Gokhale. He had been a teacher in the New English
School in Poona (which Tilak had been partly instrumental in
founding) and editor of two newspapers, the "moderate" *Dnyan
Prakash* and the more "extremist" *Kesari*, at various times in the
eighties and nineties. At the same time he had studied law. He was
one of the first members of the Sarvajanik Sabha, and he preserved
a deep reverence for both Ranade and Tilak until the end of his
life. "His independence and impartiality prevented him from becoming a partisan on one side or the other."[30] (To some extent, of
course, Sane's career illustrates the fact that amongst the followers
of Ranade and Gokhale on the one hand, and Tilak on the other,
the dividing line was often very indistinct.[31]) In 1894 Sane had
moved to Barsi, a market town in Sholapur district, to practise law.
His work as a newspaper editor and now, especially, as a small-
town lawyer gave him a sound knowledge of the rural areas. Sane
took great pains not to bring politics into the co-operative movement. Tilak, it has been claimed by a Poona Brahman who was
himself, as a member of the Indian Civil Service, Registrar in the
late twenties, "did not like Sane's mixing himself up with
Government-sponsored co-operative activities and told him that in
the end he would see his mistake."[32] Sane's ability as an orator in

29 N. A. Dravid, "Entrance to the Servants of India Society," in *Gopal Krishna Devadhar*, ed. H. N. Kunzru, p. 24.

30 Obituary notice of Sane in *Mahratta*, 6 December 1925.

31 Cf. Ganesh Vyankatesh Joshi, who remained a member of the Poona Sarvajanik
Sabha when Ranade and Gokhale formed the Deccan Sabha, but who was the con-
fidant and to some extent the speech writer for Gokhale in economic matters.

32 V. S. Bhide, "Memories and Reflections of an Old-Stager," *B.C.Q.*, April 1954,
p. 10.

Marathi, his integrity, and above all his clear thinking in co-operative matters—he was the Bombay movement's most acute critic from within—were to keep him in the forefront for the next ten years.[33]

In the Deccan, before the First World War, most of the honorary organizers were Brahmans—frequently, like Chitale and Sane, or M. R. Tarkunde of Sasvad, pleaders. Taluka-town pleaders, especially, possessed a great deal of influence amongst a litigious peasantry. In commercially-minded Gujarat it was wealth that was considered to be essential at this time. The fact that A. U. Malji of Broach, for example, was a Brahman, was only incidental; his "influence" was considered to arise from the fact that he was a mill-owner as well as a lawyer.[34] In the Karnatak the local urban politician came to the fore in the ranks of the honorary organizers: R. G. Naik was the President of Belgaum municipality,[35] and S. K. Rodda was the President of Dharwar municipality and for a time an elected member of the Legislative Council.[36] Some of these men undoubtedly worked very diligently in the co-operative cause. In 1915 Naik at Belgaum claimed to have spent the whole or parts of 181 days in co-operative work and to have despatched 387 English and 157 vernacular letters. Naranbhai Desai, who for a time attempted to guide the Kolis of the Mandvi taluka of Surat district, was apparently not far behind. They were given part-time clerks as assistants.[37] But most of the honorary organizers were, in the words of R. M. Sane, "more or less holiday workers."[38] And the comfort of the "holiday" depended to a considerable extent on how the honorary organizer was graded—first, second, or third "class" so far as travelling allowance was concerned. Here was a source of a good deal of rivalry and potential bitterness.[39]

[33] For Sane see Govind Raghunath Kale, *Barsi Central Co-operative Bank Ltd., va Barsi talukantil Sahakari Patpadya yatsa Itihas* (in Marathi), pp. 1–3.

[34] Ewbank to D.A. No. 6549 of 15 December 1913, encl. Bom. G.R.R.D. No. 905 of 30 January 1914. (Original: B.R.O., R.D. Vol. 428 of 1914.)

[35] Ewbank to D.A. No. 2123 of 9 May 1912, encl. Bom. G.R.R.D. No. 5207 of 1 June 1912.

[36] Ewbank to D.A. No. 5180 of 18 November 1912, encl. Bom. G.R.R.D. No. 11673 of 23 December 1912.

[37] Bom. R.D. Order No. 7030 of 15 July 1916, on Ewbank to D.A. No. 3036 of 10 April 1916.

[38] Sane, "Notes on Conditions precedent to the Registration of a Rural Co-operative Society," *Prov. Co-op. Conf. Procs., 1912*, p. 44.

[39] Ewbank to Govt. No. 10541 of 18 August 1917, encl. Bom. Govt. Order No. 759/51–Confl. of 24 January 1918. (I.O.R., Bom. Confl. L. Rev. Procs., Vol. 37.)

Amongst the honorary organizers, then, there were all sorts. A few, such as Sane and Devadhar, took part in co-operative work simply because they felt that good could come from it. Many others had mixed motives. Some might have been seeking titles and similar government recognition;[40] more, probably, either consciously wished to reinforce their traditional status or else fell naturally into positions which they felt, and others felt, were theirs by right. Others again, such as many of the pleaders, doubtless assisted partly in order to give themselves more contacts with potential clients. Pleaders often had money to lend, too; this could be both an advantage and a disadvantage to the societies under their aegis. And many an honorary organizer tried to use his position as a springboard to a political career. At this stage in the development of the co-operative movement the honorary organizers came mainly from the educated, "English-knowing" classes. There were few real rural leaders amongst them. They were usually reasonably "loyal"—though in the years immediately before the war, anyway, it was not very fashionable to be actively "disloyal."

The Bombay Central Co-operative Bank

The foundation of the Bombay Central Co-operative Bank meant that the Registrar had to forge yet another set of relationships with non-official Indians. The men at the Bank in Bombay were certainly of a rather different type from most of the honorary organizers of the *mofussil*. Vithaldas Thackersey and Fazulbhoy Currimbhoy were members of the Imperial Legislative Council. Sir Shapurji Broacha had charge of the investments of the Maharajah of the prosperous Indian State of Baroda,[41] and, in fact, supplied most of the fixed deposits in the early days of the Bank's operations.[42] Chunilal Mehta, a family friend of Lalubhai Samaldas,[43] was the son of Vijbhukhandas Atmaram, who was sometimes described as a "merchant prince." "If our Directors cannot get money nobody can," one of them claimed.[44] The person who pro-

---

[40] In the early days of the co-operative movement in the Bombay Presidency it had been suggested that retired Mamlatdars might take up work as honorary organizers in the hope of some titular reward. See Motilal Chunilal, "How can the assistance of non-officials be obtained?" *Prov. Co-op. Conf. Procs., 1908*, p. 37.

[41] Information from Sir Stanley Reed.

[42] Reed, Evidence, Maclagan Cttee.

[43] Natarajan, *Lalubhai Samaldas*, p. 24.

[44] Reed, Evidence, Maclagan Cttee.

vided most of the inspiration on the Board, once Vithaldas had ceased to take a very active interest in the Bank, was Lalubhai Samaldas. The Board was not, of course, typical of the Bombay business community. For one thing, most of its members were much wealthier than the average Bombay commercial man: they could afford to be interested in such matters as the co-operative movement. Politically, the Bank's Board came largely from the circles of those who were described as "Bombay Moderates" or, somewhat later, as "Bombay Liberals."[45]

The everyday management of the Bank was left in the hands of Vaikunth Mehta, except for a period when he was away, in 1914–15, during which, significantly, K. Natarajan, editor of the *Indian Social Reformer*, one of the leading voices of the "Moderates," acted as Manager. Vaikunth Mehta was only twenty-one, and had recently graduated from Elphinstone College, when he took up his post in 1912. The son of Lalubhai Samaldas, he worked as Manager for a number of years simply for "pocket money from father."[46] Indeed, the Bank in the first few months, before it took up premises in the Fort area of Bombay, operated from Lalubhai's home at Andheri.[47] But Vaikunth Mehta, though he had a gentle modesty of his own, and his father's vision and integrity, grew rapidly in independence. (In later years he was to break with his father politically—although certainly not personally—and join the Congress; he was Finance Minister in the Government of Bombay from 1946 until 1952.) Ewbank and Vaikunth Mehta often toured the societies together. A close relationship between the young Indian and the young Englishman grew up—one of those British-Indian relationships that were to be important in the years to come. Ewbank was the first European whom Mehta came to know

[45] It is perhaps significant that when Gandhi began his agitation in 1916 against indentured emigration to South Africa, two of the four men who helped him first in Bombay, Lalubhai Samaldas and Dr. Stanley Reed, were directors of the Bank, and a third, K. Natarajan, was for a time Acting Manager. See *The Story of My Experiments with Truth*, p. 295. Another director, Chunilal Mehta, was a prominent Liberal minister in Bombay in the early twenties. Lalubhai himself was a member of the Bombay Legislative Council, 1915–26, and Revenue Member for a period in the mid-twenties.

[46] The phrase was used by Sir Stanley Reed in an interview with the author. Reed made a similar statement to the Maclagan Committee many years earlier. (See Evidence, Maclagan Committee.) Reed was the editor of the leading Bombay English newspaper, the *Times of India*.

[47] See V. L. Mehta to Ewbank, 21 November 1912. (Poona, Original Circulars, I.)

well;[48] Ewbank, for his part, was soon beginning his informal letters with "My dear Vaikunth" instead of "My dear Mr. Mehta."

The Central Bank, then, was basically in good hands. But almost certainly Raiffeisen would not have approved of the Bank's structure. There was only one co-operative society amongst its 911 original shareholders, and because the share capital was fully subscribed before the final date for consideration of applications, societies at first could not become shareholders except by buying operations on the open market.[49] One director, at least, did not want to "complicate matters" by having societies as shareholders.[50] But the directors took care to distribute the shares fairly widely: the assertion that, if they had wished, "the whole capital could have been subscribed by the Directors"[51] was probably true. And, as Ewbank wrote in 1913, the directors' "primary object, which they may claim to have attained, was to place money within reach of the ryot."[52] This was the fundamental fact about the Bank. Bombay capital—largely Gujarati capital, in fact—was at last beginning to return to the *mofussil*: to the Deccan and to the Karnatak as well as to Gujarat. Although the amount concerned was comparatively small, there was a measure of philanthropy involved; the Bank cannot fairly be considered a part of some continuing tradition of Gujarati "exploitation" of the non-Gujarati parts of the Presidency. During the period from March 1911 to March 1912 the working capital of the rural co-operative societies of the Presidency increased from Rs.4,88,552 to Rs.14,47,118; about six lakhs of this increase was capital supplied by the Bank. In 1914 the figures for the rural societies' working capital and the Bank's working capital were, respectively, Rs.28,03,849 and Rs. 15,04,435. Most of the Bank's working capital was lent to rural societies. About half the working capital of the rural societies at this time, then, came from the Bank in Bombay.[53] The proportions were to remain fairly constant, though the total capital involved

---

48 Information from the late Shri Mehta.

49 Bank's evidence, *Bom. Prov. Banking Enquiry Cttee.,* 1930, Vol. IV, p. 431; *Rept., 1911–12,* p. 3; V. L. Mehta to G. F. S. Collins, Regr., D/O No. 1388 of 25 January 1927. (Poona, Nira Canal and Central Bank [N.C. & C.B.].)

50 Reed, Evidence, Maclagan Cttee. (Patiala.)

51 Reed, loc. cit.

52 *Rept., 1912–13,* p. 4.

53 For statistics, see *Rept., 1912,* pp. 17 and 20; *Rept., 1914,* pp. 27 and 29.

in the operations of the societies and the Bank was to increase considerably.

But statistics could be deceptive, as Edward Maclagan, Secretary of the Revenue and Agriculture Department of the Government of India, well knew. He believed that an undue proportion of the Bank's available funds was invested in capital-intensive operations in the canal areas.[54] A lakh or two went to societies outside the canal areas in the Bank's first years of existence,[55] but it was true that most of its funds were at first employed in the irrigated regions of Poona district. The Government of Bombay, in December 1911, had discontinued the practice of giving loans to all newly organized societies and advised such societies to apply to the Bank;[56] the Bank, however, did not always satisfy their requirements. But the societies were scattered all over the Presidency and normally demanded only small loans. How could the Bank, with its limited resources, contact all the societies in order to judge what amounts it could lend them? There was at first no one to do this work in Gujarat. When the Bank finally did appoint an "Inspector" for Gujarat it was claimed that, by the time his salary and travelling expenses had been paid, the Bank's profit was only about 1¼ per cent; it had to pay 4 per cent interest to its debenture holders and over 1 per cent sinking fund charges.[57]

The Bank's Directors asserted that when their articles of association were being drawn up they had come to "some understanding" with the Bombay Government to the effect that while the Bank was establishing itself government officials would help in all valuation work.[58] Certainly there was a clause in the agreement with the Secretary of State which specified that no loan could be granted without the sanction or recommendation of the Registrar, and this clause could in practice be made to work very much in the Bank's favour. W. W. Smart, who for a time acted as Director of Agriculture, thought that the Bank's directors were interpreting the agreement in a way which appeared to "require from the

[54] *Regrs.' Conf. Procs., 1912,* p. 8.
[55] *Rept., 1912–13,* pp. 4–6.
[56] Bom. G.R. Finance Dept. No. 4045 of 11 December 1911.
[57] V. L. Mehta to Ewbank, No. L–3–1318 of 26 March 1914, encl. Bom. G.R.R.D. No. 6606 of 1 July 1914.
[58] See Ewbank to D.A. No. 486 of 10 February 1912, encl. Bom. G.R.R.D. No. 7651 of 12 August 1912.

Registrar the business ability which they themselves should supply."[59] Suspicion of the "Bombay business interests" who dominated the Bank was still considerable. But, after some initial
hesitation, Ewbank boldly decided to undertake the responsibility
for making enquiries before loans were given to societies. He was
able to use for this work three "Special Mamlatdars" who had been
temporarily working under him, trying to remedy some of Campbell's muddles;[60] the continuation of the appointments of these
Special Mamlatdars until July 1914 was sanctioned. Ewbank used
the argument that it was "only equitable" that enquiries into the
assets of the Nira Canal societies, formed at the behest of Government, should be made by official agency. And there was little doubt
that in those early days of its existence the representatives of the
Central Bank often needed a "quasi-official position" so that their
enquiries into such matters as the size of holdings, and their encumbrances, should not be hindered by the "recalcitrance of
village officers."[61] Normally, only one Special Mamlatdar was employed on the Nira Canal; the other two Special Mamlatdars
therefore made it possible for the Bank to branch out into business
in other regions.

"Veiled Control" in the Nira Valley

In the Nira Canal area the Special Mamlatdar in charge, R. B.
Badve, exercised a "veiled control" over most of the operations
of the societies.[62] All applications from societies for loans from
the Bank had to pass through his hands and receive his approval.
He thus had "a practical power of veto in granting loans to members."[63] He controlled the staff of five "secretaries" which the societies employed between them. In effect, as Ewbank himself
recognized, "co-operative machinery was being used to fulfil the
functions of a land bank."[64] As a matter of policy it was decided
"to follow as closely as possible the main lines of the Takavi

[59] Smart to Govt. No. A.–3736 of 27 May 1912, encl. Bom. G.R. cited.
[60] See Bombay G.R. Finance Dept. No. 2292 of 15 July 1911.
[61] Ewbank to D.A. No. 486 of 10 February 1912, encl. Bom. G.R.R.D. No. 7651 of
12 August 1912.
[62] K. S. Gore, "Remarks on submitted audit memo on the Nira Canal societies for
1914." (Poona, N.C. & C.B.)
[63] Badve, "Report on the Working of the Nira Canal Societies up to the close of
the Co-operative Year 1913–1914," p. 2. (Poona, Registrar's Library.)
[64] Ewbank, *Regrs.' Conf. Procs., 1913*, p. 3.

scheme." Sahasrabudhe, the "Special Officer" in charge of the government scheme, "after retiring from government service," became the first agent of the Bank on the Canal. It was doubtful whether many realized the difference in his function. The societies were started with no members' deposits; instead, no doubt to the great relief of the Government, the Bank took over the collection of the debts of all the *takkavi* borrowers and immediately paid a sum representing the outstanding debts into the local government treasury.[65]

But the "veiled control" of the Special Mamlatdar was not complete. One of the most important aspects of the government scheme had been that the cultivators who were financed had to bring all their produce to the government shop for sale, so that repayment of loans could be enforced.[66] This was, of course, merely to imitate the normal methods of the money-lender-cum-shopkeeper. A similar practice became a feature of the Bank's scheme; indeed, all that happened was that the government shop became the Bank's shop. In effect (in spite of the Government of India's admonitions in 1904), standing crops were being treated as one of the securities for loans. But when the Bank took over responsibility, the four Circle Inspectors who had previously been employed on the Canal were now dispensed with. These men had visited borrowers several times during the growing period to encourage good agricultural practice, and, at harvest time, to ensure that all the crop actually reached the shop. Under the new scheme the committee members of the co-operative societies (and not the secretaries) were supposed to undertake these duties. Yet there was little encouragement for the committee members to perform this function; the societies were regarded as a government affair.[67] Ewbank himself was sometimes inclined to fall in with the prevailing attitude. At the end of the season in 1913 the despatch of the produce of the canal societies was being delayed by a shortage of railway wagons. Ewbank drafted a telegram to the Railway's head office which read, at first, "Government Jaggery Store suffering serious loss owing to shortage of wagons at Diksal." It was perhaps only an afterthought which led him to change the wording in the final draft to "Govern-

65 Badve, "Report . . . Nira Canal," p. 2.
66 Sahasrabudhe, "Interim Report . . . ," p. 1.
67 Badve, "Report," p. 5.

ment Co-operative Jaggery Store"—still a somewhat incongruous combination according to co-operative theory.[68]

There was a further cause of apathy in the Canal societies, though it was never specifically stated. This was the patriarchal attitude to the societies of the Raje of Malegaon. In many ways, in fact, the Nira Canal societies formed an important "aristocratic" survival (to use Campbell's terminology) in the Ewbank period. Malegaon was an *inam* village; its Raje came from an old and notable Maratha family, and his influence extended through much of the area irrigated by the Nira Canal.[69] In the original government scheme the Sardar had "consented" to "his" rayats taking *takkavi* and had stood security for them all. His *karbhari* (tax-collector) had opened the shop for the disposal of the raw sugar and had "lent the services of his relation Mr. Uplekar" to look after it.[70] Perhaps partly for his pains over the *takkavi* scheme, the Raje was nominated a member of the Legislative Council in 1910. When the co-operative scheme began, the Raje expected to have the same position under it that he had had previously. Ewbank went to some lengths to placate the Raje: "I should be extremely loth to settle matters in a way that does not command your approval; and am therefore bringing my camp to Baramati on November 8th."[71] The Raje was undoubtedly anxious to obtain for "his" rayats all the funds that he could. But the form in which those funds came—*takkavi* or co-operative loans—did not concern him. He was totally indifferent to co-operation as such.

The Raje of Malegaon did not for long have a monopoly over the patronage of the Nira Canal societies. After the Bombay banking crisis of 1913–14 these societies, because they were thought to be government backed, came to be looked upon in the Poona area as safe places for investment. Many societies obtained large deposits from "pleaders, doctors and other *pandharpeshas.*" The control which the Special Mamlatdar had over loans from the Central Bank did not apply in such cases; the committees, Badve complained, were advancing large sums "without my knowledge."[72] In the tra-

---

[68] See Draft Telegram to G.I.P. Railway, Bom., 18 March 1913. (Poona, N.C. & C.B.)

[69] The Raje of Malegaon was a "First Class Sardar," one of seven in the Deccan given powers of civil jurisdiction in their *inam* areas. See list in *Bombay Government Gazette*, pt. iii, 3 March 1910.

[70] Sahasrabudhe, "Interim Report," p. 31.

[71] Ewbank to Raje of Malegaon, No. 4976 of November 1912. (Poona, file cited.)

[72] Badve, "Report . . . Nira Canal," p. 4. The word *pandharpesha* now had a wider

dition of the area the *pandharpeshas* demanded a large say in the control of the societies.

The Nira Canal societies were, then, hardly ready for "independence"—yet if they were not given any freedom at all, they would not have the chance to develop the very qualities of responsibility which were required.[73] As in the sphere of "local self-government," it was tempting to emphasize the first consideration and ignore the second. Ewbank eventually decided, however, to risk giving the Canal societies a greater interest in the business conducted by the Special Mamlatdar and the Bank. In 1913 he made tentative approaches to G. K. Devadhar for assistance in the formation of a "Union," for the whole of Poona district, which might help with the inspection and perhaps the finance of the canal societies. The scheme fell through.[74] Nevertheless, the proposal remained under discussion between the Registrar and the Bank. In 1915 the Bank accepted the institution of an "advisory committee," appointed by the Registrar from members of the societies, as "an experimental measure."[75] It was somewhat disconcerting to find that at its first meeting the carefully selected Nira Valley Co-operative Board passed resolutions in favour of repayment of debts "by instalments," and the postponement of arbitration in cases concerned with arrears of payments. "If this is a specimen of the work of the Supervising Board," commented E. L. Moysey, who was acting as Registrar at the time, "it is not likely to be very useful."[76]

Purchase and Sale Societies

The Nira Canal societies did have one virtue, however. In a very tentative way they showed that the rural co-operative movement could undertake more than the supply of credit: indeed, they showed that, in order to survive, co-operative societies, like money-lenders, sometimes had to undertake several types of business. In

---

connotation than that implied by its original meaning of "founder" of a village. A suitable translation might be "man in white clothing," or even "white-collar worker."

[73] See *Rept., 1911–12*, pp. 3–4.

[74] Badve to Haigh, Ag. Regr., No. 261 of 31 October 1914. (Poona, file cited.)

[75] V. L. Mehta to Regr. No. R5/203 of – 1915 (exact date not given). (Poona, file cited.)

[76] Chairman, Nira Valley Co-op. Board to Regr., 22 November 1915 (translated by Badve), and Moysey's comments. (Poona, file cited.)

1912, furthermore, the Government of India, with the concurrence of the Government of Bombay,[77] passed a new Co-operative Societies Act,[78] which permitted registration to any society which had as its object "the promotion of the economic interests of its members in accordance with co-operative principles." The Government of Bombay appear to have been convinced of the necessity of experimenting with co-operative purchase and sale, although their Registrar, at this stage perhaps somewhat discouraged by the Nira Canal developments, continued to assert that "the prime need of the agriculturist is cheap and ready credit. . . . Until credit has been really cheapened and democratized it would be suicidal for societies to dissipate their funds . . . upon speculative purchase and sale."[79]

The first rural society for co-operative purchase in the Bombay Presidency was not, in fact, organized by an official directly connected with the Co-operative Department. Dr. Harold H. Mann, then Principal of the Poona Agricultural College, brought into being a society for the co-operative supply of manure on the Mutha Canal, near Poona.[80] It was one of many experiments in co-operative and other fields made in the Bombay Presidency by this far-seeing scientist, sociologist, and social worker.[81] Harold Mann, to quote one Indian estimate, was "one of those rare officials in India who are as unlike the popular conception of an official as any individual can be";[82] he "loved India with the intensity of an Indian," said the *Mahratta*, the English organ of Tilak's "party," in 1920.[83] He was always a Yorkshire puritan at heart—in India he interested himself in the causes of temperance, untouchability, and prostitution. He was responsible for sociological investigations of village life in India[84] which remain virtually unequalled for ac-

---

[77] Bom. G.R.R.D. No. 3632 of 21 April 1910.

[78] For an explanation of the Act, see India R. & A. Dept. (L. Rev.) Circular No. 13–C of 9 March 1912, in Ewbank, *Manual* (1914 ed.), pp. 209–13. For the Act itself, see Ewbank, *Manual* (1919 ed.), pp. 17–32.

[79] See *Rept., 1912–13*, p. 10, and G.R.R.D. No. 9101 of 4 October, 1913, on this report.

[80] Mann to D.A. No. 3518 of 16 November 1912, encl. Bom. G.R.R.D. No. 11465 of 14 December 1912.

[81] Even before he arrived in the Bombay Presidency he had made a notable social survey of an English village. See Mann, "Life in an Agricultural Village in England," in *Sociological Papers* (Sociological Society), 1905.

[82] *B.C.Q.*, December 1927, p. 134.

[83] *Mahratta*, 13 June 1920.

[84] *Land and Labour in a Deccan Village*, Study No. I, 1917; Study No. II, 1921.

curacy,[85] and as the first Principal of Poona Agricultural College and then as Director of Agriculture in Bombay from 1921 to 1927 he was responsible for scientific agricultural investigations of a high order. But he counted Gokhale, Gandhi, and even Tilak among his friends,[86] and in later life he described himself as "always a rebel and a reformer."[87] Naturally, some of his compatriots found this outspoken and often obstinate man, who in any case was not a member of the I.C.S., somewhat difficult to fathom.

By 1914 Ewbank felt more confident that he would be able to cope with co-operative purchase and sale. Accordingly, when V. H. Gonehalli became enthusiastic about the possibilities of co-operation as a means of agricultural improvement, Ewbank obtained permission to utilize his services chiefly in the organization of non-credit societies amongst agriculturists.[88] Gonehalli always gave the impression of immense activity, although Ewbank remained, even in 1916, somewhat sceptical. Before any non-credit society was set up, Ewbank insisted, the potential profitability of co-operative methods had to be compared with the cost of existing methods. And Ewbank still believed that "a credit society is the easiest to organize, is valuable as a training ground for more difficult enterprises and is the first condition of most of the new schemes."[89] On the whole, Ewbank's caution was necessary in a movement that tended to be somewhat unthinkingly dedicated to removing the apparently unnecessary "middleman." The middleman, Ewbank was sure, would not be "obliterated without a struggle."[90] Ewbank saw more clearly than many the attention to detail, the business ability, and members' loyalty that were necessary if non-credit societies—and for that matter credit societies—were to be a success.

[85] See Walter C. Neale, "The Limitations of Indian Village Survey Data," *Journal of Asian Studies*, Vol. XVII, No. 4 (May 1958), pp. 398–99.

[86] Information from the late Dr. Mann. Dr. Mann died in December 1961. A collection of his papers with biographical memoirs, ed. Daniel Thorner, was published in 1967 under the title *The Social Framework of Agriculture: India, Middle East, England.*

[87] F. C. Bawden, F.R.S., "Science and Agriculture: The Contribution of Harold H. Mann," in Thorner, p. xviii.

[88] Bom. G.R.R.D. No. 7330 of 7 August 1914, on D.A. to Govt., No. A–5887 of 18 June 1914.

[89] Ewbank to D.A. No. 1930 of 8 March 1916, encl. Bom. R.D. Order No. 5669 of 2 June 1916.

[90] *Rept., 1914*, p. 12.

Land as Security

The increasing emphasis on non-credit societies was not the only departure from the principles of 1904. At that time it had been laid down that the security for loans should be personal, depending primarily on the character of the man and his sureties and not on the extent of his property. This, it was thought, was what would distinguish co-operative credit from the money-lender's credit. But a Government of India Resolution of 1914, surveying the lessons that had been learnt in the co-operative field over the previous ten years, pronounced that mortgages had their uses; co-operative credit need not necessarily be personal.[91]

Campbell's small societies for poor men had had to be based almost solely upon personal credit. And Ewbank's 1914 Manual states that in the case of small loans, of up to Rs.200 or Rs.300, personal surety would usually be sufficient. But loans for larger amounts or for lengthy periods demanded a "firmer" security.[92] In the Nira Canal area a mortgage on land was almost always insisted on, this in addition to a promise to market the crop solely through the Bank. The Bank took charge of the societies' mortgage bonds.[93] Sometimes a mortgage without possession was taken. This was often sufficient; under the system of unlimited liability a borrower's land was always, in theory, liable to be sold in order to make good a default. The main object of taking a mortgage, therefore, was often simply to prevent the alienation of the land to other credit agencies.[94] But when large loans were made for the redemption of old debts, as distinct from current needs, mortgage of land was always taken. The land was then apparently leased again to its "real" owner on an "annually renewable rent note."[95] The method was familiar to the peasants—and to the money-lenders. In Bombay 43 per cent of the total amount advanced by co-operative societies during 1913–14 was secured on land in one way or another.[96] The use of mortgages in the Nira Canal area may have assisted in avoiding completely facile credit. But the reports of Badve, the Special

[91] India G.R., R. & A. Dept. (L. Rev.) No. 12–287–1 of 1 June 1914. (B.R.O., R.D. Vol. 428 of 1914.)

[92] Ewbank, *Manual* (1914 ed.), pp. 77–78.

[93] Dr. Stanley Reed, Evidence, Maclagan Cttee. (Patiala.)

[94] *Maclagan Cttee. Rept.*, p. 42.

[95] Ewbank, *Regrs.' Conf. Procs., 1913*, p. 20.

[96] *Maclagan Cttee. Rept.*, p. 41.

Mamlatdar, in 1914 were rather ominous: in "many instances," he said, defaulters in the Canal area, under pressure of "repeated dunnings . . . through the Secretaries and their peons," had paid off their debts to their societies by selling lands or other property.[97]

It was the increasing insistence on land as security which effectively stifled the growth of the co-operative movement in the Konkan, the narrow strip of the Presidency south of the city of Bombay. The population of the Konkan was, it was true, declining, and much "cultivable" land was left uncultivated.[98] Both these factors were to a considerable extent the result of the proximity of Bombay and its mills. In addition, what cultivation there was often did not require a great deal of capital. But the primary reason for the co-operative movement's lack of growth in the area was the fact that a majority of the cultivators did not have any land to mortgage. In 1921 in the three districts of Kolaba, Ratnagiri, and North Kanara there were only 92,000 "cultivating owners" as compared with 222,000 "cultivating tenants."[99] A high proportion—perhaps half—of the land was worked by tenants in other parts of the Presidency,[100] but in those areas most tenants also owned some land, which, if necessary, they could mortgage in order to raise capital from a co-operative society.[101] The *khoti* form of land tenure was dominant in Ratnagiri district and prominent in Kolaba district. The exact legal position of the *khots* (who were often Chitpavan Brahmans) was for long a matter of argument. They appear to have begun their careers under the Peshwas as farmers of the village revenues; under the British they seem to have been able to retain and indeed improve their position as revenue middlemen. They were entitled to a percentage of much of the revenue they col-

[97] Badve, "Report on the Working of the Nira Canal Societies," p. 6. A *peon* in modern India is a messenger and guard.

[98] See [Harold H. Mann] "Economic Progress of the Rural Areas of the Bombay Presidency, 1911–1922," p. 7. (Ghokhale Institute Library.) Percentage population decline, 1911–21, in Konkan districts was as follows: Thana 3.7; Kolaba 5.3; Ratnagiri 4.2; North Kanara 6.7. In all Gujarat districts there was a rise in population in the same period, in spite of the influenza epidemic of 1918. In 1921 only 39 per cent of the "cultivable" land in Ratnagiri was cultivated; the Konkan district with the highest proportion was Kanara, with 55 per cent. *Rept., 1921–22*, p. 15.

[99] Ibid.

[100] The proportion was being calculated only at the end of our period. See F. G. H. Anderson, *Facts and Fallacies about the Bombay Revenue System*, 1929, p. 51.

[101] "The completely non-owning cultivator is present only in very small numbers." *Royal Commission on Agriculture*, Vol. II, pt. i, *Evidence taken in Bombay*, p. 76: evidence of Dr. Harold Mann.

lected; in practice they acted as landlords over much of the land in their villages—*khotnisabat* land—which was held by their "tenants" on a yearly basis.[102] The co-operative movement, as it came to be organized in Bombay, could not make much progress in such circumstances.

The position of many of the inhabitants of the so-called *talukdari* areas of North Gujarat was in some ways similar to that of the tenants of the Konkan *khots*. The *talukdars* (the name seems to have been given them by the British) were a peculiar Gujarat variant of the North Indian "landlord" type of zamindar; their estates were worked by tenants-at-will. Such tenants-at-will had little or no property to pledge as security; hence the co-operative movement could make little headway in those parts of Ahmadabad, Kaira, and Panch Mahals districts where the *talukdari* system of tenure was dominant.[103]

As credit came to be increasingly bound up with legal formalities the problem of recovery of arrears, which McNeill and Campbell had seen in relation to summary procedure, began to increase. Ewbank believed that the proposals for summary procedure had been rejected for "adequate reasons."[104] Nevertheless, it was true that—as a candid Government Press Note put it in 1915—"societies had continually chafed at the delay, trouble and expense involved in filing suits in the Civil Courts." The Press Note quoted "a few eloquent examples." Up to the end of 1913 eighteen suits had been filed in Baramati, on the Nira Canal, to recover the total sum of Rs.16,191. Every case was undisputed, but the societies concerned had to pay Rs.914 in court costs and Rs.348 in pleaders' fees. There were further losses, too: interest was often disallowed for varying periods, and the debtor was usually permitted a period of six months for payment.[105]

Ewbank and his superiors decided that there was a case to be made for the appointment of non-official arbitrators (often, in fact,

102 For the position of the *khots*, see *Gazetteer of the Bombay Presidency*, Vol. X, *Ratnagiri and Savantvadi*, pp. 137–39, 203–9; Vol. XI, *Kolaba and Janjira*, pp. 162–65.

103 For the *talukdari* system, see R. D. Choksey, *Economic Life in the Bombay Gujarat, 1800–1939*, pp. 26, 70, 76; also *Gazetteer of the Bombay Presidency*, Vol. IV, *Ahmedabad*, pp. 179–86.

104 Ewbank to D.A. No. 5884 of 20 August 1914, encl. Bom. G.R.R.D. No. 598 of 18 January 1915.

105 Press Note, forwarded to editors, etc., under Govt. Letter No. 5660 of 21 May 1915. (Poona, Government Resolutions file.)

"honorary organizers") to act in such situations. The government press release on the subject was deceptively over-sanguine about the suitability of such a form of arbitration in the co-operative field: "Cases between co-operative societies and their members are always simple and intelligible, and . . . the claims are almost invariably just and supported by ample evidence."[106] But arbitration in co-operative cases appears to have been slightly more satisfactory than it had been in cases under the Deccan Agriculturists' Relief Act. The arbitration system was certainly used by members of co-operative societies. By the end of Ewbank's regime in 1919 there were nearly 1,000 arbitration cases annually;[107] by 1922 there were 1,600. As the Registrar insisted in that year, many of these cases were fundamentally the result of "carelessly giving away money."[108] Arbitration cases sometimes took up the time of officials. Under the arbitration rules of 1915 the Registrar could, if he wished, himself act as "arbitrator" in any co-operative case; furthermore, any appeals against the decisions of non-official arbitrators were to be made to the Registrar, or to the Director of Agriculture in the case of appeals against the Registrar's decisions.[109] To a large extent, in fact, Ewbank had the "summary procedure" for which McNeill and Campbell had pleaded in vain.

But, whatever authority made the award in a case concerning co-operative societies, it still had to be executed. In December 1914 Badve wrote to Haigh, the Acting Registrar, in great distress about the dilatoriness of the Revenue Department in executing decrees which the Civil Court had made against some Canal society members in October 1913. The Court had allowed the defaulters four months in which to pay. When the payments were not made, *darkhasts* ("representations") had to be obtained from the Court. It was August 1914 before they could be sent to the Collector. They were then forwarded to the Mamlatdar at Baramati. More time was lost in going through the procedure of issuing various notices; finally, the date for holding the auction of the debtors' land was fixed for January 1915. At this stage most of the worst offenders applied to the Collector for a grant of postponement of the sale of

---

106 Ibid.
107 Ewbank to Govt. No. 6318 of 22 May 1919, encl. Bom. R.D. Order No. 14140 of 3 December 1919.
108 Otto Rothfeld, Regr., *Prov. Co-op. Conf. Procs., 1922,* p. 26.
109 Press note cited.

their lands until their crops had been harvested. This was given. "I don't think that they would ever pay the money due from them within the time allowed by the Collector," Badve complained. "Certainly such things are most disheartening. . . . So long as this pusillanimous method of the civil procedure continues to govern the societies, I am afraid, the movement has little chance to succeed. . . . I may kindly be excused for being somewhat outspoken."[110] This letter was passed on to the Collector of Poona. Somewhat stung by what was, indeed, a degree of outspokenness unusual in a subordinate official, he fastened on one particular case, claiming that he had never been advised that the Court decree was one in favour of a co-operative society. This was quite possibly correct. He said he would do all he could to help co-operative societies, but he had "300 & more Civil Court decrees to deal with."[111] In January 1916 Ewbank still had to note in melancholy fashion: "As far as I know, no case yet referred to the Revenue Department has been fully disposed of."[112]

This episode does not merely illustrate the cumbrousness of the processes of the Revenue Department. It also shows how a co-operative society which resorted to decrees and *darkhasts* could very easily be thought, by the average over-worked government official as well as by the average peasant, to be little better than the money-lender. This, it would appear, was the penalty that had to be paid for the shift away from "personal credit."

The Maclagan Committee

The Government of India Resolution of 1914, which made manifest the conversion of those concerned with the formation of co-operative policy to the notion that mortgage credit had some virtues in co-operative organization, was in fact a comprehensive review of the movement's progress in the past ten years. And it announced the appointment of a committee to investigate the movement's achievements and prospects in detail; it was to be headed by Sir Edward Maclagan, the Secretary of the Government of India's Revenue and Agriculture Department.[113]

The "Maclagan Committee" had its origin, to some extent, in

110 Badve to Haigh, Ag. Regr., No. 297 of 9–10 December 1914. (Poona, N.C. & C.B.)
111 J. Mountford, Collr., Poona, to Haigh, D/O of 21–22 December 1914. (Poona, file cited.)
112 Ewbank to Collr., Poona, No. 566 of 21 January 1916. (Poona, file cited.)
113 India G. R. R. & A. Dept. (L. Rev.) No. 12–287–1 of 17 June 1914. (B.R.O., R.D. Vol. 428 of 1914.)

the Bombay banking crisis of December 1913 and early 1914. Vithaldas Thackersey lost heavily in the failure of the Specie Bank—and the responsibility in the matter which he felt so keenly was actually his, to some extent.[114] So the Government of Bombay's action earlier in 1913 in refusing to allow the Bombay Central Co-operative Bank to invest its funds in the Specie Bank—in spite of the directors' protests of the soundness of the Specie Bank's finances[115]—was justified by events. The Central Co-operative Bank itself, it is true, weathered the storm remarkably well. Its shares fell from 23 to 14¾, and some short-term deposits were withdrawn. "But it was never forced to stop or curtail its lending business or raise its rates. Any deposits that were withdrawn were at once replaced by one of the Directors [probably Lalubhai Samaldas]. At no time was it in the slightest danger." Its position, Ewbank claimed, when he wrote his annual report in 1914, was "now as strong as ever."[116] Nevertheless, when the Burma Registrar, A. E. English, noting events in Bombay, suggested a full-scale Government of India enquiry into the workings of the co-operative movement,[117] Lamb, the Revenue Member of the Bombay Government, welcomed the proposal. He hoped that the enquiry would concentrate on the stages "above that of the individual society."[118]

The official appointed to act as Secretary of the Maclagan Committee was Ewbank, the Bombay Registrar. Ewbank's horizons were broadened by his work with this Committee. He had to travel with the members of the Committee to all parts of India, to read widely, to discuss the problems of the co-operative movement with all manner of people, and finally to assist in drafting the Report.[119] Lalubhai Samaldas was a member of the Committee—though possibly only because the Viceroy himself insisted on it[120]—and his son Vaikunth Mehta accompanied him as a private secretary in all

114 See Kaji, *Vithaldas Thackersey*, p. 137.
115 Bom. G.R.R.D. No. 10309 of 13 November 1913 and enclosures.
116 *Rept., 1913–14*, p. 4.
117 L.J.K. [Kershaw?], Note, 6 July 1914. (N.A.I., R. & A. (L. Rev.) Loose "A" Procs., November 1914, File 312 of 1914.)
118 Lamb, Note, 23 August 1914, below R.D. Unofficial Reference No. 7691 of 18 August 1914. (B.R.O., R.D. Vol. 428 of 1914.)
119 Information from Sir Robert Ewbank. The value of this Report is still recognized in post-Independence India; it has been reprinted by the Reserve Bank of India.
120 There was a fierce argument as to whether he should be paid the allowance for which he asked. Hardinge intervened, ordering that he be paid Rs.1500 per month —he was, he said, "far the best man." Hardinge, Note, 27 October 1914. (N.A.I., file cited.)

provinces except Burma.[121] After Ewbank had finished his work with the Committee, he went home for a period of leave, wrote an article for the *Quarterly Review* on the co-operative movement in India,[122] and carefully considered the action to be taken in the light of his increased experience. His first memorandum on the subject was written in England.[123]

At the head of the co-operative system in the Bombay Presidency, Ewbank said, stood the Bombay Central Co-operative Bank. It had brought a good deal of money to the cultivator. Its main defect was that almost all its shares were held by individuals who were, Ewbank now asserted, "mainly concerned with realizing their dividends." (Ewbank was certainly criticizing the Bank with a good deal less reserve than before.) The Bank's directors, being unfamiliar with local needs, had to rely on the Bank's own enquiry staff and, to a greater extent, on the Registrar's staff. From July 1914 the Bank had been paying half the salaries and expenses of the Special Mamlatdars, but the directors had agreed to do so only with reluctance.[124] Such methods were expensive, and "not capable of indefinite expansion." Furthermore, supervision of this variety provided "only an outside view of the working of any particular society." In some districts, it was true, urban co-operative societies had begun lending to rural societies—sometimes, in fact, in rivalry with the Bombay Central Bank.[125] Before he became secretary of the Maclagan Committee, Ewbank had induced the urban co-operative banks at Surat, Barsi, and Dharwar to modify their constitutions so that they approximated those of the "central banking unions" of Bengal. But in Bombay the pre-1914 "district banking unions," apart perhaps from Sane's Barsi Taluka Union, had remained urban banks at heart: if money could be lent in the towns, why bother to go out into the rural areas? Such "unions" exercised little supervision over the money they lent.[126] Certainly the Bom-

121 Information from the late Shri Vaikunth Mehta.

122 Ewbank, "The Co-operative Movement in India," *Quarterly Review*, Vol. CCXXV, No. 447 (April 1916).

123 Ewbank, "Suggestions for the future development of the Co-operative System in the Bombay Presidency," written from Bolton Rectory, Cumberland, 5 August 1915. (Poona, Committee on Co-operation.) Quotations in the following paragraph are from this memorandum if no other source is given.

124 Bom. G.R.R.D. No. 6066 of 1 July 1914 and enclosures.

125 Ewbank to D.A. No. 486 of 10 February 1912, encl. Bom. G.R.R.D. No. 7651 of 12 August 1912.

126 On the Surat "Union" see evidence of Khandubhai Desai before the Maclagan Cttee. (Patiala.)

bay Central Bank was most unwilling to have such organizations acting as intermediaries between its Bombay office and the cultivator.[127] But in northern India, Ewbank noted after his Maclagan Committee experience, "unions" had become "the cardinal feature of the whole organization." The village societies of the Presidency, Ewbank thought, were "on the whole in a satisfactory condition" and in many ways could "challenge comparison with the best rural societies in any other part of India." But they had "not yet combined for mutual supervision and control"; they relied entirely on the supervision provided by the honorary organizers, and by government and bank officials.

District Banks and Guaranteeing Unions

Here, then, was a summary of the criticisms of the Bombay system implied in the Maclagan Committee Report. Ewbank's proposals for remedying the situation were also based on the Report. They involved the creation of an elaborately tiered structure of financing agencies, each with a definite interest in the agencies above and below. The Maclagan Committee used the terms "primary society," "union," "central bank" (or "district central bank"), and "provincial bank" to describe the various stages in the system which they proposed. In Bombay the ordinary village society or urban society corresponded to the Maclagan Committee's conception of a "primary society," and the Bombay Central Co-operative Bank approached its idea of a "provincial bank." The term "union," which in Bombay had previously been used to describe the rather tentative approaches to "district central banks," was now to be reserved for an institution new to the Presidency, the "guaranteeing union." This was an association of several neighbouring societies, often within a taluka, for the purposes of supervision and, at first, of arranging for its constituent societies mutually to guarantee, in a special way, loans from district central banks and from the "provincial" bank in Bombay.

When Ewbank arrived back in India he still maintained that he regarded as "crucial"[128] the recommendations that societies and district central banks should be represented in the management of

---

[127] Bom. G.R.R.D. No. 6066 of 1 July 1914 and enclosures; Evidence of Reed and Khandubhai Desai, Maclagan Cttee.; *Maclagan Cttee. Rept.*, p. 140.

[128] Ewbank quoted P. R. Cadell, Ch. Sec., Bom., to Sec., R. & A. Dept., G. of I., 12 September 1916. (Poona, Committee on Co-operation.)

the Bank in Bombay, and should be able to purchase shares so that
"within a reasonable time" they could secure a majority of the
votes at a general meeting.[129] Nevertheless, he realized that it
would be "a mistake to alienate the goodwill of the Directors on
the ground that it [the Bank] does not altogether satisfy the abstract ideal of a Provincial Bank as conceived by the committee."[130]
For their part, the directors of the Bank elected the ubiquitous and
hardly "representative" G. K. Devadhar to watch over the interests
of the societies. Arrangements were made to procure shares from
individual shareholders for societies which dealt with the Bank
and wished to have a stake in its ownership. The directors said that
they would admit other "suitable" representatives of the societies
to their Board as the interest of the societies in the share capital
increased. It was not a completely satisfactory arrangement. But
the Bank's directors did keep their word in the coming years. By
1930 seven of the directors represented societies and district central banks and seven individual shareholders. One-third of the
share capital was by that time owned by the societies.[131] Ewbank's
deference to pragmatism in 1916 was thus to some extent justified.

Ewbank wished to press ahead with the organization of central
banks in the districts. The investing classes (as they were called)
of the district towns had grown with the prosperity brought about
by the war. So it was possible, with some energetic canvassing, to
organize three new district banks for the districts of Thana, East
Khandesh, and Dharwar during 1916.[132] District central banks for
Poona and Sholapur were registered in the following year.[133] Societies were given some representation on the directorates of these
banks.

The old Surat Central Banking Union became the Surat District
Co-operative Bank under the new arrangements. In 1916 C. M.
Gandhi took over the chairmanship of this bank, and it began to
widen its interests considerably. C. M. Gandhi—shrewd, good-
natured, though often critical of officialdom—was a leading lawyer
in Surat city. The Moderates in the Congress had entrusted him
with the arrangements for the tumultuous 1907 Congress; his in-

---

129 Recommendations Nos. 167 and 168, *Maclagan Cttee. Rept.*, p. 174.
130 Ewbank quoted Cadell to G. of I., letter cited.
131 Evidence of Bombay Provincial Co-operative Bank, *Bom. Prov. Banking Enquiry Cttee.*, Vol. IV, p. 431.
132 *Rept., 1916–17*, p. 7.
133 *Rept., 1917–18*, p. 20.

creasing involvement in the co-operative movement was probably
to some extent an expression of the fact that he had no real role
to play in the politics of the Home Rule Leagues and of the Gandhian era.[134]

The Poona Central Bank soon became another arena for the
conduct of the political battles of the time. In setting up the Bank,
Ewbank began by getting in touch with such safe men as Devadhar;
M. R. Tarkunde,[135] the Sasvad pleader and honorary organizer; Go-
vindrao Kale, the Chairman of the Hadapsar society; and V. G.
Kale, the Professor of Economics at Fergusson College in Poona.
N. M. Navle, a Mali honorary organizer, was added to the list of
"promoters" to give agriculturists—of one variety, anyway—some
"representation." At a "big public meeting" held in August 1916,
Ewbank outlined the steps to be taken. The Nira Valley societies,
financed by the Bombay Central Co-operative Bank, would "of
course" be excluded from the proposed bank's purview; there
were, however, fifty-six other societies in Poona district which required funds. The Cosmos Bank, an urban co-operative bank in
Poona, was refusing deposits, and there were few branches of
joint-stock banks in the city. Village societies would provide "part"
of the working capital. Provided the bank was "economical about
staff," all should be well.[136] It was somewhat embarrassing for
Ewbank when Gonehalli, who had been put in charge of the organization of the bank, came to light with a promise of a substantial
sum from N. C. Kelkar, Tilak's lieutenant in some matters and the
editor of *Kesari*.[137] But this was in 1917, in the midst of the war. It
was not government policy to spurn the Indian politicians at this
time. At the first general meeting Kelkar was elected chairman of
the Board of Directors.[138] The election of Kelkar was the signal for
an outbreak of what appears to have been pro- and anti-Kelkar
feeling amongst the "quarrelsome Poona residents" who were
shareholders in the Bank. They turned the second annual general
meeting into "a bear-garden," Ewbank reported in 1919; he

[134] For a perceptive comment see the brief essay by V. S. Bhide in "C. M. Gandhi
—Tributes and Reminiscences," *B.C.Q.*, July 1956, p. 4. C. M. Gandhi was Hindu,
not—as are some of those taking the name Gandhi—Parsi.

[135] See Ewbank to Tarkunde, D/O of 6 June 1916, and the following office notes.
(Poona, Poona Central Co-operative Bank—A File [Poona C.C.B.–A].)

[136] Notes of Ewbank's speech at Inaugural Meeting. (Poona, file cited.)

[137] Gonehalli to Ewbank, No. 5416 of 27 August 1917. (Poona, file cited.)

[138] Proceedings of the First General Meeting of the Poona C.C.B., 1 October 1917.
(Poona, file cited.)

claimed that those "agriculturists" who had attended the meeting (they must surely have been few in number) had been disgusted by the whole proceedings. He had had to threaten the cancellation of the Bank's registration.[139] Most district central banks were much milder affairs.

The "guaranteeing union" was recommended by the Maclagan Committee for adoption throughout India, "unless experience elsewhere should belie the results obtained in Burma."[140] A. E. English, the experienced and senior Registrar in Burma, was a member of the Maclagan Committee, and it was obviously his enthusiasm for what was to a large extent his own creation that prompted Ewbank to set about organizing guaranteeing unions on his return to his post in 1916. Guaranteeing unions were virtually untried in India proper, and Ewbank's adoption of them was the greatest concession to theory which he made in his career as Registrar. That an enormous gap separated the "humble village panchayat" from the district central bank, and from the Bombay Central Co-operative Bank, was undeniable.[141] Ewbank had now come to the conclusion that the intermediate organization which would assess the rayats' credit needs and supervise the use of loans had to be formed amongst the rayats themselves. But "mere supervision and advice unweighted by any definite responsibility" were likely to prove "formal and futile."[142] Responsibility, Ewbank felt, had to include financial responsibility if it was to mean anything at all. So, if societies were to be grouped together for the purposes of mutual credit assessment and supervision, they ought to be made to some extent liable for the debts of the societies with which they were associated. A guaranteeing union would have another virtue. It would bring together the "little leaders of the labouring classes," the men with whom the "future hopes of the movement" lay,[143] and give them responsibility beyond the boundaries of their village.

Such was the vision which Ewbank had before him. The guaranteeing unions which he introduced in Bombay rested largely on a system of inter-visiting between the societies by chairmen and committee members. Small fees from the guaranteeing unions' funds

139 *Rept., 1918–19,* p. 19.
140 *Maclagan Cttee. Rept.,* p. 65.
141 *Rept., 1913–14,* p. 6.
142 Ewbank, "Guaranteeing Unions," in *Indian Co-operative Studies,* ed. Ewbank, p. 50.
143 Ibid., p. 61.

were paid for this. Guaranteeing unions were also supposed to employ a "supervisor" to assist the committee members in their duties; since, however, many guaranteeing unions in the Bombay Presidency consisted of only four or five societies, it was difficult for them to afford to pay a supervisor out of the levy of one-half of one per cent on the total working capital of the affiliated societies which they were allowed to make. With the help of the information gathered by these means, the union had to decide to what extent each society would be justified in raising capital. Each society had to accept a lump liability calculated at a rate of between Rs.20 and Rs.100 per member.[144] On the strength of this, the union applied to the central financing institution, through the Registrar, for a lump sum, which it then proceeded to distribute amongst its constituent societies. Until 1920, only the Bombay Central Co-operative Bank, amongst the co-operative banks, was permitted to handle guaranteeing-union business.[145] The maximum credit which the Bank could grant was to the value of six times the total liability of the constituent societies of the union; in practice it was usually lower. As a rule, the credit thus opened was not unrestricted. The guaranteeing union had to state for what purpose each separate loan was required by each society under its control,[146] and the Registrar still had to sanction each loan granted by the Bank in Bombay. There appeared to be sufficient checks and balances. The system was accepted by the Bank. It did not, in 1916, appear to be a system that was fraught with difficulty.

"Fluid Resource" and Famine

The Maclagan Committee had to some extent grown out of the Bombay banking crisis of 1913–14. It was therefore very much concerned with the financial structure and stability of the movement. The 1912 Act had been silent about the maintenance of what the Maclagan Committee called "fluid resource"—assets held in the form of cash or easily realizable investments in order to provide against temporary difficulties caused by such occurrences as famine or an extended period of low prices. With F. W. Johnston, the Government of India Finance Department's representative on the

---

144 Ewbank, *Manual*, 1919 ed., p. 123. In *Indian Co-operative Studies*, p. 56, Ewbank gives the maximum liability as Rs.200 per member.

145 V. L. Mehta, "Supervising Unions," *Prov. Co-op. Conf. Procs., 1922*, Appx. p. xviii.

146 Ewbank, *Manual* (1919 ed.), p. 124.

Committee, the lack of fluid resource perhaps became something of a bogy.[147] Largely at his insistence, the Committee recommended that district central co-operative banks be compelled to maintain as fluid resource "a sum sufficient to meet half the fixed deposits falling due during the ensuing year even if no fresh deposits were received and no repayments of loans made."[148] Primary societies which took deposits and utilized them in their business should, the Committee thought, maintain similar fluid resource.[149] The Committee believed that provincial co-operative banks should maintain fluid cover amounting to at least 75 per cent of their deposits at call.[150] The Bombay Central Co-operative Bank, under its agreement with the Secretary of State, had to maintain fluid resource amounting to 40 per cent of deposits at call.

A small conference of leading officials and non-officials interested in co-operation, which Ewbank convened on his return to India, unanimously resolved that, for Bombay, the standard laid down by the Committee was "impossible." Ewbank and Vaikunth Mehta, who had both been associated with the Committee, agreed that "sudden rushes are impossible and times of scarcity can be foreseen and that, at most, [primary] societies should be required to arrange that three fourths of their deposits should fall due for repayment during the harvest months." Ewbank felt, too, that no standard should be fixed for co-operative banks, either district or urban. A quarterly financial statement from such banks would enable the Registrar to make any necessary enquiries about discrepancies between liabilities and receipts; nothing further was needed. The Government of Bombay agreed with Ewbank's recommendations.[151] And, in the famine year of 1918–19, Ewbank's confidence that the co-operative system could survive times of scarcity was put to the test and, so it seemed, largely justified.

As Ewbank had prophesied, the likelihood of famine was foreseen well in advance. The monsoon of 1918 failed, but while the situation was "still developing" Ewbank laid his plans. He revealed them in a paper read to the Indian Economic Conference held at the end of 1918 and which was published in March 1919.

147 The opinion of Sir Robert Ewbank.
148 *Maclagan Cttee. Rept.*, p. 90.
149 Ibid., p. 51.
150 Ibid., p. 100.
151 See P. R. Cadell, Ch. Sec., Bom., to G. of I., R. & A. Dept., No. 8810 of 12 September 1916, and enclosures.

Obviously, extensions of the time laid down for repayment would have to be granted. District central banks, he thought, might have to carry forward at least three-quarters of their advances. The situation in the primary societies would not be so serious: "In practically all cases the deposits consist of good lying money which the depositors have no intention of withdrawing." Nevertheless, if depositors made insistent demands, they would have to be given their money: "The whole credit of the movement, particularly with outside investors, depends on the punctual repayment of debts." But, "mercifully," continued Ewbank, the position of the Bombay Central Bank would be "very strong." Not only was half its capital non-withdrawable but it commanded "ample fluid resources" amounting to eight lakhs. And with the shrinkage of trade, money should be more, rather than less, easy to obtain in a large city like Bombay.[152]

As it happened, Ewbank was able to note "with great satisfaction" that there were very few withdrawals from societies because of the famine.[153] The district central banks made remarkably good recoveries.[154] But by 1920—possibly partly as a delayed result of the famine—the quarterly statements of some of these banks were causing sufficient concern for the Registrar to issue them with warnings.[155] The later twenties were to demonstrate that for village societies, furthermore, a period of sustained low prices could make much greater demands on "fluid resource" than one season of famine. Even in 1918–19 the Registrar and the Bombay Central Co-operative Bank had to adopt a very conservative policy with regard to loans during the famine period. The finance of the following year's crops, they felt, should have first claim on the movement's resources. All necessary extensions were granted; for the rest, it was decided to "stand fast and conserve resources" until the agricultural season of 1919 should set in. This, Ewbank admitted, "might not seem a very heroic course," but in the absence of experience of famines it seemed the only proper one. He was receiving applications daily from famine-stricken villagers who had to keep family and animals alive until July. All Ewbank could do was advise them

152 Ewbank, "Co-operation and Famine," *B.C.Q.*, March 1919, pp. 196–97.
153 Ewbank, Memorandum No. 5746 of 15 May 1919. (Poona, Original Circulars, II.)
154 *Rept., 1918–19*, p. 5.
155 Rothfeld, Regr., to Govt. No. 3040 of 19 March 1920, encl. Bom. R.D. Order No. 1093 of 1 April 1920.

to apply for *takkavi*. "It may appear to some a lame conclusion," Ewbank wrote, "that after fourteen years of effort, societies in the face of famine can do nothing better than retire into their shells and wait for happier days. Nobody deplores this impotence more than the present writer." But to Ewbank the conclusion seemed "unavoidable" that the co-operative movement, "as at present constituted," would not "for many years be strong enough to tide its members over a famine on its own resources."[156]

At the time of the famine, Ewbank had written of the "very strong" position of the Bombay Central Co-operative Bank. Nevertheless, it has to be said that its position in 1918 was not quite as strong as its directors had hoped when they had framed their agreement with the Secretary of State seven years before. Its debenture capital had been intended to be three times the amount of its share capital; the intention had been to make long-term loans from such capital, mainly for the purpose of "debt redemption." In this respect the Bank had at first attempted to remain within what might be described as the "Wedderburn tradition." But by the time the debentures were on the market, the bank rate in Bombay stood at 6 per cent; the Bank's 4 per cent debentures could not attract ordinary investors. The only sources from which the Bank could raise its debenture capital were the big trust funds and charitable endowments.[157] In 1913, to the apparent surprise of the Government of Bombay as well as the Bank's directors, the Bombay High Court refused to prescribe the Bank's debentures as recognized securities under the Trusts Act and the Charitable Endowments Act, saying that the principal and the interest on the debentures were insufficiently secured.[158] The High Court judges refused at this time to give any further reasons for their decision, but the Government Solicitor surmised that they had rejected the Bank's application because, according to the agreement with the Secretary of State, the guarantee extended only to the repayment of interest on the debentures for forty-one years, and not to the repayment of the principal.[159]

156 Ewbank, "Co-operation and Famine," p. 198.
157 V. Thackersey to Ch. Sec. Bom., No. G.–3–723 of 6 March 1914, encl. Bom. R.D. Order No. 6270 of 8 June 1915.
158 Prothonotary, High Court, to Solicitor, G. of B., No. 367 of 1 July 1913 and No. 495 of 11 September 1913, encl. Bom. G.R.R.D. No. 635 of 21 January 1914.
159 Solicitor, G. of B., to Govt., No. 1005 of 18 July 1913, encl. Bom. G.R. cited.

The Government of India for some years refused to legislate so as to nullify the High Court's decision. In August 1916 the Bank sent what was meant to appear to be an ultimatum: If the Bank's debentures were not recognized as trustee securities, the directors would have to ask the Bombay Government to "take over the whole affairs of the Bank or to entrust them to a Provincial Bank which they may establish on lines which meet with the approval of the Government of India."[160] This letter produced, at last, the desired effect. The Government of India, reversing previous decisions, resolved to support the amending bill put up in the Imperial Legislative Council by Fazulbhoy Currimbhoy, a director of the Bank.[161]

Such a conclusion in the matter, however, though it doubtless provided some comfort in that it removed a long-standing grievance, came too late. Lending rates had risen sharply in Bombay, and it was now impossible to place the 4 per cent debentures in any sector of the market.[162] In all, it would appear, only about six lakhs of the twenty lakhs of debentures whose issue had been authorized by the Secretary of State had been taken up.[163]

The Bank had other long-term deposits. Nevertheless, the realization that its debentures could not be placed on the market for an indefinite number of years did enable the Registrar and the Bank to come to a tacit agreement to give up long-term financing in the meantime. Even in 1913 Ewbank had asserted that there was "a real danger in allowing societies to lock up too large a proportion of their capital in long non-productive loans and it is also unwise to pay off a debt until the sowkar's claim has been verified by some person with a knowledge of law."[164] Debt redemption was obviously hardly a matter for the ordinary village society to manage on its own. By 1916 the directors of the Bombay Central Co-operative Bank agreed. They were chastened by their experiences in the Bombay bank crisis and, perhaps, by the warnings implied in the Maclagan Committee report. They decided to cease granting long-

---

160 F. Currimbhoy to Ch. Sec., Bom., No. S.6–6 of 19 August 1916, encl. Bom. R.D. Order No. 2242 of 23 February 1917.

161 G. of I., R. & A. Dept., to G. of B., No. 151–C of 25 January 1917, encl. Bom. R.D. Order cited.

162 *B.C.Q.*, December 1917, p. 142; also information from Sir Stanley Reed.

163 *Rept., 1914–15*, p. 39. Not many more debentures were taken up after this date: see *Bom. Prov. Banking Enquiry Cttee. Rept.*, p. 89.

164 *Rept., 1912–13*, p. 6.

term loans. It was, they now said, "highly inadvisable" to advance loans for periods longer than twelve months on the basis of share capital and short-term deposits.[165]

The Bank's decision had its repercussions in the societies. The most important was that the societies, now unable to finance either "debt redemption" or long-term "improvements," became even less attractive to the large cultivator.

Gandhi

In retrospect, it might seem that the greatest triumph of the co-operative movement and its official guides in Bombay at this time was to have gained the interest of the man who is now universally known as Mahatma Gandhi. It should not be forgotten, of course, that in the war years Gandhi was still thought of primarily as a supporter of the war effort, the friend of the Bombay Governor, Lord Willingdon, the "philanthropist" working on behalf of the Ahmadabad mill employees.[166] The Co-operative Department, which had some interest in the promotion of co-operative societies amongst both handloom weavers and factory workers, gave demonstrations at Ghandi's *ashram* (spiritual community) at Ahmadabad for three months during 1916–17.[167] Ewbank and Gandhi went together on one occasion to address a meeting of millhands; presumably the aim was the formation of a society amongst them. Gandhi has given us a vivid description of this meeting. "The chawl in which they were living was as filthy as it well could be. Recent rains had made matters worse. . . . There we were, seated on a fairly worn out charpai, surrounded by men, women and children. Mr. Ewbank opened fire on a man who had put himself forward and who wore not a particularly innocent countenance. After he had engaged him and the other people about him in Gujarati conversation, he wanted me to speak to the people." Characteristically, perhaps, Gandhi dwelt on "the moral basis of co-operation" —"owing to the suspicious looks of the man who was first spoken to."[168]

---

[165] Minutes of a Meeting of the Board with the Registrar, 1 February 1916. (Poona, N.C. & C.B.) See also [fragments of] V. Thackersey to Govt. [c.1915–16]. (Poona, file cited.)

[166] Collr., Ahmadabad, *Bom. L. Rev. Admin. Rept., 1917–18*, pt. ii, p. 14.

[167] *Rept., 1916–17*, p. 21.

[168] Gandhi, "The Moral Basis of Co-operation," *Prov. Co-op. Conf. Procs., 1917*, p. 73.

"The Moral Basis of Co-operation" was the subject on which Ewbank invited Gandhi to speak at the Bombay Provincial Co-operative Conference in September 1917. Since the meeting with the Ahmadabad millhands Gandhi had been in Bihar, conducting his Champaran campaign against the indigo planters.[169] He now had practical experience of conditions in the rural areas. And this experience made him appear at the Co-operative Conference a "doubting Thomas before the Jesus of co-operation," as he put it.[170] The "so called agricultural banks" in Champaran had disappointed him. Co-operation conceived simply as an economic movement, he warned, was not a panacea for the country's ills. The moral as well as the economic aspects of the question needed to be emphasized; he was pleased to see that the Maclagan Committee had done this. But his "limited experience" in Champaran had made him question the "accepted opinion" of the money-lender.

I have found him to be not always relentless, not always exacting of the last pie. He sometimes serves his client in many ways or even comes to their rescue in the hour of their distress. My observation is so limited that I dare not draw any conclusions from it, but I respectfully enquire whether it is not possible to make a serious effort to draw out the good in the Mahajan [money-lender] and help him or induce him to throw out the evil in him. May not he be induced to join the army of co-operation, or has experience proved that he is past praying for?[171]

It was this attitude—that the problem was one of somehow reforming the money-lender, not of removing him entirely from the village—which was to characterize a good deal of Congress thought on the problem of rural indebtedness in the twenties. It was, of course, an attitude not very different from that of some British officials.

Mahadev Desai and the Honorary Organizers

Almost certainly, one of those who heard Gandhi speak at the 1917 Provincial Co-operative Conference was his future secretary and intimate biographer, Mahadev Desai.[172] Mahadev had been a

---

169 See *The Story of my Experiments with Truth,* pp. 298 et seq.

170 *Prov. Co-op. Conf. Procs., 1917,* p. 20.

171 "The Moral Basis of Co-operation," ibid., p. 74.

172 He was included in the list of delegates at the Conference as "Inspector, Bombay Central Co-operative Bank," although according to Narahari D. Parikh, *Mahadev Desai's Early Life,* p. 52, he had "left his Bank Inspector's job in August."

close friend of Vaikunth Mehta at Elphinstone College in Bombay; he had found practice as a pleader potentially somewhat unprofitable and so had taken the position of Inspector for the Bank which Vaikunth had offered. He had travelled widely on behalf of the Bank in both Maharashtra and Gujarat, often suffering a good deal of hardship, and had sent detailed if somewhat astringent reports on the societies. When, in 1916, the Gujarat Special Mamlatdar was ordered to the Nira Canal area to assist in making recoveries, Mahadev was left on his own in Gujarat. It was in this position that the hardworking, scrupulously honest Mahadev began to run foul of some of the honorary organizers. He became convinced that the "whole question" of honorary organizers needed to be reconsidered. Men should be appointed who had "a thorough knowledge of co-operative principles and of local conditions . . . men who are keenly alive to a consciousness that they are appointed, above all, to serve the people." If such men were not forthcoming, Mahadev thought, the only alternative was to have paid inspectors, three or four to a district, "exercising the closest scrutiny in matters of minute detail."[173] Now honorary organizers were officially government servants, although they were unpaid. Applications for loans from the Bank were normally sent through honorary organizers as representatives of the government. On one occasion, however, Mahadev considered that an honorary organizer had withheld a society's loan application without sufficient cause; he forwarded an application direct to the Bank. The honorary organizer protested to Ewbank, Ewbank accepted Mahadev's explanation;[174] the incident, however, appears to have been one factor which brought about Mahadev's decision to leave the Bank.[175] When Gandhi asked Mahadev to join him, one of the reasons for his request was, according to Mahadev: "I would need your knowledge of the Co-operative Movement. . . . We have to free that department from its defects."[176]

---

173 M[ahadev]. H. Desai, "Co-operation in Gujerat," *B.C.Q.*, June 1917, p. 29.

174 V. L. Mehta, quoted Parikh, *Mahadev Desai's Early Life*, pp. 41–42. Mehta also had this to say about his friend: "I shall ever remain indebted to Mahadev for having left a stamp of honesty, fearlessness and spirit of service on the newly started institution. Mahadev became acquainted for the first time with the social and economic problems of villages through his work in the Bank. . . . I cannot say whether Mahadev was more of a poet than a philosopher, but I could definitely notice the hidden poet in the descriptions he gave in his letters."

175 See Ramnikrai N. Mehta, "Rural Co-operative Credit in Bombay State," *B.C.Q.*, April 1954, p. 30.

176 Parikh, *Mahadev Desai's Early Life*, p. 54.

The Registrar was certainly increasingly conscious that the honorary organizers had their defects as well as their virtues. In January 1918 the list of honorary organizers was revised and reclassified so that an honorary organizer's position on it depended more on the value of the work that he did for the movement than on what had been termed his "social standing." Only three honorary organizers were now placed in the "first class"; they were Malji, Sane, and R. G. Naik, who were given the title of Divisional Honorary Organizer for the Northern, Central, and Southern Divisions respectively. "District Honorary Organizers" were placed in the second class for the vital travelling allowance. Then came a third group to be known as Assistant Honorary Organizers. These men were, on the whole, new to the work of honorary organizer; they all came from the rural areas and were usually chairmen of successful societies.

A good many of the old honorary organizers did not appear on the new list. Some had done little work for some time; some, Ewbank reported, were unwilling to work—and travel—in the second class after having been in the first class.[177] One of these was G. K. Chitale of Ahmadnagar. Looking back in 1933, he claimed that his decision had been taken because he had felt that it was "not consistent with the self respect of honorary organizers" to draw allowances "on the meagre scale allowed."[178] The effect of the resignations and deletions in the Deccan was that the number of Brahman honorary organizers was reduced, although this does not appear to have been a result specifically desired at this stage.[179] The new Assistant Honorary Organizers were, however, mainly from the "agriculturist" castes: Patidars, Marathas, and Lingayats. They were at first given most of the powers of the old honorary organizers, including powers of distributing money from the Bombay Central Co-operative Bank to societies "under their charge." But, when an Assistant Honorary Organizer died in the influenza epidemic of 1918 and defalcations came to light, Ewbank told the Divisional Honorary Organizers that he felt that he should forbid the Assist-

[177] Ewbank to Govt., No. 3565 of 6 April 1918, encl. Bom. R.D. Order No. 7073 of 4 July 1918.

[178] "Proceedings of the Co-operative Round Table Conference, 1933." (Poona, Typescript.)

[179] For the discussion which took place before the reorganization occurred, see Bom. R.D. Order No. 759/51–Confl. of 24 January 1918, and enclosures. (I.O.R., Bom. L. Rev. Procs., Confl. Vol. 37.) There is no mention of the caste factor.

ant Honorary Organizers to undertake this duty in future.[180] Sane
replied speedily, expressing his agreement.[181] Malji in Gujarat also
replied promptly; he thought that the incident showed that in
some instances the new Assistant Honorary Organizers did not
"own sufficient property."[182]

A Co-operative "Intelligentsia"

It was not merely *mofussil* honorary organizers who had to be
thought of as "leading non-officials" in the years from about 1916.
Shareholders in the Bombay Central Bank not unnaturally wished
to increase their say in the use of the funds which to a considerable
extent they provided for the movement. But more important than
the shareholders were a group of younger Bombay men. A few had
been drawn into the movement as a result of their personal friendship with Vaikunth Mehta: like Mahadev Desai, such men could
easily develop "nationalist" proclivities. Others were leaders of
"middle-class" urban co-operative banks and housing societies in
the city of Bombay: organizations for clerks and small businessmen, on the whole from the higher castes. One thinks especially of
S. S. Talmaki of the vigorous Sarasvat Brahman community, a
pioneer first in co-operative banking and then in the building and
letting of blocks of tenements on a "co-partnership" basis. Still
other members of the new co-operative "intelligentsia" were welfare workers in the Bombay mills, who saw co-operation as providing a framework for "loan societies." One thinks here of the
highly articulate N. M. Joshi of the Servants of India Society, at
this stage setting out on a distinguished career as a "labour leader"
—albeit as a labour leader from the outside, in the normal, indeed
perhaps in those days the inevitable, paternalistic Indian way. Such
Bombay men, then, though from somewhat diverse backgrounds,
were beginning to form themselves into an intelligent and sometimes impatient group of commentators on co-operative matters.[183]

---

[180] Ewbank, Memo to Divisional Honorary Organizers and Assistant Registrars,
No. 94 of 7 January 1919. (Poona, Original Circulars, II.)

[181] Sane to Ewbank No. 18 of 10 January 1919. (Poona, file cited.)

[182] Malji to Ewbank No. 36 of 10 January 1919. (Poona, file cited.)

[183] Since this study is concerned primarily with rural credit, developments in the
urban co-operative sphere are discussed only when they impinge on the activities
of rural co-operatives. But the Bombay urban co-operative banks and loan societies,
and especially the housing societies, deserve a study on their own. A start may be
made with two papers in *Indian Co-operative Studies,* ed. R. B. Ewbank (1920):
G. K. Devdhar and N. M. Joshi, "Co-operation amongst Factory Workers," and S. S.

It was this group which provided the main opposition to the new Co-operative Societies Rules which Ewbank considered necessary in the light of the Maclagan Committee's recommendations. He promulgated these, in draft form, in June 1917.[184] The new rules, the Bombay men considered, increased the power of the Registrar quite unnecessarily. A protest meeting was held under the auspices of the Central Bank. The draft rule which raised the most vehement objections was one which read: "No society, by itself or by the Committee or any officer, may take any action which would involve the society in the discussion or propagation of controversial opinions of a political or religious character, and the Registrar may prohibit any action, or rescind any resolution which, in his opinion, is of such tendency." The Bombay representation stated that the co-operative movement could not be entirely divorced from the life of the nation. Moreover, it was claimed, the rule might have the effect of turning away from the movement prominent co-operators who took part in politics.[185] There had been, in fact, virtually no evidence in the Bombay Presidency of co-operative societies being used for political ends, but such activities did occasionally occur in Bengal, and Ewbank believed that it was desirable to have such a rule "in reserve." Nevertheless, he agreed to modify the proposed rule so that, like the equivalent Punjab rule, it did not apply to "the Committee or any officer" but only to the society as a whole.[186]

Another proposed rule gave the Collector the right to visit all co-operative societies in his district. The Bombay meeting objected to this, too. Ewbank complained that "Bombay people . . . seem to draw their distorted views of the terror inspired by the Collector from the vapourings of the extremist press." But he thought that there was no real need for the rule from the point of view of co-operation as such, and so he withdrew it.[187]

Talmaki, "Co-operation and the Housing Problem." Vaikunth Mehta's paper in the same symposium, "Training and Propaganda," is also interesting: here, on p. 112, two years after the Russian Revolution, the word *intelligentsia* is used apparently for the first time in co-operative writings in Bombay. On N. M. Joshi as a trade union leader, see Morris, *The Emergence of an Industrial Labor Force in India*, p. 183.

[184] For these draft Rules, see *B.C.Q.*, September 1917, pp. 89–91.

[185] Fazulbhoy Currimbhoy to Ch. Sec., Bom., No.G7/562 of 28 July 1917. (Poona, 36, IX.)

[186] Ewbank to D.A. No. 1310 of 31 October 1917 encl. Bom. R.D. Order No. 6952 of 2 July 1918.

[187] Ibid.

"The vapourings of the extremist press": the phrase was becoming a favourite one amongst British officials. Almost inevitably, perhaps, Ewbank regarded the new nationalism with some disdain. Yet he had given way to a considerable extent over the draft rules, and he soon decided, rather than possibly lose altogether the sympathy of the embarrassing group of "educated young men in Bombay,"[188] to try to find outlets for them in the co-operative movement. He encouraged this vocal and highly literate group to produce a quarterly periodical, which was named the *Bombay Co-operative Quarterly*. At first it was edited by N. M. Joshi, but S. S. Talmaki and Vaikunth Mehta soon took over most of the editorial work. The first issue appeared in June 1917, complete with a "message" from "C.S.C."—obviously Campbell. ("Let us . . . proceed with light hearts and joyful countenance to the Ideal we originally had in view.")[189] The standard maintained by the *Quarterly* over the years was high. Usually one can recognize the hand of Vaikunth Mehta behind the editorial contributions—perceptive, well-written assessments of the co-operative situation in Bombay and in India as a whole. The *Bombay Co-operative Quarterly* rapidly became a national co-operative journal for India.

A further step in the working out of Ewbank's ideas about the role of the Bombay young men was taken in the founding of the Bombay Central Co-operative Institute. It was to some extent modelled on Horace Plunkett's Irish Agricultural Organization Society, though Ewbank saw "no harm in working out our own scheme for ourselves without paying too much attention to foreign models."[190] Ewbank did not at first intend the Institute to do anything more than provide "propaganda" and, in Bombay city only, some supervision.[191] But in fact Ewbank had set out on a somewhat hazardous path. F. R. Hemingway, the Madras Registrar, advised caution; otherwise Ewbank might find that he had placed control of the whole movement in the hands of "an unofficial autocracy that will be quite as unrepresentative and far less responsible than the official department." On the other hand, if real power were not given to the Institute, Ewbank would find that it would "lan-

188 Ewbank to A. E. Mathias, Regr., Central Provinces, D/O of 25 April 1918. (Poona, Bombay Provincial Co-operative Institute [B.P.C.I.], III.)
189 *B.C.Q.*, June 1917, p. 31.
190 Ewbank, Note, undated (c. 1917). (Poona, B.P.C.I., III.)
191 See "Prospectus." (Poona, file cited.)

guish in the same sort of way that our 'Provincial Union' has." This body had been set up in Madras city in 1914 for propagandist purposes only. "It now does no really useful work," Hemingway wrote, "and is in the hands of a few amiable, mildly enthusiastic men in Madras with no experience of the mofussil."[192]

As Hemingway had virtually prophesied, the Institute, given a taste of power in Bombay city, wanted a great deal more elsewhere. On two successive days in December 1919 the nationalist *Bombay Chronicle* devoted editorials to the Institute's affairs. The chief complaint of the *Chronicle* was that the Institute had no concern with "the main functions of organization, supervision and audit." "It was presumed," the paper said, "that the Institute, when started, would be entrusted with certain questions relating to the development of non-credit co-operation and would be recognized as the representative association of co-operators in the Presidency."[193] The goal of "absolute self-management in internal affairs" should always be kept in mind in the co-operative movement. "That Ideal government set before themselves when the movement was first introduced into this country, but in many a province it has been well nigh forgotten."[194] Instead, control was still centred in "the Registrar's department and its ornamental adjunct, the Honorary Organizers."[195] Almost certainly the editorial was not written by the *Chronicle*'s vitriolic editor, B. G. Horniman. It was probably written by Sayed Abdullah Brelvi, a member of the paper's editorial staff, later to become its editor.[196] Brelvi, like Mahadev Desai, was a close friend of Vaikunth Mehta. He was, in fact, virtually a member of the Lalubhai Samaldas household; Motilal Nehru called Brelvi "the aopted son of Sir Lalubhai."[197] The editorials in the *Bombay Chronicle*, therefore, almost certainly represented the opinions of the powerful Lalubhai Samaldas Mehta family.

Ewbank, for his part, was ready to say that "the goal of our policy

---

[192] F. R. Hemingway to Ewbank, D/O (Confl.) of 19 March 1918. (Poona, file cited.)
[193] *Bombay Chronicle*, 22 December 1919.
[194] Ibid., 21 December 1919.
[195] Ibid., 22 December 1919.
[196] See M. R. Jayakar, *The Story of my Life*, Vol. I, *1873–1922*, pp. 237–47, for a description of the *Bombay Chronicle*'s inner workings at this time.
[197] Natarajan, *Lalubhai Samaldas*, p. 56. G. L. Mehta, another son of Lalubhai, was assistant editor of the *Bombay Chronicle*, 1923–25. He was manager of one of Lalubhai's enterprises, the Scindia Steam Navigation Company, 1928–47, and Indian Ambassador to the United States, 1952–58.

is to restrict official control gradually to the functions definitely
assigned to the official staff in the Co-operative Societies Act and to
transfer all initiative, training, finance and development to co-
operators themselves as rapidly as efficient, representative and
democratic co-operative institutions can be created."[198] And, indeed (to quote the words of one of his subordinates), Ewbank "en-
listed the co-operation of non-officials to an extent unequalled in
India."[199] As early as 1913, furthermore, he had been speaking of
"democratizing" credit as well as cheapening it.[200] About this time
the Government of India had also begun to use the phrase "democratization of credit";[201] it had been almost forgotten since
Nicholson's time, but a revival of concern about the implementa-
tion of the ideals of "local self-government"[202] appears to have
spread to the co-operative sphere. The co-operative movement was
beginning to be thought of not only as providing an opportunity
for the growth of the Victorian virtue of "self-help," but also as a
training ground for political democracy. The Montagu declaration
of 1917 on the political future of India strengthened this notion:
the goal of the British in India was to be eventual "responsible government" for that country. Ewbank believed that he was fully within the spirit of such government policy when he stated that "the
alternative to expert official control is not control by non-official
amateurs, however philanthropic, but self-control." The Bombay
men did not agree, however. "The Central Co-operative Institute,"
Ewbank wrote towards the end of his period as Registrar, "can do
valuable propagandist and training work but it is not truly representative of the movement as a whole and is not in my opinion
suited at present for taking over any administrative work."[203]

By 1918 Ewbank also strongly opposed any extension of the control over the movement which was exercised by the district central
banks. In the United Provinces and the Central Provinces, as Ewbank had noted in 1915, the policy had been to make the district

198 Ewbank to Govt. No. 6318 of 22 May 1919, encl. Bom. R.D. Order No. 14140
of 3 December 1919.
199 D. A. Shah, Obituary Notice of Sir Janardan Madan, *B.C.Q.*, April 1957, p. 261.
200 *Rept., 1912–13*, p. 7.
201 India G.R., R. & A. Dept. (L. Rev.), No.12–287–1 of 17 June 1914. (Published
in pamphlet form.)
202 See the discussion of the Government of India's Local Self-Government Resolution of 1915 in Tinker, *The Foundations of Local Self-Government*, p. 97.
203 Ewbank to Govt. No. 6318 of 22 May 1919, encl. Bom. R.D. Order cited.

central banks not only the balancing and lending organizations of the movement but also the main supervising agencies. Ewbank now condemned such arrangements. "The small knot of professional gentlemen and landowners at headquarters,"[204] who in practice ran these banks, were too distant from the village societies to be able to supervise them directly. In his Report for 1918 Ewbank insisted on the need to keep the village society firmly in mind. "The object for the benefit of which the whole fabric has been constructed is the village society."[205] Ewbank now placed his faith firmly in the men thrown up by the village societies, the village leaders who had been brought together in the guaranteeing unions. The guaranteeing union was to be, in fact, "the axis around which co-operative administration revolves."[206] The guaranteeing unions, rather than the urban intelligentsia, the philanthropic amateurs, were to provide that means of "self-control," that truly democratic scheme of administration which Ewbank, after his fashion, undoubtedly desired.

"The Little Leaders of the Labouring Classes"

Ewbank's long career as Registrar came to an end in January 1920 with his appointment as Deputy Secretary to the Government of India in the Commerce and Industry Department.[207] He was given a general oversight over co-operation in India as part of his duties.

If we take the statistics furnished in March 1912 and in March 1920 as roughly representative of the state of the movement in Bombay at the beginning and end of Ewbank's term as Registrar, we may understand, at least to some extent, the nature of the growth which took place during this period. The number of rural societies had risen from 284 to 2,091. The average membership per rural society had increased from 45 to 75 and the average working capital per member from Rs.38 to Rs.71. In Dharwar district, the best so far as numbers were concerned, about a third of the villages had societies.[208] Co-operation, the *Bombay Chronicle* conceded,

---

[204] Ewbank, "Guaranteeing Unions," in *Indian Co-operative Studies*, ed. Ewbank, p. 51.

[205] *Rept., 1917–18*, p. 3.

[206] Ewbank, "The True Sphere of Central Banks," *B.C.Q.*, September 1918, p. 110.

[207] See *Rept., 1919–20*, p. 1.

[208] See Table II, p. 238.

was no longer merely "a fad and a craze promoted by Government"; in spite of the *Chronicle*'s disagreements with Ewbank, there would be "general regret at his going."[209] The *Chronicle* did not compliment Englishmen unnecessarily.

Yet today it is possible to see that the co-operative movement in Bombay was still in a somewhat precarious position in 1920. Ewbank had built up a force of honorary organizers and then proceeded to disband large sections of it. He had seen the Bombay Central Co-operative Bank grow from its infancy, yet, in spite of his friendship with Vaikunth Mehta, there was sometimes in his dealings with the Bank a distrust of Bombay "big business." He had organized the Institute, but he had drawn back from giving that organization real power. The distrust which Ewbank displayed of the urban elite may frequently have been justified. Yet to that elite such distrust was probably just another sign of unreasonable British dislike of "these educated classes."[210] And there were now dynamic new political ideologies which could easily draw the urban elite away from co-operative activity altogether.

Ewbank's fundamental sympathies—and, of course, those of Campbell and many other British officials of the time—were with the villager. The villager was conceived to be someone slow and simple, yet hardy and in most ways basically honest. It was with the villager, Ewbank felt, that the "future hopes of the movement" lay. The guaranteeing union, made up of the "little leaders of the labouring classes," was eventually to be the "axis" around which the movement revolved. In the meantime, official control at the top had to remain. The co-operative movement in Bombay at this time reflected to a remarkable degree, in fact, the attitudes of the British to the whole problem of the transfer of power. Democracy must start from the bottom; "unrepresentative" elites were to be distrusted.[211]

But suppose that in the co-operative sphere guaranteeing unions proved to be basically unworkable. In that case, was the only al-

209 *Bombay Chronicle*, 29 January 1920.

210 Cf. Nirad C. Chaudhuri, "Passage to and from India," *Encounter*, Vol. II, No. 6 (June 1954), p. 23.

211 Cf. Percival Spear, "From Colonial to Sovereign Status—Some Problems of Transition with Special Reference to India," *Journal of Asian Studies*, Vol. XVII, No. 4 (August 1958).

ternative to co-operative democracy (if there was not to be control by townsmen and dilettante amateurs) three or four paid inspectors, representing either government or a bank, to each district? In other words, were Mahadev Desai's conclusions on the co-operative movement basically correct?

IV

"The Peak"? 1920-1923

Otto Rothfeld

Otto Rothfeld had reached the Senior Collector's grade as Collector of East Khandesh.[1] He was a little too unorthodox in his ideas and his methods to be able to look forward to a Commissionership, and probably would have retired somewhat earlier than he did if he had not been offered the position of Registrar of Co-operative Societies.[2] The post, which he took up in 1920, gave this "brilliant, versatile, impetuous and impatient officer"[3] full scope for his abilities. "The Rothfeld regime," one who followed him as Registrar has written, "represented, perhaps, the peak which the Co-operative Idea attained in official estimation, and almost everything that he asked for or ordered was given and carried out without question."[4]

But although Rothfeld usually had his way, he was distrusted in some official circles. One Collector wrote sarcastically of "the Germanized uniform scheme" which had grown up under Rothfeld's administration of the Co-operative Department;[5] there was an element of personal rancour here, as Rothfeld, of part Hungarian extraction and with relatives in Hungary, had been interned for a brief period during the war.[6]

Rothfeld had spent some time in the Political Service before he became Collector of East Khandesh and had had time to write sev-

[1] Otto Rothfeld: Asst. Collr. and Asst. Political Agent, 1899–1916; Collr., 1916; Regr. Co-op. Socs., 1920; retd., 1923.
[2] See Rothfeld's speech, *Prov. Co-op. Conf. Procs., 1923*, p. 74.
[3] D. A. Shah, Obituary Notice of Sir Janardan Madan, *B.C.Q.*, April 1957, p. 261.
[4] V. S. Bhide, Obituary Notice of Professor H. L. Kaji, *B.C.Q.*, January 1953, p. 108.
[5] [Copy of] A. H. A. Simcox, Collr., Nasik, to Commr., C.D., D/O of 9 June 1921. (Poona, T.A.G.7.)
[6] Information from the late Shri Vaikunth Mehta.

eral reasonably successful evocations of the Indian scene.[7] Though
he toured quite extensively as Registrar—for about two hundred
days a year, in fact—one has the feeling that his comparatively
leisured life continued. His tours took him rather frequently to
those parts—Gujarat and Khandesh—which he knew well. His
annual reports were apparently tossed off in a few days with the
aid of a shorthand typist, instead of being painstakingly written
and circulated to the Assistant Registrars for comment before pub-
lication.[8] A Personal Assistant did most of the everyday work that
had previously been done by the Registrar, and many of the Registrar's powers had been delegated to the increasing number of Assistant Registrars. In some ways, then, Rothfeld represented the new
type of departmental administrator. His task, as he conceived it,
was to have the ideas; it was largely up to others to look after the
minutiae of co-operative administration. Rothfeld "saw and
planned almost fifty years ahead, leaving little unthought and un-
touched," one of Rothfeld's subordinates has written.[9] This is
perhaps an exaggeration; nevertheless, it is true that many of the
opinions which Rothfeld held are, on the face of it, similar to
those held by some in India today.

Before he took up his position as Registrar he was sent on a six-
week deputation to France and Italy to study co-operation there—
the Maclagan Committee had recommended that such experience
should form, if possible, part of the training of Registrars.[10] What
he saw there, he claimed in his report on his deputation, compelled
him "slowly to abandon the prepossessions I had in favour of non-
intervention" by the state in co-operative matters.[11] Rothfeld realized, at least partially, where the new developments which he
fostered might lead. It was hardly possible, he thought, for producers' and consumers' societies to develop "without bringing into
question long accepted opinions about property and individual
rights of every kind."[12] The co-operative movement, Rothfeld told
the Provincial Co-operative Conference in 1923, "stands for the

[7] *Indian Dust* (Oxford, 1909); *Life and its Puppets* (Oxford, 1910); *With Pen and Rifle in Kishtwar* (Bombay, 1918); *Women of India* (London, 1920). See also *Umar Khayayam and His Age* (Bombay, 1922).
[8] Information from Shri D. A. Shah.
[9] Shah, Madan Obituary cited.
[10] *Maclagan Cttee. Rept.*, p. 56.
[11] Rothfeld, *Impressions of the Co-operative Movement in France and Italy*, p. 3.
[12] Rothfeld, review of L. Smith-Gordon and C. O'Brien, *Co-operation in Many Lands*, Vol. I, in *B.C.Q.*, June 1920, p. 35.

control of all business in the interest of the people." It stood "as a barrier to prevent the onrush of the evils which have in other countries followed in the wake of the capitalist movement." He spoke quite savagely about the evidence of certain businessmen before the Tariff Committee of 1923—of "those who control the means of production" and who wished "to impose additional taxes on the peasant."[13] One instance stands out in which it might be said that Rothfeld was acting from "socialist" motives. In 1922 the Bombay Central Co-operative Bank submitted a list of banking institutions with which it desired to make deposits. One was the Peninsular and Oriental Banking Corporation, an organization obviously connected with the shipping line of that name. Rothfeld, writing to Government, recommended that deposits with the Bank be not permitted: the Corporation was, he claimed, "a striking example of a bank devoted to the interests of a capitalist concern peculiarly opposed to the ideals underlying co-operation." The Bombay Government were not impressed by such arguments, however.[14]

Rothfeld's "socialism" was chiefly the result of his capacity to think the co-operative idea through to its "logical conclusions." His practical achievement was necessarily a good deal more limited than the scope of his thought.

Dyarchy

After Rothfeld had been Registrar for a few months the Montagu-Chelmsford reforms came into effect in Bombay. Co-operation became a "transferred" subject under an Indian Minister.[15] The first Minister of Agriculture and Co-operation was Chunilal Mehta. Chunilal resigned as Chairman of the Board of the Bombay Central Co-operative Bank when he became the Minister; he was therefore obviously very familiar with the problems of co-operation. He belonged to that group of Liberals who assumed office in most provinces while Congress refused to contest the Council seats, and who have been said to have "provided the

13 *Prov. Co-op. Conf. Procs., 1923,* pp. 16–17.
14 Rothfeld to Govt. No. B.P.B./13 of 13 November 1922, encl. Bom. G.R.R.D. No. 6720 of 28 March 1914.
15 Under the Government of India Act of 1919, which brought into being at the provincial level the system which Lionel Curtis called "dyarchy," ministers responsible to the provincial legislative councils were to have charge of certain aspects of government—in general the "nation-building" departments. Revenue and "law and order" matters, amongst others, were left in the hands of men responsible directly to the provincial governors.

most distinguished and forceful ministers of the whole Dyarchy period."[16] His philosophy was perhaps somewhat paternalistic. Certainly he felt that the initiative in the Indian situation had to come from above rather than from below: "If we do desire to have progress, let us not consider what will be acceptable or what will not be acceptable to most people. Let us first see what is good—what is for the good—for the agriculturists and the co-operators in the Presidency and then see what would be the best way of carrying it out according to the wishes of the people."[17] The Liberals, it has been pointed out often enough, "did not believe in mass contact."[18]

Rothfeld was the first Registrar to be completely independent of the Director of Agriculture. But Rothfeld as Registrar, Mann as Director of Agriculture, and Chunilal Mehta as Minister worked together as a vigorous trio; the harmonizing influence between the stern Director and the somewhat flamboyant Registrar was usually the Minister.[19] During the years of their administration it certainly appeared that "rural development" had been freed from the trammels of official tardiness and even, for a time, from the trammels of official parsimony.

Yet, as Rothfeld pointed out to the Royal Commission on Agriculture, "the Secretariat" still came between the departmental administration and the Minister of a transferred subject. Rothfeld did not object to his proposals being submitted to the Finance Department: "No head of a department in this or in any other country could possibly object to his proposals, as far as they involve finance, being subject to a Finance Department." But he did object to the continuing Revenue Department surveillance of co-operative affairs:

The Registrar, let us say, or the Director brings up to the Minister certain proposals for a change in policy for discussion and approval. He goes up to him as the permanent head of a department naturally would in any country. The Minister approves of the proposals. They are then drawn up in detail. They are then submitted through the

---

16 Tinker, *The Foundations of Local Self-Government in India, Pakistan, and Burma*, p. 130.

17 *Prov. Co-op. Conf. Procs., 1922,* p. 104.

18 B. R. Ambedkar, *Ranade, Gandhi and Jinnah,* p. 82.

19 Cf. Mann, when a "Development Commissioner" was suggested, following a Punjab example, in order to bring together the activities of the Co-operative and Agriculture Departments: "my Development Commissioner is the Minister." *Regrs.' Conf. Procs., 1926,* p. 54. Chunilal Mehta by this time had ceased to be Minister, however.

Revenue Secretary, and, in conformity with the old Secretariat system, the Revenue Secretary naturally thinks himself entitled not merely to criticise the form of the proposals and to see that they are put up in a correct form, but also to start revising the matter of the proposals already approved by the Minister.[20]

Rothfeld failed to mention in this account that under the reforms he himself was not purely an administrative head. He was also a member of the Legislative Council. His duties there took up a good deal of his time;[21] one suspects, however, that the verbal duels of the Council Chamber were enjoyable to a man of his temperament. It should also be added that Chunilal Mehta's position as Minister was not as powerful as it might have been if Lloyd,[22] the Governor, had called joint meetings of ministers. Chimanlal Setalvad, the first Indian member of the "reserved" half of the administration, claimed that under Lloyd the ministers were "reduced to shadows."[23] Responsibilities and powers, then, were as yet vaguely defined, both in law and by precedent.

Congress, Brahmans, and Non-Brahmans

For a time, of course, during the Non-Co-operation campaign of 1920–22, all those who participated in the reforms scheme, and indeed British government in India itself, were under strong attack from the Congress. Although at the end of his period as Registrar and in retirement[24] Rothfeld professed himself to be strongly in favour of the rapid transfer of political power to India hands—he appears to have expected Indian self-government by about 1930[25]—he was opposed to the brand of politics represented by Gandhi and the Congress in the early twenties. In his 1921 Report, Rothfeld noted that he had spent a good deal of time in Gujarat, inspecting the societies there, because, he claimed, they were affected by "political conditions."[26] There is, in fact, no conclusive

[20] *Royal Commission on Agriculture*, Vol. II, pt. i, *Bombay Evidence*, pp. 166–67. Cf. *Indian Statutory Commission*, Vol. VII, *Memorandum submitted by the Government of Bombay*, pp. 292–98.

[21] *Rept., 1922–23*, p. 3.

[22] Sir George Lloyd: M.P. (Unionist) 1910–18; Govr., Bom., 1918–23; M.P., 1924–25; High Commissioner for Egypt and Sudan, 1925–29; Baron, 1925.

[23] *Bombay Chronicle*, 22 October 1924. See also *Indian Statutory Commission*, Vol. cited, p. 5.

[24] See *Prov. Co-op. Conf. Procs., 1923*, p. 74, and *Prov. Co-op. Conf. Procs., 1926*, p. 97.

[25] Ibid.

[26] *Rept., 1920–21*, p. 1.

evidence available to show that cultivators at this time refused to pay debts owing to co-operative societies because they considered the societies to be British-sponsored. It is true, however, that in 1920–21 arrears in Surat district increased from Rs.22,000 to Rs.1,14,300.[27] Rothfeld and the Government of Bombay traced some of this increasing "contempt for the law" to the attitudes to which, they thought, the Non-Co-operation campaign gave rise.[28]

In fact, as we shall see, there were other reasons for the malaise of the co-operative movement in parts of Gujarat. And Non-Co-operation in the Bombay Presidency at this time was largely confined to Gujarat. In the Deccan and in the Karnatak the situation was greatly complicated by the growing importance of rivalry between Brahman and non-Brahman castes. In 1875, it will be remembered, Maharashtrian Brahmans had on the whole been left alone at the time of the Deccan Riots. Nevertheless, the growing "politicization" of life in the Deccan, and the increasing emphasis on the "rights" of special groups, especially at the time of the introduction of the Montford reforms, exacerbated such tensions as there were between Brahmans and non-Brahmans in the area.[29] In 1911–12, furthermore, Shahu Chhatrapati, Maharajah of the Deccan State of Kolhapur, and a Maratha, had set about reviving the Satya Shodhak Samaj (Truth Seeking Society), a non-Brahman organization which had been founded by a Mali, Jotirao Phule, in 1873, but which had been moribund since the beginning of the century, if not earlier.[30] In this activity the Maharajah had the assistance of his Chief Revenue Officer, Bhaskarrao Vithoba Jadhav, who as early as 1907 had organized what was termed the Maratha Educational Conference. In 1919, however, Jadhav fell out of favour in Kolhapur. He transferred his activities in organizing the Satya Shodhak Samaj to nearby British districts, especially Satara.[31] Within a year or two, it would appear, he was also organizing co-operative societies. In the Karnatak, rivalry between Brahmans

27 Ibid., p. 8.

28 Bom. G.R.R.D. No. P.53 of 8 December 1921.

29 For a general discussion of Brahman–non-Brahman tension in Bombay see *Indian Statutory Commission*, Vol. cited, pp. 226–30; also pp. 437–80, passim.

30 A. B. Latthe, *Memoirs of His Highness Shri Shahu Chhatrapati, Maharaja of Kolhapur*, II, 376–77.

31 Maureen L. P. Patterson, "A Preliminary Study of the Brahman versus Non-Brahman Conflict in Maharastra" (M.A. Diss., University of Pennsylvania, 1952) p. 101. See also Patterson, "Caste and Political Leadership in Maharashtra," *Economic Weekly*, 25 September 1954.

and non-Brahmans by this time may well have become more in-
tense than in most parts of the Deccan,[32] although it is not so well
documented. The conflict in the Karnatak was given a peculiar
twist by the fact that the Lingayats, who in any case professed to
stand apart from the Hindu community, spoke Kanarese, whereas
the Brahmans often had Marathi as their native tongue.

In the days of the Home Rule Leagues, and in the first year or so
of the political campaigns of 1919–22—that is, while the "national
movement" in the Deccan and the Karnatak appeared to be both
powerful and Brahman-dominated—British officials might well
have been tempted to use the co-operative movement to foster political aims. Certainly co-operatives appear to have been used for
such purposes in Bengal in the twenties.[33] There was perhaps a hint
of the possibilities in Bombay in a report by E. L. Moysey, Collector of Satara and a man with some experience of co-operative societies, since he had acted as Registrar for a time in 1915. As he
surveyed the membership of recently founded co-operative societies in his district he exclaimed: "The Non Co-operation movement will, I believe, find no foothold among these fine leaders of a
sturdy peasantry."[34] This was a time, after all, when British officials
in the Deccan, with Moysey prominent amongst them, were engaged in organizing "Loyalty Leagues," "Leagues of Peace and
Progress," and "Patels' Associations" amongst the Marathas.[35] In
the Karnatak, a British official was pleased to report in 1919 that
the Lingayats, and the local Marathas also, were beginning to
think that "Home Rule" would be "the Rule of a Brahmin Oli-
garchy."[36]

There is not sufficient evidence to enable us to come to a definite
conclusion as to the degree of association, if any, between a man
such as Moysey and a man such as Jadhav in the promotion of co-
operative societies in Satara district at this time. But it needs to be

[32] The opinion of the Government of Bombay in their submission to the Indian
Statutory Commission. See *Indian Statutory Commission,* Vol. cited, p. 476. Some
useful hints on the Brahman–non-Brahman situation in the Karnatak are contained
in A. T. Tansley, "The Early Non-Brahmin Movement and 1917," unpublished
working paper, Department of History, University of Western Australia, 1968.

[33] J. H. Broomfield, *Elite Conflict in a Plural Society: Twentieth Century Bengal,*
p. 272.

[34] Moysey, quoted *Bom. L. Rev. Admin. Rept., 1919–20,* p. 28.

[35] See Commr., S.D., *Bom. L. Rev. Admin. Rept., 1918–19,* p. 30; Commr., C.D., *Bom.
L. Rev. Admin. Rept., 1920–21,* p. 30.

[36] Commr., S.D., *Bom. L. Rev. Admin. Rept., 1918–19,* p. 30.

noted that irrigation had recently made a considerable difference to the south of Satara district; the times were now a good deal more propitious for co-operatives than they had been at the time of Campbell's conspicious lack of success in Satara. The promotion of societies amongst Marathas in that district could not have proceeded as it did if the coming of irrigation had not provided some incentive. As it was, the growth of Maratha solidarity enabled the Marathas in Satara district to avoid some—but not all—of the errors made by their confrères in the Nira Valley of Poona district twenty years before.

Whatever links there were between government and the non-Brahman movement in the Deccan and the Karnatak soon disappeared. For by the end of the first great Non-Co-operation campaign it was becoming apparent that the Brahman "national" leadership in the Deccan and in the Karnatak was in considerable disarray, under the combined impact of the death of Tilak, Gandhian mass politics, and the non-Brahman challenge. The non-Brahman leadership was generally neutral, if not actively hostile, towards Congress aims. There was, then, no longer the need for British officials to take quite so seriously the injunctions of Montagu, the reforming Secretary of State (who in any case had now disappeared from the scene), to enter the "political" life of India and actively to build up support for government policies.[37] Furthermore, the Satya Shodhak Samaj, according to some, had shown violent proclivities in Satara district.[38] And, so far as the co-operative movement was concerned, officials were not at all sure what the disappearance of Brahman leadership, such as it was, would lead to.

Even Moysey had been concerned about the effects of anti-Brahman feeling on co-operative societies: "I feared at one time that the Satya Shodak movement was going to disturb and divide these Societies which largely owe their inception to Brahmins like Mr. Rajadnya, but this undesirable and unjust symptom of anti Brahman feeling appears, I am glad to say, to have died down." So

[37] See Montague to provincial governors, 24 January 1918: Edwin S. Montagu, *An Indian Diary*, pp. 216–17.

[38] But cf.: "The Collector [of] Satara reports that the violence attributed to the teachings of [the Satya Shodhak Samaj] is very much exaggerated and that it may be said that the violence that has taken place has been in spite of, rather than in consequence of, its admonitions." Commr., C.D., *Bom. L. Rev. Admin. Rept., 1920–21,* p. 30.

wrote Moysey in 1920.[39] R. N. Rajadnya was District Honorary Organizer in Satara and to some extent was able to preserve his position in the face of the non-Brahman onslaught. But we may be sure that there was some rejoicing in the non-Brahman camp when, in 1922, a Brahman Assistant Honorary Organizer in Satara district was convicted of embezzlement.[40]

Rothfeld's attitude to the controversy between Brahmans and non-Brahmans was hardly impartial. As one whose service had hitherto been mainly in Gujarat and its fringes, he was, perhaps, somewhat lacking in understanding of the troubles of the Deccan. He was sarcastic about the Sholapur cultivators who "seem to have persuaded themselves in some mysterious way that this is primarily a Brahmin movement."[41] But he did not hesitate to point out, with even more sarcasm, that in the majority of cases of defalcation in 1923 "the offenders belong to the educated class and to a community which holds the first rank in the Deccan and the Southern Mahratta Country and prides itself on its power and purity."[42] Rothfeld appeared to some to be aiding the non-Brahman cause in a circular which he issued in 1921. A secretary of a society in the Sholapur district misappropriated Rs.300 belonging to the society. He was discovered and given a stiff sentence by the Collector. Now this secretary was a Brahman, a *watandar kulkarni*, that is, a hereditary village accountant. Kolhapur had begun to replace *watandar kulkarnis*, who had charge of the accounts of single villages, with *talatis*, who had control of several villages;[43] the Government of Bombay had been encouraging a similar but voluntary process in British districts.[44] Rothfeld, in this situation, issued a circular which stated that "under no circumstances" should a *watandar kulkarni* be a secretary of a co-operative society.[45] Rothfeld could hardly have pressed the point if a society had particularly desired a *kulkarni* as secretary; nevertheless, the circular was seen to be the beginning of the end of another of the *kulkarnis'* perquisites. Speakers at the 1921 Provincial Co-operative Conference felt that

39 Moysey, loc. cit.

40 *Rept., 1922–23*, p. 39.

41 Ibid., p. 10.

42 Ibid., p. 39.

43 Latthe, *Memoirs of Shahu Chhatrapati*, II, 511; for the opposition of the Kolhapur *kulkarnis*, see Dep. Collr., Belgaum, quoted *Bom. L. Rev. Admin. Rept., 1918–19*, p. 30.

44 See *Bom. L. Rev. Admin. Rept., 1914–15*, pt. ii, pp. 14–15.

45 Rothfeld, Circular No. P.O.L.–12 of 2 May 1921. (Poona, loose.)

the circular "indirectly breathes hatred against the Brahmin community in general."[46] There were black sheep in all groups, it was said, but a group should not be judged by its dishonest minority. Possibly it was in order to placate Brahman feeling that Janardan Madan, the Civilian who acted as Registrar for part of 1922 while Rothfeld was on leave, issued another circular about the place of *patils* (village headmen, who were almost without exception non-Brahman) in the work of the societies. There were instances, he said, in which *patils* took advantage of their position in the societies, and in such cases they should be removed from the societies' committees. But, even so, "great care" should be taken to ensure proper enquiry in such cases; the *patils*, unlike the *kulkarnis*, were cultivators, and usually "influential" in the villages in a potentially useful way.[47] Madan, as an Indian, was treading delicately in a potentially explosive situation.

The fact was, of course, that in some senses the co-operative movement in Maharashtra had been a Brahman affair. Until the coming of Assistant Honorary Organizers, towards the end of Ewbank's period as Registrar, the majority of honorary organizers in Maharashtra had been Brahman; most District Honorary Organizers were still Brahman. To repeat what has been pointed out earlier: men aspired to be honorary organizers from many motives, but at least to some extent Brahmans had fallen naturally into their traditional leadership roles in the co-operative movement. In the villages themselves positions as secretaries of societies had frequently been given to *kulkarnis*, who, because they had to be literate in order to perform their duties as accountants, were almost invariably Brahman. But in the years before the First World War such Brahman dominance in the co-operative movement in Maharashtra went largely unnoticed. It needed the activities of the Satya Shodhak Samaj to make men aware of the situation.

This is not to say that men had been unaware of more general problems of caste in the co-operative movement. One of those who was particularly affected by the rise of non-Brahman sentiment in the co-operative movement after the war was R. M. Sane, the Brahman Divisional Honorary Organizer for the Central Division. Before the war, in 1912, he had complained almost in Tilak fashion of the "promiscuous mixing of people of various social classes in one

46 E.g. V. M. Bakre, *Prov. Co-op. Conf. Procs., 1921*, p. 21.
47 Madan, Circular No. 160 of 7 April 1922. (Poona, Original Circulars, II.)

society."[48] Ewbank, then Registrar, had made no comment. But
some years later Ewbank had gone as far as recommending "sub-
committees" for individual *wadas* in a village if a society's membership was becoming much more than about a hundred.[49] Ewbank, then, had been prepared to "accept caste as a basic fact of
society and make use of it,"[50] but he had still felt that the village
as such was "a very real unit."[51] In 1919, however, a proposal was
put forward—actually by a Brahman auditor of societies—for complete division of large societies on the basis of caste.[52] Sane opposed
this suggestion when his opinion was asked by Ewbank, perhaps
partly because his own Brahman community was now beginning
to suffer through rivalries between castes. The "depressed classes"
had practically no property, he said, so it would be impossible for
them to form their own societies. Sane preferred to see division, if
it had to come, on the basis of faction;[53] significantly, perhaps, Sane
does not appear to have considered "faction" as synonymous with
"caste."

By 1920 Sane was very depressed by the role that caste was coming to play in the co-operative movement, especially in his home
district of Sholapur. Writing in *Kesari*, that is, in Tilak's paper,
read primarily by Brahmans, he condemned the non-Brahman cry
that the co-operative movement was run by Brahmans for their
own benefit. The chief purpose of the movement, he said, was to
raise the economic and moral standards of the people. With such
an aim, the main group who benefited were the non-Brahmans.
The Brahmans who led the movement did so simply because they
were educated. If the non-Brahmans really wanted the Brahmans
to go, they would go—and the movement would suffer. But the
non-Brahmans should not blame the Brahmans for all the faults of
the co-operative movement if at heart they were not prepared to do
without the Brahmans.[54]

48 Sane, "Notes on Conditions precedent to the Registration of a Rural Co-operative
Credit Society," *Prov. Co-op. Conf. Procs., 1912,* p. 44.

49 Ewbank to D.A. No. 2489 of 31 March 1916, encl. Bom. R.D. Order No. 6400 of
27 June 1916. *Wada,* in this context, means an area in a village normally inhabited
by one particular caste.

50 *Rept., 1917–18,* p. 11.

51 Ewbank to D.A., letter cited.

52 K. R. Kulkarni, Auditor, S.D., to Regr. (through Asst. Regr., S.D.) No. 781 of
21 May 1919. (Poona, Original Circulars, II.)

53 Sane to Ewbank, No. 272 of 5 June 1919. (Poona, file cited.)

54 Sane, *Kesari,* 29 June 1920.

In fact, the non-Brahmans were increasingly prepared to do without the Brahmans; Sane himself resigned as Divisional Honorary Organizer in 1923 and died in 1925. For a time there was indeed something of a leadership vacuum in the co-operative movement in the rural areas of the Deccan and the Karnatak; non-Brahmans with the education and the capacity which was required were not easy to find in the 1920s. It is true that in Poona city at this time N. C. Kelkar and D. V. Gokhale (another of Tilak's leading followers) became more and more immersed in the affairs of the Poona Central Co-operative Bank. But their interest in such matters, though in one sense a continuation of the long-standing Brahman interest in banking, was (like C. M. Gandhi's earlier activities in Surat) to a large extent a reflection of their rejection in local politics. The 1922 municipal election, for example, virtually marked the end of "advanced class" domination of Poona Municipality.[55] Kelkar's insistence in 1923 that he would remain on the Board of the Poona Bank only if there were a cessation of party feeling seems largely to have cured that Bank of its squabbles.[56] But the cure appears still to have left that Bank as something of an outpost of Chitpavan Brahman power in Maharashtra.

"A Self-governing Movement"?

Otto Rothfeld once wrote in an annual report that the "lines of development" which he wished to see the co-operative movement follow were those "by which Government control and Government supervision are reduced to a bare minimum and on which the societies are left to work out their own salvation as individual units in a self-governing movement."[57] Yet, obviously, when Rothfeld wrote this he did not have either Congress politicians or caste politicians in mind as the future leaders of the co-operative movement. Nor did he see the "humble villager" as a potential leader in the way that Ewbank had done; Rothfeld was too sophisticated an intellectual for that. His socialism, such as it was, was of the essentially urban variety. It certainly did not prevent him from relying "with confidence upon educated and moderate opinion among

[55] See Y. B. Damle, "Caste in Maharashtra," *Journal of the University of Poona, Humanities Section*, No. 9, 1958, p. 93; also M. P. Mangudkar, "Municipal Government in Poona (A Case Study)" (Ph.D. thesis, University of Poona, 1957), p. 34.
[56] Minutes of Annual General Meeting, Poona Central Co-operative Bank, 24 June 1923, and following papers. (Poona, Poona C.C.B.-A.)
[57] *Rept., 1922–23*, p. 33.

commercial and professional leaders of Bombay."[58] For under
Rothfeld the Bombay Central Co-operative Institute was allowed
to assume a much more important role in the movement than that
which Ewbank had intended it to assume. Rothfeld brought forward a scheme for affiliating societies to the Institute on payment
of a very small fee and also for opening up Divisional and even
district branches of the Institute. During 1921, the enthusiastic
V. H. Gonehalli, just back from England, and now assuming the
name of Naik, was given the task of reorganizing the Institute
along these lines. He succeeded remarkably well. Over 1,000 societies joined. Divisional branches were formed in Gujarat, Maharashtra, and the Karnatak.[59]

With the rise of the Institute the place of the honorary organizers in the movement began to decline. Vaikunth Mehta, for one,
was all in favour of this. After a clash with an honorary organizer
in one of the canal areas he wrote to Rothfeld: "I have very often
conveyed to you officially and in private conversation my own
opinion of the system of honorary organizers. You have been inclined to agree with me and have assured me and so had the Hon.
Mr. Mehta that it was only a question of time before this system
which puts a premium on irresponsibility was replaced by an
agency more amenable to rational discipline. . . . My personal view
is that a body of persons who are neither responsible to Government nor are organically connected with banks or the Institute
should have no place in the movement."[60] Rothfeld, however, did
not take any action in the matter of honorary organizers. He probably preferred to let the institution die a slow death. In fact, it had
quite a long life in front of it.

The control of the non-official side of the movement—the upper
ranks of the honorary organizers, the banks, and the Institute—
remained in the hands of the educated urban minority. Rothfeld
believed that the primary societies would always need "advice,
supervision and inspection from outside."[61] This was very different
from the "self-control" which Ewbank had advocated. Rothfeld in
one place claimed that he would like to see the outside control

---

[58] *Rept., 1920–21*, p. 5.
[59] V. H. Naik, *Prov. Co-op. Conf. Procs., 1921*, pp. 124 et seq.
[60] V. L. Mehta to Rothfeld, D/O of 17 September 1923. (Poona, Bombay Provincial
Co-operative Bank [B.P.C.B.].)
[61] *Royal Commission on Agriculture*, Vol. II, pt. i. *Bombay Evidence*, p. 169.

coming increasingly from the Institute and the financing agencies. He would not, however, hand over all powers of supervision to the Institute until it had "a trained and numerically adequate staff." In order to maintain this staff the funds of the Institute needed to be "nearly doubled." Any such increase implied not only an increase in the subscriptions but also an increase in the government grant.[62]

In practice, Rothfeld probably exercised as much control over the movement as his predecessors, if not more. Hubert Calvert, the Punjab Registrar, who was a member of the Royal Commission on Agriculture, asserted that the Bombay Registrar's office issued circulars "to an extent unknown in other Provinces."[63] The trio of distinguished Punjab Co-operative officials, Calvert, Strickland, and Darling,[64] certainly went further *in theory* than did those in most other provinces in advocating the "self-management" of societies. Yet Rothfeld claimed that there was a "very much larger percentage" of societies in Bombay which were "entirely self-managing (which write out their own accounts and conduct their whole business very well) than is the case in the Punjab or in any other Province."[65] Rothfeld's outlook towards official control was conditioned by his Continental experience. "Why do you think official control is necessary? Why not educate a society to manage its own affairs?" Calvert asked Rothfeld, now retired, when he came to give evidence before the Royal Commission. Rothfeld replied:

I find it very difficult to put what I mean into words. I have not that trust in human nature and I know of no countries, except Denmark and England, which have been able to carry on the co-operative movement without a good deal of official control. The circumstances of certain intensely individualist countries like Denmark and England are very different from those of India, and to my mind the analogy appears to be rather with the practice in France and practically every other European country. . . . If the co-operative movement is ever going to do what, after all, we as co-operators look forward to as the

[62] *Rept., 1922–23*, p. 33.

[63] *Royal Commission on Agriculture,* Vol. cited, p. 175.

[64] Hubert Calvert, Regr., Punjab, 1916–26; C. F. Strickland, Dep. Regr., 1922–26, Regr., 1926–27; Malcolm Darling, Joint Regr., 1920–21, Regr., 1927–31. Of these Sir Malcom Darling is probably the best known, because of his extraordinarily readable accounts of the rural Punjab, but Calvert and Strickland were also forceful administrators.

[65] Ibid., p. 174.

ideal, and that is, almost to be the State itself in all its economic aspects, it appears to me essential that the State in its political aspects should also to some extent control the co-operative movement in as much as it will also be controlled by it.[66]

This point of view was poles apart from that of many in high government circles in the India of the time. In theory, if not always in practice, the approach of a Calvert to the problem of authority in India was fundamentally that of a well-meaning Englishman, at heart a liberal. Rothfeld, on the other hand, approached the problem in a peculiarly doctrinaire and (some must have thought) a peculiarly Continental way.[67]

Rothfeld's views on the general question of control were probably to some extent the result of his experiences with guaranteeing unions. Even before he became Registrar, there were signs that the guaranteeing unions were not working as they should. Henry Wolff had written to Ewbank expressing the opinion that societies might overlook the defects of other societies within the unions in order to obtain similar treatment themselves. And this was exactly what was happening. Even Ewbank had had to admit that the half-yearly forecasts of the unions to the Bombay Central Co-operative Bank were often too high, and that intervisiting was not taking place as frequently as it had been planned that it should. He had issued a circular announcing that a Special Mamlatdar, or a person appointed by him, would visit each union annually and make specific enquiries on these points.[68] Yet the guaranteeing unions had been intended to eliminate the work of the Special Mamlatdars. Once the Registrar felt that he had to check, in a way that was more than formal, the recommendations of the unions to the Central Bank in Bombay, the whole purpose of the guaranteeing unions was beginning to disappear.

---

[66] Ibid.

[67] But it is perhaps worthwhile pointing out that the agricultural policy of fascism provoked some admiration in the Punjab. See *Royal Commission on Agriculture*, Vol. VIII, *Evidence taken in the Punjab*, especially evidence of F. L. Brayne of Gurgaon fame, p. 82: "I suppose some sort of Mussolini influence is necessary to awaken the people." Malcolm Darling, pp. 595 et seq., was less enthusiastic, and he knew Italy well. It should be remembered, too, that this was only 1926: fascism had yet to reveal some of its uglier facets.

[68] *Rept., 1918–19*, p. 21.

Rothfeld at first went no further than to express the opinion that Ewbank had been somewhat over-optimistic about guaranteeing unions.[69] Even in 1921 he did little more than endorse the opinion of Madan, his senior Assistant Registrar, that "Union members are not yet sufficiently actuated with a sense of social service to do their work properly without the stimulus of either reward or fear. . . . With, however, proper supervision and guidance, the spread of the Union system seems to me to be the only way for effecting that supervision over societies which at present is necessary and which in some provinces is now undertaken by official agency."[70] But by 1922 Rothfeld was very concerned about the conditions of the guaranteeing unions. Proximity was essential in grouping societies together in a guaranteeing union. Because of the scattered nature of the societies in Bombay, only sixty-six guaranteeing unions had been formed. Yet, since on the whole the guaranteeing unions were formed in the more prosperous areas, they absorbed fifty-three lakhs of the Rs.1,60,00,000 working capital of the rural societies of the Presidency. Rothfeld thought this state of affairs somewhat dangerous.[71] Registrations of guaranteeing unions had virtually ceased; only two, in fact, had been registered since 1920.[72]

Strangely, the faults of the guaranteeing-union system were never, so it would seem, analyzed in detail. The basic fault appears to have been that the "guarantee" came into operation only as a last resort. The procedure in case of default was outlined by Ewbank in this way: "The defaulting society is first cancelled and the joint unlimited liability of its members enforced to the uttermost. It is only if at the end of the liquidation any deficit remains, the payment of which has been guaranteed by the union, that the other union societies are required to make it good in proportion to the degree of liability accepted by each of them." Ewbank added, significantly, that "as no case has yet arisen in India or Burma, in which the union guarantee has been actually enforced, it is difficult to decide which system will bear the strain best and prove in

---

[69] Rothfeld, Review of Ewbank, ed., *Indian Co-operative Studies*, *B.C.Q.*, June 1920, p. 36.
[70] Madan, Note, *Prov. Co-op. Conf. Procs., 1921*, p. 67; also quoted in part in *Rept., 1920–21*, p. 10.
[71] *Rept., 1921–22*, p. 8.
[72] Cf. *Rept., 1919–20*, p. 6.

practice most equitable to its members."[73] This was written in 1919. In the years following, the societies completely opposed any change in the procedure. The limits on borrowing under the guaranteeing-union system were such that the enforcement of joint unlimited liability in the one defaulting society almost always covered the loss. This was what Rothfeld meant by the "illusory" nature of the guarantee.[74] But at the same time the credits available under the system, enhanced by the "supervision" that was supposed to be an essential part of it, were high enough to encourage reckless recommendations by societies in the unions. They knew that almost certainly they would not be affected if the loans they recommended could not be recovered. The result of the continuance of such a system could easily have been a large number of liquidations. Another fault of the guaranteeing-union system was that, from the beginning, no effort was made to train the committees of the unions and their meagre, poorly paid staff. Ewbank had plainly expected too much from "the little leaders of the labouring classes."

The 1922 Provincial Co-operative Conference appointed a strong committee to consider the whole question of guaranteeing unions. The committee reported to the Conference of the following year. It "unanimously held that for the purposes of supervision it was necessary to have some agency intermediate between the primary society and the central financing agency." While the committee had "great doubts" about the efficacy of guaranteeing unions, and did not believe more should be registered, it did not wish the existing ones to be dissolved unless the members wished it. It was proposed, however, to form "supervising unions" for the purpose of supervision only.[75] These unions would have areas larger than the areas which guaranteeing unions served "so that," as the Registrar's Report for 1924 stated, "more societies could be affiliated and a better committee and a well paid supervisor could be appointed."[76] Rothfeld, however, did not "feel any certitude," as he wrote his final Report, that the new supervising unions would do "all that is required in the matter. The fact is that it is extremely difficult to find any unpaid workers in this Presidency who are

---

[73] Ewbank, "Guaranteeing Unions," in *Indian Co-operative Studies*, p. 57.
[74] *Rept., 1922–23*, p. 10.
[75] *Prov. Co-op. Conf. Procs., 1923*, Appx. p. 49.
[76] *Rept., 1923–24*, p. 10.

content to do persistent and continuous detailed supervision and inspection of a kind which secures little applause or public recognition."[77]

Takkavi

Guaranteeing unions had arisen as a result of the recommendations of the Maclagan Committee. There was one other important recommendation of the Maclagan Committee upon which Ewbank had acted much more slowly. It concerned the distribution of *takkavi* through and to societies. The Maclagan Committee had believed that in times of scarcity short-term loans under the Agriculturists' Loans Act should be made to societies and should be left to them to distribute.[78] It was claimed that minor government officials extracted so much by way of perquisites when distributing *takkavi* that villagers would sometimes prefer to borrow from co-operative societies, although the societies' rates of interest might be on paper considerably higher than the rate charged by Government.[79] Similar arguments, the Committee thought, applied to long-term loans under the Land Improvements Loans Act.[80] Campbell, if he read the Maclagan Committee's Report, must have felt that his beliefs were at last being justified.

It was not, however, until the prospect of a considerable amount of freedom from Government of India surveillance began to open up in 1919 that Ewbank felt able to give the matter any concentrated thought. In March of that year he informed Government that he believed co-operative society members should have the option of taking *takkavi* either from their society or from Revenue Department officers. He thought that no loans should be given by societies under such a system for more than five years.[81] There was no thought, however, of merging *takkavi* in the general funds of co-operative societies; it was plain that each society would have to maintain separate accounts for general co-operative society funds and *takkavi* funds, and that some organization would have to be responsible for making elaborate checks before *takkavi* loans were granted.

[77] *Rept., 1922–23*, p. 11.
[78] *Maclagan Cttee. Rept.*, p. 176, Recommendation No. 201.
[79] Ibid., p. 117.
[80] Ibid., p. 176, Recommendation No. 202.
[81] Ewbank to Govt. No. 2373 of 3 March 1919, encl. Bom. R.D. Order No. 3552 of 4 April 1919.

Rothfeld did not entirely agree with Ewbank's proposals. He thought that few land improvements could be made within five years; co-operative societies, however, certainly could not afford to lend their own funds even for five years. "The only solution," in his opinion, was "State aid." He quoted the examples of France, Italy, and Hungary.[82] But "State aid" should be dispensed through co-operative societies. Rothfeld belonged to the school of thought which believed that advances under the Agriculturists' Loans Act did more harm than good. Short-term "doles," he told the Agricultural Commission, merely "touched the fringe of the problem" and, in fact, retarded the growth of the co-operative movement. Except in a few backward areas, he would limit the distribution of short-term government loans to famine years.[83] And, if a co-operative society existed in a village, there should be no alternative to applying to the society for a *takkavi* loan of any description. To some extent Rothfeld managed to persuade Chunilal Mehta and the Bombay Government of the justice of his cause. In the rules that were framed in 1922, the emphasis was placed on loans for land improvement. In villages where there were co-operative societies, advances under the Land Improvements Loans Act would in future be made only through the agency of such societies. Government would place an annual allotment of three lakhs at the disposal of the Bombay Central Co-operative Bank, which would issue a loan on receipt of a certificate from the Registrar that the loan would be utilized for a valid purpose. Individual members of the societies had to apply through their district banks to the Bombay Central Co-operative Bank.[84] The procedure had not been properly tested when Rothfeld gave up his position as Registrar.

Provincial Bank and District Banks

Almost inevitably, another Registrar meant yet another round of examination and reorganization of the upper reaches of the finance of the movement. That they "had gradually been getting into a condition rightly criticized by the Manager of the Provincial Bank in strong terms can hardly be denied," Rothfeld wrote

---

[82] Rothfeld to Ch. Sec. No. 4303 of 5 May 1920. (Poona, T.A.G.4.)

[83] See especially Rothfeld's evidence, *Royal Commission on Agriculture*, Vol. II, pt. i, p. 171.

[84] See *Bom. Prov. Banking Enquiry Cttee. Rept.*, p. 85.

in his first Administration Report. Ewbank had left the correspondence on the matter for Rothfeld to deal with, together with
"valuable" notes.[85] None of Vaikunth Mehta's actual letters on
the subject, or of Ewbank's and Rothfeld's notes, appear to have
survived. But it may be taken that the substance, at least, of Mehta's submissions is contained in two editorial contributions which
appeared in the *Bombay Co-operative Quarterly* in December 1919
and June 1920.[86]

The exact nature of the relations which should exist between
the Central Bank in Bombay and the district banks, the first article
began, remained undefined. The district banks were showing
themselves to be unable to meet the requirments of the societies in
their charge.

The consensus of opinion, especially among rural co-operators, is that
the results are in no degree commensurate with the energy spent on
developing the new organizations. In some of the districts which have
local banks in their midst, complaints are rife that adequate capital
is not collected, that much time is taken in sanctioning loans, that demands are put off for insufficient grounds, that no effort is made by the
banks to entertain a field staff and that the management cannot ascer-
tain the needs and difficulties of societies. . . . The delays of the original
arrangements have only been slightly reduced.[87]

The suggestion was put forward, not for the first time, that co-
operative banks should be organized on a taluka rather than on a
district basis.[88] In cases where men and capital were not available
in taluka towns, "branches of the provincial or district bank should
be started, the former only in areas outside the jurisdiction of existing local banks."[89]

Rothfeld spent most of February and March 1920 discussing
these questions. He concluded that none of the district banks was
in a position to finance all the societies in its district itself. District
banks did not have the capital, and they were very willing to follow

---

[85] *Rept., 1919–20*, p. 3. The "Provincial Bank" referred to was, of course, the organization that was still known officially as the Bombay Central Co-operative Bank.
[86] "Co-operative Finance in the Bombay Presidency," *B.C.Q.*, December 1919, pp.
155–61; "Provincial Co-operative Finance," *B.C.Q.*, June 1920, pp. 16–25. Shri R. M.
Talpade, for many years editor of the *B.C.Q.*, assured the present writer that the first
article was by Vaikunth Mehta; the second article is little more than an elaboration
of the first.
[87] *B.C.Q.*, June 1920, pp. 17–18.
[88] *B.C.Q.*, December 1919, p. 157.
[89] Ibid., p. 158.

Ewbank's injunction to the Poona Bank to be "economical about staff."[90] But at the same time Rothfeld felt that district banks should be "the main unit of finance"; therefore, "they must be strengthened and their share capital rapidly increased." Until the district banks could finance all the societies in their districts, the Central Bank in Bombay would continue to do direct business with societies in areas not covered by district banks. Legal steps were taken to have the name Bombay Central Co-operative Bank changed to the more accurate Bombay Provincial Co-operative Bank—though these were not brought to a conclusion until 1923.[91] The "likelihood of erecting efficient Taluka Banks in present conditions," Rothfeld wrote, "seemed almost hopeless to all who knew the actual conditions of those small towns."[92]

In spite of Rothfeld's desire to foster the activities of the district central banks, many of the more significant developments at this time took place under the aegis of the Provincial Bank.

As we have seen, there was one particular facet of the old Nira Canal *takkavi* scheme which the Bank had rapidly recognized as virtually essential in any scheme for the large-scale financing of cash crops. This was the intimate connection between the provision of credit and the organization of supply and marketing, a connection provided by the Bank's branch and "shop" at Baramati. In spite of all the setbacks of the Nira Canal co-operatives, the Bank believed that its basic principles of operation in the area were sound.[93] From 1917, therefore, the Bank felt justified in beginning to set up more branches with shops, on the Baramati model, to serve the recently organized societies in the newly irrigated areas along the Godavari and Pravara canals in Ahmadnagar district, and in the south of Satara district. A branch was opened at Kopargaon in January 1917.[94] A branch at Islampur followed in 1920, and others at Belapur and Nira in 1923.[95]

---

90 See above, chapter 3.

91 Bank's evidence, *Bom. Prov. Banking Enquiry Cttee.*, IV, 429.

92 *Rept., 1919–20*, p. 4.

93 For a lucid explanation of the methods which the Bank adopted from the money-lender, see *Fifteenth Annual Report of the Bombay Provincial Co-operative Bank (for the year 1925–26)*. (Poona, B.P.C.B.)

94 For this branch, see V. L. Mehta to Rothfeld No. R.11/660 of 17 March 1922. (Poona, file cited.)

95 See Map in Bank's *Annual Rept., 1925–26*.

The goal which the Bank had in mind was that of financing primary societies only in areas served by a branch.[96] The virtual limitation of the societies directly financed by the Bank to those in a few cash-crop areas made it possible to create a well-paid and well-trained staff to undertake the duties which, in the original Nira Canal co-operative scheme, had been undertaken by the Special Mamlatdar. The Bank had now, apparently, built up enough of a reputation to be able to do without the official prestige which was normally attached to that personage. When a branch had been working for a year or two, the Bank normally associated with it what was termed an Advisory Committee, but after the initial experiences with the Nira Canal societies' Advisory Committee the Bank saw to it that such a committee remained purely "advisory," and reserved the right of nominating some of the members. An Advisory Committee's primary task was to act as a sounding board for grievances. Here, then, were the possible beginnings of a new system of finance, by-passing the district central banks, based on trained guidance from above, and acknowledging the democratic principles of co-operation only to a limited extent.

The chief reason for this expansion of the Bank's activities was, of course, the opening up of new irrigation areas. Yet there was also a very definite feeling that boom times had come to stay and that rapid development was worthwhile financially. "The year was remarkable for the prosperity of the trade and the exceptional prices realised for the jaggery," read the audit memorandum on the Bank's branch at Baramati for the year 1920–21. "Naturally a remarkable decrease in the overdue arrears is also visible. The same have come down from Rs.1,19,080 – 4 – 9 to Rs.35,427 – 13 – 8."[97] Malji, the Gujarat Divisional Honorary Organizer, came down to look at the Nira Canal societies. Their condition, he reported, was "more or less enviable when compared with credit societies in other parts of the country."[98] Many began to think—over-optimistically, as it happened—that the troubles of the Nira Canal societies in the preceding decade had been caused simply by low prices.

96 Ibid., p. 7.
97 Audit memo., Baramati branch, B.C.C.B., year ending 31 March 1921. (Poona, B.P.C.B.)
98 Malji to Madan, Ag. Regr., 1 February 1922. (Poona, P.S.8.)

The Bhils

The principles upon which the Provincial Bank operated in the canal areas were adopted with appropriate modifications in the work amongst the Bhils of the Panch Mahals. Here, the Bank was prepared to lose money as a measure of philanthropy, though in fact it did so only on a comparatively small scale.[99]

The Bhils were to be found scattered through much of central India, and (in the old Bombay Presidency) especially in the districts of Panch Mahals and West Khandesh. Many villages in those areas had a few Bhil families, for in the past they had acted as village watchmen. In the more isolated "jungle" areas there were villages populated almost completely by Bhils. (One says "villages," although in fact one of the distinguishing features of Bhil life was that the Bhils normally lived in their fields rather than in nucleated settlements.) The Bhils had taken to settled agriculture to a greater extent than many other "tribal" groups in India; indeed, it could be argued that it was their attempt to bridge the gap between the roaming tribal existence and the settled life which made them peculiarly vulnerable to certain forms of economic exploitation.

The Bhil, claimed David Symington, in a brilliantly written if perhaps somewhat shrill report produced shortly before the Second World War,

begins the cultivating season in debt and without ready money, and consequently he has to borrow to meet the cost of cultivation, to feed himself and his family for part of the year, and to get drunk occasionally. The sowcar is accommodating at this time of the year. You only have to ask in order to get Rs.5 for cloth, Rs.40 for bullocks, or Rs.2 for liquor. True, you may have to work on the sowcar's premises for a day or two without pay, but the chances are you will then get an extra rupee to get drunk with before going through the formality of affixing your thumb on the necessary promissory note; the contents of which are mercifully not revealed or pleasantly explained away. Cash is thus readily available in small doles to meet all the Bhil's immediate necessities, which are very few. The sowcar will also advance money for land revenue; and frequently, especially in Nawapur taluka, actually pays the Bhil's assessment himself at the taluka office.[100]

99 Bank's *Annual Rept., 1925–26.* The dividend paid by the Bank during 1921–23 had been 7½ per cent. (Maharashtra State Co-operative Bank, Bombay [B.S.C.B.], Registrar [Regr.] file.)

100 D. Symington, *Report on the Aboriginal and Hill Tribes of the Partially Ex-*

At harvest time, Symington reported, a high proportion of the crops was taken by the *saukar*. "One thing is certain . . . the Bhil Khatedar never sells his crop, but hands it over bodily in part payment of an inextinguishable debt."[101] If the Bhil owed money to two or more *saukars*, his crop was "pounced upon" by a *saukar*'s agent—often a fierce Pathan from the North-West Frontier—as soon as it was ripe.[102]

Four men were largely responsible for the extension of co-operative activity to the Bhil areas. There was Vaikunth Mehta of the Provincial Bank, who sincerely desired it to engage in some really self-sacrificing work. There was Rothfeld, who had been an Assistant Collector in the area and hence knew its needs. There was D. A. Shah, the newly appointed Assistant Registrar for Gujarat, a gifted and devoted man. Finally, there was A. V. Thakkar, "Thakkar Bapa," the engineer who had become a social worker, the Gandhian in the Servants of India Society, the father of the Bhil Seva Mandal and, indeed, of Hindu concern for the aboriginals.[103]

From the beginning, it was realized that an attack on the problem of the Bhils could not begin simply with one or two credit societies. Credit, purchase, and sale facilities had to be supplied from the beginning. Such work could not possibly be done by the Bhils on their own. It was here that the Bank stepped in with its offer to open a branch at Dohad, in the midst of the Panch Mahals. To provide sufficient custom, fifty or sixty societies had to be organized all at once. "You cannot start one society at a time and then add to it as time goes on," said Shah, when describing the work some years later. [104] Both the Bank and Government were fairly generous in supplying supervisory staff, including a Special Mamlatdar. They soon found that staff even for the routine work would have to be supplied too. In spite of careful training,[105] the Bhil group secretaries could not handle the work. So three caste Hindus had to be em-

---

cluded Areas in the Province of Bombay (1939), p. 6. Mr. Symington has recently discussed his work with the Bhils in a book published under the pseudonym James Halliday, *A Special India*, pp. 145–160. For a brief modern anthropological discussion of the Bhils, see Karve, *Maharashtra, Land and its People*, pp. 16–17.

101 Symington, *Report*, p. 7.

102 Ibid., p. 12.

103 For Thakkar, see Gujarat Research Society, *Shri Thakkar Bapa Commemoration Volume*, particularly the chapter by G. V. Mavlankar; also Thakkar, *The Problem of the Aborigines in India*.

104 Shah, *Prov. Co-op. Conf. Procs., 1929*, p. 46.

105 Shah to Madan, Regr., No. A.G.C., of 12 October 1923. (B.S.C.B., Regr.)

ployed as clerks at Dohad. "The class of men who could do writing work well," wrote Shah truthfully, "would not be able to do the field work, spend nights at Bhil villages and mix freely with the Bhils."[106]

The Bank's "branch" system was carried to its logical, "frankly paternal,"[107] conclusion amongst the Bhils. Like the *saukar*, the Special Mamlatdar and the Manager of the Bank's branch had to "practically . . . take charge of the whole life of the Bhils."[108] Arrangements had to be made to enable the branch to pay the revenue assessments on behalf of the members of the societies. If the Bhils were allowed to pay it direct, claimed Rothfeld, they would be "robbed on their way by the Savkars or their Pathan Bullies."[109] Perhaps, however, the Bank employed people whose task was not altogether unlike that of the "Pathan Bullies" against whom Rothfeld delighted in crusading. Even the Bank found that the Bhils had to be "goaded" into making repayments. It employed "menial servants" who went ahead of the Bank's Inspector and who stayed behind to see that orders were carried out.[110]

The co-operative society had in fact completely taken over the role of the *saukar*, the only difference being that its terms of business were strictly fair. Perhaps the term "co-operative" could hardly be used to describe the system. But Symington, who saw it in action in the late thirties, believed it should be the model for the backward areas of the rest of the Presidency. "The co-operative movement," he wrote, "can never succeed in backward tracts unless it is so closely controlled as to cease to be truly co-operative."[111]

The Kadva Patidars

Developments in the Olpad taluka of the Surat district, in Gujarat, would have provoked more admiration from the co-operative purist. There, in the twenties, some remarkable cotton-sale societies sprang up and flourished amongst the Kadva Patidars.

On the whole, credit societies had not had much success in Gujarat so far. Mahadev Desai, a shrewd observer, had little doubt that the relevant question was "Is the present type of society suitable?"

---

106 Shah to Madan No. A.D.M./4 of 7–8 June 1924. (B.S.C.B., Asst. Regr., Surat.)
107 *Rept., 1926–27*, p. 19.
108 *Rept., 1927–28*, p. 21.
109 Rothfeld to Collr., Panch Mahals, No. A.G.C./109 of 21 April 1923. (B.S.C.B., Regr.)
110 Shah to Madan No. A.D.M./4 of 7–8 June 1924. (B.S.C.B., Asst. Regr., Surat.)
111 Symington, *Report*, p. 51.

Agriculturists of good credit in Surat and Kaira districts could obtain loans, either from professional money-lenders or from agriculturist money-lenders, at a rate of interest varying from 6 to 7½ per cent. Unless the societies could afford to reduce their rate of interest from their usual 9⅜ per cent, the movement had "no chance of having the popularity it has had in many parts of the Deccan."[112] The evidence appears to suggest, furthermore, that in the more prosperous parts of Gujarat some of the substantial agriculturists were not merely uninterested in co-operative societies; they were opposed to them. Indeed, it was asserted that they felt that co-operative societies stood in the way of their efforts to build up their holdings at the expense of the smaller cultivators, and to retire from field work altogether.[113] For the Kadva Patidars[114] of the Olpad area, however, credit societies had had a certain appeal. A leader had arisen amongst the Kadva Patidars who could play upon the anti-Bania sentiment that was to be found in the caste at this time.[115] Purshottamdas Itcharam Patel had been educated almost entirely in Gujarati, but had spent periods abroad in Mauritius and Burma, and it is claimed that during a year in South Africa he learnt "the benefits of working together" in Gandhi's Civil Resistance Movement.[116] By

[112] M. H. Desai, "Co-operation in Gujerat," *B.C.Q.,* June 1917, pp. 26–31.

[113] Khandubhai Desai, Evidence, Maclagan Cttee. (Patiala.) It is practically impossible to obtain satisfactory statistics to back up Khandubhai's assertions.

[114] The term *Patidar* originally referred only to one who was a "joint proprietor" of a village under the *Narvadari* form of land tenure, which was prevalent in much of Gujarat. But the distinction between *Patidar* and the simple *Kanbi,* or cultivator, tended to die out in the nineteenth century, especially in Surat district. See *Gazetteer of the Bombay Presidency,* Vol. II, *Surat and Broach,* p. 52; Cf. ibid., Vol. III, *Kaira and Panch Mahals,* p. 31. We have earlier observed a similar process occurring in connection with the term *Maratha.* There are three main divisions of the Patidars: Leva, Kadva, and Anjana. The Leva Patidars tend to be the wealthiest; a modern study states baldly that the Leva "do not themselves work in the fields," whereas the Kadva do. (Kusum Nair, *Blossoms in the Dust: The Human Factor in Indian Development* (1961), p. 177.) The *Bombay Gazetteer* reported in 1901 that the Leva and the Kadva "eat together but do not intermarry": Vol. IX, pt. i, *Gujerat Population, Hindus,* p. 163.

[115] Shri Anil Bhatt, of the Centre for the Study of Developing Societies, New Delhi, has surveyed the Patidar caste journals of the period. I am grateful to him for much useful information. I would refer here also to his paper on the role of the Patidar Yuvak Mandal in the national movement in Gujarat, in *Caste and Politics in India,* ed. Rajni Kothari (forthcoming). Another who has assisted me with information about the Patidars is Dr. D. F. Pocock, of the University of Sussex.

[116] C. M. Gandhi, "Glimpses of the Co-operative Movement," *B.C.Q.,* April 1954, p. 16. Cf. D. A. Shah, "Let us remember our own pioneers in time," *B.C.Q.,* March 1946, p. 160, and P. T. Parikh, *A Brief History of the Co-operative Movement in the Surat District,* Appx.: "Surat District Co-operative Bank Ltd., Souvenir of the Silver Jubilee Celebrations 23rd December, 1934," p. 53.

1915 his Sonsek Co-operative Credit Society was prosperous and well managed and was lending money to other credit societies in the neighbourhood.[117] In that year Ewbank made him an honorary organizer.[118]

But even amongst the Kadva Patidars the success of mere credit societies appears to have been limited: "Rapid as their growth was," says a history of the co-operative movement in the Surat district, somewhat dolefully, "decay of some of the societies was equally rapid."[119] The example which led to the break-through in the field of cotton co-operatives appears to have been set by the Agriculture Department. In 1914–15 the Department began encouraging growers of cotton grown from improved seed which the Department had supplied to pool their cotton and have it ginned and sold in bulk.[120] Cotton produced in this way provided its growers with a higher profit than cotton that was not so produced. In 1919–20 some Kadva Patidars of the Sonsek area, again under the leadership of Purshottamdas Patel, began to imitate some of the methods of the Agriculture Department—using, however, a variety of standard seed different from that of the Agriculture Department. There was a genuine difference of opinion over the most profitable variety of seed to be chosen for standardization and pooling. [121] The cotton-sale co-operative society which thirteen Sonsek men formed in 1919 and registered in 1921, had a membership of 300 by 1924, and there were several other societies nearby.[122] In 1926 Purshottamdas Patel and his colleagues (who now included, it is worthwhile noting, a graduate of Elphinstone College, Bombay)[123] opened their first co-operative ginning and pressing factory. Finally, in 1930, the various cotton so-

---

117 Khandubhai Desai, Evidence, Maclagan Committee. In 1915 F. G. Pratt, Commr., N.D., in a somewhat sceptical report, claimed that the growth of the co-operative movement in Olpad taluka was "due to some extent to official or demi-official nursing": *Bom. L. Rev. Admin. Rept. 1914–15*, pt. ii, p. 50. But he may have been referring merely to the activities of Purshottamdas Patel as honorary organizer.

118 Bom. R.D. Order No. 4889 of 10 May 1916.

119 P. T. Parikh, *Brief History*, p. 19.

120 J. B. Shukla, *Life and Labour in a Gujarat Taluka*, pp. 257–58. This work is a detailed study of Olpad taluka, published in 1937. See also *Royal Commission on Agriculture*, Vol. II, pt. i, *Bombay Evidence*, pp. 13 and 14 (evidence of Harold Mann), and p. 576 (evidence of Bhimbhai M. Desai, Dep. D.A., Gujarat). I have discussed the Gujarat cotton societies with Shri D. A. Shah, Asst. Regr. in Gujarat at the time of their formation.

121 Evidence of Mann and Desai, ibid. Desai wished to put all non-credit co-operative societies under the control of the Agriculture Department: ibid., p. 577.

122 Shah, "Co-operative Cotton Sale in Gujarat," *Prov. Co-op. Conf. Procs., 1924*, Appx. p. lviii.

123 Balubhai Kalidas Patel. See P. T. Parikh, *Brief History*, Appx. p. 54.

cieties which had sprung up in the Surat district organized themselves as the Southern Gujarat Co-operative Cotton Sales and Ginning Societies Union. A headquarters was set up in Surat city with a
highly paid management in touch with day-to-day market fluctuations and with large buyers. By this time, it should be added, the
disagreements with the Agriculture Department over the type of
seed to be sown had disappeared.

What was the secret of the success of the cotton societies of Gujarat? Finance supplied by the Surat District Central Bank[124] and
marketing contacts provided by the Bombay Provincial Co-operative Bank[125] played their part. The Co-operative Department was
sympathetic to the early developments but, perhaps because of Agriculture Department opposition, gave no assistance by way of finance or staff. "From the beginning," D. A. Shah, the Assistant
Registrar in charge of Gujarat at that time, has declared, "Sonsek
Pioneers stood on their own legs."[126] A determination to prove that
their judgement about seed was as good as the Agriculture Department's probably boosted morale in the early days; (fortunately for
the societies their judgement was not proved entirely wrong). Then
there was the leadership of Purshottamdas Patel, a man whose
horizons had been extended overseas. In addition, the societies
were willing to pay, and the scale of their operations was such that
they were able to pay, for skilled management—even though that
management came from amongst the Kadva Patidar community
itself, from amongst those who sometimes, in fact, still took part in
agricultural operations during the monsoon.[127]

But at first sight the most obvious reason for the Kadva societies'
success in Olpad taluka is what might be termed "caste solidarity."
Like the Leva Patidars, the Kadva Patidars had been involved in
promoting various "reforms" within their own community—especially marriage and dowry reform—since the early years of the century. Perhaps because they were less wealthy than the Leva Patidars
they were more inclined to put into practice the somewhat pious resolutions of the four great Patidar "caste conferences" held between
1910 and 1917. Many of those resolutions related to marriage matters: the Kadva Seva Mandal, founded in 1917–18 as a result of the

124 P. T. Parikh, p. 85.
125 See Provincial Bank's *Annual Rept., 1925–26*, p. 13. (Poona, B.P.C.B.)
126 Shah, "Let us remember our own pioneers in time," *B.C.Q.*, p. 159.
127 Ibid.

conferences, was responsible in 1922 for the abolition amongst the Kadva Patidars of the custom of conducting marriage ceremonies (including infant marriages) only once in ten years. But for our purposes a resolution of the third conference, held in May 1914, is of particular importance. It called for the establishment of more co-operative societies. This conference, it is worth noting, was held in Surat, close to the taluka of Olpad.[128]

"Solidarity seeking," a modern Indian political scientist has asserted, "is something inherent in the very character of Patidars."[129] Yet Patidar caste solidarity was not necessarily of assistance to the co-operative movement in the twenties. Patidar caste solidarity in Bardoli, another Surat taluka, was directed almost entirely into political channels. It was from Bardoli that the latter stages of the Non-Co-operation campaign of 1920–22 were managed, and it was on the no-tax campaign in Bardoli that the attention of political India was focussed for much of 1928. On the other hand, the Kadva Patidars of Olpad taluka did not, generally speaking, become enthusiastic about the national movement until 1928; in the earlier twenties their main energies were devoted to the co-operative movement. The most likely explanation for this state of affairs would appear to lie in the differences in prosperity of the two talukas. Bardoli was a wealthy taluka, considerably more wealthy than Olpad. It was the sort of taluka where the Patidar families—generally Leva by caste—could afford to have the occasional younger son working full time in the national cause; it was also the sort of taluka where the co-operative movement simply was not required. Olpad taluka, however, was an area where rainfall and more especially drainage were somewhat less reliable than they were in Bardoli.[130] The holdings of the Kadva Patidars of Olpad were generally "economic," but not very much larger than "economic." In Sonsek, the little

---

128 See G.R.R.D. No. 7135 of 31 July 1914, and enclosure.

129 Anil Bhatt, personal communication. Much of the preceding paragraph is based on information provided by Shri Bhatt. Mahadev Desai, and the nationalist leaders who often made Bardoli their headquarters, were well aware of the existence of the "closely knit organization" of the Patidars. See M. Desai, *The Story of Bardoli, being a History of the Bardoli Satyagraha of 1928 and its Sequel*, p. 36. It is worthwhile adding here that in the opinion of Anil Bhatt the earlier leaders in social reform amongst both the Kadva and Leva Patidars were almost all young men who had little or no knowledge of English; in general, too, Bhatt believes, the importance as leaders of the Africa-returned can be exaggerated.

130 *Papers relating to the Revision Survey Settlement of the Olpad Taluka of the Surat Collectorate*, 1897, *S.R. G. of B.*, N.S., No. ccclxi, pp. 3–4.

village upon which many of the developments in the co-operative field were based, the average area which a peasant took up for cultivation was, in or about 1931, 16.2 acres.[131] Thirteen of the twenty-eight landholders in the village cultivated between 15 and 30 acres (was it sheer coincidence that it was thirteen men who founded the Sonsek cotton-sale society?); only three landholders cultivated more than 30 acres and none more than 40 acres.[132] It would appear likely that the Sonsek Kadva came from precisely the group of medium cultivators for whom co-operatives could perform a real service.

Yet we would be unwise to conclude, even at this point, our search for explanations of the success of the cotton co-operatives in the Olpad taluka. Mere credit co-operatives amongst cotton growers, it was true, went "only half the way in helping the farmer, leaving him, all of a sudden, in the lurch at the most critical time,"[133] that is, when the time for marketing arrived. The cotton co-operatives illustrated once again the fact that co-operative marketing procedures could be more helpful to peasants growing "cash" crops than credit co-operatives alone. But co-operative marketing—as Ewbank had always insisted and as Harold Mann and Otto Rothfeld, Director of Agriculture and Registrar of Co-operative Societies, stressed in a joint memorandum in 1923—was not something to be entered into lightly.[134] The chain of "middlemen" employed in moving cotton from the rural village to the Bombay mill, or overseas, might seem to be extraordinarily lengthy, inefficient, and costly.[135] But in fact only certain links in the chain were vulnerable. The *banias* who bought cotton in the village, and the *adatyas* (middlemen) who, if the cultivator brought his cotton to market himself, sold the cotton to the ginning factory, did not usually gain

---

131 Shukla, *Life and Labour*, p. 93.

132 Ibid., p. 94. Shukla, p. 91, gives the following figures for land actually owned: Number of holders with 51–60 acres, one; 41–50, none; 31–40, one; 21–30, three; 15–20, one; 11–15, seven; 6–10, seven; and 1–5, six. None held less than one acre.

133 M. L. Dantwala, *Marketing of Raw Cotton in India*, p. 64.

134 See Mann's evidence, *Royal Commission on Agriculture*, Vol. II, pt. i, p. 15. "The repeated and frequent failure of amateur attempts to replace the present [marketing] system by something apparently much simpler shows either that the system on the whole works well, or else that there are vested interests in it so powerful as to be able to resist any but very well considered changes backed by very general support of the producers. Probably both alternatives are correct. But I am not sure that, except in a few cases in the Bombay Presidency, we know very much about the whole course of the marketing of any product." Ibid., p. 12.

135 See diagram in *Bom. Prov. Banking Enquiry Cttee. Rept.*, p. 101.

excessively.[136] It was at the ginning factory, partly as a result of the manipulations of the "weighman" when the cotton was received, that most of the disputes and the potentialities for profiteering occurred.[137] It is not surprising, then, that at first, when the Sonsek co-operators confined their activities to the sale of unginned seed cotton, they did not reduce their costs very considerably. It would seem that sometimes, in fact, in their earliest years of operation, they lost money.[138] "Caste solidarity" doubtless carried them through at this point. But in the long run, success could come only through profitability, and that profitability does not seem to have become assured until Purshottamdas Patel and his men had gone a stage further in their operations and themselves had undertaken first the ginning and then the sale of the processed cotton. To a degree, then, co-operation came almost spontaneously to the Kadva Patidars; caste solidarity served them well. But ultimately it was economics that governed their fortunes.

"Philanthropy and Sentimentality"

In an article published in *Kesari* shortly before he withdrew from most of his activity in the co-operative movement, the perspicacious R. M. Sane gave his views on the progress of the movement in areas where, on the whole, it had certainly not arisen in any way spontaneously. The issue of *Kesari* in which Sane wrote his article happened to be that in which the death of Tilak was announced and tributes paid to him; hence it was a widely read issue.[139] In some co-operative circles Sane's rather pessimistic article was considered to be "sensational."[140]

On the basis of the statistics of the numbers of new societies, Sane wrote, the movement appeared to be progressing. The accounts of societies often showed, on the surface, a profit. But when one went into the villages one found a different situation. A loan from a society had to be repaid within a fixed time. That being so, most members, Sane claimed, borrowed from money-lenders to pay their

---

136 Indian Central Cotton Committee, *Report on Eight Investigations into the Finance and Marketing of Cultivators' Cotton, 1925–28*, pp. 28, 39. Mann claimed to have "organized" this enquiry; see his evidence, *Royal Commission on Agriculture*, Vol. II, pt. i, p. 12.

137 *Report on Eight Investigations*, pp. 26, 39.

138 Information from Shri D.A. Shah.

139 *Kesari*, 3 August 1920.

140 *B.C.Q.*, September 1920, p. 106.

debts to the society. Two months later they would borrow from the society to pay the money-lender. But, said Sane, the peasant would pay as much interest on those two months' borrowings as he would pay to the society in a year. Sane did not profess to be completely pessimistic about the prospects of co-operative societies, however. Very occasionally, he had come across villages which had genuinely benefited from a co-operative society. Such villages showed what could be done. For one-third of the farmers of India, Sane asserted, it was not worthwhile doing anything. But for the remaining two-thirds something could be done. If the rayats themselves did not understand what was good for them, because they were illiterate, then the educated must help. Sane used the analogy of a doctor. If the doctor recommended a medicine, but the patient would not take it, the patient's relatives and friends had to consider it their duty to persuade—even to force—the patient to take the medicine. The same attitude was necessary so far as co-operative societies were concerned. It would seem (we may comment) that the old paternalism, similar to that of Chunilal Mehta, was still manifesting itself. It was doubtless an indigenous paternalism of the best kind, but there was to be a diminishing role for such paternalism in the India, democratic yet caste-conscious, that was beginning to emerge.

What basis in reality had Sane's picture of the co-operative society member as one caught up in a vicious circle of borrowing here and paying there? The *Bombay Co-operative Quarterly*, though it joined with Sane in calling for an economic enquiry into these charges,[141] commented that such an enquiry probably would not reveal anything not already known to "close students" of the movement. However, it felt that the days were certainly past when it was "undesirable to uproot the tender plant again and again and examine whether its growth was healthy."[142] Rothfeld's examination of the plant tended to verify Sane's charges. "Taking the Presidency as a whole,"[143] he wrote in his Report for 1923, "it is believed that the annual expenditure in money, mainly borrowed, for current cultivation amounts to about Rs.25 to Rs.30 crores." Rothfeld did not give any calculations to show how he arrived at this figure;[144]

141 Ibid., p. 75.
142 Ibid., p. 106.
143 That is, including Sind.
144 In 1922 he had estimated the total requirements at Rs.25 crores, again giving no calculation. See Rothfeld, "Note on Indian Rural Finance: Remarks on Note by Mr. Simcox." The "Mr. Simcox" referred to is A. H. A. Simcox, Collr., Nasik, who

the Bombay Provincial Banking Enquiry Committee, basing their calculations to some extent on "reliable" data from the Department of Agriculture, came to the conclusion that the total cash requirements for cultivation of the Presidency as a whole in 1930 came to about Rs.32½ crores.[145] Rothfeld knew that the total number of agriculturists in the Presidency was about two million. Of these, 208,000, or nearly 11 per cent, were members of credit societies. Even if only twenty crores were required by the agriculturists annually, the co-operative society members, supposing them to represent a fair cross-section of cultivators, would require two crores. In fact, however, many co-operative society members came from irrigated areas and other areas requiring large amounts of capital. Therefore they needed at least two and a half crores annually. The total amount lent to individuals by credit societies with unlimited liability in 1922–23 was Rs.1,15,03,380.[146] Rothfeld thus calculated that the cultivators who were members of co-operative societies were obtaining from the societies only a little over two-fifths of what they required for current agricultural operations. They were still far from abandoning the *saukar*.[147]

Yet Rothfeld did not conclude that the solution in all areas was simply to provide more money for the co-operative movement. Even in 1921 he had "strong doubts" about co-operative societies ever succeeding in the dry areas of the Deccan.[148] He felt, in fact, that in many cases where the cultivator's business was unprofitable the only solution was for him to sell his land and go and work in a factory in Bombay. [149] Rothfeld knew that this idea would be unpopular. But, he told the Provincial Conference of 1922, "as far as I am concerned I consider the most serious enemies of the movement—far more serious than any joint stock banks—are Philanthropy and Sentimentality. There is far too much of a tendency to deplore the state of poor cultivators, of uneconomical cultivators, and in consequence there is a risk of giving them money which has

---

was something of a latter-day opponent of the policy of promoting co-operative societies. (Poona, T.A.G.6.)

145 *Bom. Prov. Banking Enquiry Cttee. Rept.,* p. 62. It should be noted that no allowance is made in any of these calculations for the cultivator's requirements for marriages and other social observances.

146 *Rept., 1922–23,* p. 48.

147 Ibid., p. 8.

148 *Rept., 1920–21,* p. 18.

149 Rothfeld to D. A. Vichare, M.L.C., No. Misc. of 17–20 January 1921. (Poona, T.A.G.3.) See also *Prov. Co-op. Conf. Procs., 1922,* p. 53.

been earned, hard-earned, by another man who is really economical."[150] Rothfeld's final thoughts on the matter while he held the position of Registrar were these: "I think that in the Deccan co-operative credit should not be the main instrument of co-operation but that greater reliance should be paid [sic] upon the consolidation of holdings, the spread of joint cultivation, and of the extension of co-operative sale and co-operative purchase of agricultural requisites."[151]

Consolidation of Holdings and "Joint Cultivation"

Rothfeld's conclusions about the consolidation of holdings and the spread of joint cultivation were also, on the whole, those of Mann, the Director of Agriculture. Mann told the Royal Commission on Agriculture that it was his policy to try to organize the whole rural community on co-operative lines.[152] He attempted to promote two new developments. One was simply co-operative consolidation of fragmented holdings; the other was co-operative farming with, on occasion, some surrender of interests in land.

Keatinge, as Director of Agriculture, had been greatly concerned about the fragmentation of already scattered holdings which occurred under Hindu law each time land passed from father to sons. In 1916 he had brought forward a draft of a bill, which was to be purely permissive, giving rightholders of an "economic holding" the power to register it in the name of one of them. Each Collector was to decide what constituted an "economic holding" in his district. Once registration had been effected, partition or transfer to more than one person would be prohibited.[153] Both the Government of Bombay and the Government of India were wary of the proposal; Mann claimed, in fact, that Keatinge had "met with almost united opposition from almost every side."[154] But by the twenties the Punjab system of societies for the voluntary co-operative consolidation of holdings was meeting with some success.[155] By

---

[150] Ibid., p. 27.

[151] *Rept., 1922–23*, p. 14.

[152] Mann's evidence, *Royal Commission on Agriculture*, Vol. II, pt. i, p. 69.

[153] Keatinge to Ch. Sec. No. 10457 of 11 November 1916. (Printed "for official use," Poona, Government Resolutions file.) See also Keatinge, *Agricultural Progress in Western India*, pp. 63–88, 195–253.

[154] Mann, *Prov. Co-op. Conf. Procs., 1922*, p. 97.

[155] See Darling, *The Punjab Peasant in Prosperity and Debt*, pp. 240 et seq; also *Royal Commission on Agriculture Rept.*, pp. 138–140.

"consolidation" was meant simply the exchange of scattered fragments for a compact block or a few compact blocks. Mann felt very strongly that government efforts in this direction in Bombay would still be regarded with suspicion. Indeed, Mann was to some extent arguing his predecessor's brief rather than his own: in one of his village studies he had come to the conclusion that the problem was "in part, settling itself." Landholders in the village of Pimple Saudagar, at least, were often "subletting" small or distant fragments of land to cultivators able to make better use of them.[156] But, Mann told the 1922 Provincial Co-operative Conference, "if mutual consent to consolidation is to be obtained by anybody that body is the Co-operative movement."[157] In the voting at the Conference, Mann appeared to win the approval of the "old Co-operators" present for the idea of making experiments in "co-operative" consolidation, although there seems to have been some division on the matter in the non-official ranks.[158]

Rothfeld told the Conference that he had "very little faith in the voluntary method in this Presidency"; this was hardly a surprising confession from a man such as he. Rothfeld claimed that it was "almost impossible to draw any inference from what has been achieved in the Punjab." There was "an extraordinary want of cohesion" in the villages of Bombay, he said. In the Punjab, Rothfeld thought, there were "very strong united communities," in spite of major religious differences. "Here we are all faced with divisions of interest from the Legislative Council . . . down to the Village Panchayats." But at the same time Rothfeld believed that any interference with the Hindu system of inheritance would be politically unwise. He agreed with Mann that fragmentation, as it actually existed in the villages, should be dealt with first; legislation should not at present be directed against future subdivision as a result of inheritance.[159]

Societies for "joint cultivation" were a much more radical proposal. These societies would be for those who agreed to pool all

156 *Land and Labour in a Deccan Village,* Study No. I, pp. 49–50.
157 *Prov. Co-op. Conf. Procs., 1922,* p. 98.
158 Ibid., p. 101.
159 Ibid., pp. 100–103. Cf. Rothfeld's evidence, *Royal Commission on Agriculture,* Vol. II, pt. i, p. 168. Keatinge's notions on fragmentation do not appear to have been put into effect finally until 1947 (in the Bombay Prevention of Fragmentation and Consolidation of Holdings Act of that year). Some of the tortuous history of his proposal may be traced in I.O.R., Bom. Legal Procs., 1917 and 1918, and again in *Bombay Government Gazette,* pt. V, 7 July 1927, pp. 41 et seq.

their labour, their implements, and for a time, their interest in land. We have no indication as to where Mann obtained his ideas on this subject; if he—or, perhaps, Rothfeld—had been influenced by recent events in Russia, they took good care not to mention the fact. Certainly the notion of "joint cultivation" on a co-operative basis was a new one to most in the co-operative movement in Bombay. At the 1921 Provincial Co-operative Conference most of the leading delegates were politely non-committal about such societies, although according to the official record the Conference "unanimously" passed a resolution recommending that experiments in joint cultivation be made.[160]

At the 1922 Conference, Mann reported in detail on the progress of his experiments. They had been made in two villages, Bhambora in Ahmadnagar district and Arjunsonda in Sholapur. The Bhambora society was based on the lease of land for ten years to a co-operative society with unlimited liability. The second experiment was based on the lease of land to what was, in effect, a limited company. It was chiefly the first experiment to which Mann drew the attention of the Conference. The village chosen was one which had been deeply affected by famine. "The credit of the people had gone . . . 80 per cent of their bullocks had died and the land was rapidly passing out of cultivation." Mann claimed that the only alternative

---

[160] *Prov. Co-op. Conf. Procs., 1921*, pp. 55–57. In the 1930s, after his retirement from Bombay, Mann went to the Soviet Union as an adviser on tea cultivation. At that time he was certainly very interested in Soviet collective farming. (See "The Collective Farm System in Russia," reprinted from the *Indian Co-operative Review* (Madras), Vol. IV, No. 2, 1938, in Mann (ed. Thorner), *The Social Framework of Agriculture*, pp. 338–347.) But this is not to say that as early as 1921 Mann had become interested in what had hitherto been the very tentative Soviet experiments in collective farming; 1921 was the year, furthermore, of the "New Economic Plan" and the reversion to an emphasis on individual peasant farming and the market mechanism in the Soviet Union. It is, of course, just possible that Mann had been influenced at this stage by Rothfeld, who in turn may have been influenced by the Hungarian Karolyi, or even Bela Kun. But the impression I gained from an interview with Dr. Mann before his death was that his personal relations with Rothfeld were not very close. In the forties and fifties Mann insisted that compulsory co-operative farming was unnecessary in India. See "Note on the [Bombay] Plan of Economic Development for India," 1944, in *The Social Framework*, pp. 296–97; "The General Report of the All India Rural Credit Survey," *Indian Economic Review*, Vol. III, No. 4, 1957, reprinted in *The Social Framework*, especially p. 315. In "The Central Mechanized Farm at Suratgarh," *Economic Weekly*, 1960, pp. 1827–28, reprinted in *The Social Framework*, pp. 332–37, he asserted that if large mechanized co-operatives were created in India the peasants could become, "as in the Russian collectives . . . essentially labourers on a large estate in whose management they would have little part."

to the cultivators' abandoning their lands was a co-operative farming society. He was ready to admit that the task of organizing such a society was made easier because the villagers' credit had disappeared. The society's by-laws were fairly rigorous. No member could withdraw from the society if the land which he had brought in was essential to the continuation of the work of the society. Besides the Managing Committee there was a "Committee of Control," consisting of two outsiders appointed by the Registrar. Predictably, the main difficulty was the suspicion of the people. They thought that the society might be a preliminary to the loss of their land altogether. The only way round this problem was to enlist the help of local leaders: "No amount of assurance by anyone else, but the men they knew well, would convince them."

In the first year the cultivators were permitted to work the land which they had previously held; the society provided bullocks, ploughs, and seeds out of funds totalling Rs.15,000 lent by the Bombay Provincial Co-operative Bank and the Ahmadnagar Famine Fund. The produce was divided into three parts. One part, subject to the payment of land revenue, was given to the owners. Another part was given to those who actually cultivated the land, and the third part went to the society for its provision of the means of cultivation. In the first year the society appeared to be making a good profit. Mann claimed that the cultivators had obtained, through the working of the society, cheaper credit than they could have expected before, bullocks and seeds without having to incur further debt, and better terms for the sale of produce than the local money-lenders-cum-traders would have given.[161]

Rothfeld was enthusiastic, and wanted to go even further. A sub-committee of the Conference had recommended that "the whole question of economic cultivation would be much simplified if co-operative farming could be extensively undertaken without interfering with actual ownership."[162] Rothfeld was willing to agree to experiments along these lines. "But I do not want it to be understood by this acquiescence," he added, "that I, in any way, mean to express any personal preference for such methods of joint cultivation with actual ownership. I strongly believe in the possibility of

161 *Prov. Co-op. Conf. Procs., 1922,* pp. 109–11.
162 Ibid., p. 98.

Co-operative Farming Societies of lands not owned by cultivators."[163]

Here, then, was Rothfeld the socialist, due, in fact, to retire in a
week's time. Such an utterance contrasted rather strangely with
the caution of Rothfeld the member of the Indian Civil Service,
who at the previous Provincial Co-operative Conference had spok-
en against interfering with the Hindu law of inheritance. The conflict between the two aspects of the man was always apparent.

Brilliance without Tenacity

How are we to sum up the administration of Rothfeld the Indian
Civil Servant? The terse comment of the *Bombay Co-operative
Quarterly* when Rothfeld retired from the position of Registrar
and from the I. C. S. is perhaps the most revealing of all. "His "vigorous personality," the journal noted, had left an impression on
every field—urban co-operative banking, housing co-operatives, co-
operative marketing—"with the possible exception of agricultural
credit."[164]

The most damaging figures are those of overdues. In 1920–21
they climbed from 8¼ to 18 lakhs.[165] In 1921–22 they rose to 19½
lakhs. At the end of March 1923 they amounted to 31 lakhs, or over
18 per cent of the working capital of the movement.[166] Rothfeld
claimed that these figures were "somewhat confusing. In the first
place as considerable efforts were made to recover the current demand punctually and to recover outstandings as well, the working
capital was rapidly reduced by the recoveries during the last month
in the financial year. Hence the overdues which bulk larger as per-
centages at the end of the year than if they were compared to the
maximum capital in the winter." Even so, the figures were "alarm-
ing."[167]

Rothfeld had, in fact, issued a circular stating that overdues
should be reduced by at least a half by the end of March 1923.[168]
But there was much that circulars—which Calvert correctly saw as

[163] Ibid., p. 102.
[164] *B.C.Q.*, December 1923, p. 236.
[165] *Rept., 1920–21*, p. 8.
[166] *Rept., 1921–22*, p. 9.
[167] *Rept., 1922–23*, p. 9.
[168] Rothfeld, Circular No. S.R.A.D.M.–39 of 1922, published in *B.C.Q.*, March
1923, p. 315.

issuing from the Registrar's office in an ever-increasing stream—
would not do. One of the offending areas was that part of Ahmadnagar district irrigated by the new Godavari and Pravara canals. "It
is respectfully suggested that this tract may also be visited by R.
[the Registrar]," wrote Rothfeld's Personal Assistant by the side of
a copy of a letter from Vaikunth Mehta to the Assistant Registrar
for the Central Division, which was very obviously on the subject
of overdues in the new canal areas. "Justification?" Rothfeld wrote
in his imperious hand underneath.[169]

Admittedly Rothfeld did not have the staff he wished for. There
are complaints about "retrenchment" even in his Report for
1922.[170] Nevertheless, he had a considerable number of men under
him. The sanctioned strength of the superior staff of the Co-
operative Department on 31 March 1923 was seven Assistant Registrars, two Special Auditors, thirty-seven Auditors, and ten paid
Organizers. Of these, the appointments of one Assistant Registrar
and two Organizers were held "in abeyance" through lack of
funds.[171]

Rothfeld indicated that the Banks must undertake some of the
supervision work while this staff shortage persisted.[172] At the same
time, he believed that the staff of the Institute should be greatly
increased if it was to engage in serious supervision work. For this,
however, the funds of the Institute would need to be "nearly
doubled." This implied a rise in the government grant to the Institute.[173]

Rothfeld undoubtedly realized what was happening to the
movement. Comparatively few societies were organized during his
last year as Registrar. Consolidation was required, he wrote—"the
internal state of the movement made this necessary."[174] Yet simply
to realize what was happening was not enough. Rothfeld was a
brilliant man. In a modern Planning Commission he would quite
possibly be a triumphant success. But the co-operative movement
in the Bombay Presidency in the early twenties still needed the

169 V. L. Mehta to Asst. Regr., C.D., No. R.10–B.C.C.B. of 24 January 1921. (Poona,
B.P.C.B.)

170 *Rept., 1921–22*, p. 1. For the effect of Bombay's financial troubles on the movement after the Reforms scheme came into operation see chap. 5.

171 *Rept., 1922–23*, p. 1.

172 Rothfeld, Circular No. A.D.M./34 of 1923, "Programme of Work for the year
1923." (B.S.C.B., Regr.)

173 *Rept., 1922–23*, p. 33.

174 Ibid., p. 6.

stolid, more conventional qualities of the average Indian Civil Servant, as well as ideas and an insistent pen. The co-operative movement still needed, in other words, someone who was felt by members of societies in remote corners of the Presidency to be a real person, someone to turn to in times of trouble, and also someone liable to descend at any time, someone, in fact, to be feared. If Ewbank laid too much emphasis on the "humble village panchayat," Rothfeld did not give it enough attention.

V

Reality, 1923–1930

Economic Conditions

By the end of Rothfeld's time as Registrar it was beginning to be possible to discuss the rural areas of the Bombay Presidency with information that was rather more precise than that upon which the Deccan Riots Commission and Sir Richard Temple in the seventies, the authors of the various reports on the working of the Deccan Agriculturists' Relief Act, and even George Curtis in 1912, had based their generalizations. L. J. Sedgwick's 1921 Bombay Census Report explored, for example, the question of the occupations of those in the rural sector with a good deal more thoroughness than the reports of his predecessors.[1] And the social and economic investigations of Harold Mann—especially, perhaps, his detailed surveys of two Deccan villages and his masterly study of the "Economic Progress of the Rural Areas of the Bombay Presidency 1911–1922"[2]—made all previous enquiries into rural conditions in Bombay look somewhat amateurish by comparison. Sometimes, of course, Mann's enquiries, because they revealed the inadequacy of the data available, served to complicate rather than to clarify the picture. But at least many of the right questions were being asked. As answers to these questions were attempted, the roots of some, at least, of the economic difficulties of the Presidency in the twenties, and even in the thirties, became apparent.

The decade 1911–12 to 1921–22, Harold Mann wrote in 1924, had been "a time of very great stress and strain, of changes the like of which have not taken place during the last ninety years at least."[3]

---

[1] L. J. Sedgwick, *Census of India, 1921*, Vol. VIII, *Bombay*, pt. i, pp. 212–17.

[2] Mann, "Economic Progress of the Rural Areas of the Bombay Presidency, 1911–1922," Government of Bombay, 1924. (Gokhale Institute Library, Poona.)

[3] Ibid., p. 3.

His claim may not have been altogether wide of the mark; the decade was certainly one of transition. It would seem, for example, that the appearance of increasing productivity and increasing prosperity for the ordinary peasant over the years from about 1879 to about 1911–12 (with an interruption at the end of the nineteenth century) was in part the result of a fairly prolonged and fairly general increase in the so-called cultivated area of the Presidency. The second decade of the century saw no such general increase;[4] the third decade actually saw, in all regions of the Presidency, a slight decrease in the cultivated area, in other words a throwing up of unprofitable occupancies.[5] The apparent increase in productivity prior to about 1911–12 was also, in part, the result of an increase in double-cropping. But in the years 1912–13 to 1921–22, while there was a further increase of 20 per cent in the double-cropped area in Gujarat, there was a decline of 7 per cent in the Deccan and 3 per cent in the Karnatak.[6] The process of expansion seems, then, to have been decelerating and in places coming to a halt. So it is not altogether surprising that, according to a recent but already almost definitive study, the decade 1911–21 saw the beginnings in Bombay of a disparity (serious by the time of Independence) between the rate of population growth and the foodgrain output rate.[7] It must be said, however, that these beginnings were to some extent masked by the toll taken by the influenza epidemic at the end of the war.[8]

Reality was masked during and immediately after the war in another way, which happened to be important for the health of the co-operative movement as it had developed in the Bombay Presidency. The high prices received for sugar during these years disguised the fact that in the Nira Canal area, by 1918, five thousand acres had been put out of production as a result of that bane of so many Indian canals, salination. Water had been used too lavishly; little attention had been paid to drainage. The topsoil had become salty, the subsoil "stinking with sulphurated hydrogen."[9] Harold Mann, whose original training had been as a chem-

[4] Ibid., p. 10.

[5] See Quinquennial Statements of Holdings in Government Rayatwari Area in the Districts of the Bombay Presidency Proper, in *Bom. L. Rev. Admin. Repts., 1916–17,* pt. i; *1921–22; 1926–27.* Also *Bom. Prov. Banking Enquiry Cttee. Rept.,* p. 51.

[6] Mann, "Economic Progress," p. 19.

[7] George Blyn, *Agricultural Trends in India, 1891–1947: Output, Availability and Productivity* (1966), p. 100.

[8] See Mann, "Economic Progress," p. 5.

[9] Mann, "The Economic Results and Possibilities of Irrigation," in Mann (ed.

ist, conducted some of the most rigorous enquiries into this condition and its possible remedies, but his research yielded increasingly pessimistic results. Some of the best land had been rendered "permanently barren." But Mann was, as usual, concerned also about social consequences. Many of the Malis in the Nira Canal region could afford to move on to the newly opened Godavari Canal areas, in Ahmadnagar district. But other cultivators—generally Marathas—could not afford to do so.[10] As Ewbank had put it in 1916, "They blunder on in hopes of making a coup."[11] In the years from 1919 to 1923 sugar prices gave many some hope. But it was to be false hope.

Cotton prices during the war and immediately after it were more erratic than sugar prices. But in 1919–20 cotton produced "almost unheard of" profits. 1920 was also a peak year for *jowari* and *bajri* prices.[12] In that year Harold Mann published the results of an enquiry into the effects of rising prices on rural prosperity, based largely upon work he had carried out in his two Deccan village studies. In both places, he found, interest rates had hardly risen at all—certainly not to the extent to which prices had risen. The land revenue assessment, under the thirty years' settlement, had not changed. The wages of labour had risen, on the other hand, as had rents. Mann assumed, for the purposes of this enquiry, a 50 per cent rise in prices and wages. In these circumstances, he calculated, the economic position of proprietors who did no field work would not be greatly improved unless they had very large debts, the interest rate upon which would remain virtually static while receipts rose. Those who depended upon self-cultivated land alone for their

---

Thorner), *The Social Framework of Agriculture*, p. 329. This paper was originally published in the *Indian Journal of Agricultural Economics*, Vol. XIII, No. 2, 1958.

10 Mann, loc. cit.; also Mann, "Economic Conditions in some Deccan Canal Areas," *B.C.Q.*, December 1918, p. 126, and Mann and V. A. Tamhane, *The Salt Lands of the Nira Valley* (1910).

11 Ewbank, Memo., encl. Ewbank to Collr., Poona, 21 January 1916. (Poona, N.C. & C.B.)

12 1918–19 was a famine year and 1920–21 was a year of great scarcity; "peaks" in these years should be disregarded. The series *Agricultural Statistics of India*, Vol. I, gives "Harvest Prices" of Principal Crops in the Bombay Presidency, 1917–30. In the twenties the compilers seem to have taken advantage of the annual appearance of the series to amend certain figures given in earlier volumes. In Table 3, p. 239, which must have only limited reliability, later estimates are normally given. In defence of these statistics it can be said that they tally fairly well with the index of agricultural prices constructed by Dharm Narain, *Impact of Price Movements on Areas under Selected Crops in India, 1900–1939*, pp. 167–69.

income, and who had possessed sufficient land to maintain themselves before the rise in prices, would generally be better off. The
economic position of peasants who had previously managed to
make ends meet partly through work on their own land and partly
through wage labour would be marginally improved. But the position of those whose condition had already been one of "insolvency"
before the price rise would often be one of still further decline.[13]

Mann was somewhat hesitant about applying the results of these
two Deccan studies to the whole Presidency. But, assuming that his
results were not entirely irrelevant outside the Deccan,[14] it would
appear that the medium peasants, those who cultivated their land
themselves with, perhaps, little or no reliance on agricultural
labourers, fared reasonably well in the years immediately before
1922. Such men were often the mainstay of co-operative societies.
But Mann's study of the effects of a price rise contained certain
largely hypothetical elements: he himself later showed, for instance,
that between 1912–13 and 1921–22 the increase in the monetary
value of the agricultural produce of the Presidency proper which
entered the markets at harvest time was in fact not 50 per cent but,
rather, something in the order of 80 per cent.[15] And he could say
little about the extent of the rise in rents.[16] In 1926 he made a new,
on-the-spot survey of Jategaon Budruk, the village which he had
first surveyed in 1917. The results of this resurvey were presented
briefly to the Royal Commission on Agriculture. While the percentage of families in Jategaon Budruk who were "solvent" was
slightly higher in 1926 than it had been in 1917, it was now clear
that solvency had to be bought increasingly by supplementary
wage-earning. The number of families in the village who depended

13 Mann, "The Effects of Rise of Prices on Rural Prosperity," in Mann (ed. Thorner), *The Social Framework of Agriculture*, pp. 104–17, first published in the *Proceedings* of the Madras Conference of the Indian Economic Association, 1919–20. The
paper also forms Chapter VII of Mann and Kanitkar, *Land and Labour in a Deccan
Village*, Study No. II (1921). Mann found it difficult to explain why rural interest
rates should remain virtually static. "The only reason we can think of for this is
that the rate of interest was already so high . . . that it can hardly rise further and
hence is independent of moderate rises in the value of money elsewhere." Since loans
from money-lenders were often renewed annually, one might add, the raising of
interest rates should have been comparatively easy. Perhaps we have here a situation
of qualified "dualism" between urban and rural economies.

14 Mann, "Economic Progress," p. 61.

15 Ibid., p. 55.

16 Ibid. Recent settlement reports, a valuable source of information on rent levels,
were rather few in number at this time.

solely upon agriculture had diminished in proportion to the total number of families.[17] The agricultural wages upon which some of the solvent relied for part of their income were capable not only of rising rapidly but also of falling with equal speed. And wages could fall at a time when rural interest rates may well have remained almost as unresponsive to financial trends as they had been at a time of rising wages and prices.[18] Insofar as the Jategaon Budruk studies gave some clue as to what was happening in the dry farming areas of the Deccan, and perhaps beyond, they implied that the average co-operative society member in those areas probably belonged to a group that was diminishing in importance, or at least changing its character.

At such a time of "stress and strain" money-lending groups, of both the professional and the "agriculturist" variety, must surely have tried to capitalize on the situation. One would certainly hardly expect them to lie dormant. But, as in the eighties and nineties, it is extraordinarily difficult to come to any very definite conclusions in the matter. The Bombay Provincial Banking Enquiry Committee of 1929–30 felt that there was still a "tendency" for land to pass from "agriculturists" to "non-agriculturists," but the Committee admitted that their figures were "not quite reliable."[19] In reality, their figures give the impression that between 1917 and 1927 there was virtually no increase in the amount of land held by "non-agriculturists" in the Central and Southern Divisions of the Presidency, that is, in the Deccan and the Karnatak. The Banking Enquiry Committee went on to speak, as so many official enquiries had done since the eighties, of the "rise of the agriculturist money-lender."[20] One might expect to find, in this

[17] *Royal Commission on Agriculture,* Vol. II, pt. i, *Bombay Evidence,* pp. 16(i)–16(ii).

[18] On rural wages see *Season and Crop Reports of the Bombay Presidency, 1926–27,* p. 22; *1927–28,* p. 23; *1928–29,* p. 21. Rural wages could be paid in cash or in kind or in both. Statistical data on the subject were notoriously unreliable: see the note by J. A. Woodhead, Secretary, G. of I., Commerce Dept., 1930, in front of the I.O.R. copy of the last (37th) issue of India, Department of Statistics, *Prices and Wages in India,* 1923. Reliable data on interest rates are also very difficult to come by. But the average rate of interest in Jategaon Budruk in 1917 was 23.8 per cent. (Mann and Kanitkar, *Land and Labour in a Deccan Village,* Study No. II, p. 120.) At the end of the twenties the Bombay Provincial Banking Enquiry Committee estimated the average interest rate in the Deccan-Karnatak famine tract to be 24 per cent. (See their *Rept.,* p. 55.)

[19] *Bom. Prov. Banking Enquiry Cttee. Rept.,* p. 52.

[20] Ibid.

situation, an increase in the number of occupancies held by those who have been called the "rich peasants." Such an increase might well have been brought about through the use by "agriculturist money-lenders" of such methods as foreclosure; they were certainly not legally restrained, in the way the "non-agriculturist" money-lenders were, by the Deccan Agriculturists' Relief Act. But when one comes to examine the quinquennial statements of size and distribution of holdings of "agriculturists" for the years 1917, 1922, and 1927, one again finds that there are no essential changes over the decade. Except in one district, Bijapur, in the acreage ranges over 25 acres there are no marked increases in the number of "agriculturist" landholders and the total acreage involved. Even in Bijapur it is the total acreage of "agriculturists'" holdings in the 100–500 acres range that increases—from 431,700 acres in 1917 to 513,518 acres in 1927—rather than the number of holders, which actually decreases from 2,832 to 2,716. There is, of course, at this time of population increase, a marked rise in all areas of the number of holdings of less than five acres. But at the top end of the scale there does not appear to be any strong tendency towards aggregation amongst the "agriculturist" communities.[21]

It may well be, of course, that a decade—especially the decade 1917–27—is not a long enough span of time in which to discover trends. Unfortunately the statistics on holdings 1917–27 are not directly comparable with those of the last investigation of this matter, that of 1905.[22] And in 1932 the system of gathering such statistics was changed yet again. Furthermore, these statistics were still subject to all the old difficulties over the definition of "agriculturist" and "non-agriculturist,"[23] although the introduction of the Record of Rights had led to the disappearance from the statistics of the man who paid revenue but who was not the "real" holder.[24] Registration statistics were still of little value. As F. G. H. Anderson put it, in the Bombay Registration Report for 1920–22, if all

---

[21] See Quinquennial Statements of Holdings in *Bom. L. Rev. Admin. Repts., 1916–17*, pt. i; *1921–22*; *1926–27*.

[22] Commrs., C.D. and N.D., *Bom. L. Rev. Admin. Rept., 1916–17*, pt. i, p. 14.

[23] Cf. *Bom. Prov. Banking Enquiry Cttee. Rept.*, p. 51.

[24] See F. G. Hartnell Anderson, *Manual of Revenue Accounts of the Villages, Talukas and Districts of the Bombay Presidency* (5th ed., reprinted 1940), p. 53, on the effects of the amended Land Revenue Code of 1913. There was still the possibility, however, of a three months' delay between a man's purchase of land and the entry of his name in the Record of Rights: see G. S. Curtis, Evidence, Maclagan Cttee. (Patiala), and cf. also *Bom. Prov. Banking Enquiry Cttee. Rept.*, p. 188.

the explanations given by district officers for rises and falls in registration statistics were accepted, "a new natural phenomenon" could be said to have come into existence, an effect which had "opposite and contradictory causes."[25]

The failure of the quinquennial statements to show a marked increase in the numbers and size of large holdings amongst both non-agriculturists and agriculturists possibly illustrates one important aspect of the rural credit situation in the Bombay Presidency at this time. Whatever may have been the position in the nineteenth century, and especially before the Deccan Riots and the Deccan Agriculturists' Relief Act, by the 1920s most loans from money-lenders were not advanced on the security of property. There were, of course, the "sales" that were in reality mortgages, often insisted on in the case of large loans. But the Bombay Provincial Banking Enquiry Committee of 1929–30 believed that small loans from both "agriculturist" and "non-agriculturist" money-lenders were "almost invariably given on personal security." Only between 27 and 36.5 per cent of all loans given in the districts by private persons were on the security of property.[26] Most of the loans were on "personal account." Co-operative societies, on the other hand, as we have seen, increasingly advanced loans on the security of land—sometimes with an additional lien on crops grown. The proportion of agricultural loans from co-operative societies in Bombay secured on land was already 43 per cent in 1913–14.[27] By the early 1950s it was in the vicinity of 75 per cent.[28]

The peculiarly ambivalent attitude of many officials and non-officials to the "agriculturist money-lenders" found expression in the Report of the Bombay Provincial Banking Enquiry Committee. The Committee thought that "several" of these agriculturist money-lenders had "an eye on their debtors' lands."[29] The Indian Central Banking Enquiry deduced from this that the Bombay

25 *Report on the Administration of the Registration Department in the Bombay Presidency, 1920–1922*, p. 2.
26 *Bom. Prov. Banking Enquiry Cttee. Rept.*, p. 56.
27 *Maclagan Cttee. Rept.*, p. 41.
28 Reserve Bank of India, *All-India Rural Credit Survey, Report of the Committee of Direction*, Vol. II, *The General Report* (1954), p. 233. This is not to say, of course, that there was a steady progression from before the First World War to the time of the *Rural Credit Survey*. I have been unable to find any statistics on the type of security demanded by societies in the intervening period; the Bombay Prov. Banking Enquiry Cttee. could produce no statistics on the matter. (See their *Rept.*, p. 157.)
29 *Bom. Prov. Banking Enquiry Cttee. Rept.*, p. 64.

Committee meant that "the agriculturist moneylender is often more exacting than the professional moneylender."[30] But the Bombay Committee in fact emphasized their belief that, in general, the agriculturist money-lender, "though often grasping," was "easy in his dealings with his brother agriculturist and is under the influence of public opinion in the village."[31] In this assertion they were, of course, to some extent merely echoing the opinion of the Arthur Commission of 1912. Nevertheless, one suspects that the agriculturist money-lender in Bombay was of a somewhat more gentle disposition than, say, the agriculturist money-lender of Punjab.

Certainly by the 1920s a number of officials in the Bombay Presidency were beginning to realize that it was not simply what a man owned that mattered; it was also the amount of land that he cultivated. Sedgwick in the 1921 Census Report claimed that "many cultivators have about 50 per cent of their own land and 50 per cent of rented land."[32] There was no simple distinction in the Bombay Presidency between "landholder" and "tenant." Many a cultivator was both landholder and tenant; he could be landholder, tenant, and labourer as well. At last it was realized that in Bombay the unit of cultivation was frequently larger than the owned holding. In this situation, it was claimed (perhaps with a little too much optimism), "tenancy" was often a not undesirable characteristic. There was, for example, more tenancy in Gujarat than there was in the Deccan, but this fact certainly did not indicate that Gujarat was poorer than the Deccan.[33] The actual amount of land that was cultivated under tenancy was calculated as the second revision settlements began to be made in the middle 1920s; on the whole, the settlement reports produced at this time showed the correctness of many of Sedgwick's assertions of 1921.[34] These settlement

---

[30] *Indian Central Banking Enquiry Committee, 1931, Majority Report,* p. 75, quoted *Rural Credit Survey, General Report* (1954), p. 169.

[31] *Bom. Prov. Banking Enquiry Rept.,* p. 53. See also ibid., p. 64.

[32] *Bombay Census Rept., 1921,* pt. i, p. 216.

[33] Ibid., p. 217.

[34] See *Papers relating to the Second Revision Settlement of Satara Taluka of the Satara District, 1923,* S.R. G. of B., N.S., No. dcxxxv, p. 7; *Papers relating to the Second Revision Settlement of the Karad Taluka of the Satara District, 1925,* S.R. G. of B., N.S., No. dcxxxi, p. 4. For a broader analysis, apparently based on statistics from a number of unpublished second revision settlement reports from other parts of the Presidency, see F. G. H. Anderson, *Facts and Fallacies about the Bombay Land Revenue System* (1929), p. 50. Anderson published this tendentious but useful tract on his retirement from the position of Settlement Commissioner, in the midst of the Bardoli crisis.

reports tend to confirm one's impression that while the average co-operative society member in the twenties certainly possessed some land, and was an "economic" cultivator, he may not necessarily have actually possessed an "economic holding." Unfortunately there are no statistics to enable us to make a more precise statement on the matter.[35]

The Registrars

When Rothfeld left the Co-operative Department it appeared to many people that there was "hardly anything that could be suggested or attempted for years to come."[36] Though the number of rural societies in Bombay and their membership increased by more than half between 1924 and 1930, and their working capital more than doubled,[37] there were no really important changes in the structure of the movement. The Provincial Bank, the district banks, the supervising unions, the village societies—all remained. The Registrar, the Institute (now known as the Bombay Provincial Co-operative Institute), and the honorary organizers played, with some adjustments, more or less their accustomed roles. Yet it was during this period that the real weaknesses—and some of the strengths—of the co-operative movement became fully apparent.

With Rothfeld's departure the days when a Registrar's personal eccentricities could sometimes dominate the co-operative movement were virtually at an end. For one thing, the elected element in the Legislative Council could hardly be expected to permit the indefinite continuation of such a state of affairs in a "transferred" field. Nevertheless, the co-operative movement still to some extent revolved about the person of the Registrar, the more so, perhaps, as the effects of Rothfeld's neglect of certain aspects came to be felt. Three men held the position of Registrar during the next seven years—two Indians and one Englishman. Jarnardan Madan[38] was

---

35 Rothfeld went so far as to claim that "the pure cultivator in this Presidency has by this time almost ceased to exist." *Rept., 1922–23,* p. 14.

36 D. A. Shah, Obituary Notice of Sir Janardan Madan, *B.C.Q.,* April 1957, p. 261.

37 The number of rural societies in the Bombay Presidency in 1924 was 3,050; in 1930 it was 4,779. Membership increased from 220,616 to 343,642; working capital of the rural societies from Rs.1,97,61,913 to Rs.4,10,06,469: *Rept. 1923–24,* pp. 72–75, and *Rept., 1929–30,* pp. 124–27.

38 Janardan Atmaram Madan: Asst. Collr., Bom., 1909; Asst. Regr. Co-op. Socs., 1919; Ag. Regr., 1919, 1921; Regr., 1923; Joint Sec., Royal Commission on Agriculture, 1926; Chairman, Bom. Prov. Banking Enquiry Cttee., 1929; Sec., R.D., 1934; Commr., 1936; Adviser to Govr., 1939; Kt., 1942.

Registrar from 1923 to 1926, G. F. S. Collins[39] during some of 1926 and much of 1927, and V. S. Bhide[40] for the remainder of the period.

Madan had been carefully groomed for the position. He had already had a good fourteen years' service as a Civilian, including three as senior Assistant Registrar under both Ewbank and Rothfeld. Like Rothfeld, he had been sent on a visit to England and Europe to study co-operation before taking over as Registrar.[41] Madan's position as Registrar has been described as "both very difficult and very comfortable."[42] His position was comfortable in that many major decisions had been made before he took charge, difficult in that he could not attract attention to himself, in the way that Rothfeld did, simply by making major decisions. Madan had to make his mark by hard, painstaking work on the details of administration. Perhaps he was assisted by the fact that he was an Indian. "I can go and see him at his house, I can join him at tea and talk to him at any time without reserve," said G. K. Devadhar.[43] On the other hand, Madan was capable of writing curt, often commanding notes to non-officials.

Madan went on to a distinguished career after he left the position of Registrar. But his successor, Collins, who held the post for just over a year, rapidly became convinced that the movement had been allowed to deteriorate and that vigorous measures were required. His opinions were perhaps a reflection not so much on Madan as on Rothfeld: he could note in his 1927 Report that in the area around Poona "a large part of the arrears" dated back six or seven years.[44] It is possible to detect in his writings a certain British relish for the exposure of corruption and incompetence in India; in his administration he was inclined to hack mercilessly at a limb before he had had time to discover whether or not it was made up completely of dead wood. Nevertheless, he, more than anyone else, was responsible for pinpointing the undoubted faults of the movement.

[39] Godfrey Fernando Strafford Collins: Asst. Collr., Bom., 1912; Ag. Regr., 1926; Sec., Home Dept., 1929; Private Sec. to Govr., 1934; Commr., Sind, 1935; Sec., R.D., 1937; Advisor to Govr., 1942; K.C.I.E., 1945.
[40] Vithal Shivaram Bhide: Asst. Collr., Burma, 1915; Asst. Collr., Bom., 1919; Regr., 1927; Sec., R.D., 1939; Commr., 1942.
[41] See Bom. G.R.R.D. No. 6728 of 17 March 1923.
[42] Shah, Madan Obituary Notice (n. 36 above), p. 261.
[43] *Prov. Co-op. Conf. Procs., 1925*, p. 113.
[44] *Rept., 1926–27*, p. 16.

V. S. Bhide was thoroughly Indian at heart; many of his friends, for instance, came from Poona Brahman circles. Yet, perhaps partly because he came after Collins, he, too, pursued a fairly ruthless policy. But Bhide's policy was neither arbitrary nor inelastic. It definitely left room for development. One factor which Bhide's policy could not allow for completely, of course, was the final setting in, after the Wall Street collapse, of the disastrous economic depression.

Retrenchment

Throughout the period the Co-operative Department was dogged by sheer lack of funds. This state of affairs was not altogether the result of diminishing prosperity in the Presidency. To some extent, rather, it was inherent in the system of finance which was introduced with the reforms. Under the scheme drawn up by the Financial Relations Committee of the Government of India (the "Meston Committee") during 1919 and 1920, the provinces' main source of income was to be the land revenue. The central government was given control of income tax and customs duties. Bombay's chief source of revenue was thus inherently inexpansive —or, rather, it could be expanded only every thirty years, at the time of revision settlements, and then, so it seemed in the twenties, at the risk of provoking a Bardoli type of satyagraha. The Bombay Government, it would appear, was perfectly correct in claiming that the Presidency had been better off before the reforms. Deficit budgets were necessary in 1921 and 1922, and from 1925 until 1928.[45]

Under the reforms scheme the Legislative Council had the right to reject a demand for a grant for a transferred department, and unless expenditure was required simply in order to keep the department in being, the Governor had no right to interfere. With "retrenchment" a necessity, it is not very surprising that the Legislative Council sometimes decided to reject the demands of the Co-operative Department. The Council did the same to the demands of the Education and the Sanitary Departments. In spite of the fact that Bhide could claim that "almost all the members of the Legislative Council. . . are in one way or another connected with the

---

[45] For the Meston settlement and Bombay see *Indian Statutory Commission*, Vol. VII, *Memorandum submitted by the Government of Bombay*, pp. 562 et seq.; T. M. Joshi, *Bombay Finance (1921–46)*, pp. 21–39; P. Thomas, *The Growth of Federal Finance in India*, pp. 346–48.

Movement"[46]—it was usually only a very tenuous connection—the benefits provided by the older established "nation-building" departments were probably just as obvious to the average Council member as those provided by the Co-operative Department, if not more so. One thing was certain: co-operators now had to work through their representatives in the Legislative Council if they wanted the movement to have more government money. But the members of the Council were not sure that they did want the movement to have more money, if that money was to be spent on more official staff.[47] The Legislative Council persistently refused, for example, to sanction a grant for the post of Deputy Registrar, even though the establishment of the position had been sanctioned by the Secretariat.

In his Report for 1928 Bhide produced a table giving Government expenditure per member of the societies in Bombay and in the other provinces for the year 1926–27. Bombay was far behind the Punjab and the Central Provinces.[48] Staff were required in the Central Provinces to repair a structure which had almost collapsed in the early twenties. But the figures for the Punjab, where there were no abnormal conditions, clearly show where the emphasis in fact lay in that province. A great deal of money was spent in the Punjab on a force of government "inspectors"; indeed Mahadev Desai, in the days of his association with the co-operative movement, might well have approved. There was much talk in the Punjab about the virtues of non-official control in the co-operative movement. But practice was often rather different from theory.[49]

---

[46] *Rept., 1927–28*, p. 63.

[47] Cf. Rothfeld's peevish complaint in 1923, when "retrenchment" was just beginning: "It is of course for the members of the Council of the Presidency to decide whether the country prefers lower taxation or lower development. It cannot have both and the view taken may possibly be correct that the country is not ripe for being rapidly developed." *Rept., 1922–23*, p. 6.

[48]

	Rupees	Annas	Pice
Madras		14	2
Bengal	1	0	0
Bombay	1	0	7
Punjab	1	11	9
Central Provinces	1	6	5
United Provinces		13	3

Source: *Rept., 1927–28*, p. 19.

[49] Auditors in the Punjab were employed by the non-official Punjab Co-operative Union, and largely paid by fees from societies; in practice they were under the government inspectors. See Bhide to Govt. No. ADM.–135 of 29 August 1927, encl. Bom. G.R.R.D. No. 3818/24 of 22 February 1928. The Punjab's finances were not in such a parlous state as Bombay's, largely, it would appear, because of the high receipts from irrigation dues. See Calvert, *The Wealth and Welfare of the Punjab*, 2d ed., p. 415.

It would seem that Bhide was largely justified in speaking, after retiring, of the "Punjab School of Co-operation," with its emphasis on official direction and initiative."[50]

The "Punjab School" had its representative on the Royal Commission on Agriculture in Hubert Calvert. It is very likely that he was responsible, possibly with Madan,[51] one of the Secretaries of the Commission, for much of the section on co-operation in the final Report. "If co-operation fails," the Commission claimed, "there will fail the best hope of rural India."[52] But the members of the Commission felt it necessary to recommend, "for the immediate future, a continuance of official guidance and, to some extent, of official control." They believed that "every effort" should be made to build up "a highly educated and well trained staff of officials" in all provinces.[53] Bhide used this recommendation as a text in his efforts to obtain more staff. The Agriculture Commission, he wrote in 1928, had given their "authoritative opinion . . . and as a result of the detailed discussions that will take place with reference to their recommendations it is to be hoped that a comprehensive programme of State assistance to the Movement will be drawn up and a substantial portion of the State assistance will take the shape of an increase to the existing staff of the Department."[54] But Bhide's hopes, which for a time were possibly genuinely high, were soon dashed. Rothfeld commented acidly from retirement:

As things are, with the Co-operative Department's budget as it is, it is hypocrisy for Government, the Registrar, or anyone else to speak of his supervising societies. The plain fact is that he cannot do it with the staff allowed him. With a considerably smaller number of societies and about half the working capital five years ago I made it tolerably clear that I could no longer go on accepting any appreciable responsibility as Registrar for the guidance or at any rate the supervision of societies. If I were Registrar now, I should absolutely refuse to accept any at all, until the Legislature cared to pay for an adequate staff; take it or leave it![55]

---

[50] Bhide, Obituary Notice of Sir Janardan Madan, *B.C.Q.*, April 1957, p. 252.
[51] See Bhide, loc. cit.
[52] *Royal Commission on Agriculture Report*, p. 450.
[53] Ibid., p. 451.
[54] *Rept., 1927–28*, p. 64.
[55] Otto Rothfield [he had changed the spelling of his name], "Societies and their Supervision," *B.C.Q.*, June 1929, p. 5.

Bhide eventually showed signs of adopting a policy somewhat along these lines. During 1930 Assistant Registrars were instructed virtually to cease registering new societies.[56] In the same year Bhide had an interview with the Governor at which he stressed the need for additional staff in the higher grades. But there was no thought of asking the Governor to intervene in Legislative Council affairs.[57]

If more staff could not be obtained, the existing staff could at least be used to the best advantage. Madan, in particular, set high standards for his staff. The touring of Assistant Registrars was often "spasmodic," without any regular plan, he complained in one of his 1925 circulars.[58] More circulars to the Assistant Registrars followed on delayed replies to letters, incomplete diaries, and slackness generally. Auditors, too, were the subject of some of Madan's caustic little notes. "I find that Auditors usually spend several days at headquarters every month doing 'office work.' Usually there is very little office work for them."[59] Another circular reminded the Auditors that it was essential that the societies' accounts be audited in the village. "It is very necessary and desirable that the Auditor should sleep in the village and thus have an opportunity of meeting the members of the societies in the evening."[60] Probably taking his cue from Madan, and also passing on some of Madan's rebukes, one rather loquacious Assistant Registrar exhorted his Auditors to "make the most of the immense opportunites you get of acquainting yourselves with the village conditions."[61] But auditing was dull work, and for a townsman away from home and family, the villages were dull places; no doubt some auditors regarded such efforts to inspire enthusiasm as somewhat naïve.

Madan was the first Registrar to suggest that with the increasing proximity of societies the ratio of one auditor to a hundred societies was perhaps somewhat high.[62] It was left to Bhide to develop

---

56 *Rept., 1929–30*, p. 15.

57 See Bhide to Asst. Private Sec. to Govr., D/O of 12 February 1930. (Poona, loose.)

58 Madan to all Asst. Regrs., Circular No. ADM.–83 of 6–10 November 1925. (Poona, Sub-circulars.)

59 Madan to all Asst. Regrs. and Auditors, Circular No. ADM.–83 of 21–25 November 1924. (Poona, file cited.)

60 Madan to all Asst. Regrs. and Auditors, Circular No. ADM.–83 of 8 May 1925. (Poona, file cited.)

61 Asst. Regr., C.D., to Auditors, C.D., No. CLR.–2 of 28 March 1924. (Poona, file cited.)

62 Madan to Govt., No. EST.–146 of 31 August 1925, encl. Bom. G.R.R.D. No. 4830/24 of 12 October 1925.

this suggestion. A new class of "sub-auditors" was brought into being; Bhide believed that with the increasing numbers of university graduates becoming available, it would be possible to obtain lower-paid men who could accomplish much of the work satisfactorily. The glut of graduates (so disturbingly familiar to those who have known India in the second and third quarters of the twentieth century) meant that there need be no increase in the number of comparatively well paid auditors—men whom Campbell, Ewbank, and Rothfeld had felt to be so necessary. And although Ewbank, now back in Bombay after several years with the Government of India, advised against such a move, Bhide recommended that fees be charged from well-established agricultural societies, in proportion to the amount of working capital, sufficient to cover a considerable part of the cost of the audit. Bhide was certain, however, that audit should continue to be conducted by government officials. "In a Province which more than others has adopted the policy of conducting the movement by non-official agency, it is the ultimate, and in fact the only, form of control and supervision which the Registrar has over the societies."[63]

A New Act

Official control over the movement had hitherto been exercised by means of the wide discretionary powers vested in the Registrar under the all-India Acts of 1904 and 1912. "Take away or reduce the discretionary powers of the Registrar," Ewbank had said, "and it at once becomes necessary to substitute statutory control for his general powers and to extend the Co-operative Societies Act by at least 100 more sections."[64] Rothfeld, however, with a mind that was always yearning for precise definition, had not been daunted by this warning. The provisions of the 1912 Act, he believed, were "rather vague," or, as they were "often called by some confusion of thought, simple."[65] He decided that with the coming of the reforms a new, provincial Act was required. Such an Act would set out in detail what had been learnt in Bombay about the control of co-operatives in the years since 1912.

[63] Bhide to Govt., No. ADM.–135 of 29 August 1927, encl. Bom. G.R.R.D. No. 3818/24 of 22 February 1928.

[64] Ewbank to Govt., No. 6318 of 22 May 1919, encl. Bom. R.D. Order No. 14140 of 3 December 1919.

[65] Rothfeld, Note, "Co-operative Jurisprudence," 1 September 1923, (B.S.C.B., Regr.)

The bill which Rothfeld drafted in 1922 did not reach the Legislative Council until July 1924, by which time he had retired. To attempt to define by means of legislation what had hitherto been chiefly defined by rules promulgated under the 1912 Act, and by pure convention, was, of course, to invite strong criticisms from "non-officials" both within and without the movement. As soon as the bill was published, it was condemned by the *Bombay Chronicle* for failing to take notice of "the changed political outlook" in the Presidency.[66] The bill was referred to a Select Committee, which reported in October. Much to the satisfaction of the *Chronicle*, this Committee recommended that any rules framed under the proposed new Act should be supplied to the Legislative Council, which would be called upon to express its approval by means of a Resolution. Apparently the officials on the Select Committee gave way to the non-officials on this point.[67]

The bill was referred to another Select Committee and finally subjected to three days of minute examination by the legally minded members of the Legislative Council. L. B. Bhopatkar, the Chitpavan Brahman chairman of the Poona Central Co-operative Bank, and a man soon to be prominent in militant Hindu Mahasabha politics, took the lead in this examination. Those "non-officials" who followed him apparently wished to construct a complete system of boards of appeal, so that decisions could be contested at all levels.[68] But Bhopatkar and his men did not gain a great deal of support from some other groups, such as the non-Brahmans, and, of course, little from the official element in the Council. When all was done, Madan could report that "the Bill as finally passed differs very little from the one originally drafted by Mr. Rothfeld."[69] The net effect of the Act was defined by Rothfeld when he was questioned by the Royal Commission on Agriculture. "Has not Bombay gone further than any other Province in India in its legislative control over societies?" Calvert asked him. "I

[66] *Bombay Chronicle*, 10 July 1924.

[67] See *Bombay Chronicle*, 10 October 1924.

[68] For the Report of the Second Select Committee, see *Bom. Legislative Council Procs.*, Vol. XV, Appx. C. For the Bill, see ibid., 23–25 July 1925.

[69] *Rept., 1924–25*, p. 37. Interestingly enough, most of the co-operative developments in Palestine in the days of the Mandate, and the many experiments in co-operation in Israel, have taken place on a legal basis provided by an Ordinance of 1933 which was based very largely on the Bombay Act of 1925. See G. of I., Ministry of Community Development and Cooperation, *Report of the Study Team on the Working of the Cooperative Movement in Yugoslavia and Israel*, 1960, p. 66.

suppose so," Rothfeld replied. But he immediately qualified his answer by saying: "We have more definitely stated in our legislation the points where we consider that control by the Registrar must continue than any other Province has done, but we confine ourselves strictly to these."[70]

Perhaps the most immediate result of the new Act was a vast increase in the work of arbitration in the matter of the recovery of societies' dues. The 1925 Act provided for the appointment of three arbitrators instead of one if one of the parties so desired. The decision as to the number of arbitrators had previously been the Registrar's. Almost always, defaulters now opted for three arbitrators, as part of their delaying tactics, knowing that it would be difficult to find three quickly. The number of honorary workers willing and fit to act as arbitrators, Collins claimed, was decreasing rapidly, and almost all the cases had to be assigned to government auditors. This meant a considerable increase in their work and in the work of their immediate superiors, the Assistant Registrars.[71]

The new Act also contained, perhaps as a compensatory measure, provision for the immediate reference to the Revenue Department of cases in which decisions had been reached. There was now no need for an application to be made to the Civil Court before the work of recovery could begin. But, as the economic recession deepened, Revenue Department officials were genuinely unable to handle all the cases—there were 12,133 in 1929.[72] Additional staff had to be provided, therefore, at the societies' and the defaulters' expense.[73]

Brahmans and "Holiday Lectures"

At such a time as the passing of the new Act the role of the honorary organizers and the Institute naturally came into question. Madan realized that "political affairs" were now absorbing all the time of a good number of potential non-official leaders of the co-operative movement.[74] He criticized the Institute for not making enough effort to enrol members,[75] and by 1926 he was ready to admit that honorary organizers might at some future date

---

[70] Rothfeld, evidence, *Royal Commission on Agriculture,* Vol. II, pt. i, pp. 174–75.
[71] *Rept., 1926–27,* p. 45.
[72] *Rept., 1928–29,* p. 60.
[73] *Rept., 1929–30,* p. 79.
[74] *Rept., 1923–24,* p. 40, and *Rept., 1924–25,* p. 39.
[75] Ibid., p. 31.

be "an anachronism." But it was necessary to find some means of keeping up their enthusiasm for a number of years to come.[76]

With Collins there came a decided reaction against the Institute. "The decrease of Honorary Organizers must depend on the increase of Supervising Unions and not on the strengthening of the Institute. The latter by its constitution has no legal authority, and therefore no power of supervision over the Societies which have joined it, and it is not a Union of Societies."[77] Collins, in fact, appears to have been profoundly suspicious of some of the townsmen who were members of the Institute.

As if to confirm the policy of Collins, the Report of the Royal Commission on Agriculture, which appeared in 1928, stated boldly: "To the failure to recognize the limitations inherent in the system of utilising honorary workers must be largely attributed the very serious defects in the movement."[78]

It cannot be said that Bhide had any strong desire to work through non-official agency, although at first he was inclined to think that, if more officials were not available, the appointment of more honorary organizers was the best method available of securing a modicum of supervision. Bhide consulted Ewbank on the question of the future of the Institute. Ewbank, to quote Bhide, was "emphatically of opinion that the Institute cannot undertake supervision, and he goes so far as not to be in favour of District branches of the Institute, although he agrees that Divisional branches were necessary. He adds that it might be possible at some future stage to replace the Institute by a Provincial Union as a giant and final federation of Supervising Unions, and it could then be entrusted with supervision, and possibly even audit." Bhide accepted Ewbank's opinion.[79]

The grand edifice which Rothfeld had envisaged would now never be built. Rothfeld, writing from his retreat in Spain to R. M. Talpade, the Institute's senior executive officer, fulminated against the direction the movement was taking: "We have a very powerful and multiform enemy to fight; and we must throw our challenge down boldly." The letter was published in the *Bombay*

---

[76] *Rept., 1925–26*, p. 3.
[77] *Rept., 1926–27*, p. 3.
[78] *Royal Commission on Agriculture Report*, p. 451.
[79] Bhide to Govt., No. ADM.–135 of 29 August 1927, encl. Bom. G.R.R.D. No. 3818/24 of 22 February 1928.

Co-operative Quarterly.[80] Rothfeld's attempts at intervention in the movement after he retired were doubtless intensely irritating to some people.

At the end of the decade, opinion, both official and non-official, was definitely swinging against the honorary organizers. A Karnatak correspondent of the *Bombay Chronicle* complained that "holiday lectures by those who think themselves superior beings" were of no use in taking "the message of co-operation to the doors of the ryot."[81] The Karnatak was one of the centres of anti-Brahman feeling. Anti-Brahman feeling remained high in the Deccan, too. "Now if I want to stand for a [sic] membership they would not take me," complained G. K. Chitale, one of the Brahman honorary organizers who had retired in 1918.[82]

Since 1923 it had been the Government of Bombay's policy to reduce Brahman recruitment to paid positions in government service.[83] It was almost inevitable, therefore, that sooner or later there should be a government demand for the reduction of the numbers of Brahman honorary organizers of co-operative societies. Such a demand came in 1929. It would appear, in fact, that the Government of Bombay rejected the first list of District Honorary Organizers that Bhide submitted in response to their demands. In his final list "only a few Brahmin names" appeared, "particularly of those who have up to this time distinguished themselves by their work and have proved very useful to the movement. It would be a great loss to lose their services and their names have accordingly been included." "I am not making any remarks regarding Taluka Honorary Organisers," Bhide continued (with, perhaps, what might be construed as a certain Brahmanical hauteur); "the powers of appointing and removing them have been delegated to me." Nevertheless, in the revised list of Assistant Honorary Organizers for the Central Division there were twenty Marathas and only four Brahmans.[84]

---

80 Rothfield [Rothfeld] to Talpade, 19 January 1930, published in *B.C.Q.*, March 1930, pp. 214–15.

81 A Co-operator, "Co-operation in the Karnatak," *Bombay Chronicle*, 2 April 1929.

82 Chitale, Evidence, *Bom. Prov. Banking Enquiry Cttee.*, Vol. II, p. 403.

83 Bom. G.R. Finance Dept. No. 2610 of 17 September 1923. (I.O.R., Bom. Financial Procs. Vol. 11319.)

84 Bhide to Govt. No. EST.–74 of 20 September 1929, encl. Bom. G.R.R.D. No. 517–A of 7 October 1929. It would be a mistake to read too much into this letter. "British" ideas of impartiality had made reasonable headway amongst senior Indian officials. From the point of view of efficient administration of the co-operative move-

In his 1930 Report Bhide stated that he now believed that in some parts of the Presidency, at least, the money spent on travel allowances for honorary organizers could probably be spent in other ways.[85] The co-operative movement was now not attracting as honorary workers men of the same calibre and status as those who were drawn into it in the early days. He pointed to the fact that the Institute, also, was now recruiting very few members, and those who were recruited did not take the same interest in the work as the older members.

The cry for more and more deofficialization of the Movement is raised every now and then, but very few people are now coming forward to accept responsibility for the efficient conduct of the various types of institutions. Honorary agency is of course the very foundation of the Movement and is welcomed everywhere, but we certainly do not want honorary agency of a type which undertakes an important piece of work today, does it half-heartedly for some time and moves on to something else leaving the institutions concerned to take care of themselves as best they can.[86]

Supervising Unions

Both Collins and Bhide planned to give to the supervising unions the work that had been done by the honorary organizers. But the success achieved by the supervising unions was, in the somewhat ironic words of a committee which examined their work in 1933, "commensurate with the resources available."[87] The pivot of the union organization was the paid supervisor. It had been hoped, in 1924, that the supervising unions would be self-supporting after three years,[88] but many failed to achieve this aim. The pay which had been proposed for a supervisor at the beginning was Rs.40 to Rs.60 a month.[89] Actually, most unions seem to

---

ment in Maharashtra it did not matter greatly at this time that the Registrar was a Brahman. I have found no overt hints of feeling against senior Brahman officials of the Co-operative Department in the 1920s; Maratha abuse was directed against non-official Brahman leaders. We must beware, in fact, of seeing too many of the problems of the twenties in terms of group interest and group conflict.

[85] *Rept., 1929–30,* p. 4.

[86] Ibid., p. 81.

[87] *Report of the Bombay Co-operative Supervision Committee,* 1933, p. 7.

[88] Madan to V. L. Mehta (official, but part of the letter containing number has been destroyed by insects), 26–31 January 1925. (B.S.C.B., Regr.)

[89] Madan to Govt., No. EST.–127 of 18 September 1924, encl. Bom. G.R.R.D. No. 2062/24 of 18 November 1924.

have paid a sum of about Rs.35 to Rs.40. The result in 1933—a depression year, when employment was particularly difficult to obtain—was that out of the 122 supervisors in the Presidency, only 14 had received any university education. Even of those, 9 had passed none of the co-operative diploma examinations which the Institute had been conducting. The number of supervisors who had passed the matriculation examination was 47, "of whom only 28 have passed the test prescribed for appointment to [a] supervisor's post and three are lent by the Co-operative Department."[90]

Qualified men were sometimes available, however, though their services were not utilized. According to strict co-operative theory, Bhide wrote in his Report for 1930, the selection of supervisors ought to be left to the supervising union itself. Yet to give the supervising union these powers was to make "opportunities for sheer jobbery on an extensive scale."[91] Bhide had been quite definite for some years that "representatives of the rural societies on the Union Board of Management are hardly likely to make a proper choice."[92] When it came to village life, Bhide was a man of no illusions. He decided to set up "District Supervision Boards" to review the work of the supervisors. These consisted of the Assistant Registrar of the Division, a representative of the Institute, and a representative of the financing institution. But in spite of these Boards, there were instances in 1930 of "unions insisting upon the appointment of incompetent and untrained persons mainly for local, personal and factious reason."[93]

Bhide had a plan under which primary societies would compulsorily contribute to a provincial supervision fund at a flat rate of one-half of one per cent of their working capital. He also hoped for the creation of a provincial cadre of supervisors.[94] But there were protests from the wealthy districts at the idea of their supporting co-operative work in the poorer districts.[95] As a compromise, it was agreed that funds should be pooled within each district.[96]

90 *Supervision Cttee. Rept.*, p. 17.
91 *Rept., 1929–30*, p. 43.
92 *Rept., 1927–28*, p. 37.
93 *Rept., 1929–30*, p. 43.
94 Bhide's speech, *Prov. Co-op. Conf. Procs., 1929*, p. 61. See also A. U. Malji's speech, ibid., p. 52.
95 Ibid., pp. 55–59.
96 Ibid., pp. 61 ff.

The problem of supervision remained in 1930. But at least the nature of the problem was clear. Madan, who chaired the Bombay Provincial Banking Enquiry Committee in 1929, and whose opinions had probably changed little in the three years since he had been Registrar, put the problem succinctly into words:

The whole point is this. The Movement is based on democratic principles. . . . But our people in the villages are not yet literate enough or competent enough to work a democratic institution and especially so when it deals with large amounts of money; and the society goes bad because the generality of members are not able to control the actions of the men at the top. If the members themselves are unable to control it, there must be some one else . . . who would be able to control it when necessity arises; and if that is necessary . . . what kind of control should it be?[97]

"An Absurd Position"

There was, of course, one kind of control which under certain conditions could have been extremely effective. This was control by the financing institution. Rothfeld, in one of his commentaries from afar, underlined the point that he had made at the end of his career as Registrar—that, in the absence of other agencies, the district banks should take an increasing part in supervision activities.[98] But his was very much a lone voice. Why was there this reluctance in the co-operative movement to adopt the type of control that was both normal and reasonably effective in the everyday commercial world?

The chief reason had been given by Ewbank: the townsmen who ran the banks were out of touch with the rural societies. The district banks, furthermore, simply did not wish to pay for the staff which would keep them in touch with the societies. Only the Provincial Bank had an adequate, properly trained, and well-paid staff. "Many of the District Banks," Collins complained in 1927, "are paying dividends of 8, 9 and 10 per cent. while their outdoor staff is neglected."[99] The district banks were able to do this because much of the money which they obtained as deposits was never used for making loans to societies. Instead, it was frequently reinvested

---

[97] Madan, questioning Bhide, *Bom. Prov. Banking Enquiry Cttee.*, Vol. II, p. 259.
[98] Rothfield [Rothfeld], "Societies and their Supervision," *B.C.Q.*, June 1929, p. 4.
[99] *Rept., 1926–27*, p. 35.

in the Provincial Bank in Bombay. In 1924 the Karnatak Central Bank, by far the largest district bank and by far the worst offender, put approximately thirty-nine lakhs on deposit with the Provincial Bank and lent twenty-six lakhs to societies. Its expenditure on "Establishment and Contingencies" was a mere Rs.14,796. (The Poona District Bank, with roughly two lakhs on loan to societies, paid Rs.17,893 for its staff.)[100] In 1927 the Karnatak Central Bank's deposits with the Provincial Bank reached the high figure of Rs.1,01,90,630; it gave loans amounting to Rs.14,96,831 and its staff expenses came to Rs.22,343.[101] The Provincial Bank, in turn, sometimes had to deposit such funds with trading banks because it did not always have a sufficient outlet for investment in the co-operative sphere. The amount of interest which these deposits earned was often little more than that which the Provincial Bank paid the district banks.

The situation first caused real concern in 1924. At the beginning of that year the Provincial Bank had about 43½ lakhs on loan to co-operative banks and societies, nearly 16 lakhs invested in government securities, and 36 lakhs on fixed deposit with commercial banks.[102] The Bank's investments in the co-operative movement were only slightly greater than they had been three years before.[103] "It is an absurd position," Vaikunth Mehta wrote to Madan, "for a Bank like ours to drain away money from the mofussil for being deposited in commercial banks."[104] Certainly, it was hardly for this purpose that the Bank had been set up. At the same time, it was not good policy to refuse deposits; they were "the result of the confidence built up after years of steady work on the part of this Bank and Central Banks."[105]

Actually, the increase in deposits was also the result of a gradual decrease in the interest rate on government borrowings. The co-

100 *Rept., 1923–24*, pp. 100–101. The figures given under "loans to Provincial and Central Banks" cover, in the case of district banks, only "loans" to the Provincial Bank; loans to other district (central) banks were not permitted. See Madan, Note, "Investment of Surpluses of District Central Banks," 24 March 1924. (B.S.C.B., Regr.) Although it was apparently contemplated, both in this note and in Circular No. B.C.B.-21 of 14 April 1924, that district banks should be permitted to make direct deposits in commercial banks, judging from the tables in the Annual Reports such deposits were rarely made.

101 *Rept., 1926–27*, pp. 114–15.

102 V. L. Mehta, Note for Board of B.P.C.B., 15 January 1924. (B.S.C.B., Regr.)

103 Mehta to Madan, D/O of 4 March 1924. (B.S.C.B., file cited.)

104 Mehta to Madan, D/O of 15 January 1924. (B.S.C.B., file cited.)

105 Mehta, note for B.P.C.B. Board cited.

operative banks had now begun to attract the larger investor.[106] Deposits continued to flow in during the later twenties, as they had done at the time of the 1918–19 famine, largely because of the decrease of investment opportunities caused by the contraction of trade.[107] This very fact, of course, is an indication of the strong and increasing connections of the district banks with the trading and money-lending classes. These organizations were in peril of becoming completely un-co-operative, as some cotton-sale societies in the Karnatak became: "The merchant members become the enemies of the society when its business begins to extend and they find their own business curtailed."[108]

In spite of the tendency towards a lowering of urban interest rates, the district central banks and rural societies persisted in paying high rates of interest on fixed deposits. In some cases, Collins wrote, they still paid "the same rates of interest as they had been paying during the War or immediately after the War when the rate of interest on Government securities was over 6 per cent. Rural Managing Committee members are afraid of losing their deposits if they lower the rates of interest, and the directors of Central and urban banks are proud and gratified to see the large funds pouring into their banks. The law of supply and demand is not fully understood."[109] It was certainly an extraordinary situation.

"The Proof of the Pudding"

Some district banks, of course, worked closely with the Department. When Collins sent out a circular in which he went so far as to "direct" an interest rate on deposits of no more than 6¼ per cent,[110] these banks fell into line. But some did not. "One sometimes feels," Bhide wrote, "that the principle of internal autonomy has been allowed to proceed too far and it would have been much better if a certain measure of departmental control had been retained over Central Banks." Under the Agreement with the Secretary of State the Provincial Bank's loans had to be sanctioned by the Registrar. But the Registrar had no such control over the loans

[106] See Audit Memo. of B.P.C.B. for 1924–25. (Poona, B.P.C.B.)
[107] *Rept., 1926–27,* p. 6.
[108] Ibid., p. 24.
[109] Ibid., pp. 6–7.
[110] Collins, Circular No. A.G.C.–42 of 18 June 1927. (Poona, Circulars, 1916–30.)

of the district central banks. Where the district banks were dependent to some extent on the Provincial Bank for finance, the existence of this clause in the Agreement enabled the Registrar to bring some indirect pressure to bear on them.[111] But the offending banks were usually the wealthier ones, which had no need of funds from the Provincial Bank.

Such difficulties with the district banks led Collins to reverse Rothfeld's policy of developing these organizations. Instead, he encouraged the Provincial Bank to open up more branches, chiefly in reasonably wealthy but largely unirrigated districts such as West Khandesh—a district which the Provincial Bank financed directly.

Madan had been keen on the conversion of branches of the Provincial Bank, with their Advisory Committees, into independent "Purchase and Sale Unions." The canal areas might be a special case, but he was definitely opposed to the Provincial Bank's exercising in unirrigated areas the same sort of control as it had in the canal areas. "Nothing must be done which would in any way sap the independence and sense of responsibility of these societies."[112] This was the authentic voice of the enthusiast for co-operative principle. But Collins appears to have had little time for such democratic notions. In fact, when the Pravara Canal societies demanded a fully independent Purchase and Sale Union and the Bank proposed to meet them half way, Collins rejected the idea outright.[113]

It was "the belief of the Department," Collins wrote, that the work done by the branches of the Provincial Bank in "facilitating the operations of primary societies, in providing more adequate and prompt finance, in developing up-country banking and setting to other central banks the example of maintaining direct touch with affiliated societies, is perhaps the greatest force in the present progress of the movement."[114] Bhide thought similarly: "The proof of the pudding is in the eating," he told the Provincial Banking Enquiry Committee, "and the eating has been very good so far."[115] There was, however, one vital factor which inhibited the indefinite expansion of the Provincial Bank's system. A large, well-

111 Bhide to Govt., No. 359/2 of 22 December 1928. (Poona, B.P.C.B.)
112 Madan to V. L. Mehta, No. 359/2 of 30 November 1925. (Poona, file cited.)
113 Collins to A. C. Desai, Asst. Regr., Bombay City, No. 359/2 of 11 April 1927. (Poona, file cited.)
114 *Rept., 1926–27*, pp. 31–32.
115 Bhide, Evidence, *Bom. Prov. Banking Enquiry Cttee.*, Vol. II, p. 267.

trained staff cost a great deal of money. By its Agreement with the Secretary of State, the Bank was forbidden to make loans at more than 8 per cent. Interest of 4 per cent had to be paid to debenture holders. Shareholders usually had to be paid a dividend of about 7½ per cent; depositors normally expected 6 per cent. By comparison, the expenses of maintaining the Bank's staff—about 2½ to 3 per cent on loans made—were extremely high. Lalubhai Samaldas virtually admitted this in reply to the rigorous questioning of the indigenous bankers' representative on the Provincial Banking Enquiry Committee. But, he said, "we are doing business which other banks do not do. As the Chairman of the Co-operative Bank, I like the bank to spend money so that it may be in direct touch with the agriculturists."[116]

Experiments Forgotten

If Rothfeld's policy on district banks was openly reversed by his successors, his policy on other more unusual, and possibly more important, subjects was quietly forgotten, particularly during the regimes of Collins and Bhide. To a large extent, of course, this neglect was understandable. As Rothfeld's basic administration was shown to be somewhat unsound his more unorthodox ideas were naturally put out of mind. There were financial and staffing problems too, and the conventional forms of co-operation were creating problems enough. One suspects, also, that, at the level of the Secretariat, the task of maintaining, in the face of an increasingly bitter nationalism, what A. D. Gorwala has called the "security state,"[117] was taking up the time of most of the most highly thought of administrators. The tough-minded Collins, for example, went from the Co-operative Department to, within a very short time, a key post in the struggle with the nationalists, that of Secretary of the Home Department of the Government of Bombay.

Everyone had less time for the experiments which had been made in the first flush of enthusiasm after the Montford reforms. The first ventures in "co-operative farming," for instance, failed, and nothing further was done in the field in Bombay for many a year. Madan's first Report, that for 1924, spoke of "bad management" in the two joint cultivation societies at Bhambora and Ar-

116 Lalubhai Samaldas, questioned by H. V. Desai, ibid., p. 26.
117 A. D. Gorwala, *The Role of the Administrator: Past, Present and Future*, pp. 4–5.

junsonda.[118] In the following year the registration of the Bhambora society was cancelled.[119] It is unfortunate that no records relating to these failures appear to have survived. Harold Mann, in his wide-ranging final report as Director of Agriculture, written in 1927, spoke of his conviction that, in the task of "rural reconstruction," "it is not one man or one department which is concerned." Rural reconstruction involved, amongst other things, "the consolidation of holdings," "the communal or co-operative holding of implements," and "the organization of purchase of supplies and sale of produce."[120] But Mann no longer spoke of "co-operative farming." Collins, as might be expected, had little sympathy for the notion of co-operative farming. Joint farming societies, he wrote in his departmental report for 1927, submitted at about the same time as Mann's, were "not likely to succeed in the present state of education and co-operative development."[121]

Collins was, however, fundamentally sympathetic towards Rothfeld's policy of distributing *takkavi* through societies. But the fact was that the delays inherent in Rothfeld's system had, Collins said, "disheartened people in some areas, and there are some societies and even district banks and Collectors who will favour a return [to the old system] unless a speedier method of operation can be devised."[122] Applications had to go not only to the society itself and its central bank, but also "to local officers of the Co-operative or Agricultural Departments, often to the Deputy Director of Agriculture and invariably to the Assistant Registrar and the Registrar of Co-operative Societies." None of these officers had the time for the work. Yet the banks, receiving only nominal remuneration for handling the distribution of *takkavi*, could not fairly be expected to undertake the work of dealing with applications. At least the revenue authorities had their own "on the spot" agency—"ill-equipped though it may be." Of the Rs.3,50,000 allotted by Government annually from 1923–24 for Land Improvement Loans through co-operative societies, no more than Rs.2,09,570 was ever taken up in one year; in 1928–29 only Rs.50,097 was taken up.[123]

118 *Rept., 1923–24,* p. 17.
119 *Rept., 1924–25,* p. 15.
120 *Annual Report of the Department of Agriculture in the Bombay Presidency, 1926–27,* p. 21.
121 *Rept., 1926–27,* p. 27.
122 Ibid.
123 *Bom. Prov. Banking Enquiry Rept.,* p. 86.

Land Mortgage Banks

The question of the supply of long-term agricultural credit from the capital actually raised by co-operative organizations, rather than from state funds merely administered by co-operative societies, had been shelved since the Provincial Bank's failure to get most of its debentures taken up. Madan did not altogether agree with Rothfeld that the supply of long-term credit was necessarily a function of the state. But it was primarily the need to find an outlet for surplus co-operative funds which prompted him to investigate the possibilities of "co-operative land mortgage banks."[124] Such banks would concentrate on the supply of long-term credit, generally to those reasonably substantial cultivators who did not find the co-operative movement very attractive. Madan eventually realized, as others had realized before him, that it was impossible to finance long-term loans, for purposes of "debt redemption" or "agricultural improvement," by means of short-term capital. By 1926 he had come to the conclusion that it would be desirable to have separate institutions for such long-term business and that "it would not be proper to entrust this work to existing organizations except at the top where . . . I propose that the Provincial Bank should undertake the work of floating debentures and make itself financially responsible for their repayment."[125]

The Provincial Bank saw here the opportunity of getting rid of its old, unsold debentures. It was impossible, however, to place them on the market except at a large discount. The Bank began looking to Government for help. At first they obtained no response, but eventually, probably to the surprise of many, the Government of Bombay decided to take up two lakhs of the debentures, at a discount which "would not involve Government in any loss."[126] The Land Mortgage Department of the Provincial Bank came into existence in August 1929, and three co-operative land mortgage banks were set up, at Broach, Dharwar, and Pachora in Khandesh. Each bank was given the services of a government Land Valuation Officer.

124 "I think the kind of society which will absorb and usefully absorb a large amount of capital is the Land Mortgage Bank." Madan to V. L. Mehta, D/O of 18 January 1924. (B.S.C.B., Regr.)
125 Madan to Govt., No. A.G.C.–151 of 18 May 1926, encl. Bom. G.R.R.D. No. 6576/24 of 26 September 1927.
126 *Report of the Land Mortgage Committee,* 1934, p. 2.

The establishment of these banks came at a time when the full effects of the depression were being felt. Their business was therefore very limited. By 1933 there had been only 181 borrowers from all three banks, and overdues were 40 per cent of the demand. The Land Mortgage Department of the Provincial Bank had suffered a paper loss of Rs.15,000. Constitutional defects had been discovered in the land mortgage banks, too. Only borrowers or intending borrowers were eligible for membership; consequently, in unfavourable years the Boards of these banks did not bring much pressure on the borrowers to secure repayment.[127]

It was perhaps fortunate that the activities of the early land mortgage banks were so limited, and that lessons were learnt without too much money being lost. The Bombay Committee which investigated the problem of Land Mortgage in 1933–34 spoke of "simmering discontent" in the rural areas, caused by the effects of the depression. "Political parties," the Committee claimed, "anxious to take advantage of the situation, have the provision of Land Mortgage Credit with State assistance as the main point of their programme."[128] The Committee probably exaggerated when they said that land mortgage was the "main plank" of political programmes at this time.[129] Nevertheless, the Congress at this time was beginning to gain a foothold amongst the Maratha peasant community. Fears of rural discontent may well have been partly responsible for the Government of Bombay's establishment of ten new state-assisted land mortgage banks in the districts, and a Provincial Land Mortgage Bank, in 1935—two years before the flurry of agrarian legislative activities brought about by the Congress government of 1937–39.

"Weeding Out"

Land mortgage banks, it seemed, could not provide an outlet for all the surplus capital in the co-operative movement. It appears to have been this fact which brought about Madan's decision to begin to expand the credit movement again. For about a year he had continued the policy of consolidation which had been fol-

---

127 Ibid., pp. 3–4.
128 Ibid., p. 6.
129 Although "Debt Redemption Boards" are certainly mentioned in the *Report of the Peasant Enquiry Committee of the Maharashtra Provincial Congress Committee,* 1936, pp. 67–70. It could be argued that the "main plank" of this report is a reduction in land revenue.

lowed by Rothfeld in the last months of his regime. But during 1925 and 1926 he began to accept a fairly large number of new registrations. In 1926 the number of agricultural societies went up from 3,377 to 3,868, an increase of 491, as against 327 and 181 in the previous two years.[130] Madan took care, however, to encourage the formation of new societies only in comparatively prosperous districts like East and West Khandesh. Very few new societies were registered in the potential famine districts of the Deccan.[131] When the extension of the Nira Canal into Sholapur district was contemplated in 1924, Madan wrote to Vaikunth Mehta emphasizing his wish that the Bank and the Institute should organize societies and carry out propaganda at least two years before the water became available.[132] He was determined to avoid a repetition of the troubles of the societies on the sections of the Nira Canal which had already been opened.

It cannot be said that Madan was negligent in his attitude to arrears. As soon as he became Registrar he gave orders to all auditors and district banks to submit to him a monthly account of the progress they were making in reducing unauthorized arrears. The statistics of unauthorized arrears—arrears which had not been authorized as "extensions" by the committees of the societies— came down from 20 per cent of the amount due for repayment in 1922–23 to 19.6 per cent in 1923–24, 17.8 per cent in 1924–25, and 14 per cent in 1925–26.[133] To some extent, at least, these figures must be a reflection of Madan's energetic touring, his attention to detail, and his ceaseless exhortation.

Yet Collins, when he became Registrar, felt it necessary to look very critically at the state of arrears and the state of the movement generally. His report for 1927 is in some ways similar to Haigh's report for 1915. It is essentially the work of an able and efficient outsider, with no longstanding attachments to the co-operative movement, who knew that his appointment was merely a temporary one, but who was determined to make his mark in all that he did.

According to Collins, co-operation might appear to be flourishing in East and West Khandesh, but in both districts there was "a

[130] *Rept., 1925–26*, p. 7.
[131] Ibid., p. 6.
[132] Madan to Mehta, No. SRMX/1079 of 6–10 April 1924. (B.S.C.B., Regr.)
[133] Undated Note on Arrears (c. 1932). (Poona, loose.)

noticeable desire on the part of the members to run before they can walk." Arrears were very heavy in East Khandesh, and, Collins claimed, repayments had been "deliberately withheld" by co-operative society members. The Karnatak was still "the main centre of co-operative activity." But in Dharwar, "enthusiasm has waned, the leading members have discovered that Government control is not as extensive as they imagined, and there is often open defiance and violation of bye-laws. Added to which has been the introduction of party strife which has been spreading all over the Karnatic."[134]

Collins concentrated his attention on the Deccan. There, he thought, apart from South Satara, the movement was "in a sorry state." In Poona district, including the Nira Canal area, the proportion of the amount due for collection which was made up of unauthorized arrears in July 1927 was 81 per cent, according to Collins's calculations. In the area close to Poona city it was becoming obvious that many of the defaulting members had "no intention of paying of their own accord. . . . Pleaders are employed to dispose of the lands and crops before they can be attached, and there is a general combination to prevent bidding when they are put up to auction."[135] That it had become necessary to put up for auction the crops and lands of co-operative society members was a sad reflection on the state of the movement. Yet ignominious liquidations were to a considerable extent the result of over-generous financing in the earlier years, and lack of supervision—both official and non-official—in more recent times. Many of the societies about Poona city, such as the one-time showpiece, Hadapsar society, had been financed chiefly through the labours of the Servants of India Society, and G. K. Devadhar in particular. By the twenties Devadhar had too many enthusiasms to be really effective in all things.

Collins believed that the position in the canal areas was even more serious than in the dry areas of the Deccan. The immediate cause of the problem there, he admitted, was the fall in the price of *gul* (unrefined sugar); "but the real and lasting cause is the lack of responsibility and a disinclination to repay which is common to other Deccan Societies."[136] As prices fell the members began to "wriggle out of" bringing their *gul* to the Bank's shop, and during

134 *Rept., 1926–27*, pp. 9–10.
135 Ibid., p. 16.
136 Ibid., p. 17.

the 1926–27 season, "sepoys" had to be employed to watch them at harvest time so that they would honour their agreement to bring all their produce to the financing agency.[137] It is possible that the rayats felt that there were too many Brahmans connected with the Bank's shop. A prominent cultivator in the Godavari Canal area explained to a Special Mamlatdar that he had not sent his carts of *gul* to the Bank's shop because of "exceptional circumstances." "I take it," the Special Mamlatdar wrote, "that these carts were sent only to patronize a shop opened by an influential Mahratta on this side." However, under the influence of the local supervising union, the Special Mamlatdar claimed, with an air of confidence, "things will come to a normal level next year." Unfortunately, the chairman of the supervising union happened to be the offender himself.[138]

Collins began to despair of co-operatives ever succeeding in the canal areas. In such circumstances it was not unnatural to examine the alternatives to co-operation. By August 1927 he had reached the conclusion that "the correct system of finance for Canal areas is one of land banks in each area for the big cultivators." When such banks had been formed, "it would be possible to have co-operative societies for the ordinary cultivators if the circumstances showed there was a demand for them."[139] The wheel had almost come full circle. Agricultural banks had been rejected in favour of co-operative societies; now co-operative societies were being rejected in favour of a form of agricultural bank. Collins's conclusions were an ironic commentary on the extraordinarily difficult problems posed by the canal areas.

To some extent Bhide continued Collins's general policy. Registration of societies in the Deccan ceased altogether in 1928.[140] A policy of "weeding out" the bad members in all societies was followed. The aim was to have societies with memberships no larger than fifty. "A scale of about 10 per cent. of the population of the village might be a safe standard for the present," Bhide thought.[141] There was obviously to be no attempt to cater for the whole village

137 Ibid., p. 18.
138 R. W. Potnis, Special Mamlatdar, Belapur, to V. L. Mehta, No. 399 of 1 July 1926. (Poona, B.P.C.B.)
139 Collins to B. F. Madon, Chairman, B.P.C.B., No. 240 of 10 August 1927. (B.S.C.B., Regr.)
140 *Rept., 1927–28,* p. 8.
141 Ibid., p. 12.

in existing circumstances. Those who simply would not pay their dues, regardless of the character of the season, "must clearly be taught a lesson and be made to feel the full rigour of coercive processes." Societies were everywhere being "encouraged freely to refer bad cases to arbitration."[142] Bhide was "not at all sorry" that as a result of his policy the all-round rate of increase in 1928–29 showed a considerable fall.

Yet the policy of liquidation and of "weeding out" had a negative, tragic air about it. This is exemplified in Bhide's comments on the societies around Poona originally sponsored by G. K. Devadhar and the Servants of India Society: "A number of pensioners and other middle-class folk in Poona City invested the greater part of their savings in these societies by way of deposits. . . . In my first year as Registrar, some of these disillusioned, needy depositors used to come to me regularly and make enquiries as to when they were to get back their money. My replies could only be dim and discouraging."[143]

Congress were naturally not slow to take advantage of the discontent caused by arbitration and liquidation proceedings. Gandhi had lost all interest in the government-sponsored co-operative movement: "I am engaged in running the greatest co-operative society that the world has ever seen."[144] After the floods in North Gujarat in 1927 Vallabhbhai Patel and Narahari Parikh showed signs of commencing an agitation against government policy on co-operatives in that area. To enforce the recovery of arrears after such a calamity was, they felt, completely unjust. Vallabhbhai Patel spoke on the subject at a public meeting in Bombay.[145] But Shah, the capable Assistant Registrar in Surat, and Vaikunth Mehta visited Patel and apparently managed to smooth matters over.[146] It was not so easy to smooth over agitation about co-operative societies in Bardoli taluka, the scene of the Congress's most concen-

142 Ibid., p. 61.
143 Bhide, "Memories and Reflections of an Old-Stager." *B.C.Q.*, April 1954, pp. 8–9.
144 *Bombay Co-operative News*, April 1925, p. 24. The *Bombay Co-operative News* was an ephemeral monthly published by the Institute.
145 *Indian National Herald*, 22 August 1927. See also ibid., 5 September 1927 (letter protesting against Patel's allegations from President of Kaira District Branch, Bombay Provincial Co-operative Institute) and 13 September 1927 (Patel's reply).
146 See Shah to Mehta, D/O of 3 October 1927, and Mehta's draft reply. (B.S.C.B., Asst. Regr., Surat.)

trated efforts. "Government have devised makeshifts in the shape
of Co-operative Societies," wrote a Congress worker in the southern
part of that taluka. "They may at best offer them [the rayats]
money at moderate interest and tempt them to run into more debt.
They cannot *give* them any relief. If it can at all be given, it can be
given by the Charka and by taking away the temptation of
Drink."[147]

Co-operation in the Matar taluka of Kaira district came under
Congress fire at the end of the decade. The Matar taluka was poorly
drained and inhabited more by backward Dharalas than by Patidars. It was therefore hardly a typical Gujarat taluka. In 1918 it
had been the subject of an investigation by a Servants of India
Society group led by G. K. Devadhar. This committee appears to
have spent only a few days making their "survey," but this was long
enough for them to recommend concentrated co-operative activity
in the area.[148] Their recommendations, unfortunately, were
heeded. By 1928 the unauthorized arrears in the taluka amounted
to 1½ lakhs.[149] The Assistant Registrar for Gujarat thought that
the situation called for the "early cancellation" of many societies.
"Any attempt in that direction will, however, be utilised by the
critics of the movement to hold it up to the public eye as a measure
of oppression."[150] Action was postponed until 1929. When it was
taken, co-operatives, as prophesied, were immediately condemned
as oppressive. Vallabhbhai Patel, Narahari Parikh, and Mahadev
Desai were members of a committee led by J. C. Kumarappa which
"investigated" economic conditions in Matar taluka. Co-operation
was condemned for its "lack of principle," its "want of human
touch," its "lack of expedition."[151] The powers of the local honorary organizer as arbitrator were criticized (surely Mahadev Desai
had a hand in this) because they were "beyond the protection of
the Civil Court."[152] Two "addresses," obviously Congress-inspired,
were quoted. One had been presented to Wilson, the Governor of

[147] Extract from *Young India*, 24 March 1927, originally published in Gujarati in
Navajivan, quoted Mahadev Desai, *Gandhiji in Indian Villages*, p. 349.

[148] G. K. Devadhar, A. V. Thakkar, and N. M. Joshi, *Report of an Inquiry into the
Agricultural Situation in Matar Taluka in the District of Kaira* (1918), p. 15.

[149] G. H. Desai, Personal Asst. to Regr., Note, 4 May 1928. (Poona, Matar Taluka.)

[150] S. G. Almoula, Asst. Regr., Surat, No. A.G.C. of 15 April 1928, below No. 51 of
29 February 1928 from Reserve Auditor, Matar. (Poona, file cited.)

[151] J. C. Kumarappa (Director), *A Survey of Matar Taluka (Kaira District)*, 1931,
p. 99.

[152] Ibid., p. 103.

Bombay, when he had visited the taluka. "The co-operative society movement," it read, "which stands for a great principle and holds out a promise of making this world a much better place for all to live in, has proved itself, to us at least, a veritable curse of the Gods."[153] An address presented when Irwin, the Viceroy, paid a visit included this passage: "The co-operative movement has on the whole proved a bane to this taluka and instead of diminishing our indebtedness has contributed to it in great measure."[154]

A Way Out

So ran the nationalist indictment of the co-operative movement. To some extent, it must be said, the Congress criticism of the harsh policy largely initiated by Collins had some validity. Bhide soon realized that one effect of Collins's activities was that sums of money which had hitherto been classed as "authorized extensions" in the statistics were simply transferred to another column, "unauthorized arrears." The result had been that in 1926–27 the figures for unauthorized arrears had suddenly leapt from 14 per cent to 29 per cent of the amount due for repayment.[155] So while Bhide continued to be "not at all sorry," in the style of the ultra-efficient Civilian, about the increase in arbitration and liquidation proceedings, at the same time, somewhat more quietly, he began to take a more reasoned attitude to the problem of arrears.

In a telling passage in his Report for 1927–28 Bhide pointed out that co-operative society arrears could not be seen in isolation. In the Central Division of the Presidency (roughly, the Deccan), land revenue and *takkavi* collections were considerably reduced. During 1926–27, "in spite of the existence of the best possible Government agency for collection work," only 86.5 per cent of the revenue demand and 87 per cent of the *takkavi* demand had been collected. Furthermore, the amount demanded by the Revenue Department of a peasant in one year was not infrequently a good deal lower than the total amount the peasant owed to a co-operative society. It was hardly a matter of surprise, therefore, that the cultivators did not show "excessive eagerness" to pay the co-operative society's dues

---

153 Ibid., p. 100.
154 Ibid., p. 101.
155 Undated Note on Arrears cited.

fully, especially in a bad year, and especially when official supervision (unlike Revenue Department authority) was in places almost "non-existent."[156]

In his 1928–29 Report, Bhide showed that out of 4,317 agricultural credit societies as many as 1,467 had no overdue arrears whatsoever. There were 490 societies with unauthorized arrears of less than 10 per cent of the demand, which Bhide considered to be "almost negligible." This was not an unfair statement: the percentage of unauthorized arrears during the latter years of Ewbank's period as Registrar, for instance, had varied between 7 and 8 per cent.[157] Thus in 1929 there were 2,317 societies—almost half the total number—in which arrears were not at all serious.[158] Furthermore, the societies in real difficulties were concentrated in a few areas, to be found, Bhide said, in the districts of Ahmadabad, Kaira, Poona, Ahmadnagar, Sholapur, Bijapur, Ratnagiri, and Kolaba.[159] Now in Ratnagiri and Kolaba, the home of the *khoti* tenure, and in Ahmadabad, the home of the Gujarati *talukdari* tenure, the co-operative movement had never been viable, largely because a very high proportion of the cultivators in those districts possessed no land of their own. In Kaira, as we have seen, the movement had appealed only to the backward; the prosperous Leva Patidars had little need of it. Poona, Ahmadnagar, Sholapur, and Bijapur were all potential famine districts; even where they were irrigated, difficulties arose, in part because "widespread calamity" had overtaken the sugar industry.

Bhide's analysis was entirely in keeping with the insistence of several Season and Crop reports of the middle and late twenties that the man with the "economic holding," who cultivated his fields himself and who did not employ a great deal of labour, was not suffering greatly.[160] Such a person, we have already seen, was the co-operative society's most promising recruit, and such a person, Dr. Dharm Narain has recently shown, produces mainly for maintenance. He sells a smaller proportion of his crop and is therefore less at the mercy of "market forces" than either the very small

---

[156] *Rept., 1927–28*, p. 18.
[157] Undated Note on Arrears cited.
[158] *Rept., 1928–29*, pp. 18–19.
[159] *Rept., 1929–30*, p. 17.
[160] *Bombay Season and Crop Reports, 1924–25*, p. 21; *1926–27*, p. 22; *1927–28*, p. 23.

peasant (who frequently has to make "distress sales") or the large farmer.[161]

Even in the "cash-crop" canal areas, Bhide realized, in some way or another the credit cycle had to be set going again. Co-operative societies were there; they were almost the only possible source of finance for some of their members. Even if co-operative societies were not perhaps the best way of financing the larger cultivators, even if some of the cultivators should not be growing sugar cane at all, still, something had to be done as a temporary measure, until better times dawned. After a visit to the canal areas in December 1928 Bhide put forward detailed proposals for future activity. The terms on which fresh finance would be made available were slightly liberalized, and the Provincial Bank's Senior Inspector was given more freedom to act without continual reference to the Registrar in person.[162] Significantly, the search for a way out of the impasse led to greater independence for the Bank, not (as it would have in earlier years) to greater dependence of the Bank on the government.

One of those who played a significant part in constructive developments at the end of the twenties, particularly during Bhide's regime, was Gunvantrai Desai, the Registrar's Personal Assistant. Towards the end of Collins's period a series of letters passed between Desai and Vaikunth Mehta on the problem of the maintenance of "fluid resource" in primary societies. At the time of the examination of the Maclagan Committee's recommendations Ewbank and Mehta had not felt this to be a serious problem. Mehta had now been forced to change his ideas, under the stress of continuous demands for repayment from private depositors in societies. As Desai pointed out on one occasion, under the system of unlimited liability "almost all of the co-operative loans are given to persons who collectively are always solvent in the end."[163] But the

---

161 Dharm Narain, *Distribution of Marketed Surplus of Agricultural Produce by Size-level of Holding in India 1950–51*, especially pp. 35–37. Dr. Narain, examining a period later than ours, finds that peasants with holdings of 5–15 acres sell on average less than 30 per cent of the value of their total output. Those with 0–5 acres sell on average 33.6 per cent; those with 15–20 acres have a "marketed surplus" of 30.1 per cent, and this rises to 51.4 per cent with those cultivating over 50 acres. Of course the actual figures vary with the area and with the crop sown. R. C. Desai, *Standard of Living in India and Pakistan 1931–32 to 1940–41*, p. 121, would seem to provide an essential gloss on Narain's work at this point.

162 *Rept., 1928–29*, p. 41.

163 Gunvantrai Desai, Office Note, 29 November 1928. (Poona, B.P.C.B.)

aim had to be to stop a society's deterioration before the point of liquidation was reached. Mehta felt that this could be assured to a greater extent if societies were compelled to maintain fluid resource cover with their financing agencies.[164] Desai felt, however, that the real remedy was to fix "maximum" and "normal" credits for each society, and to prohibit all borrowings in excess of the maximum laid down, either from central co-operative banks or from private depositors, including even deposits from members.[165]

The idea of maximum and normal credits went back as far as the Maclagan Committee,[166] and the resulting guaranteeing unions. But with the failure of the guaranteeing unions, the system of maximum and normal credits continued in operation, in a revised form, only in the societies directly financed by the Provincial Bank. Under the Provincial Bank's system, the general meeting of a society each year fixed in advance the extent of credit which it was prepared to give each individual member. The Bank would then examine the resulting "normal credit statement," and, in the light of its own information, decide on the maximum credit which it was prepared to give the society. The system was introduced, Vaikunth Mehta wrote, "not only to provide prompt and adequate finance, but also to see that all such finance as is provided is given under proper safeguards and after due inquiry. It is not an uncommon experience to find office bearers appropriating large portions of a society's funds themselves."[167] But there was a loophole for societies in the system as it existed. Any amount of money could be obtained as local deposits, over which the Registrar and the financing agency had no control. This is what had happened in the Poona area especially. Hence Desai's insistence in 1927 that all types of borrowings beyond the societies' "maximum credits" should be prohibited.

Bhide and Mehta agreed. Both village societies and district banks, Bhide wrote, generally followed "no systematic policy" and were "inclined alternately to stop finance altogether (almost as a result of panic) and grant it too freely as soon as the outlook appears promising." He proposed to insist on maximum and normal credits to a much greater extent than before.[168]

---

164 V. L. Mehta to Gunvantrai Desai, D/O of 10 May 1927. (B.S.C.B., Regr.)
165 Desai to Mehta, D/O of 5 May 1927. (B.S.C.B., file cited.)
166 See *Maclagan Cttee. Rept.*, pp. 38, 62.
167 Mehta to Madan, D/O of 20 November 1924. (B.S.C.B., file cited.)
168 *Rept., 1927–28,* p. 17.

Foundations Laid

"The main structure of the co-operative movement is quite sound," Bhide claimed in his Report for 1928–29.[169] Bhide was not altogether incorrect in his assertion. There had been no large-scale failure and there was not going to be one. But few in 1929 thought that the economic depression which had set in in some industries in 1922–23 would deepen a great deal further. In fact, prices of most agricultural products—not only of sugar and cotton—suffered on the average a 40 to 50 per cent drop in the months after May 1930.[170]

Co-operative societies, naturally, were affected. Between 1929–30 and 1936–37 the number of agricultural credit societies in the Bombay Presidency declined from 4,317 to 3,718; membership dropped from 262,569 to 198,203.[171] But the fall was in neither case catastrophic. Unreliable members and unreliable societies were weeded out. By 1935 there was new hope, and this not only because prices showed vague signs of lifting. "The movement . . . after the period of 'dry-docking' for repairs has been rendered 'sea-worthy,' " K. L. Panjabi, the Registrar, reported. "Unfortunately, the only obstacle in further development of the rural credit movement is the lack of adequate staff."[172] By 1937, and the coming to power of a Congress government in Bombay, even this defect was beginning to be remedied. The post of Deputy Registrar, for instance, was at last filled, by an Indian Civilian, S. M. Ikram, a Muslim, who was to be closely connected with the co-operative movement throughout the war years.

Bombay was not the only province in which the co-operative movement showed considerable powers of survival during the depression. "Surprisingly enough," writes Professor Walter Neale of the United Provinces, "the sharp fall in the prices of agricultural produce in the thirties did not hurt agricultural co-operative societies, though it slowed their growth."[173] The existence of such a situation in the United Provinces may perhaps occasion some surprise.

169 *Rept., 1928–29*, p. 41.
170 V. L. Mehta, *A Plea for Planning in Co-operation*, p. 2. Cf. Narain, *Impact of Price Movements*, Table 2, pp. 167–69.
171 *Rept., 1929–30*, p. 12; *Rept., 1936–37*, p. 13.
172 *Rept., 1934–35*, p. 13.
173 Walter C. Neale, *Economic Change in Rural India: Land Tenure and Reform in Uttar Pradesh, 1800–1955*, p. 177.

But the resilience of the co-operative movement of the Bombay Presidency in the thirties should not be thought of as the result of the operation of chance factors. For one thing, although very low prices probably meant that "medium" peasants had to market somewhat more than they did at other times, it is likely that they still often remained amongst those who were least affected by the market situation. For the backbone of the co-operative movement in some districts, therefore, the thirties may not have been basically different from much of the twenties. So far as co-operative organization was concerned, the basis for survival had been laid to a large extent by Ewbank and Rothfeld, and especially, perhaps, in the patient attention to detail of Bhide, Gunvantrai Desai, and Vaikunth Mehta. In the thirties, Vaikunth Mehta, although hardly in favour politically with the Government for much of the period, at last emerges from behind the scenes as in some ways the most powerful figure in the co-operative movement in Bombay. This surely is a mark of the coming of age of the movement. Vaikunth Mehta's hand was to a considerable extent behind the influential report of the Provincial Banking Enquiry Committee of 1930.[174] The so-called Mehta-Bhansali Committee, which investigated the workings of the co-operative movement in 1937, at the request of the new Congress government, was made up of Vaikunth Mehta and the comparatively new Registrar of the day, M. D. Bhansali. Inevitably, the recommendations of the Mehta-Bhansali Report were largely those of Vaikunth Mehta. And they were virtually all based upon the experience of the years before 1930. The termination of the system of honorary organizers, the use of normal credit statements, the encouragement of co-operative marketing: all these recommendations arose from the formative years which we have discussed.[175]

Thus, when after war-time affluence had achieved amongst some groups what was probably a greater reduction in real terms of agricultural indebtedness than all the measures of the previous seventy years,[176] when, in 1946, Vaikunth Mehta became Finance Minister in a Congress Government of Bombay, it was found that

[174] *Rept., 1929–30*, p. 4.

[175] *Report on the Reorganization of the Co-operative Movement in Bombay*, unofficial version published Bombay Provincial Central Co-operative Banks Conference, 1937. The "official" version was not published, but there is no reason to doubt the basic authenticity of the "unofficial" version.

[176] See Government of India, Policy Committee on Agriculture, Forestry and

many of the lessons of the first thirty years of the Bombay co-operative movement's history had been learnt reasonably well. Statistically, at least, the co-operative movement moved ahead in Bombay, and in the successor states of Gujarat and (especially) Maharashtra.[177] It was but natural—since the co-operative movement was, as ever, the work of human beings—that not all the lessons of the early days in Bombay should have been learnt.

Fisheries, *Report of the Agricultural Finance Sub-Committee* (D. R. Gadgil, Chairman) [1946] p. 7; Reserve Bank of India, *All-India Rural Credit Survey*, Vol. I, *The Survey Report*, pt. i, 1956, pp. 178–83, 208, 218.

[177] In 1964, the latest year for which all-India figures are available, Maharashtra was said to have 19,938 agricultural credit societies, 98.7 per cent "coverage" of villages and 38.91 per cent "coverage" of rural population. The relevant Gujarat figures were 8,190, 100 per cent and 31.59 per cent respectively. (Reserve Bank of India, *Review of the Co-operative Movement in India, 1962–64*, 1966, p. 47.) The *Economic Weekly* of Bombay, commenting on a similar review for 1960–62, asked: "If co-operation has indeed been so successful in Maharashtra, why have not the Co-operation Departments of other States and the Central Government thought it fit to study and analyse this phenomenon?" *Economic Weekly*, 3 July 1965, p. 1058.

VI

Past and Present

The Past

It has been said that the historian "who commits himself to a generalization is digging a pit into which he will later assuredly fall, and nowhere does the pit yawn deeper than in the realm of rural history." The writer was an authority on medieval England, Eileen Power;[1] her words have been quoted by a brilliant historian of the European and more particularly the Russian peasantry,[2] and they may equally well be applied to the history of the Indian peasantry in the nineteenth and twentieth centuries. Historians of India have been too concerned with such matters as "imperialism" and "nationalism," so that we have only begun to explore—sometimes from the very pits of which Eileen Power spoke—the seams below the surface. Nevertheless, a few tentative conclusions must be ventured at this stage.

The analysis of the Deccan economy presented by the Deccan Riots Commission in the mid-1870s needs to be subjected to further close examination. But the Commission's analysis cannot be dismissed out of hand. The professional money-lender probably was aggregating land at the expense of the peasantry in the years before 1875. Yet the riots of 1875 were by no means solely a protest against such a process; it is difficult, in fact, to explain them primarily in economic terms. It is almost as difficult to comment accurately on the situation in the Deccan after 1875 as it is to comment on conditions before that year. No reliable and extensive

---

1 Eileen Power, "Peasant Life and Rural Conditions (c. 1000 to c. 1500)," *Cambridge Medieval History*, Vol. VII, p. 716.
2 Jerome Blum, *The European Peasantry from the Fifteenth to the Nineteenth Century*, p. 1.

statistics were gathered on the subject of the transfer of land from agriculturists to non-agriculturist money-lending groups in the twenty years after the Deccan Riots Commission. Yet it was on the assumption that large-scale transfers of this nature were taking place in Bombay and elsewhere, and that such transfers had to be brought to an end, that the co-operative movement was founded in India. The Co-operative Societies Act of 1904 was imposed upon an unwilling Government of Bombay by a "Punjab"-dominated Government of India. The Government of Bombay probably painted a somewhat over-optimistic picture of the rural situation in the Presidency at this time—they certainly did in the second decade of the century—but at the same time the Government of India appear to have misinterpreted much of the information that was available to them.

So far as the Bombay Presidency was concerned, then, the validity of the economic justification put forward in 1904 for the Co-operative Societies Act appears to have been somewhat doubtful. But the fact remains that the Act was introduced; its working after 1904 is our main concern. The Act's failures in Bombay do not stem mainly from the initial insufficient understanding of the extent to which land was being transferred from the peasant to the money-lender.

One might suppose that the years from about 1904 form part of the "statistical era" in India's history, even if, in certain respects, the later nineteenth century does not. But statistics must be treated cautiously even in the twentieth century. Co-operative societies, for example, may increase in number but not in quality; this is true also of membership. The figures for loans may rise, but arrears may rise more rapidly. An apparent increase in total working capital may be made up of funds which are not utilized in the movement. At a rather more fundamental level we also flounder, basically because the full survey of the economic effects of the co-operative movement in the Bombay Presidency, which Sane and others demanded in the twenties, was never undertaken wholeheartedly. The nearest approach to such a survey in our period is the Bombay Provincial Banking Enquiry Committee's Report of 1930, a rounded and useful discussion of the whole subject of banking and credit in the Presidency, but the fruit of only six months' activity by a largely amateur group and a few very brief surveys of local areas by "sub-committees," again made up mainly of amateurs—

often dignitaries in the co-operative movement. The Banking Enquiry Committee estimated, for instance, that in 1930 about 10.7 per cent of the rural population of the Presidency came "within the fold" of the co-operative movement,[3] but it made no attempt to estimate the extent to which the credit needs of even that 10 per cent were fulfilled by the co-operative movement. Such an attempt had been made, however, by Rothfeld in 1923. He believed that only about two-fifths of the credit needs of co-operative society members were met by their societies.[4] If that were the case in 1930, about 4 per cent of the credit needs of the Presidency's rural population would have been met at that time by co-operative societies.

Certainly the Government of Bombay had no reason in 1930 to think of co-operation as a panacea for such rural ills as there were, even if (after their initial objections to the co-operative idea had been forgotten) they had tended to think of it in this way in earlier years. By 1930 the Government of Bombay were both more aware of the nature of rural ills than they had been in, say, the years immediately before the First World War, and less able to cope with them. The work of people such as Harold Mann had given them a new understanding of economic change, and lack of change, in the rural areas, but the "security state" and depressed economic conditions made concerted action well-nigh impossible.

The co-operative movement, then, does not appear to have provided any very decisive challenge in Bombay to the money-lender of either the "professional" or the "agriculturist" varieties. The same would appear to be true of most of the rest of India. Indeed, the now famous Rural Credit Survey of 1951–52 found that only 3.2 per cent of India's cultivating families used co-operatives for any of their borrowings; only 3.1 per cent of the total borrowing of India's cultivating families came from co-operatives.[5] But 58.6 per cent of her cultivating families (a figure that might, of course, surprise those who see rural India as utterly submerged by indebtedness) had to borrow from some source or other.[6]

[3] *Bom. Prov. Banking Enquiry Cttee. Rept.*, p. 157. The figures for Dharwar, Broach, and East Khandesh districts were 27.8, 24.8, and 18.7 per cent respectively.

[4] See above, p. 172.

[5] Reserve Bank of India, *All-India Rural Credit Survey, Report of the Committee of Direction*, Vol. II, *The General Report*, 1954, pp. 230, 157.

[6] Ibid., p. 230. Even such recent statistics have been heavily criticized as unreliable: see Daniel and Alice Thorner, "The All-India Rural Credit Survey Viewed as a Scientific Enquiry," in their volume *Land and Labour in India*. (Originally published in the *Economic Weekly*, Special Number, June 1960.)

One basic reason for the existence of this state of affairs is obviously enough: the co-operative society often simply could not compete with the money-lender of either the "professional" or the "agriculturist" variety. On paper the Bombay societies' interest rates—in 1929, from 9⅜ per cent to 12½ per cent[7]—were often lower than the rates of the money-lenders, as these were calculated by the Bombay Provincial Banking Enquiry Committee. This Committee claimed that the "most usual" rate charged by the money-lenders was 24 per cent in the famine tracts of the Deccan and the Karnatak.[8] But the "usual" money-lenders' rate for loans to Leva Patidars in Gujarat seems to have been about 6 per cent. Furthermore, as Campbell realized in the early days of the movement, the money-lender rarely expected to recover his principal. His rates were therefore not as high as they appeared to be at first sight. One might well ask, in fact, how any co-operative society could continue to exist alongside a money-lender who offered loans at rates that were not always as high as they might seem, and who was less concerned about repaying capacity than a well-run co-operative society could afford to be. The Indian peasant may be illiterate, but he is not completely naïve as a man of business. The main objection to this line of argument was provided by Sane: the co-operative society so often provided not an alternative to dealings with the money-lender, but an addition to them.

A further possible reason for the lack of success of the co-operative movement in the Bombay Presidency prior to 1930 may perhaps be suggested by Dr. Ravinder Kumar's argument that the principal beneficiaries of the movement in rural Maharashtra in the earlier years of its development were the group, essentially limited in number, whom he calls the "rich peasants."[9] Unfortunately Dr. Kumar rarely defines this term. The "rich peasants" are generally contrasted in his work with the "great majority," the "poor peasants"; only very infrequently does Dr. Kumar acknowledge the existence of a middle group,[10] men who frequently cultivated, in the Deccan in our period, some twenty to forty, or perhaps sometimes fifty acres of unirrigated land. (They may not actually

---

[7] Lalubhai Samaldas, Evidence, *Bom. Prov. Banking Enquiry Cttee.*, Vol. II, p. 24.
[8] *Bom. Prov. Banking Enquiry Cttee. Rept.*, p. 55.
[9] Ravinder Kumar, *Western India in the Nineteenth Century*, pp. 262–63.
[10] Ibid., p. 216. Here Dr. Kumar is, in fact, following the 1883 report by H. Woodward mentioned above, p. 32.

have owned such an amount.) In Gujarat, with which Dr. Kumar is not concerned, such men usually cultivated between fifteen and thirty acres of reasonably good land. Such a group needs to be distinguished. Most of the available evidence points to the conclusion that the vast majority of the wealthy peasants in our period simply were not interested in co-operative societies: they could manage without them, and they were shy of unlimited liability. One can, of course, define "rich" peasants so as to include the group we have called the "medium" peasants, and indeed one suspects that a Marxist would see "medium" peasants as being of the same essentially exploitative nature as "rich" peasants. The Marxist claim is that a co-operative movement in a non-socialist economy "largely and objectively" serves the interests of "capitalist" elements.[11] In Bombay in the twenties, however, such a claim would seem to be more applicable to the shareholders in many of the district central co-operative banks than to any element within the peasantry.

But, assuming that the "middle" peasantry provided some of the most stable membership of the co-operative movement in Bombay, it must be admitted that this group was limited in size and, if Mann's surveys of Jategaon Budruk had any wider application, by the twenties shrinking as a proportion of the total rural population. Furthermore, many in this group, as Dr. Dharm Narain's studies have shown, had comparatively few connections with the market. (This fact surely casts some doubt on the assertion that the "middle" peasantry were essentially bound up with the "capitalist" sector of the economy.) Members of the "middle" peasantry often had less need of the money-lender's credit than either the "rich" peasants producing "cash crops" or the "poor" peasants who periodically had to make "distress sales." This in turn meant that there were only limited possibilities amongst such people for co-operative societies to provide competition with the money-lender, and furthermore, only limited opportunities for co-operative societies to combine credit with marketing—an operation in other circumstances generally very much to the societies' advantage. It was not possible for the co-operative movement to develop indefinitely amongst the "medium" peasants.

Now to say that the "medium" peasants provided some of the

[11] See, e.g., Mihailo Vučkovič, *A Century of Yugoslav Cooperation*, Belgrade, 1956, p. 13.

most stable membership of the co-operative movement in Bombay in our period is not to deny that many attempts were made, especially by the Bombay Provincial Co-operative Bank, to develop co-operative societies amongst other groups—amongst the sugar-cane growers of the canal areas, for example, who produced largely for the market, or amongst the very backward Bhils, who were also compelled to market much of their production. Indeed, as we have seen, the Provincial Bank invested a considerable proportion of its time and capital in the canal areas. It is debatable, however, whether these ventures—in the canal areas as well as amongst the Bhils about whom Symington wrote so vividly—can be called truly "co-operative." It might be claimed, in fact, that by the twenties the activities of the Provincial Bank were becoming increasingly like those of an "agricultural bank." Agricultural banks differed from co-operative societies in two principal ways. In the system proposed by Wedderburn, for example, there was no place for local thrift and local management, in theory the two essentials of co-operation. But it must be said that although local thrift and local management were not emphasized in the Provincial Bank's operations, they by no means disappeared. A system which was half way between co-operation and agricultural banks was thus being evolved; it could be said, in fact, that the tensions which for so long had existed between the two forms of organization were being resolved in practice.

Certainly it does appear that by the twenties the Provincial Bank—with its efficient and well-paid staff, with its branches in close contact with dependent societies and exercising strict control over them, with its linkage of credit to marketing—was, so far as prices permitted, proving its worth from an economic point of view. There seems little doubt that the Bhils, for example, were receiving a fairer deal from the Provincial Bank than they had previously received from the money-lenders. But the Provincial Bank's system was not truly "democratic." One could take a pragmatic view, like that of Bhide: the proof of the pudding was in the eating. But one could also take a more definite stand on co-operative "principles."

Probably the most important feature of the co-operative movement in Bombay in our period was the perpetual controversy between officials and non-officials, and also, it must be noted, within these two groups, over the application of these principles, and especially that concerning "democratic" control. Co-operation was given to the peasants of India, and of Bombay in particular, not because they asked for it, but because some of the "Guardians," to use Philip Mason's phrase,[12] thought it would be good for them. In the institution of the official Registrar, actively fostering societies, there was, whether the "Guardians" liked it or not, the nucleus of a whole apparatus of state control. Yet partly because of lack of money and, at times, lack of official enthusiasm, and partly because of a genuine desire to use the co-operative movement for fostering what were considered to be the virtues of "self-help" and of democracy, the aim of the government in the first twenty years of the movement's existence was always, professedly, to prepare the movement for eventual self-control. One must say "professedly" because even in the early days the British administrator—and the British-trained Indian administrator, for that matter—sometimes had their doubts as to whether the movement could ever control itself with efficiency and without a large increase in corruption.

Nevertheless, in the early years in Bombay the non-official side of the movement was emphasized to a far greater extent than in most other provinces. The honorary organizers undoubtedly helped to some extent in breaking down the natural suspicion which the Indian masses felt towards a new scheme of government; they built up new relationships with each other and with their British rulers. As Campbell put it, in language that now seems so very dated although he was writing only sixty years ago: "If co-operation has done nothing more it has anyhow afforded a delightful occasion for friendly work side by side of a Government Registrar with philanthropic Native gentlemen."[13] Professor Hugh Tinker has suggested that the "Colonial" period in India's history "will be seen, eventually, as a partnership; its keynote not British achievement or Indian nationalism but a partnership between Indians and British."[14] The story of the co-operative movement in Bombay before about 1918 appears at first sight to bear out this theory. But the theory hardly applies to the co-operative movement in the twenties. Partly because of the increase in caste animosities, and partly because of the increase in political activity, the non-official side of the movement eventually became a rather innocuous

[12] Philip Woodruff [Mason], *The Men Who Ruled India,* Vol. II, *The Guardians.*
[13] *Rept., 1906–7,* pp. 1–2.
[14] Hugh Tinker, "1857 and 1957: The Mutiny and Modern India," *International Affairs,* Vol. XXXIV, No. 1 (January 1958), p. 59.

appendage, for which Collins and Bhide, as representatives of the government, had little time.

The honorary organizers were not rejected in favour of that other group of non-official amateurs with an interest in the co-operative movement, the Bombay Provincial Co-operative Institute. The later government attitude to these urban dilettantes, whose interest they had originally fostered, is understandable enough; it may have helped make nationalists out of some solid Bombay citizens, however. And it was not proposed to give control of the co-operative movement to the co-operative banks, especially the district central banks. The Provincial Bank, which combined a measure of philanthropy with integrity and sound business sense, was perhaps the best prospect amongst all potential non-official controlling bodies. But it had surrendered its direct interest in many parts of the Presidency to the district central banks after the Maclagan Committee's report. On the whole, too, its directors, men such as Lalubhai Samaldas and Chunilal Mehta, were too closely connected with the government (especially in the twenties), and too moderate in all their attitudes, to wish to make any sustained challenge to the government. It is true that (rather than any individual Registrar) the Provincial Bank's extraordinarily able Managing Director, Vaikunth Mehta, was in many ways the most important single figure in the co-operative movement in Bombay in our period. He was no "Moderate" in his political attitudes. Yet while his father remained on the directorate Vaikunth did not lead the Bank into a confrontation with the government; Lalubhai died in 1936, and provincial autonomy came in the following year.

The honorary organizers, the Institute, the co-operative banks— none assumed control of the co-operative movement. Yet insofar as the British aimed to foster "democracy" in and through the co-operative movement, they aimed to foster it not so much amongst the urban "middle classes" as amongst the agriculturists of the villages. The co-operative movement must be seen, in fact, as one side of the British attempt to revive what some of them imagined to be the village community of the past. Charles Gonne in 1883 believed that it was possible to speak of "traditions of village co-operation." Frederick Nicholson claimed that co-operative societies "not merely popularized but democratized credit." Dupernex quoted Metcalfe on the "little Republics" of the Delhi territory. Campbell, most emphatically, believed that he was "re-introducing the

'Panch' system." Ewbank enthused over the "little leaders of the labouring classes," thrown up by the "humble village panchayat," around which he could build a system of guaranteeing unions.

Now the village communities of the Delhi area may at one time have been "little Republics." But as the Collector of Ahmadnagar insisted in 1901 and as Lalubhai Samaldas pointed out in 1902, conditions in the Deccan and in Gujarat were vastly different from the conditions Dupernex knew or claimed to know in northern India. There were, it is true, certain indigenous tendencies in western India towards what might be called, in a very broad sense, "co-operation"; the Collector of Surat in 1901, it will be remembered, noted the existence in his villages of "combinations" to build temples, bridges, and other village amenities.[15] But no human society can survive without some tendencies towards "co-operation" or "cohesion" of this variety.[16] In western India, whatever may have been the situation centuries before the coming of the British, by the end of the eighteenth century certain opposing tendencies, in the realm of property relationships as in other spheres, appear to have been already in operation. These tendencies may perhaps be termed (again using a word in a very broad sense) "competitive." The British impact undoubtedly strengthened such pre-existent tendencies. So, although it is possible to exaggerate the importance of family, faction, caste, and class conflict in the "modern" Indian village, the fact remains that, in our period at least, the western Indian village often did not possess a great deal of real unity. But the basic point to be made here is that even if indigenous tendencies towards "co-operation" had been a great deal stronger, they still would not necessarily have provided a basis for co-operative societies. A co-operative society in rural India was essentially a "Western" innovation; it had a "chairman," a "secretary," a "committee," it kept "minutes" (or was supposed to do so), it had a status in law created by a British government in India. Even the

15 See above, p. 47. One might also note in this connection the *phad* system of Khandesh, for mutual help in irrigation, and the custom in Maharashtra of "having *irjik.*" On the *phad* system, see Government of India, Ministry of Community Development, Panchayati Raj and Cooperation, *Sahakari Samaj: A symposium on the cooperative movement in India*, 1962, pp. 4–5, and A. H. A. Simcox, Collr., Nasik, "Note on Deccan Irrigation," Easter Day, 1921. (Poona, found in an untitled file of miscellaneous papers of interest, preserved by Shri Chiplunkar, one-time Record Keeper.) *Irjik* is discussed by Henry Orenstein in *Gaon: Conflict and Cohesion in an Indian Village*, p. 231.

16 See on this topic (with special reference to Maharashtra), the excellent work of Orenstein in *Gaon*.

Kadva Patidars of Olpad taluka, strongly conscious of their interests in uniting as a caste, had to have some sort of basically Western
model of a "co-operative society" before them before they could
come together successfully in their cotton-sale ventures. The co-
operative movement, as we have said, was "given" to India; without the British presence it could not have come into existence.

This is not to say, however (with, perhaps, the followers of J. H.
Boeke[17]), that the co-operative movement's failure to develop very
rapidly in Bombay in the years before 1930 was essentially the
result of its being a Western intrusion, almost totally foreign to
the Indian peasant. To make such a claim would be again falsely
to assert, although this time in a negative way, the extreme importance of the "traditional" background. Voelcker's words about
the Indian peasant in 1893, which we quoted earlier in this study,
were echoed by Harold Mann in 1929. "After long experience of
Indian farmers in many parts of India," wrote Mann, "I think
that this idea of innate conservatism amongst the rural classes is
not correct, and possibly they are really less averse to change than
a very large proportion of the farmers of western countries."[18] The
western Indian peasant would have taken more enthusiastically
to the notion of co-operative societies in the years prior to 1930 if
those societies had appeared, or been made to appear, more relevant to the condition in which he found himself.

The Present

Yet we have claimed that by 1930 many of the foundations had
been laid in western India for those post-Independence developments which have led to an apparently, considerable expansion in
co-operative activity in recent years. One must first of all strike
a familiar cautionary note: statistics do not show all. But the fact
remains that long before the recommendations of the Rural Credit
Survey of the early 1950s (from which many developments in the

17 See W. F. Wertheim et al., eds., *Indonesian Economics: The Concept of Dualism
in Theory and Policy*. Professor Gunnar Myrdal, in *Asian Drama: An Inquiry into
the Poverty of Nations*, Vol. II, p. 876, n. 1, quotes a succinct expression of Boeke's
views on co-operation from *Economics and Economic Policy in Dual Societies*, Haar-
lem, 1953, p. 303.
18 Mann, "The Agriculture of India," in Mann (ed. Thorner), *The Social Framework of Agriculture*, p. 292. (Originally published in the *Annals of the American
Academy of Political and Social Science*, Vol. CXLVI, pt. ii, September 1929.) Cf. also,
for further confirmation of this view, M. L. Dantwala, "Intensive Agricultural Development," *Economic and Political Weekly*, 17 June 1967, p. 1081.

modern Indian co-operative movement are often thought to flow), it had been discovered in Bombay that it was often necessary to integrate co-operative credit with marketing; from the Bombay Provincial Co-operative Bank's experience in the canal areas, and its insistence on "normal credit statements" has come, so it would seem, the "crop loan" scheme,[19] successfully implemented in several parts of India even if it has not fully lived up to the expectations of those who drafted the Rural Credit Survey. Long before the five-year plans, Rothfeld and Mann had warned that it was folly to expect co-operation on its own, or even co-operation backed by legislation such as the Deccan Agriculturists' Relief Act, to cure the Deccan, and indeed rural India as a whole, of their troubles. It was of no use forgetting about the problem of rainfall. It was also of no use seeing the "money-lender" in isolation. He was part of a larger economic system; he provided, in fact, what was frequently the villager's only direct link with that essentially urban-oriented system, and while that system continued in operation he was often quite an efficient link. To some extent today, in circumstances that are somewhat more propitious than those of the 1920s, these facts of Indian rural life are beginning to be understood by politicians and planners. Even the first halting attempts at "co-operative farming" in western India were made in our period, although it must be said that this subject still remains in India one of the least understood aspects of the co-operative movement.[20] So far as the administration of the movement is concerned in Bombay the essential battles had again been fought before 1930. The state is able to be the "dominant partner" in the movement in western India today largely because, in the years with which we have been concerned, the urban dilettantes, the co-operative banks, and the village societies had all lost, sometimes by default, in the contest for the control of the movement.

There are still, it is true, those in India today who wish to see the control of the movement firmly in the hands of the villagers: the Nicholson of 1895 and the Dupernex of 1900 have their spirit-

---

[19] See Bombay State Co-operative Bank, *Report of Crop Loan Evaluation Committee, 1958*, pt. i, p. 18; *1911–1961: The Maharashtra State Co-operative Bank Limited, Golden Jubilee Souvenir*, p. 24.

[20] For the controversy surrounding "co-operative farming" after the Nagpur Congress of 1959, see I. J. Catanach, "Congress and Co-operatives in India," *Political Science*, Vol. XIII, No. 2 (September 1961).

ual descendants amongst a few officials and rather more politicians (mainly of the Gandhian variety) in modern India. The Draft of the Third Five Year Plan quoted a statement by the National Development Council to the effect that "the foundation of any democratic structure had to be democracy in the village."[21] And the now famous resolution of the Nagpur meeting of the Congress, in 1959, stated that in future in India "the organization of the village should be based on village panchayats and village co-operatives."[22] Beside such views, however, one has to place the harshly "realistic" views of an Indian survivor of the I.C.S. of British days, Shri M. R. Bhide (another of the name). From 1957 until 1967, and especially from 1959 to 1964, Shri Bhide exercised a key role in official policy-making on the co-operative movement in India.[23] "It is often forgotten by policy-makers and plan drafters," Shri Bhide has said, "that cooperatives are essentially business organizations for the economic welfare of their members. The moral aspect is very important indeed. . . . Conditions have, however, changed in the last hundred years and mutual aid and mutual knowledge and mutual obligations, important as they are, have to be balanced with the other aspect viz., sound business." Co-operative societies, he continued, are "not philanthropic or charitable institutions—the earlier this is realised, the better for everyone."[24] And on the role of government Shri Bhide has had this to say: "Cooperatives . . . cannot claim complete autonomy particularly when they ask for and receive financial, technical and other assistance from the State on an increasingly large scale. It

[21] Government of India, Planning Commission, *Third Five Year Plan: A Draft Outline*, 1960, p. 159.

[22] *Times of India*, Bombay, 9 January 1959.

[23] Shri Bhide, after a distinguished career in the Punjab, was Adviser to the Planning Commission, 1957–59; Secretary, Ministry of Community Development, Panchayati Raj and Cooperation (with particular oversight of the co-operative movement) 1959–64; Deputy Governor, Reserve Bank of India, 1964–67; Chairman, Life Insurance Corporation of India since 1967. He appears to have been singled out for his post in connection with the India-wide co-operative movement by an old and famous Punjab Registrar, visiting India at the request of the Indian government. See Sir Malcolm Darling, *Report on Certain Aspects of Co-operative Movement in India*, Government of India, Planning Commission, 1957, p. 8. Thus the "Punjab" influence continues!

[24] M. R. Bhide, "Planning and Cooperation" in Indian Institute of Public Administration, *Planning in India: Short-Term Course Lecture Summaries (August 3–29, 1959)*, 1961, p. 9.

must be realized that in the changed circumstances of today there can be no complete autonomy for anyone."[25]

What appears to have happened to the co-operative movement in India, including the movement in those areas which used to be within the so-called Bombay Presidency, is that while some—at least while Jawaharlal Nehru lived—continued to call for a greater emphasis on "democratization" at the local level, senior officials such as Shri M. R. Bhide—and, of course, countless petty auditors, supervisors, and the like—have seen to it that a somewhat different system has been developed. Here, in fact, is an example of the dichotomy between word and deed in Indian agricultural policy which has been so keenly sensed by Professor Gunnar Myrdal.[26]

The system which has been developed is by no means unlike that of the Bombay Provincial Co-operative Bank in the Bhil and canal areas in our period. But a great deal more capital now comes from government and quasi-government sources, rather than from the private sector. Indeed, one suspects that government-provided capital is not infrequently too freely available through co-operative societies[27]—and this at a time when unlimited liability is no longer being stressed.[28] There is no doubt that in this changed situation co-operatives have begun to be strongly favoured, in some areas, by the "rich peasants."[29] The system, like the Bombay Provincial

[25] M. R. Bhide, "Cooperation in a Planned Economy" in International Cooperative Alliance, *Cooperative Leadership in South-East Asia* (seminar on Cooperative Leadership . . . New Delhi, November 1960), 1963, p. 38.

[26] Gunnar Myrdal, *Asian Drama: An Inquiry into the Poverty of Nations,* Vol. II, especially pp. 877–81 and chapter 26.

[27] In Maharashtra, in 1964, 45 per cent of the working capital of the Maharashtra State Co-operative Bank came from "borrowings" (excluding deposits and owned funds). Much of this appears to have come from loans from the Reserve Bank of India. The Gujarat percentage was 31. (Reserve Bank of India, *Review of the Co-operative Movement in India, 1962–64* (1966) pp. 24, 37.) Most present-day state governments provide participatory share capital in district and "apex" ("provincial") co-operative banks; many state governments provide additional funds directly or stand guarantee for loans to the "apex" banks from such institutions as the State Bank of India.

[28] In 1964, 63.7 per cent of all Indian agricultural credit co-operatives were constituted on a limited liability basis. Ibid., p. 49.

[29] Such men have benefited from the failure of land revenue assessments in recent years to rise at the rate at which the value of money has fallen: see A. M. Khusro, "Land Revenue: A Plea for Progression," *Times of India,* Bombay, 18 April 1963; and Ashok Mitra, "Tax Burden for Indian Agriculture" in *Administration and Economic Development in India,* ed. Braibanti and Spengler. Those "rich peasants" of Maharashtra who produce sugar have also benefited from the protected—perhaps over-protected—nature of the Indian sugar industry since 1931. It may perhaps be added

Bank's system, is not completely "un-co-operative." But there are some who feel that too much of the original vision has been lost, and others who feel that the co-operative movement has no need to help those already well able to help themselves.

It is proper that in modern, democratic India there should continue to be concern about the problem of local participation in the co-operative movement. The Western world, in fact, has recently begun to rediscover the meaning and importance of "participation" at the local level; it would be unfortunate if, at this very moment, "participation" came to be regarded as unnecessary in India. At the same time one wonders whether it might not be both more honest and more efficient if the supply of credit and possibly marketing facilities to some groups—the wealthy and, perhaps, the very poor—in modern rural India were carried out by agricultural banks proper rather than by co-operative societies. The failure of the Egyptian Agricultural Bank sixty years ago did not in itself demonstrate the fundamental unsuitability of agricultural banks for the supply of credit, particularly long-term credit, in under-developed countries.[30] The Egyptian failure showed merely the absolute necessity of keeping lender and borrower in the closest possible relationship. Provided a well-managed bank was prepared to pay a large, qualified, and honest staff to maintain this relationship, the supply of credit through such an institution would be perfectly feasible. But the scale of operations would have to be large to be economic; such a bank or banks could afford to deal only with "rich peasants," or, if a definite element of philanthropy were involved, with the very poor as well.[31] Co-operation's em-

---

here that Dr. Ravinder Kumar's reasons for asserting that the "rich peasants" benefited most from the co-operative movement in British times are understandable enough: he has seen the "rich peasants" today enjoying prosperity as members of co-operatives, and he has confined his study of the co-operative movement in Bombay virtually to the Campbell period. He has assumed that Campbell's "aristocratic" societies, if they were ever typical, remained typical.

[30] See B. O. Binns, *Agricultural Economy in Burma* (1948), especially Appx. B, Extract from a memorandum by Mr. L. Dawson of the pre-war Dawson's Bank in Burma; see also Binns, *Agricultural Credit for Small Farmers* (1952), passim.

[31] About such people Shri M. R. Bhide has this to say, in tones reminiscent of Otto Rothfeld: "25% to 30%, if not more, of the cultivators have uneconomic holdings by any standard that may be applied. . . . These persons, however much you help them by way of credit, supplies, etc., can have little or no repaying capacity and as such they cannot benefit to any appreciable extent through co-operative societies. For this class of cultivators what is really needed is a scheme for relief and rehabilitation. This is a task which I am afraid cooperatives cannot handle and the State will have to come to their assistance." "Planning and Cooperation," *Planning*

phasis on local thrift and local leadership would be absent; but the economic gains might outweigh, in the estimation of many a peasant, losses of a somewhat more nebulous variety.

Many another peasant, of course, even if he were found by such a bank to be an acceptable customer, might still find its operations more cumbersome than those of a local money-lender. The money-lender's system, Harold Mann reminded the authors of the Rural Credit Survey in 1957, "can be and is oppressive but it works, and it enables the small cultivator to continue to exist."[32] There is still, sometimes, a place for the money-lender in the India of today.

But we have ventured far enough into matters which are not really within the province of the historian. It must suffice to say that the best hope for the co-operative movement in India, if it is to remain reasonably true to its ideals, would appear to lie, as in the past in the old Bombay Presidency, with the "middle peasantry." Amongst that group there is still hope of some worthwhile non-economic ends—as well as some more purely economic ends—being secured by co-operative means.

---

in India, pp. 8–9. Shri Bhide adds that "the State can, of course, use cooperatives as agencies for this work." But his heart is obviously not in such a proposal.

[32] Mann, "The General Report of the All-India Rural Credit Survey," in Mann (ed. Thorner), *The Social Framework of Agriculture,* pp. 313–14. This paper is reprinted from the *Indian Economic Review,* Vol. III, No. 4, 1957. For another, somewhat earlier, considered opinion by Mann on the co-operative movement, see "Village Betterment in the New India and Pakistan," in *The Social Framework,* pp. 301–2. (Reprinted from the *Asiatic Review,* Vol. XLIV, No. 158, 1948). "The introduction of co-operative societies was thought to herald a new day. . . . Brilliant successes there have been, and that in almost every Province, but there has been little sign of the growth of a co-operative commonwealth such as some of us looked forward to in the early days." There is a certain pathos here.

Appendix

TABLE I

LAND HOLDINGS IN GOVERNMENT VILLAGES
POONA AND AHMADNAGAR DISTRICTS, 1875–76

Size of Holding (acres)	Number	
	Poona	Ahmadnagar
Not exceeding 5	12,444	3,712
5 to 10	9,525	5,012
10 to 20	14,402	14,462
20 to 50	22,404	22,271
50 to 100	9,031	12,770
100 to 200	2,587	3,514
200 to 300	346	351
300 to 400	69	87
400 to 500	17	26
More than 500	23	21

SOURCE: *Jamabandi Rept., S.D., 1875–76*, pp. 209–10.

TABLE II

AGRICULTURAL CO-OPERATIVE CREDIT SOCIETIES WITH UNLIMITED LIABILITY IN THE BOMBAY PRESIDENCY (EXCLUDING SIND)

District	Number of Societies			Membership			Working Capital (in rupees)*		
	1919–20	1924–25	1929–30	1919–20	1924–25	1929–30	1919–20	1924–25	1929–30
Ahmadabad	37	66	90	3,669	4,851	5,737	1,08,998	3,17,391	5,54,255
Broach	95	136	174	6,513	9,216	10,112	3,93,831	7,07,627	14,66,263
Kaira	58	107	139	4,571	8,995	11,719	1,73,113	4,67,447	6,52,474
Panch Mahals	21	97	159	2,865	6,194	7,932	73,592	2,17,772	4,61,120
Surat	136	144	160	7,666	8,254	8,899	5,98,433	7,92,633	12,18,517
Thana	39	40	112	3,463	4,373	6,175	1,85,011	1,90,395	3,77,239
Ahmadnagar	75	90	123	5,201	5,030	5,333	4,28,355	9,16,057	10,82,993
East Khandesh	138	264	529	8,993	17,051	28,397	6,31,260	18,33,783	45,58,488
West Khandesh	33	157	273	2,084	7,720	11,706	90,810	8,37,110	23,13,345
Nasik	71	104	245	4,126	5,267	9,507	3,75,923	5,08,150	14,88,277
Poona	155	187	180	11,484	14,541	13,297	15,15,996	37,38,369	34,90,097
Satara	148	177	244	18,103	15,762	17,805	10,56,927	14,12,849	18,43,752
Sholapur	106	121	156	9,385	10,181	11,383	7,33,194	10,75,361	11,74,620
Belgaum	137	169	194	13,269	18,472	21,344	7,48,198	13,97,169	22,24,463
Bijapur	94	123	173	8,482	10,701	12,059	4,44,280	8,94,947	12,60,923
Dharwar	342	432	470	28,487	37,725	38,421	24,97,287	44,39,199	50,51,724
Kanara	54	77	90	3,606	8,221	9,622	1,34,996	5,47,875	8,61,681
Kolaba	33	28	53	2,045	2,066	2,234	55,388	59,715	73,368
Ratnagiri	33	38	44	2,565	8,637	3,868	98,769	2,01,814	1,60,309

SOURCE: *Annual Reports on the Working of Co-operative Societies in the Bombay Presidency, 1919–20, 1924–25, 1929–30.*

* Working Capital is taken to be share capital, loans and deposits from all sources, and reserve fund.

TABLE III

HARVEST PRICES OF JOWARI, BAJRI, GUL (RAW SUGAR), AND CLEANED
COTTON IN THE BOMBAY PRESIDENCY, 1916–17 TO 1929–30
(price per maund 82 2/7 lb.)

	Jowari		Bajri		Gul		Cleaned cotton	
	Rs.	As.	Rs.	As.	Rs.	As.	Rs.	As.
1916–17*	3	0	3	6	9	4	32	13
1917–18*	4	3	4	6	8	10	45	7
1918–19	9	13	10	1	11	7	49	6
1919–20	6	6	6	7	15	12	42	9
1920–21	6	7	7	4	14	1	24	10
1921–22	6	10	7	8	14	14	35	11
1922–23	3	14	4	9	12	7	43	0
1923–24	4	2	4	8	10	0	58	0
1924–25	4	12	5	5	12	3	45	7
1925–26	4	14	5	7	11	0	42	8
1926–27	5	0	5	6	9	1	40	0
1927–28	4	9	4	11	8	6	39	12
1928–29	4	9	5	2	9	15	33	0
1929–30	4	12	5	10	9	5	32	0

SOURCE: *Agricultural Statistics of India*, Vol. I, 1917–18 to 1929–30, Table VII.

* Average Annual Market Prices.

Bibliography

Abbreviations used in the footnotes are in brackets.

I. UNPUBLISHED OFFICIAL RECORDS

A. OFFICE OF THE REGISTRAR OF CO-OPERATIVE SOCIETIES, MAHARASHTRA STATE, POONA

1. RECORD ROOM [POONA.]

A word is necessary on the material seen here. All papers in the Co-operative Department in the old Bombay State were, after about 1920, given a classification *A, B, C,* or *D. A* class or "policy" papers were supposed to be permanently preserved. *B* indicated that papers should be kept for thirty years, *C* class papers were to be retained for five years, and *D* class papers were normally destroyed after a year. The result of the introduction of the system has been that few post-1920 papers on individual co-operative societies—of the variety which would interest the historian looking for "case histories"—have survived the weeding process. From the departmental point of view, of course, some destruction of the exceptionally bulky records was obviously necessary. And fortunately the Co-operative Department has been blessed with Record Keepers who have realized the historical value of some of the earliest documents in their possession. Fortunately, too, the files of the Maharashtra State Co-operative Bank fill in some of the gaps from 1920.

Only the more important files consulted at the Registrar's Office are listed here. A brief explanation is given of their contents.

"Government Resolutions" on Co-operation. Unless it is otherwise specified in footnotes, all references to Bombay Government Resolutions and Orders, and their enclosures, are to this series of files.

"Spare Copies" of Bombay Government Resolutions.

"Establishment of C.C.S. in India." The beginnings.

"D.A.8" and "D.A.24." Files relating to Co-operation originally kept by the Director of Agriculture.

"Permanent EST." Permanent Establishment.

"ADM. S.O.7." Standing Orders.

"Original Circulars, I," "Original Circulars, II," "Circulars, 1916–1930." Originals of Circulars issued by the Registrar, and correspondence relating to them.

"Miscellaneous XVIII, Orders on Audit and Inspection."

"Nira Canal and Central Bank." [N.C. & C.B.] The Bombay Central Co-operative Bank and its work, to 1920.

"Bombay Provincial Co-operative Bank." [B.P.C.B.] The post-1920 continuation of the previous file.

"Decentralisation." Documents relating to the Decentralisation Commission, 1907–1909.

"Subordination of Regr. to D.A." (i.e. Director of Agriculture).

"Committee on Co-operation." Documents relating to the Maclagan Committee, 1915.

"Poona Central Co-operative Bank—A." [Poona C.C.B.-A] Permanent file on this Bank.

"Bombay Provincial Co-operative Institute, III." [B.P.C.I., III] The establishment and early years of the Institute.

"T.A.G.3," "T.A.G.4," "T.A.G.7." Takkavi and Co-operation.

"36, IX," "P.S.8." Miscellaneous.

"Matar Taluka."

"Proceedings of the Co-operative Round Table Conference, 1933."

2. REGISTRAR'S LIBRARY [POONA, REGISTRAR'S LIBRARY]

Sahasrabudhe, B. B. "Interim Report for the First Crop Year 1908–1909 of the Nira Canal Tagai Loans Scheme, Poona District." G. of B., 1909.

Badve, R. B., "Report on the Working of the Nira Canal Societies up to the close of the Co-operative Year 1913–1914." G. of B., 1914.

B. MAHARASHTRA STATE RECORD OFFICE, BOMBAY [B.R.O.]

Revenue Department Volumes [R.D. Vols.]: 96 of 1874; 35, 118 of 1875; 5 of 1876; 80 of 1908; 60 of 1911; 428 of 1914.

Judicial Department Volumes [J.D. Vols.]: 10 of 1873; 7, 52 of 1874; 36, 81, 82 of 1875.

General Department Volumes [G.D. Vols.]: 7 of 1874; 13, 15 of 1875.

C. MAHARASHTRA STATE CO-OPERATIVE BANK, BOMBAY [B.S.C.B..]

"Registrar" [Regr.] 1920–30. Correspondence with the Registrar.

"Asst. Regr. Surat" 1920–30. Correspondence with the Assistant Registrar for Gujarat.

D. LIBRARY OF THE GOKHALE INSTITUTE OF POLITICS AND ECONOMICS, POONA

[Harold H. Mann.] "Economic Progress of the Rural Areas of the Bombay Presidency 1911–1922." Government of Bombay, 1924.

E. NATIONAL ARCHIVES OF INDIA, NEW DELHI [N.A.I.]

Typescript of selections from the private papers of Gopal Krishna Gokhale.

Revenue, Agriculture and Commerce (Land Revenue and Settlement) Proceedings, 1875.

Revenue and Agriculture (Agriculture) Proceedings, 1909.

Revenue and Agriculture (Land Revenue) Proceedings, 1914.

"Reports on the Native Papers published in the Bombay Presidency," 1874–77.

"Selection of Papers on Agricultural Indebtedness and the Restriction of the Power to Alienate Interests in Land." 3 vols. Revenue and Agriculture Department, 1898.

F. FROM THE PUNJAB RECORD OFFICE, PATIALA [PATIALA.]

Typescript of the Minutes of Evidence, Bombay, Committee on Co-operation in India, 1914–15.

G. INDIA OFFICE LIBRARY [I.O.L.] AND INDIA OFFICE RECORDS [I.O.R.], LONDON

The Indian papers of James Caird. Home Miscellaneous Series, Vol. 796. [Caird Papers.]

Lee-Warner (Sir William Lee-Warner) Political and Miscellaneous Private Papers. (Uncatalogued in 1968.) "Deccan Ryot, Series I," "Deccan Ryot, Series II," "Series V."

The private papers of Sir Richard Temple. [Temple Papers.] MSS. Eur. F.86/214: "Native Opinion in India."

Revenue Letters from the Governor-General of India in Council to the Secretary of State for India [Rev. Letters from India], 1895–1909.

Revenue Despatches from the Secretary of State for India to the Governor-General of India in Council [Rev. Despatches to India], 1895–1909.

India (Government of India) Land Revenue Proceedings [L. Rev. Procs.], Vols. 4762; 7068; 9219.

India Judicial Proceedings, Range 206, Vol. 66.

India Legislative Proceedings, Vol. 6172.

Bombay (Government of Bombay) Land Revenue Proceedings, Vols. 4762; 5777; 6239; 8592.

Bombay Confidential Land Revenue Proceedings, Vol. 37 (1918.)

Bombay Judicial Proceedings, Vols. 9078; 9338.

Bombay Legislative Proceedings, Vol. 6237.

Bombay Financial Proceedings, Vol. 11319.

"Report on the Economic Condition of the Masses of the Bombay Presidency by the Director of Land Records and Agriculture," 1888. (In India Office Parliamentary Collection, No. 221.)

H. BRITISH MUSEUM, LONDON [B.M.]

Correspondence and Papers of the 1st Marquis of Ripon. Add. MSS. 43596.

I. PUBLIC RECORD OFFICE, LONDON

The private papers of the 1st Earl of Cromer. F.O. 633, Vol. XIV.

J. BODLEIAN LIBRARY, OXFORD

The private papers of Lord MacDonnell, especially those relating to the Famine Commission, 1901. MSS. Eng. hist. c. 356.

K. ARCHIVES OF THE SOCIETY FOR THE PROPAGATION OF THE GOSPEL IN
    FOREIGN PARTS, LONDON [S.P.G.]

Missionary Reports Received, 1898–1909, especially the Reports of Canon
C. S. Rivington.

L. HORACE PLUNKETT FOUNDATION, LONDON

The private papers of Sir Horace Plunkett.

II. PUBLISHED OFFICIAL SOURCES

A. PARLIAMENTARY PAPERS [P.P.]

Select Committee on the Affairs of the East India Company, Minutes of Evidence, Vol. III. 1831–32 (735–III) xi.
Report by James Caird, Esq., C.B.; with Correspondence. 1880 (C. 2732) liii.
Report of the Indian Famine Commission, 1878–79, pt. iii, (Famine Histories).
    1881 (C. 3086-I) lxxi, pt. i.
Copy of Correspondence respecting Agricultural Banks in India. 1887 (340)
    lxii.
*Statement exhibiting the Moral and Material Progress and Condition of India
    during the decennial period from 1882–83 to 1891–92.* 1894 (43) lix.
Report on the Finances, Administration and Condition of Egypt and the Progress of Reforms, 1895. 1896 (C. 7978) xcvii.
Report of the Indian Famine Commission, 1901, and Papers Relating Thereto.
    1902 (Cd. 876) lxx.
*Statement exhibiting the Moral and Material Progress and Condition of India
    during 1901–2 and the nine preceding years.* 1903 (249) xlvi.
*Reports by His Majesty's Agent and Consul General on Egypt and the Soudan,
    1903 and 1904.* 1904 (Cd. 1951) cxi; 1910 (Cd. 5121) cxii.
Report of the Royal Commission on Decentralisation in India. 1908 (Cd.
    4360) xliv. *Minutes of Evidence, Bombay.* 1908 (Cd. 4367) xlvi.
Report of the Royal Commission on Agriculture in India. 1928 (Cmd. 3132)
    viii. *Evidence taken in Bombay*, Vol. II, pts. i and ii; *Evidence taken in
    Punjab*, Vol. VIII, 1927 (Non-parl.)
Report of the Indian Statutory Commission. Vol. I, Survey. 1929–30 (Cmd.
    3568) xi. Vol. II, *Recommendations.* 1929–30 (Cmd. 3569) xi. Memorandum
    Submitted by the Government of Bombay: *Evidence*, Vol. VII, 1930 (Non-parl.)

B. GOVERNMENT OF INDIA

*Abstract of the Proceedings of the Council of the Governor-General of India
    assembled for the purpose of making Laws and Regulations*, 1879, 1903–04.
Agricultural Statistics of India, 1884–85, 1894–95, 1915–16 to 1929–30.
Burns, W. *Sons of the Soil. Studies of the Indian Cultivator.* 1941.
Darling, Malcolm. *Report on Certain Aspects of [the] Co-operative Movement
    in India.* Planning Commission, 1957.

Note on Land Transfer and Agricultural Indebtedness in India. [1895.]

Prices and Wages in India, 1923.

Proceedings of the Conference of Registrars of Co-operative Societies held on 25th September 1906 and the following days, and semi-annually to 1928. [*Regrs.' Conf. Procs., 19—.*]

Report of the Agricultural Finance Sub-Committee appointed by the Government of India on the recommendation of the Policy Committee on Agriculture, Forestry and Fisheries. [1946.]

Report of the Bombay Provincial Banking Enquiry Committee, 1929–30. Vol. I, Report [*Bom. Prov. Banking Enquiry Cttee. Rept.*]; Vols. II–IV, Evidence. 1930.

Report of the Commission appointed to Enquire into the Working of the Deccan Agriculturists' Relief Act (1891–92). 1892.

Report of the Committee on Co-operation in India. 1915. [*Maclagan Cttee. Rept.*] (Republished, Reserve Bank of India, Bombay, 1957.)

Report of the Committee on Co-operative Credit. Ministry of Community Development and Co-operation (Department of Co-operation), 1960.

Report of the Indian Central Cotton Committee, 1919. 1919.

Report of the Indian Industrial Commission, 1916–1918. 1918.

Report of the Select Committee on the Establishment of Co-operative Credit Societies in India. 1901.

Report of the Study Team on the Working of the Cooperative Movement in Yugoslavia and Israel. Ministry of Community Development and Cooperation, 1960.

Report of the Working Group on Co-operative Policy. Ministry of Community Development and Co-operation (Department of Co-operation) 1959.

Revenue and Agriculture Department (Land Revenue) Resolution No. 12–287–1 of 17 June 1914, on the Progress of Co-operation. (Published in pamphlet form, 1914.)

Sahakari Samaj: A Symposium on the cooperative movement in India. Ministry of Community Development, Panchayati Raj and Cooperation, 1962.

Selection from Papers on Indebtedness and Land Transfer. 1895.

Selections from the Records of the Government of India [S.R. G. of I.], Home Department, No. ccxlii, *Papers relating to the Deccan Agriculturists' Relief Act during the Years 1875–94.* 2 vols. 1897.

Third Five Year Plan: A Draft Outline. Planning Commission, 1960.

C. Government of Bombay

Department of Agriculture Bulletins:

Ambekar, G. R. *The Crops of the Bombay Presidency,* pt. ii. No. 146, 1928.

Keatinge, G. *Note on Cattle in the Bombay Presidency.* No. 85, 1917.

Mann, Harold H., and Tamhane, V. A. *The Salt Lands of the Nira Valley.* No. 39, 1910.

Padhye, R. G. *Sugar Industry in Western India and Methods of Sugar Manufacture.* No. 116, 1924.

Patil, P. C. *The Crops of the Bombay Presidency,* pt. i. No. 116, 1924.

Anderson, F. G. Hartnell. *Manual of Revenue Accounts of the Villages, Talu-*

kas and Districts of the Bombay Presidency. Corrected up to 31st July 1940. 1940.

Annual Report relating to the Establishment of Co-operative Credit Societies in the Bombay Presidency during the year ending 31st March 1905, and the following years, under varying titles, to 1937. [*Rept., 19—.*]

Bombay Government Gazette, 1904, 1910, 1927.

Bombay Legislative Council Proceedings, 1922–30.

Census of India: Census of the Bombay Presidency taken on the 21st February 1872, pts. i and ii. 1875.

Mead, P. J., and Macgregor, G. Laird. *Census of India, 1911,* Vol. VII, *Bombay,* pt. i. 1912.

Sedgwick, L. J. *Census of India, 1921,* Vol. VIII, *Bombay,* pt. i. 1922.

Chaplin, William. *A Report exhibiting a view of the Fiscal and Judicial System of Administration introduced into the Conquered Territory above the Ghauts under the Authority of the Commissioner in the Dekhan.* 1824.

Enthoven, R. E. *The Tribes and Castes of Bombay.* 3 vols. 1920–22.

Gazetteer of the Bombay Presidency: Vol. IV, *Ahmedabad,* 1879; Vol. XVII, *Ahmednagar,* 1884; Vol. XXIII, *Bijapur,* 1884; Vol. XXII, *Dharwar,* 1884; Vol. IX, pt. i, *Gujerat Population, Hindus,* 1901; Vol. III, *Kaira and Panch Mahals,* 1879; Vol. XII, *Khandesh,* 1880; Vol. XI, *Kolaba and Janjira,* 1883; Vol. XVIII, *Poona,* pts. i–iii, 1885; Vol. X, *Ratnagiri and Savantvadi,* 1880; Vol. II, *Surat and Broach,* 1877.

Jamabandi Reports [for the various Divisions of the Bombay Presidency] 1871–72, 1875–76, 1884–85, 1891–92, 1895–96 (continued as) *Land Revenue Administration Reports* [*Bom. L. Rev. Admin. Repts.*] 1903–04 to 1930–31.

[Mann, Harold H.] *Statistical Atlas of the Bombay Presidency.* 3d ed. 1925.

[Nayak, N. V.] *Fifty Years of Co-operation in the Bombay State.* 1957.

Proceedings of the Co-operative Conference held in Bombay, December 15–18, 1908, and semi-annually, under varying titles, to 1929. From 1921 to 1929 such Reports were published by the Bombay Provincial Co-operative Institute. [*Prov. Co-op. Conf. Procs., 19—.*]

Proceedings of the Council of the Governor of Bombay, assembled for the purpose of making Laws and Regulations. 1901–02.

Report of the Committee on the Riots in Poona and Ahmednagar, 1875, with *Appendices.* 3 vols. 1876. [*Deccan Riots Rept.*]

Report of the Co-operatives Supervision Committee. n.d. [? 1934.]

Report of the Land Mortgage Committee, 1934.

Reports on the Administration of the Registration Department in the Bombay Presidency, 1876–77 to 1920–22.

Rothfeld, Otto. *Impressions of the Co-operative Movement in France and Italy.* 1920.

Season and Crop Reports of the Bombay Presidency, 1903–4 to 1930–31.

Selections from the Records of the Bombay Government, New Series: [*S.R. G. of B., N.S.*]

　　No. cli. *Papers relating to the Revision of the Rates of Assessment on the*

Expiration of the first Settlement in the Old Indapur, Bhimthari, Pabal, and Haveli Talukas of the Poona Collectorate. 1877.

No. clvi. *Papers and Proceedings connected with the passing of the Deccan Agriculturists' Relief Act . . . 1877–1880.* 1882.

No. clxxvi. *Revision Settlement of 126 Villages in the Old Bagalkot Taluka of Bijapur.* 1886.

No. cclxxviii. *Character of Land Tenures and Survey Settlement in the Bombay Presidency.* Revised ed. 1908.

No. ccclxi. *Papers relating to the Revision Survey Settlement of the Olpad Taluka of the Surat Collectorate.* 1897.

No. dcxxxi. *Papers relating to the Second Revision Settlement of the Karad Taluka of the Satara District.* 1925.

Symington, D. *Report on the Aboriginal and Hill Tribes of the Partially Excluded Areas in the Province of Bombay.* 1939.

D. OTHER OFFICIAL PUBLICATIONS

Annual Report on the Working of Co-operative Credit Societies in the Punjab for the year 1904–1905, and, under varying titles, for 1907, 1913, 1927. Government of the Punjab.

Hansard's Parliamentary Debates, 3d Series, 1877, 1887; *Parliamentary Debates,* 4th Series, 1901, 1903.

Ibbetson, D. C. J. *Report on the Revision of Settlement of the Panipat Tahsil and Karnal Parganah of the Karnal District, 1872–1880.* Allahabad, 1883.

The Imperial Gazetteer of India. 26 vols. Oxford, 1907–09.

Karve, I., *Maharashtra—Land and Its People.* (Maharashtra State Gazetteers, General Series.) Government of Maharashtra, 1968.

Nicholson, F. A. *Report regarding the Possibility of Introducing Land and Agricultural Banks into the Madras Presidency.* Government of Madras. Vol. I, 1895, reprinted 1915; Vol. II, 1897. (Vol. I reprinted Reserve Bank of India, Bombay, 1960.)

Report on the Working of Co-operative Credit Societies in the Lower Provinces for the year 1904–1905; Report on the Working of Co-operative Credit Societies in Bengal for the year 1906–1907, and for 1916–1917. Government of Bengal.

Voelcker, J. A. *Report on the Improvement of Indian Agriculture.* London, 1893.

III. CONTEMPORARY PERIODICALS AND NEWSPAPERS

The Bombay Chronicle, 1919–24, 1929.

The Bombay Co-operative News, 1924–26.

The Bombay Co-operative Quarterly [B.C.Q.], 1917–57.

The Bombay Gazette, 1875–1881.

Chambers's Journal, 1883.

The Indian Agriculturist, 1901.

The Indian National Herald, 1927.
Kesari, 1920. [In Marathi.]
The Madras Weekly Mail, 1891–92.
Mahratta, 1920–25.
The Quarterly Review, 1916.
The Quarterly Journal of the Poona Sarvajanik Sabha, 1879–81.
The Servant of India, 1910.
The Times of India Illustrated Weekly, 1907.
Young India, 1921–22.

IV. OTHER WORKS

A. BOOKS

Altekar, A. S. *A History of Village Communities in Western India*. Bombay, 1927.
Ambedkar, B. R. *Ranade, Gandhi and Jinnah: Address delivered on the 101st Birthday Celebration of Mahadev Govind Ranade*. Bombay, 1943.
Anderson, F. G. H. *Facts and Fallacies about the Bombay Land Revenue System Critically Expounded*. Poona, 1929.
Anstey, Vera. *The Economic Development of India*. 4th ed. London, 1952.
Baden-Powell, B. H. *The Land Systems of British India*. 3 vols. Oxford, 1892.
Baer, Gabriel. *A History of Landownership in Modern Egypt, 1800–1950*. London, 1962.
Barrier, Norman G. *The Punjab Alienation of Land Bill of 1900*. Durham, N.C., 1966.
Bauer, P. T. *West African Trade: A Study of Competition, Oligopoly and Monopoly in a Changing Economy*. Cambridge, 1954.
Belshaw, Cyril S. *Traditional Exchange and Modern Markets*. Englewood Cliffs, N.J., 1965.
Bhatia, B. M. *Famines in India: A Study in Some Aspects of the Economic History of India (1860–1945)*. Bombay, 1963.
Binns, B. O. *Agricultural Credit for Small Farmers*. Rome, 1952.
———. *Agricultural Economy in Burma*. Rangoon, 1948.
Black, R. D. Collison. *Economic Thought and the Irish Question, 1817–1870*. Cambridge, 1960.
Blum, Jerome. *The European Peasantry from the Fifteenth to the Nineteenth Century*. Washington, D.C., 1960.
———. *Lord and Peasant in Russia from the Ninth to the Nineteenth Century*. Princeton, 1961.
Blyn, George. *Agricultural Trends in India, 1891–1947. Output, Availability and Productivity*. Philadelphia, 1966.
Bombay State Co-operative Bank. *Report of Crop Loan Evaluation Committee*, part i. Bombay, 1958.
Boserup, Ester. *The Conditions of Agricultural Growth: The Economics of Agrarian Change under Population Pressure*. London, 1965.

Braibanti, Ralph, and Spengler, Joseph J., eds. *Administration and Economic Development in India.* Durham, N.C., 1963.

Brayne, F. L. *Socrates in an Indian Village.* London (Mysore imprint), 1929.

Broomfield, J. H. *Elite Conflict in a Plural Society: Twentieth Century Bengal.* Berkeley and Los Angeles, 1968.

Buchanan, Daniel Houston. *The Development of Capitalistic Enterprise in India.* New York, 1934.

Butterfield, Herbert. *History and Human Relations.* London, 1951.

Calvert, Hubert. *The Law and Principles of Co-operation.* 2d ed. Calcutta, 1921.

———. *The Wealth and Welfare of the Punjab.* 1st ed. Lahore, 1922; 2d ed. Lahore, n.d. [1936].

Cambridge Medieval History. Vol. VII. Cambridge, 1932.

Chandra, Bipan. *The Rise and Growth of Economic Nationalism in India: Economic Policies of Indian National Leadership, 1880–1905.* New Delhi, 1966.

Choksey, R. D. *Economic Life in the Bombay Deccan (1818–1939).* Bombay, 1955.

———. *Economic Life in the Bombay Gujarat (1800–1939).* Bombay, 1968.

———. *Economic Life in the Bombay Karnatak (1818–1939).* Bombay, 1963.

———. *Economic Life in the Bombay Konkan (1818–1939).* Bombay, 1960.

Clark, Colin, and Haswell, Margaret. *The Economics of Subsistence Agriculture.* 2d ed. London, 1966.

Clark, G. Kitson. *The Making of Victorian England.* London, 1962.

The Complete Peerage. London, 1910–1959.

Dandekar, V. M., and Khudanpur, G. J. *Working of Bombay Tenancy Act, 1948: Report of Investigation.* Poona, 1957.

Dantwala, M. L. *A Hundred Years of Indian Cotton.* Bombay, 1948.

———. *Marketing of Raw Cotton in India.* Bombay, 1937.

Darling, Malcolm Lyall. *At Freedom's Door.* London, 1949.

———. *The Punjab Peasant in Prosperity and Debt.* 1st ed. London [Mysore imprint], 1925; 4th ed. Bombay, 1947.

———. *Rusticus Loquitor: or, The Old Light and the New in the Punjab Village.* London, 1930.

———. *Wisdom and Waste in the Punjab Village.* London, 1934.

Desai, A. R., ed. *Rural Sociology in India.* Revised ed. Bombay, 1959.

Desai, Mahadev. *Gandhiji in Indian Villages.* Madras, 1927.

———. *The Story of Bardoli: Being a History of the Bardoli Satyagraha of 1928 and Its Sequel.* Ahmadabad, 1929.

Desai, M. B. *The Rural Economy of Gujarat.* Bombay, 1948.

Desai, R. C. *Standard of Living in India and Pakistan 1931–32 to 1940–41.* Bombay, 1953.

Deshpande, C. D. *Western India: A Regional Geography.* Dharwar, 1948.

Devadhar, G. K., Thakkar, A. V., and Joshi, N. M. *Report of an Inquiry into the Agricultural Situation in Matar Taluka of the District of Kaira.* Bombay, 1918.

Dewey, Alice G. *Peasant Marketing in Java.* New York, 1962.

Dictionary of National Biography. London, 1885–1959.

Digby, Margaret. *Horace Plunkett, an Anglo-American Irishman.* Oxford, 1949.

———. *The World Co-operative Movement.* London, n.d. [?1951].

Digby, Margaret, and Gretton, R. H. *Co-operative Marketing for Agricultural Producers.* Rome, 1952.

Digby, William. *"Prosperous" British India: A Revelation from Official Records.* London, 1901.

Diskalker, P. D. *Resurvey of a Deccan Village: Pimple Saudagar.* Bombay, 1960.

Dupernex, H. *People's Banks for Northern India: A Handbook to the Organization of Credit on a Co-operative Basis.* Calcutta, 1900.

Ewbank, R. B., ed. *Indian Co-operative Studies.* Bombay, 1920.

Farmer, B. H. *Pioneer Peasant Cultivation in Ceylon: A Study in Asian Agrarian Problems.* London, 1957.

Farquhar, J. N. *Modern Religious Movements in India.* New York, 1915.

Firth, Raymond, and Yamey, B. S., eds. *Capital, Saving and Credit in Peasant Societies: Studies from Asia, Oceania, the Caribbean and Middle America.* London, 1964.

Furnivall, J. S. *Colonial Policy and Practice: A Comparative Study of Burma and Netherlands India.* Cambridge, 1948.

Gadgil, D. R. *Economic Effects of Irrigation: Report of a Survey of the Direct and Indirect Benefits of the Godavari and Pravara Canals.* Poona, 1948.

———. *The Industrial Evolution of India in Recent Times.* 4th ed. Calcutta, 1942.

Gadgil, D. R., with the assistance of M. V. Namjoshi. "Origins of the Modern Indian Business Class." Mimeographed. New York, 1959.

Gadgil, D. R., and Dandekar, V. M. *Primary Education in Satara District: Reports of Two Investigations.* Poona, 1955.

Gadgil, D. R., and Gadgil, V. R. *A Survey of Farm Business in Wai Taluka.* Poona, 1940.

Gandhi, M. K. *An Autobiography, or, The Story of my Experiments with Truth,* trans. Mahadev Desai. 2d ed. Ahmadabad, 1940.

———. ed. Shriman Narayan. *Co-operative Farming,* Ahmadabad, 1959.

Ghurye, G. S. *Caste and Class in India.* Bombay, 1951.

Gopal, S. *The Viceroyalty of Lord Irwin, 1926–1931.* Oxford, 1957.

———. *The Viceroyalty of Lord Ripon, 1880–1884.* Oxford, 1953.

Gorst, Sheila. *Co-operative Organization in Tropical Countries: A Study of Co-operative Development in Non-Self-governing Territories under United Kingdom Administration, 1945–1955.* Oxford, 1959.

Gorwala, A. D. *The Role of the Administrator, Past, Present and Future.* Poona, 1952.

Gujarat Research Society. *Shri Thakkar Bapa Commemoration Volume.* Bombay, n.d. [1952].

Gune, Vithal Trimbak. *The Judicial System of the Marathas.* Poona, 1953.

Gupte, K. S. *The Dekkhan Agriculturists' Relief Act. (Act XVII of 1879.) As modified to the 31st March 1928.* Poona, 1928.

Habib, Irfan. *The Agrarian System of Mughal India (1556–1707).* Bombay, 1963.

Halliday, James (pseudonym for David Symington). *A Special India.* London, 1968.

Hanson, A. H. *The Process of Planning: A Study of India's Five-Year Plans, 1950–1964.* London, 1966.

Hardinge of Penshurst, Baron. *My Indian Years, 1910–1916.* London, 1948.

Harrison, Selig S. *India: The Most Dangerous Decades.* Princeton, 1960.

Hough, Eleanor M. *The Co-operative Movement in India Before Partition and in Independent India.* 3rd ed. Calcutta, 1953.

Hoyland, John S. *Gopal Krishna Gokhale. His Life and Speeches.* Calcutta, 1933.

Indian Central Cotton Committee. *General Report on Eight Investigations into the Finance and Marketing of Cultivator's Cotton, 1925–28.* Bombay, n.d. [?1929].

Indian Institute of Public Administration. *Planning in India: Short-term Course Lecture Summaries (August 3–29, 1959).* New Delhi, 1961.

International Cooperative Alliance. *Cooperative Leadership in South-east Asia.* (Proceedings of a Seminar, New Delhi, November 1960.) Bombay, 1963.

Jagalpure, L. B., and Kale, K. D. [revised A. M. Macmillan]. *Sarola Kasar (Study of a Deccan Village in the Famine Zone).* Ahmadnagar, 1938.

Jain, L. C. *Indigenous Banking in India.* London, 1929.

Jayakar, M. R. *The Story of my Life.* Vol. I, *1873–1922.* Bombay, 1958.

Joshi, T. M. *Bombay Finance (1921–1946).* Poona, 1947.

Kaji, H. L. *Co-operation in Bombay: Short Studies.* Bombay, 1930.

———. *Life and Speeches of Sir Vithaldas Thackersey.* Bombay, 1934.

Kale, Govind Raghunath. *Barsi Central Co-operative Bank Ltd., va Barsi talukantil Sahakari Patpadya yatsa Itihas.* (In Marathi.) Barsi, 1954.

Kale, V. G. *Gokhale and Economic Reforms.* Poona, 1916.

Kapadia, K. M., ed. *Professor Ghurye Felicitation Volume.* Bombay, n.d. [?1954].

Karve, D. G. *Ranade: The Prophet of Liberated India.* Poona, 1942.

Karve, Irawati. *Hindu Society—An Interpretation.* Poona, 1961.

Keatinge, G. *Agricultural Progress in Western India.* London, 1921.

———. *Rural Economy in the Bombay Deccan.* London, 1912.

Keer, Dhananjay. *Dr. Ambedkar, Life and Mission.* Bombay, 1954.

———. *Mahatma Jotirao Phooley, Father of our Social Revolution.* Bombay, 1964.

Kellock, James. *Mahadev Govind Ranade, Patriot and Social Servant.* Calcutta, 1926.

Kumar, Dharma. *Land and Caste in South India: Agricultural Labour in Madras Presidency in the Nineteenth Century.* Cambridge, 1965.

Kumar, Ravinder. *Western India in the Nineteenth Century.* London, 1968.

Kumarappa, J. C. (Director). *A Survey of Matar Taluka (Kaira District).* Ahmadabad, 1931.

Kunzru, H. N., ed. *Gopal Krishna Devadhar*. Poona, 1939.

Lambert, Richard D., and Hoselitz, Bert F., eds. *The Role of Savings and Wealth in Southern Asia and the West*. Paris, 1963.

Landes, David S. *Bankers and Pashas: International Finance and Economic Imperialism in Egypt*. London, 1958.

Latthe, A. B. *Memoirs of His Highness Shri Shahu Chhatrapati, Maharaja of Kolhapur*. 2 vols. Bombay, 1924.

Lawrence, Walter Roper. *The India We Served*. London, 1928.

Lefebvre, Georges. *The Coming of the French Revolution*. Trans. R. R. Palmer. New York, 1957.

——. *La Grande Peur de 1789*. Paris, 1932.

Lewis, Oscar (with the assistance of Victor Barnouw). *Village Life in Northern India. Studies in a Delhi Village*. Urbana, Ill., 1958.

Limaye, P. M. *The History of the Deccan Education Society (1880–1935)*. Poona, 1935.

Low, D. A. *Soundings in Modern South Asian History*. London, 1968.

MacDonagh, Oliver. *A Pattern of Government Growth, 1800–1860: The Passenger Acts and their Enforcement*. London, 1961.

Mann, Harold H. *Rainfall and Famine: A Study of Rainfall in the Bombay Deccan, 1865–1938*. Bombay, 1955.

Mann, Harold H. *The Social Framework of Agriculture. India, Middle East, England*. Ed. Daniel Thorner. Bombay, 1967.

Mann, Harold H., and Kanitkar, N. V. *Land and Labour in a Deccan Village*. Bombay, 1917.

——. *Land and Labour in a Deccan Village: Study No. II*. Bombay, 1921.

Marriott, McKim, ed. *Village India: Studies in the Little Community*. Chicago, 1955.

Mayer, Adrian C. *Land and Society in Malabar*. Bombay, 1952.

Mehta, J. M. *A Study of Rural Economy of Gujarat: Containing Possibilities of Reconstruction*. Baroda, 1930.

Mehta, Vaikunth L. *A Plea for Planning in Co-operation*. Poona, 1942.

——. *Studies in Co-operative Finance*. Poona, 1927.

Mehta, V. L., and Bhansali, M. D. *Report on the Reorganization of the Co-operative Movement in Bombay*. Bombay, 1937.

Metcalf, Thomas R. *The Aftermath of Revolt: India, 1857–1870*. Princeton, 1964.

Montague, Edwin S. *An Indian Diary*. ed. Venetia Montagu. London, 1930.

Moon, Penderel. *Strangers in India*. London, 1944.

Morris, Morris David. *The Emergence of an Industrial Labor Force in India: A Study of the Bombay Cotton Mills, 1854–1947*. Berkeley and Los Angeles, 1965.

Mukerji, Kshitimohan. *Levels of Economic Activity and Public Expenditure in India: A Historical and Quantitative Study*. Bombay, 1965.

Mukherji, P. *The Co-operative Movement in India*. 2nd ed. Calcutta, 1917.

Mukhtyar, G. C. *Life and Labour in a South Gujerat Village*. Calcutta, 1930.

Myint, H. *The Economics of the Developing Countries*. London, 1964.

Myrdal, Gunnar. *Asian Drama: An Inquiry into the Poverty of Nations*. 3 vols. London, 1968.

Nair, Kusum. *Blossoms in the Dust: The Human Factor in Indian Development.* London, 1961.

Naik, K. N. *The Co-operative Movement in the Bombay State.* Bombay, 1953.

Naik, K. N., ed. *Fifty Years of Co-operation: Golden Jubilee Souvenir.* Bombay, 1954.

Naik, T. B. *The Bhils, a Study.* Delhi, n.d. [1956].

[Nanavati, Manilal B., and Parikh, Natvarlal.] *Bhakdad. Social and Economic Survey of a Village: A Comparative Study (1915 and 1955).* Bombay, 1957.

Nanda, B. R. *Mahatma Gandhi: A Biography.* London, 1958.

Narain, Dharm. *Distribution of the Marketed Surplus of Agricultural Produce by Size-level of Holding in India 1950–51.* New Delhi, 1961.

———. *Impact of Price Movements on Areas under Selected Crops in India 1900–1939.* Cambridge, 1965.

Natarajan, K. *Gopal Krishna Gokhale: The Man and His Message.* Bombay, 1930.

Natarajan, S. *Lalubhai Samaldas.* Bombay, n.d. [?1937].

Neale, Walter C. *Economic Change in Rural India: Land Tenure and Reform in Uttar Pradesh, 1800–1955.* New Haven, Conn., 1962.

Nehru, S. S. *Caste and Credit in the Rural Area.* Calcutta, 1932.

1911–1961. The Maharashtra State Co-operative Bank Limited. Golden Jubilee Souvenir. Bombay n.d. [?1961].

Nurkse, Ragnar. *Problems of Capital Formation in Underdeveloped Countries.* Oxford, 1953.

O'Dwyer, Michael. *India as I Knew It, 1885–1925.* London, 1925.

Orenstein, Henry. *Gaon: Conflict and Cohesion in an Indian Village.* Princeton, 1965.

Pandit, Y. S. *Economic Conditions in Maharashtra and Karnatak.* Poona, 1936.

Parekh, H. T. *The Bombay Money Market.* Bombay, 1953.

Parikh, Narahari D. *Mahadev Desai's Early Life.* Trans. from the Gujarati by Gopalrao Kulkarni. Ahmadabad, 1953.

———. *Sardar Vallabhbhai Patel.* Vol. I. Ahmadabad, 1953.

Parikh, P. T. *A Brief History of the Co-operative Movement in the Surat District.* Surat, n.d. [?1936].

Park, Richard L., and Tinker, Irene, eds. *Leadership and Political Institutions in India.* Princeton, 1959.

Patel, G. D. *Agrarian Reforms in Bombay: The Legal and Economic Consequences of Abolition of Land Tenures.* Bombay, 1950.

Patwardhan, R. P., and Ambekar, D. V., eds. *Speeches and Writings of Gopal Krishna Gokhale.* Vol. I, *Economic.* Bombay, 1962.

Philips, C. H., ed., with the co-operation of H. L. Singh and B. N. Pandey. *The Evolution of India and Pakistan, 1858 to 1947: Select Documents.* London, 1962.

Polanyi, Karl; Arensberg, Conrad M.; and Pearson, Harry W. *Trade and Market in the Early Empires: Economics in History and Theory.* Glencoe, Ill., 1957.

Qureshi, Anwar Iqbal. *The Future of the Co-operative Movement in India.* Madras, 1947.

Ragnekar, D. K. *Poverty and Capital Development in India: Contemporary*

Investment Patterns, Problems and Planning. London, 1958.

Raj, K. N. *The Monetary Policy of the Reserve Bank of India: A Study of Central Banking in an Undeveloped Economy.* Bombay, 1948.

The Ranade Industrial and Economic Institute. Poona, 1910.

Ranade, M. G. *Essays in Indian Economics.* Bombay, 1899.

Ratcliffe, S. K. *Sir William Wedderburn and the Indian Reform Movement.* London, 1923.

Ray, S. C., ed. *Agricultural Indebtedness in India and its Remedies, being Selections from Official Documents.* Calcutta, 1915.

Reed, Stanley. *The India I Knew, 1897–1947.* London, 1952.

Report of the Peasant Enquiry Committee of the Maharashtra Provincial Congress Committee. Poona, 1936.

Report of the Seventeenth Indian National Congress held at Calcutta on the 26th 27th and 28th December 1901. Calcutta, 1902.

Report of the Proceedings of the Nineteenth Indian National Congress held at Madras on the 28th 29th and 30th December 1903. Madras, n.d. [?1904].

Report from the Sub-committee of the Poona Sarvajanik Sabha appointed to collect Information to be laid before the East India Finance Committee on matters relating to India. Poona, 1873.

Reserve Bank of India. *All-India Rural Credit Survey. Report of the Committee of Direction.*

    Vol. I. *The Survey Report,* pt. i. Bombay, 1956.

    Vol. II. *The General Report.* Bombay, 1954.

Reserve Bank of India. *Review of the Co-operative Movement in India, 1962–64.* Bombay, 1966.

Rogers, A. *The Land Revenue of Bombay.* 2 vols. London, 1892.

Rudé, George. *The Crowd in History: A Study of Popular Disturbances in France and England, 1730–1848.* New York, 1964.

Rudolph, Lloyd I., and Rudolph, Susanne Hoeber. *The Modernity of Tradition: Political Development in India.* Chicago, 1967.

Sargant, N. C. *The Lingayats: The Vira-Saiva Religion.* Bangalore, 1963.

Sayers, R. S., ed. *Banking in the British Commonwealth.* Oxford, 1952.

Sen, Surendranath. *Administrative System of the Marathas. (From Original Sources.)* 2d ed. Calcutta, 1925.

Shah, Vimal and Sarla. *Bhuvel: Socio-Economic Survey of a Village.* Bombay, 1949.

Shukla, J. B. *Life and Labour in a Gujarat Taluka.* Bombay, 1937.

Singer, Milton, ed. *Traditional India: Structure and Change.* Philadelphia, 1959.

Singh, Tarlok. *Poverty and Social Change: A Study in the Economic Reorganization of Indian Rural Society.* Calcutta, 1945.

Sivaswamy, K. G. *Legislative Protection and the Relief of Agriculturist Debtors in India.* Poona, 1939.

Sovani, N. V., and Dandekar, V. M., eds. *Changing India: Essays in Honour of Professor D. R. Gadgil.* Bombay, 1961.

Spate, O. H. K., and Learmonth, A. T. A., with the collaboration of A. M. Learmonth and a chapter on Ceylon by B. H. Farmer. *India and Pakistan:*

A General and Regional Geography. 3d ed. London, 1967.

Srinivas, M. N., ed. *India's Villages. (A collection of articles originally published in "The Economic Weekly" of Bombay.)* Calcutta, 1951.

Stokes, Eric. *The English Utilitarians and India.* Oxford, 1959.

Strickland, C. F. *An Introduction to Co-operation in India.* London [Bombay imprint], 1922. 3d ed. as *Co-operation in India: A Student's Manual.* [Mysore imprint] 1938.

Sydenham, Lord (George Sydenham Clarke). *My Working Life.* London, 1927.

Sykes, W. H. *Land Tenures of the Dekkan.* London, 1835.

Tahmankar, D. V. *Lokamanya Tilak: Father of Indian Unrest and Maker of Modern India.* London, 1956.

Thakkar, A. V. *The Problem of Aborigines in India.* Poona, 1941.

Thomas, P. *The Growth of Federal Finance in India, being a survey of India's public finance from 1833 to 1939.* Madras, 1939.

Thomas, P. J., and Sundarama Sastry, N. *Indian Agricultural Statistics. (An Introductory Study.)* Madras, 1939.

Thorburn, S. S. *Musalmans and Money-lenders in the Punjab.* Edinburgh, 1886.

Thorner, Daniel. *The Agrarian Prospect in India: Five Lectures on Land Reform delivered in 1955 at the Delhi School of Economics.* Delhi, 1956.

Thorner, Daniel and Alice. *Land and Labour in India.* Bombay, 1962.

Tignor, Robert L. *Modernization and British Colonial Rule in Egypt 1882–1914.* Princeton, 1966.

Tinker, Hugh. *The Foundations of Local Self-Government in India, Pakistan, and Burma.* London, 1954.

Trivedi, A. B. *Wealth of Gujerat.* Jaipur, 1943.

Venkatasubbaiya, V., and Mehta, Vaikunth L. *The Co-operative Movement.* Allahabad, 1918.

Vučkovič, Mihailo. *A Century of Yugoslav Cooperation.* Belgrade, 1956.

Wacha, Dinshaw Edulji. *Speeches and Writings of Sir Dinshaw Edulji Wacha.* Madras, n.d.

Wallace, Anthony F. C., ed. *Men and Cultures. Selected Papers of the Fifth International Congress of Anthropological and Ethnological Sciences, Philadelphia, September 1–9, 1956.* Philadelphia, 1960.

Wedderburn, W. *Agricultural Banks for India.* [Bombay, ?1882].

———. *A Permanent Settlement for the Dekkan.* Bombay, 1880.

Wengen, G. D. van. *Social Aspects of the Co-operative Movement in Ceylon and Southern India.* Amsterdam, n.d. [1957].

Wertheim, W. F., et al., eds. *Indonesian Economics: The Concept of Dualism in Theory and Policy.* The Hague, 1961.

Wolff, H. W. *Co-operation in India.* London, n.d. [1919].

———. *People's Banks.* 2d ed., London, 1910. 3d ed., London, 1919.

Wolpert, Stanley A. *Tilak and Gokhale: Revolution and Reform in the Making of Modern India.* Berkeley and Los Angeles, 1962.

Woodruff, Philip (pseudonym for Philip Mason). *The Men Who Ruled India.* Vol. II, *The Guardians.* London, 1954.

B. Articles and Papers

Acharya, Hemlata. "Creative Response in Indian Economy: A Comment." *Economic Weekly.* Vol. IX, 27 April 1957.

Beals, Alan. "The Government and the Indian Village." *Economic Development and Cultural Change.* Vol. II, No. 5 (June 1954).

Bhatia, B. M. "An Enquiry into the Condition of the Agricultural Classes in India, 1888." *Contributions to Indian Economic History.* Vol. I, 1960.

Bhattacharya, Sabyasachi. "Laissez faire in India." *Indian Economic and Social History Review.* Vol. II, No. 1 (January 1965).

Brebner, J. Bartlet. "Laissez-faire and State Intervention in Nineteenth Century Britain." *Journal of Economic History.* Supplement VIII, 1948.

Catanach, I. J. "Agrarian Disturbances in Nineteenth Century India." *Indian Economic and Social History Review.* Vol. III, No. 1 (March 1966).

———. "Congress and Co-operatives in India." *Political Science.* Vol. XIII, No. 2 (September 1961).

———. "Democracy and the Rural Co-operative Movement: Some Reflections on the Indian Experience." *Second International Economic History Conference, Aix-en-Provence, 1962, Proceedings.* Vol. II. Paris, 1965.

Chaudhuri, Nirad C. "Passage To and From India." *Encounter.* Vol. II, No. 6 (June 1954).

Cohn, Bernard S. "Recruitment of Elites in India under British Rule." (Paper presented to the Conference on Modern South Asian Studies, Cambridge, July 1968.)

Damle, Y. B. "Caste in Maharashtra." *Journal of the University of Poona,* Humanities Section No. 9, 1958.

Dantwala, M. L. "Intensive Agricultural Development." *Economic and Political Weekly,* Vol. II, 17 June 1967.

Das Gupta, Ashin. "The Character of Traditional Trade." (Paper presented to the Conference on Modern South Asian Studies, Cambridge, July 1968.)

Dumont, Louis, and Pocock, D. F. Editorial in *Contributions to Indian Sociology.* No. 1, April 1957.

Fukazawa, Hiroshi. "Lands and Peasants in the Eighteenth Century Maratha Kingdom." *Hitotsubashi Journal of Economics.* Vol. VI, No. 1 (June 1965).

Geertz, Clifford. "The Rotating Credit Association: A 'Middle Rung' in Development." *Economic Development and Cultural Change.* Vol. X, No. 3 (April 1962).

Grover, B. R. "Nature of Land-Rights in Mughal India." *Indian Economic and Social History Review.* Vol. I, No. 1 (July–September 1963).

Hasan, S. Nurul. "The Position of the Zamindars in the Mughal Empire." *Indian Economic and Social History Review.* Vol. I, No. 4 (April–June 1964).

Kannangara, A. P. "Indian Millowners and Indian Nationalism before 1914." *Past and Present.* No. 40 (July 1968).

Khusro, A. M. "Land Revenue: A Plea for Progression." *Times of India.* 18 April 1963.

Kirk, George, "Lord Cromer of Egypt: A Retrospect." *Harvard Library Bulletin.* Vol. XII, No. 3 (Autumn 1958).

Kulkarni, A. R. "Village Life in the Deccan in the 17th Century." *Indian Economic and Social History Review*. Vol. IV, No. 1 (April 1967).

Kumar, Ravinder. "The Deccan Riots of 1875." *Journal of Asian Studies*. Vol. XXIV, No. 4 (August 1965).

Leacock, Seth, and Mandelbaum, David G. "A Nineteenth Century Development Project in India: The Cotton Improvement Program." *Economic Development and Cultural Change*. Vol. III, No. 3 (July 1955).

McCormack, William. "Lingayats as a Sect." *Journal of the Royal Anthropological Institute of Great Britain and Ireland*. Vol. XCIII, pt. i (January–June 1963).

MacDonagh, Oliver. "The Nineteenth-century Revolution in Government." *Historical Journal*. Vol. I, No. 1 (1958).

McLane, John R. "Peasants, Money-lenders and Nationalists at the End of the 19th Century." *Indian Economic and Social History Review*. Vol. I, No. 1 (July–September 1963).

Mann, Harold H. "The Agriculture of India." *Annals of the American Academy of Political and Social Science*. Vol. CXLV, pt. ii (September 1929).

Masselos, James C. "Liberal Consciousness, Leadership and Political Organization in Bombay and Poona, 1867–1895" (synopsis of Bombay Ph.D. thesis). *Indica*. Vol. II, No. 2 (September 1965).

Metcalf, Thomas R. "The British and the Moneylender in Nineteenth-century India." *Journal of Modern History*. Vol. XXXIV, No. 4 (December 1962).

Morris, Morris David. "Economic Change and Agriculture in Nineteenth Century India." *Indian Economic and Social History Review*. Vol. III, No. 2 (June 1966).

Neale, Walter C. "The Limitations of Indian Village Survey Data." *Journal of Asian Studies*. Vol. XVII, No. 3 (May 1958).

Orenstein, Henry. "Caste and the Concept 'Maratha' in Maharashtra." *Eastern Anthropologist*. Vol. XVI, No. 1 (1963).

Owen, Roger. "The Influence of Lord Cromer's Indian Experience on British Policy in Egypt 1883–1907." *St Antony's Papers*. No. XVII (Middle Eastern Affairs No. 4), 1965.

Pandit, D. P. "Creative Response in Indian Economy: A Regional Analysis." *Economic Weekly*. Vol. IX, 23 February and 2 March 1957.

Panikar, P. G. K. "Rural Savings in India." *Economic Development and Cultural Change*. Vol. X, No. 1 (October 1961).

Pocock, David F. "Inclusion and Exclusion: A Process in the Caste System of Gujerat." *Southwestern Journal of Anthropology*. Vol. XIII, Spring 1957.

———. "The Movement of Castes." (Summary of a Communication to the Royal Anthropological Institute, 28 April 1955.) *Man*. Vol. LV, Article 79, May 1955.

Raychaudhuri, Tapan. "The Agrarian System of Mughal India." *Enquiry*. New Series, Vol. II, No. 1 (Spring 1965).

Shah, A. M. "Political System in Eighteenth Century Gujarat." *Enquiry*. New Series, Vol. I, No. 1 (Spring 1964).

Spear, Percival. "From Colonial to Sovereign Status—Some Problems of Transition with Special Reference to India." *Journal of Asian Studies.* Vol. XVII, No. 4 (August 1958).

Sovani, N. V. "British Impact on India before 1850–57." *Cahiers d'histoire mondiale.* Vol. I, No. 4 (April 1954).

——. "Economic Conditions in Maharashtra." *Journal of the University of Poona.* Humanities Section No. 9, 1958.

Spodek, Howard. "The 'Manchesterization' of Ahmedabad." *Economic Weekly.* Vol. XVII, 13 March 1965.

Srinivas, M. N. "Caste in Modern India." *Journal of Asian Studies.* Vol. XVI, No. 4 (August 1957).

——. "The Dominant Caste in Rampura." *American Anthropologist.* Vol. LXI, No. 1 (February 1959).

——. "A Note on Sanskritization and Westernization." *Far Eastern Quarterly.* Vol. XV, No. 4 (August 1956).

Stokes, Eric. "Traditional Elites in the Great Rebellion of 1857: Some Aspects of Rural Revolt in the Upper and Central Doab." (Paper presented to the Conference on South Asian Elites, Cambridge, April 1968.)

Tansley, A. T. "The Early Non-Brahmin Movement and 1917." Unpublished working paper, Department of History, University of Western Australia, September 1968.

Thorner, Daniel. "The Village Panchayat as an Instrument of Social Change." *Economic Development and Cultural Change.* Vol. II, No. 3 (October 1953).

Tignor, Robert L. "The 'Indianization' of the Egyptian Administration under British Rule." *American Historical Review.* Vol. LXVIII, No. 3 (April 1963).

Tinker, Hugh. "Authority and Community in Village India." *Pacific Affairs.* Vol. XXXII, No. 4 (December 1959).

——. "1857 and 1957: The Mutiny and Modern India." *International Affairs.* Vol. XXXIV, No. 1 (January 1958).

——. "People and Government in South Asia." *Transactions of the Royal Historical Society.* Fifth Series, Vol. 9, 1959.

C. Unpublished Theses

Bonner, Edna R. "The Economic Policy of the Government of India, 1898–1905." M.A., University of London, 1955.

Driver, P. N. "The Co-operative Developments in the Bombay Presidency, with special reference to the Bombay Deccan." M.A., University of Bombay, 1932.

Dutia, Bhupendra Padmasinh. "Economic Aspects of Production and Marketing of Cotton in India." Ph.D., University of London, 1956.

Mangudkar, M. P. "Municipal Government in Poona, 1882–1947. (A Case Study.)" Ph.D., University of Poona, 1957.

Patterson, Maureen L. P. "A Preliminary Study of the Brahman versus Non-Brahman Conflict in Maharastra." M.A., University of Pennsylvania, 1952.

Tucker, Richard P. "M. G. Ranade and the Moderate Tradition in India 1842–1901." Ph.D., Harvard University, 1966.

Glossary

Some terms are explained in more detail in the main body of the book. In general, terms used only once and explained in the text are not included here.

bajri	A small millet
balutedar	A village artisan
bania	A trader who is generally also a money-lender. *Bania* castes belong to the Vaisya *varna* (q.v.) and are traditionally trading castes.
bhadralok	In Bengal, the "respectable people": men who did not undertake manual work and who generally possessed an education in English
Bhatia	Caste of Kutch and Sind, now largely a trading community
Bhil	Name of an "aboriginal" tribe; member of that tribe
charkha, charka	A small spinning wheel
charpai	A wooden bedstead covered with netted string or webbing
chawl	A block of tenements
Chitpavan	A Maharashtrian Brahman caste
crore	Ten millions
Deshasth	A Maharashtrian Brahman caste
inam	Rent (revenue)-free land; hence *inamdar*, the holder of such land
jowari	A millet
Kaliparaj	Dark-skinned people
Koli	Member of a Gujarat tribe
kulkarni	In Maharashtra, a village accountant and registrar, normally a Brahman
kunbi; Kunbi	A cultivator; also the name of a number of cultivating castes
lakh	One hundred thousand (often 100,000 rupees)
mali; Mali	Gardener; caste name
mamlatdar	Revenue officer in charge of a taluka (q.v.)
Marwari; Marwadi	A person from Marwar; a money-lender originating from that area
miras	Land held by hereditary "proprietorship"; hence *mirasdar*, one who holds such land

mofussil (mufassal)	The country as opposed to the town
panch, panchayat	Literally, a committee of five; used to describe an association of any number of persons, instituted for objects of an administrative or judicial nature
Pathan	A member of the most important Muslim tribe of the North-West Frontier
Patidar	A cultivating caste in Gujarat
rayat (ryot)	A cultivator, a peasant
rayatwari (ryotwari)	Revenue settlement between Government and peasant without intermediaries
Sarasvat (Saraswat)	A Brahman caste
saukar (savkar, sowcar, sowkar, sawkar)	A money-lender
swadeshi	"Of one's own country": applied to an early twentieth century movement to foster Indian business, and, in Bengal, to boycott all or most things British
takkavi (tagai, taccavi, takavi)	An advance of money from Government to an agriculturist
taluka	A subdivision of a district, generally consisting of 100–200 villages
talukdar	In Gujarat, the holder of an estate
Vaisya	The third *varna* according to the Hindu system, made up mainly of trading castes
varna	(Literally "colour".) A division of the Hindu community. There are four *varnas*: Brahmans, Ksatriyas, Vaisyas, and Sudras. Each *varna* is made up of a large number of separate castes.
watan	An hereditary office and the land which goes with it; hence *watandar*, one who holds such an office

Index

tural indebtedness in, 24, 36–39; peasantry of, 37, 58; co-operative societies in, 133, 153; consolidation of holdings in, 173, 174
Punjab Alienation of Land Act of 1900, 40, 41, 92, 93
"Punjab School of Co-operation," 192
Purandhar taluka (Poona), 29
Purchase and sale societies, 109–111, 204. *See also* Co-operative Marketing; Cotton-sale societies

Raddis, 98
Raiffeisen-type co-operative societies, 31, 43, 44, 104
Railways, 16, 35, 107
Rainfall, 6, 7, 15, 65, 168, 231
Rajadnaya, R.N., 147, 148
Ranade, Mahadev Govind, 25, 26n49, 49, 91, 100
Ratnagiri district, 113, 215
Rayats, 12, 27, 29, 68, 80, 84, 108, 122, 211. *See also* Cultivators; Peasants
Rayatwari land tenure, 5, 16
Record of Rights, 33, 91, 92, 185
Reed, Sir Stanley, 61n27, 102n41, 103n45, 46, 112n93
Reforms. *See* Dyarchy
Registrars' Conferences: of 1906, 60; of 1911, 74; of 1908, 82
Registrars of co-operative societies, 3, 7, 51, 52, 141; duties of, 53, 59, 133; McNeill, 56, 57; Campbell, 61–64; Director of Agriculture and, 75, 76; banks and, 83, 102, 105, 106, 109, 127, 203, 204, 217; Ewbank, 95, 96, 97; and honorary organizers, 131, 135; Rothfeld, 140, 141; role of, 188–190
Registration Department, Bombay, 33; reports of, 33, 185, 186
Registration records, 24, 25, 33. *See also* Record of Rights
Rents, 182, 183
Reserve Bank of India, 186n28, 220n177, 223n5
Retrenchment, 178, 190–194
Revenue and Agriculture Department, Government of India, 36, 84
Revenue Department, Bombay, 17, 18, 115, 116, 143, 157, 196, 214, 215
Revenue, land. *See* Land revenue
Riots. *See* Deccan Riots Commission; Deccan Riots of 1875
Ripon, Lord, 4n6, 28, 29
Rivington, Canon C.S., 57, 58, 64
Rodda, S.K., 101
Rothfeld, Otto, 143–149 *passim*, 163, 164, 188, 189, 194, 206, 207; background,

140–142; on co-operative movement, 151, 152, 153, 154, 158, 159, 169; on district banks, 160, 201, 204, 205; doubts about co-operative movement, 171, 172, 173, 174; and joint cultivation, 175, 176; retirement of, 177, 178, 179; and control of co-operatives, 195, 196, 197, 198; on retrenchment, 191n47, 192
Royal Commission on Agriculture of 1927–28, 53, 143, 153, 158, 173, 183, 192–197 *passim*
Royal Commission on Decentralisation in India of 1907–08, 71, 72, 73, 74
Rural Credit Survey of 1951–52, 223, 230, 231, 235
Russia, 175, 221

Sahasrabudhe, B.B., 88, 107
Sale deeds, 17, 18, 33
Salination (Nira Canal area), 181
Samaldas, Sir Lalubhai, 102, 103, 117, 135, 228, 229; and formation of Bombay Central Co-operative Bank, 78–86
Sandhurst, Lord, 39, 40
Sane, R.M., 118, 170, 171, 222, 224; an honorary organizer, 99–102, 131, 132; and rise of non-Brahman sentiment, 149, 150, 151
Sasvad (Poona), 87, 121, 147
Satara district, 11, 21, 34, 75, 96, 145, 146, 147, 160
Satyagraha, 190
Satya Shodhak Samaj, 145, 147, 149
Saukars, 49, 50, 69, 162, 163, 164, 172. *See also* Money-lenders
Secretary of Home Department (Bombay), 205
Secretary of State (Bombay), 203, 205
Secretary of State for India, 36, 147, 203, 205
Security: land as, 24, 112–116; crops as, 53, 231
Sedgwick, L. J., 180, 187
Select Committees, 48, 195
Self-government, 144. *See also* Local self-government
"Self-management," 152, 153
Servants of India Society, 99, 100, 132, 163, 210, 212, 213
Setalvad, Sir Chimanlal, 144
Shah, D.A., 163, 164, 167, 212
Share capital: of Provincial Bank, 86, 87, 120, 126, 128; of district banks, 120, 160
Shareholders: of urban co-operative banks, 79; of district banks, 120, 203, 225
Sholapur, 24, 41, 148, 215